MW01103496

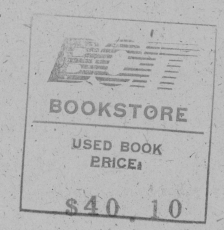

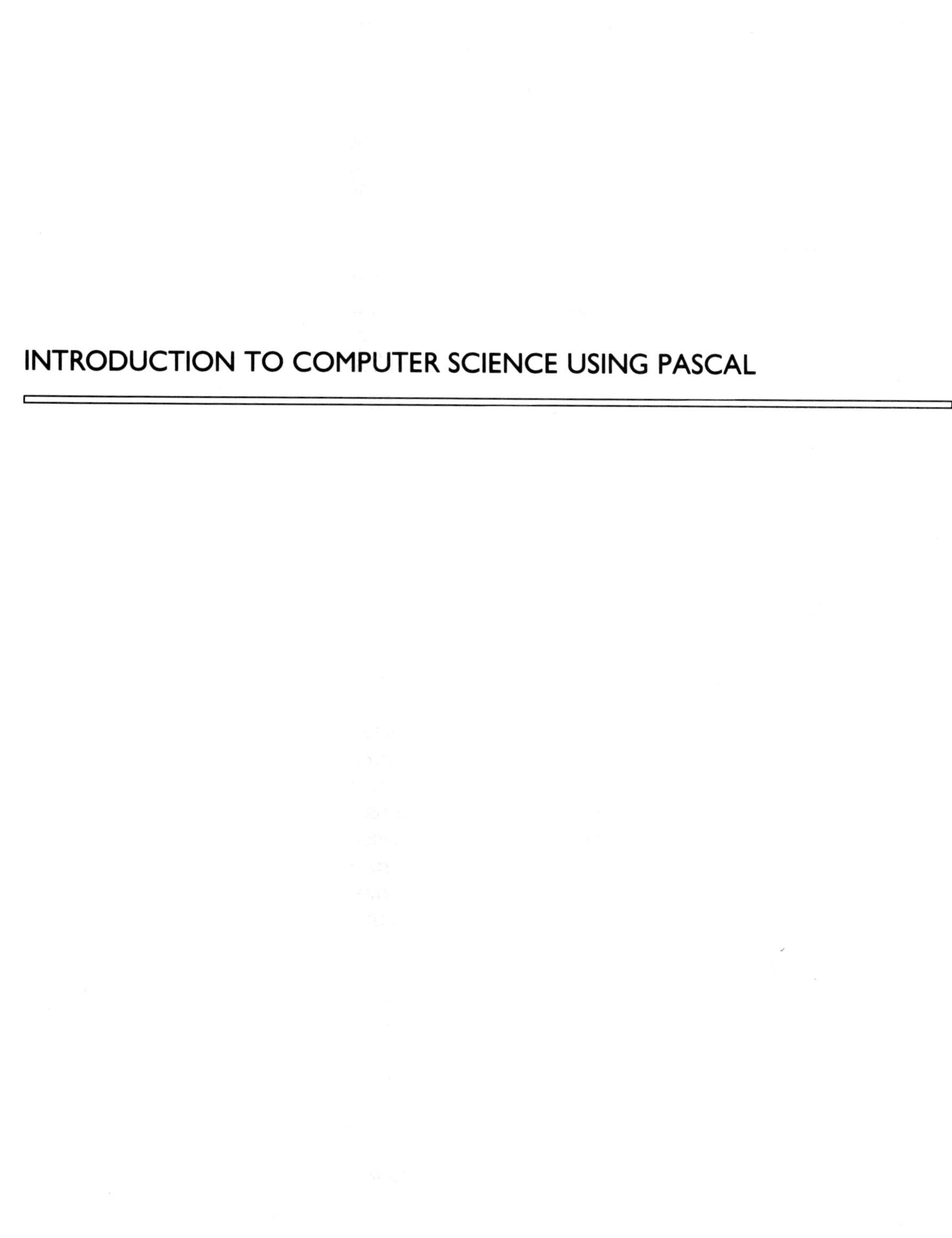

INTRODUCTION TO COMPUTER SCIENCE USING PASCAL

INTRODUCTION TO COMPUTER SCIENCE USING PASCAL

João P. Martins

Wadsworth Publishing Company
Belmont, California
A Division of Wadsworth, Inc.

Computer Science Editor: Frank Ruggirello
Special Projects Editor: Judith McKibben
Editorial Associate: Reita Kinsman
Production Editor: Vicki Friedberg
Designer: James Chadwick
Print Buyer: Randy Hurst
Permissions Editor: Robert M. Kauser
Copy Editor: Betty Duncan-Todd
Technical Illustrator: Jeannie Schrieber, Salinda Tyson, Ben Turner Graphics
Compositor: Graphic Typesetting Service
Cover Design: James Chadwick
Cover Illustration: Mark McGeoch Design Group
Signing Representative: Dawn Beke

Printed in the United States of America 34
1 2 3 4 5 6 7 8 9 10—93 92 91 90 89

LIBRARY OF CONGRESS
Library of Congress Cataloging-in-Publication Data
Martins, João P.
Introduction to computer science using Pascal / João P. Martins.
p. cm.
Bibliography: p.
Includes index.
ISBN 0-534-09402-3
1. Pascal (Computer program language) 2. Electronic digital computers—Programming. I. Title.
QA76.73.P2M338 1989
005.13'3—dc19 88-3219
CIP

To my children, João Pedro and Maria Leonor.

May computers help them grow in a better world than I did.

BRIEF CONTENTS

CONTENTS

Chapter 4 Development of Programs 75

Chapter 5 Elementary Data Types 91

Chapter 6 Control Structures 1: Sequencing 121

Chapter 7 Control Structures 2: Selection 159

Chapter 8 Control Structures 3: Repetition 183

Chapter 9 Subprograms Revisited 205

PREFACE

"Take some more tea," the March Hare said to Alice earnestly.

"I've had nothing yet," Alice replied in an offended tone: "so I ca'n't take more."

"You mean you ca'n't take less," *said the Hatter: "it's very easy to take* more *than nothing."*

Lewis Carroll, *Alice's Adventures in Wonderland*

In the last 35 years, computers have become essential objects in our everyday life. Simultaneously with the technologic development of computers, a new branch of science has emerged, *computer science,* which studies computers and their related processes.

This book presents a general introduction to computer science and programming. Its main goal is to supply an insight on the activity of programming and to convey the underlying computer science concepts. The topics covered are presented from a computer science perspective rather than from a programming perspective; our main concern is to teach computer science concepts rather than a particular programming language.

In particular we consider the following aspects: (1) The study of the *methodology of problem solving using computers,* which involves the study of the methods used to define a problem, the study of the methods used to find its solution (or solutions), the study of the ways of describing that solution using algorithmic languages, and the techniques for coding the solution in a well-structured program; (2) the study of the *general concepts underlying programming languages* and their application to the Pascal programming language; and (3) *an introduction to the main areas of computer science,* giving the necessary background to pursue more advanced topics.

Coverage

The material covered in an introductory computer science course has naturally changed as computer science has developed as an independent scientific discipline. The most recent curriculum for a first course in computer science (CS1) (Koffman, Miller, and Wardle 1984) was presented in October 1984 by the Association for Computing Machinery. The material proposed for CS1 is covered fully in this book. The objectives of CS1 are to

- ☐ Introduce a disciplined approach to problem-solving methods and algorithm development
- ☐ Introduce procedural and data abstraction
- ☐ Teach program design, coding, debugging, testing, and documentation using good programming style
- ☐ Teach a block-structured, high-level programming language
- ☐ Provide a familiarity with the evolution of computer hardware and software technology

This book also addresses some of the objectives proposed for a second course in computer science (CS2) (Koffman, Stemple, and Wardle 1985), such as to

- ☐ Teach the use of data abstraction using data structures other than those normally provided as basic types
- ☐ Provide an understanding of the different implementations of these data structures
- ☐ Introduce searching and sorting algorithms
- ☐ Provide a foundation for further studies in computer science

Although it covers the material proposed for CS1 and most of CS2, this book has goals that go beyond the objectives of the CS1/CS2 program, namely to

- ☐ Introduce fundamental concepts from computer science and the theory of programming languages
- ☐ Provide a clear understanding of the syntax and semantics of a language
- ☐ Provide a feeling for interactive programs and user-friendly interfaces

The language used to express the solutions of our problems, Pascal, was developed by Niklaus Wirth in the early 1970s (Wirth 1971; Jensen and Wirth 1974; Jensen, Wirth, Mickel, and Miner 1985). Although developed mainly as a tool to teach programming, Pascal is used in many practical applications. Pascal has become the most popular language used to teach programming because it gives rise to well-structured and well-organized programs and has enough expressive power to deal elegantly with fundamental programming concepts. These are the main reasons why Pascal was chosen for this book. It should be stressed, however, that our goal is not to teach Pascal (thus, some of its features are left out). We use Pascal to teach *how* to program in *any* programming language.

The book contains enough material for a two-semester course, but it also can be used for a one-semester course by covering only Chapters 1–10.

Why this text is different

There are several aspects that make the presentation in this book unique.

1. It represents a general introduction to computer science and programming not just an introduction to Pascal. (This is the main reason that some aspects of Pascal, for example, variant records, are not covered in this book.) It uses Pascal[1] as a tool to express the concepts presented, but the main goal of the book is to introduce fundamental concepts from computer science, such as top-down design of algorithms and data structures, procedural and data abstraction, testing and debugging strategies, proper documentation, and information hiding.
2. It covers concepts in the theory of programming languages that are not usually covered in introductory books, for example, full discussion of the scope and lifetime of variables, parameter-passing techniques, and garbage collection. These concepts are introduced using Pascal as a tool, and whenever possible the alternatives used in other programming languages are discussed.
3. It places a heavy stress on the distinction between (and clear understanding of) syntax and semantics, and language and metalanguage. To master any programming language, it is not only important to be able to talk *in* the language (write programs) but also to be able to talk *about* the language (using English or some other language as a metalanguage). This is stressed throughout the book.
4. Procedures are introduced very early in the book (in fact, they are the first aspect of Pascal to be covered), which allows the use of procedural abstraction from the beginning. The first Pascal programs that we develop use procedures and talk about *what* procedures do, without the student's knowledge of *how* to write a complete procedure.

1. ISO Standard Pascal (Cooper 1983) is followed throughout.

5. Recursion is introduced in Chapter 9, and the chapters that follow draw heavily on recursive programs.
6. The methodology for developing abstract data types is explained in clear terms, and three complete examples of abstract-data-type development are explained and their implementation fully discussed.

Organization and content

The following is a chapter-by-chapter description of the book.

- ☐ Chapter 1, "Computers and Algorithms," discusses the nature and main characteristics of a computer and introduces a fundamental concept in computer science—the concept of an algorithm. Algorithms are defined, and their characteristics are presented. It shows examples of informal algorithms: a cooking recipe, crocheting instructions, and instructions to assemble objects. Based on these examples, it introduces the concepts of procedural and data abstraction.
- ☐ Chapter 2, "Syntax and Semantics," introduces the concepts of syntax and semantics. It gives an introduction to the Backus–Naur formalism (BNF) and to syntax charts. These two formalisms are used throughout the book. Based on the syntax and semantics, it discusses the kinds of errors that may exist in a computer program: syntactic and semantic errors.
- ☐ Chapter 3, "Structure of a Program," describes the structure of a Pascal program. It shows examples of Pascal programs while presenting examples of equivalent programs written in other programming languages. It introduces the idea of procedure and discusses how procedures are defined and used in Pascal. It explains how procedures can be used to implement procedural abstraction and develops a Pascal program that uses procedures.
- ☐ Chapter 4, "Development of Programs," describes the phases that the development of a program goes through, lists the goals for writing a good program, and describes a number of tools for attaining those goals. It discusses techniques for top-down design with an emphasis on modularization and good documentation. Approaches for debugging and testing are also discussed.
- ☐ Chapter 5, "Elementary Data Types," discusses what data types are and introduces Pascal's elementary data types. It introduces the notions of constant and variable, discusses the attributes of a variable (name, type, value, range, and lifetime), and explains how to define constants and declare variables in Pascal. It also introduces user-defined types by describing enumerated and subrange types.
- ☐ Chapter 6, "Control Structures 1: Sequencing," is the first of three chap-

ters discussing control structures. It covers sequencing and introduces the compound statement and three simple Pascal statements: the assignment statement, the input statement, and the output statement. The input and output statements are presented stressing interactive programming and user-friendly communication.

- ☐ Chapter 7, "Control Structures 2: Selection," describes the need for making choices among the statements of a program and introduces two control structures: the `if` and `case` statements. It discusses when to use `if` and when to use `case` statements.
- ☐ Chapter 8, "Control Structures 3: Repetition," introduces the concept of loops, and discusses the advantages of using loops and the kinds of loops available in Pascal: `while`, `repeat`, and `for`. The syntax and semantics of each of these statements is fully presented, and examples of their use are given. The chapter ends with a comparison of the three statements and a discussion of when to use each of them.
- ☐ Chapter 9, "Subprograms Revisited," explores more deeply the notion of procedure introduced in Chapter 3 and introduces the concept of function. It explores the concept of block-structured program, discussing scope and lifetime of variables. The methods of parameter passing are introduced, and examples are given for each one of them. Finally, complete programs are presented.
- ☐ Chapter 10, "Structured Data Types 1: Arrays," is the first of a sequence of chapters that discusses data structures. It starts by showing the severe limitations of the exclusive use of elementary data types and introduces the concept of data structure. Arrays are defined, methods for manipulating arrays are described, and examples of programs that use arrays are given. It discusses some applications of arrays, namely, the representation and manipulation of character strings, sorting, and searching and presents several sorting and searching algorithms. It introduces the notion of analysis of algorithms and applies these ideas to the sorting algorithms presented.
- ☐ Chapter 11, "Structured Data Types 2: Records," introduces the need for another data structure, records, by showing some limitations of arrays. It discusses the characteristics of records and shows some examples using records and arrays of records.
- ☐ Chapter 12, "Structured Data Types 3: Sets," discusses the data structure `set` and shows examples of programs using sets.
- ☐ Chapter 13, "Structured Data Types 4: Files," introduces the concept of a file, discusses the operations that a Pascal program can perform on files, and presents an example of their usage.
- ☐ Chapter 14, "Dynamic Data Types: Pointers," describes the need for a data type that enables the creation of structures whose size is not predetermined and introduces the concept of a pointer. It discusses how pointers are created, manipulated, and destroyed and shows some

examples of programs using pointers. It discusses the concepts of memory management: manual updates (used in Pascal), reference counters, and garbage collection.

- Chapter 15, "Abstract Data Types," introduces the concept of abstract data type. It discusses the advantages of using abstract data types and the methodology to be followed to define and implement them. This discussion contains some insights on the evolution of programming and the urge to make programs more modular.
- Chapter 16, "The Stack as an Abstract Data Type," introduces the concept of stacks, discusses their use in computer science, and presents an example that uses stacks. It compares two possible representations for the stack data type.
- Chapter 17, "The List as an Abstract Data Type," discusses the concept of a list and ways of representing it in Pascal. It shows examples of lists using different representations.
- Chapter 18, "The Tree as an Abstract Data Type," introduces trees, discusses alternative ways of representing trees in Pascal, and uses the concepts in an application: tree sort.
- Chapter 19, "Hardware and Software," introduces the main hardware components, describes main memory and auxiliary memory devices, and discusses the cycle of execution of statements by the CPU. It introduces the concept of an abstract machine and discusses the options available for building an abstract machine. Based on the notion of abstract machine, it presents the levels of a computer, discussing what each level does. This chapter is independent of the other chapters and can be read anytime after Chapter 1.
- Appendix A, "Representation of Characters," discusses how characters are stored inside the computer, giving the full ASCII character code.
- Appendix B, "Syntax of the Pascal Language," contains a BNF grammar defining the full syntax of Pascal. The rules of this grammar are sorted by the nonterminal symbol on the left-hand side, making it easy for students and instructors to find definitions.
- Appendix C, "Pascal Identifiers," contains a list of Pascal's reserved and standard identifiers.

Additional features

"The best way to explain is to do it."
Lewis Carroll, *Alice's Adventures in Wonderland*

Chapter exercises

At the end of each chapter is a set of exercises that tests whether the goals of the chapter have been attained. The exercises are grouped into three categories: review questions (indicated by the symbol ✓), questions of medium difficulty (indicated by the symbol **?**), and hard questions (indicated by the symbol **!**).

Class testing

This manuscript has been tested with freshman students over a four-year period in the Instituto Superior Técnico (School of Engineering, Technical University of Lisbon, Portugal) and in the Department of Computer Science, State University of New York at Buffalo.

Acknowledgments

Many people have directly or indirectly contributed to the present form of this book.

William J. Rapaport and Ernesto Morgado have made detailed comments on the several drafts of the book and contributed to its final form with stimulating and fruitful discussions. Anthony Ralston helped define its coverage.

Stuart C. Shapiro helped shape my mind about what computer science really is. António Gouvea Portela had a major influence on my computer science career, and without his help this book would never have been written.

Maria dos Remédios Cravo thoroughly revised the manuscript, uncovering errors and problems, and Diana Santos pointed out some additional errors.

Many thanks also go to the reviewers of the book for their suggestions: Margaret Mize Cline, Western Kentucky University; Wanda Dann, State University of New York at Morrisville; Ray Ford, University of Iowa; Peter Gingo, University of Akron; Henry Gordon, Kutztown University of Pennsylvania; Don Greenwell, Eastern Kentucky University; Michael P. Johnson, Oregon State University; Abraham Kandel, Florida State University; Doris Lidke, Towson State University; Kenneth W. Loach, State University of New York at Plattsburgh; Robert J. McGlinn, Southern Illinois University at Carbondale; David McNab, University of Illinois; Bruce R. Maxim, University of Michigan; Seymour V. Pollack, Washington University of St. Louis; William J. Rapaport, State University of New York at Buffalo; Mary Lou Soffa, University of Pittsburgh; and Henderson Yeung, California State University at Fresno.

My thanks also to Frank Ruggirello, Vicki Friedberg, James Chadwick, Judith McKibben and the rest of the Wadsworth staff, who contributed much to the final form of the book.

I would also like to thank the freshman students of the Instituto Superior Técnico, who over a period of years have gone through several versions of this book, in particular, Rui Neves, who helped me with some of the programs in Chapters 17 and 18, and António Leitão for converting part of the manuscript in LATEX.

The Centro de Informática do Instituto Superior Técnico provided the computing resources for the preparation of the book. In particular, I thank Jean Silva, my weekend computing companion, for all his help on file transfer and recovery.

I also thank Maria Helena Varandas for her careful preparation of the book's figures.

Finally, a heartful thanks to my family for their patience, encouragement, and lost weekends.

CHAPTER 1

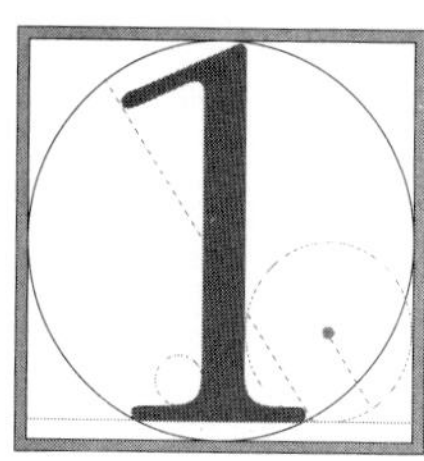

This chapter discusses the nature of a computer and its main characteristics and introduces a fundamental concept in computer science—the concept of an algorithm. We show examples of some algorithms used in everyday life: a cooking recipe, crocheting instructions, and car model–building instructions. Based on these examples we informally describe the two parts of a program: declaration of data and description of actions to be performed on the data. The notions of procedural and data abstraction are also introduced and their advantages discussed.

COMPUTERS AND ALGORITHMS

We must recognize the strong and undeniable influence that our language exerts on our ways of thinking, and in fact defines and delimits the abstract space in which we can formulate—give form to—our thoughts.
Niklaus Wirth (1974, p. 249)

In the last 35 years, computers have become essential objects in our everyday life. Computers are used routinely for mundane tasks such as producing utility bills and bank statements, controlling traffic, and handling reservations. There are computers in automobiles, cameras, and home appliances. In the past few years, with the advent of personal computers, computers have spread from institutions to private homes; personal computers will soon become tools used by everyone. It is almost impossible for the average American to spend a full day without somehow making use of a computer: in a telephone, a television set, or a pocket calculator.

Alongside the technologic development of computers, a new branch of science has emerged, **computer science,** which studies computers—how to design them, how to make them work, how to make them friendly, how to define their limitations, and, most of all, how to stretch their capabilities and to guide them in new directions.

This book introduces some of the important concepts of computer science and teaches how to instruct a computer to perform tasks. This is done by developing a sequence of steps that the computer follows, using a notation that the computer understands. This written sequence of steps is called a program, and writing programs is called programming—a challenging and fascinating intellectual task, which is not hard but that requires a great deal of discipline. The goal in this book is to give a disciplined introduction to programming, to teach the steps involved in developing a program, and, most of all, to teach how to write structured, efficient, and error-free programs.

1.1 Main characteristics of a computer

One of the most common misconceptions about computers is that they are only huge calculating machines. Computers do much more than arithmetic computations. In general terms, a computer is a machine whose purpose is to manipulate symbols. The symbols manipulated by the computer are used to represent information. By *information,* we mean data, facts, and ideas, independent of the form in which they are represented. Information can be transmitted from person to person, can be extracted from nature by observation and measurements, and can be acquired through books, films, television, and so forth. Computers, then, are machines that convey and manipulate information. A **computer** can thus be defined as an *information-manipulating machine.*

Although computers can differ in size, appearance, and cost, they share four fundamental characteristics: They are automatic, universal, electronic, and digital.

A computer is said to be *automatic* in that, once it has been given the right information, it works by itself without human intervention. This does not mean that a computer starts working by itself; rather, it computes the solutions to problems by itself. To solve problems the computer must be given instructions, called a program, on how to go about solving them. The instructions of a program are specified in a language that the computer understands, and they state exactly how the work has to be carried out, or executed. While the work is being executed, the program is stored inside the computer's memory.

A computer is said to be *universal* because it can perform any work whose solution can be described by a program. While executing a given program, a computer can be considered a special purpose machine. For example, while computing the salaries of employees, the computer can be considered a payroll machine; while generating business letters or a piece of text, the same computer can be regarded as a word-processing machine. The word *universal* stems from the fact that computers can execute *any* program, solving problems in different application areas. While solving a given problem, the computer manipulates the symbols that represent the information for that particular problem without assigning any specific meaning to those symbols. It should be stressed, however, that computers cannot solve all types of problems. The class of problems that can be solved by computers was studied before the first electronic computers had been built. During the 1930s several mathematicians (Church, Gödel, Kleene, Post, Turing, and others) tried to define formally the class of functions that could be mechanically computed. Although the methods used by these mathematicians were different, all formalisms turned out to be equivalent in that they all defined the same class of functions, the **partial recursive functions.** It is now believed that the partial recursive functions are *exactly* the computable functions. This belief is stated in the "Church–Turing Thesis."[1]

A computer is *electronic.* The word *electronic* refers to the components of the machine. These components are responsible for the high-speed operations performed by the machine. Depending on the technology used in these components, computers can be divided into several generations. Although some controversy exists concerning the classification of computers into generations, the following classification is generally accepted: *First-generation computers* (circa 1944–1959; for example, the Harvard Mark I, ENIAC, and IBM 704) used vacuum tubes as main components. *Second-generation computers* (circa 1959–1964; for example, the CDC 1604, IBM 7094, and Burroughs B5000) used transistors as their main components. *Third-generation computers* (circa 1964–1975; for example, the IBM 360 and 370 series, Burroughs 5500, and Digital PDP-8) used integrated circuits as their main components. *Fourth-generation computers* (circa 1975–present; for example, the Digital VAX series, CRAY-1, and CDC 7600) use very large-scale integrated (VLSI) circuits as their main components. Each succeeding generation of computers is smaller, faster, and cheaper than the preceding.

Most modern computers are *digital.* Digital computers represent information as discrete binary digits. For example, in a digital computer the number 14 might be represented as 01110 (the binary numeral for 14).

Before proceeding, let us summarize the fundamental points covered in this section.

1. A computer is an information-manipulating machine.
2. The computer works by following the instructions of a program, which is stored inside the machine.
3. A computer manipulates information without needing human intervention: It is automatic.
4. A computer manipulates information representing many different areas: It is universal.
5. A computer uses electronic components to manipulate the information: It is electronic.
6. A computer represents information as discrete binary digits: It is digital.

---

1. A discussion of partial recursive functions and the Church–Turing Thesis is far beyond the scope and level of this book. If you have a strong background in mathematics and are interested in this subject, you can deepen your knowledge of this topic by reading Brainerd and Landwebber (1974), Hennie (1977), or Kleene (1974).

In the next section, the characteristics of a program—the set of instructions used by the computer to perform a specific task—are discussed.

1.2 Algorithms

As previously discussed, a computer works by following a program—a sequence of instructions that specifies *exactly* what has to be done. As we will see, this program is an algorithm written in what is called a programming language. In this section the concept of an algorithm and its main characteristics are discussed.

An **algorithm** is a finite sequence of well-defined, unambiguous instructions for solving a particular problem, each of which can be executed mechanically in a finite length of time and with a finite amount of effort. Before proceeding, let us take a closer look at our definition of an algorithm. First, an algorithm consists of a *finite sequence* of instructions. This means that an algorithm has a given number of instructions and that there exists an ordering of these instructions. Second, the instructions of an algorithm are *well-defined* and *unambiguous.* It is clear what each instruction means and that they do not contain multiple meanings. Third, each instruction can be executed *mechanically,* that is, without requiring imagination from the agent who is executing the instruction. Finally, the instructions are to be executed *in a finite length of time* and *with a finite amount of effort.* This means that each instruction terminates.

An algorithm is always associated with a given goal, that is, with the solution of a particular problem. The execution of the instructions of the algorithm guarantees that its goal will be attained.

The word *algorithm* is a phonetic variation of the pronunciation of the last name of the Arab mathematician Abu Ja'far Mohammed ibu-Musa al-Khowarizmi, who lived in the ninth century and developed a set of algebraic rules to perform arithmetic operations with decimal numbers. Al-Khowarizmi was also the creator of the word *algebra.*

The description of a sequence of actions plays a fundamental role in our everyday life and is related to our ability to communicate. We are constantly conveying or following sequences of instructions—for example, instructions to fill out forms, to operate devices, to get to some place, and to assemble objects. The following are some descriptions of sequences of instructions followed in our daily life. We will begin with the following recipe for Meringue Layer Cake from *The Classic French Cuisine,* Donon (1959, pp. 282–283).

MERINGUE LAYER CAKE

6 egg whites
1 and ½ cups powdered sugar
½ teaspoon vanilla extract

2 egg whites
½ cup powdered sugar
few drops of vanilla extract

Beat the 6 egg whites until they are stiff but not dry, and gently fold in the 1 and ½ cups of powdered sugar, little by little. Fold in the ½ teaspoon of vanilla.

Cover two well-buttered baking sheets with white paper or dredge them with flour. With a 9-inch plate as a guide, outline 4 circles.

Put the meringue in a pastry bag fitted with a round tube 1 inch in diameter. Cover one of the circles completely with a layer of meringue. Ring each of the remaining three with meringue to form a wreath 1 and ½ inches wide. Sprinkle with confectioner's sugar and bake in a slow oven (250°F) until the meringue is dry. This may take an hour or more.

Make another meringue with the 2 egg whites, ½ cup of powdered sugar, and vanilla extract. Arrange the wreaths of meringue on top of a solid circle, with uncooked meringue between them to make them set together. Put the remaining meringue in a pastry bag, and with a fancy tube decorate the top and sides of the cake at will. Return the layer cake to the oven at still lower temperature, about 200°F, for an hour or longer, until the meringue is thoroughly dry and very lightly browned. Cool the cake and fill the center with ice cream or with whipped cream flavored with vanilla extract, and garnish with candied violets.

The Meringue Layer Cake recipe comprises two distinct parts: a description of the objects to be manipulated (this description does not contain every object to be manipulated, for example, the "pastry bag") and a description of the actions to be performed on those objects. The second part of this recipe is a finite sequence of well-defined instructions (for someone who knows how to cook and thus understands the meaning of expressions like "beat the 6 egg whites"). Almost every one of them can be executed mechanically in a finite period of time and with a finite amount of effort. In other words, the second part of this recipe is very close to being an algorithm.

As a second example, let us consider the following crocheting pattern from the *Pingouin Magazine* No. 45:[2]

MARACAS STITCH

Chain stitch: ch.

Single crochet: sc.

Double crochet: dc.

4 Double Crochet Closed Together: * yo, insert hook in 1st, yo, draw through 1 loop, yo, draw through 2 loops*. Repeat ** 3 more times, always inserting hook in the same stitch, then * yo, draw through all 5 loops on hook, ch 1*.

Instructions for Maracas Stitch:

Row 1: On a chain base: 1 sc in each ch, 1 ch to turn.

Row 2: 1 sc, * 4 dc closed together, 1 sc in each of the following 2 sc*, 1 ch to turn.

Row 3 and all odd rows: 1 sc in each stitch.

Row 4 and all even rows: Work like row 2 but stagger the 4 dc closed together by 1st toward the left.

As opposed to the Meringue Layer Cake recipe, the instructions for this crocheting pattern do not list the objects being manipulated (although it is implicitly assumed that we will be using yarn and needles); they just show the sequence of actions to be performed. Also, unlike the recipe, the Maracas Stitch pattern uses special symbols in its description. These symbols are of two kinds: those that are supposed to be known by any person who can read crocheting instructions—for example, "yo" (for yarn over)—and those that are defined for this particular stitch—for example, "ch" and "4 dc closed together."

The first part of these instructions contains the definition of new symbols: First, the symbols "ch," "sc," and "dc" are defined as being chain stitch, single crochet, and double crochet, respectively (notice that this only assigns a new name to something that is already known); then a new stitch is defined. While reading the description of the Maracas Stitch, a person *learns* the stitch known as "4 dc closed together." The second part of these instructions uses the symbols that were defined previously.

The description of this stitch is a finite sequence of well-defined instructions (again, for someone who knows how to crochet and thus understands the meaning of—knows the sequence of actions corresponding to—single crochet, yarn over, and so on), each of which can be exe-

2. Reprinted with permission from *Pingouin Magazine.*

cuted mechanically (there are crocheting machines) in a finite period of time with a finite amount of effort. In other words, this is another informal example of an algorithm.

As a third example, let us consider the following (incomplete) sequence of instructions to build a model car, taken from the instruction sheet for the COX 1:24 scale 1964 Ferrari.[3]

PRELIMINARY INSTRUCTIONS

Read the step by step instructions and study the exploded view prior to actual assembly to become familiar with the parts and procedure. Each part is defined in the text with a call-out number keyed to the exploded view of the car.

When a part has been removed from the trees, trim the excess flash and pits from it. Use a sharp knife such as an X-acto or the equivalent.

ASSEMBLY INSTRUCTIONS

1. Locate the body bottom (R-1), rear spacer (R-2) and the "A" Arm (P-1). Carefully scrape the plating from the inside of the fork, from the area around the end locator holes, shock absorber tie points between the locator pins, and from the inside of the transmission locator hole.
2. Apply a thin coat of cement to the scraped portion of the "A" Arm fork and push the spacer into the fork. The shoulder of the spacer should be flush with the top of the fork. Apply a thin coat of cement to the inside of the body-bottom boss and insert the "A" Arm and the spacer unit. Check alignment.
3. Locate the transmission cover halves (P-2), scrape plating from the seam surfaces, from the locator in the left half, from the sides of the slot, the area around the locator holes for the disk brakes, and the two small slots at the top of the cover which receive the upper control arms. CAUTION: do not break off locator pins. Apply a light coating of cement to the seam surfaces and cement the two halves together. Clamp with a spring type clothespin and set aside.

The instructions for building the kit consist of a description of the objects to be manipulated—the parts of the kit (shown in Figure 1.1), the cement, and an X-Acto knife (referred to in the instructions)—and a description of the sequence of actions to be followed (there are 27 steps in the complete set of instructions, only the first 3 were described here).

---

3. Reprinted with permission from COX Hobbies, Inc.

FIGURE 1.1 Instructions for the 1964 Ferrari.

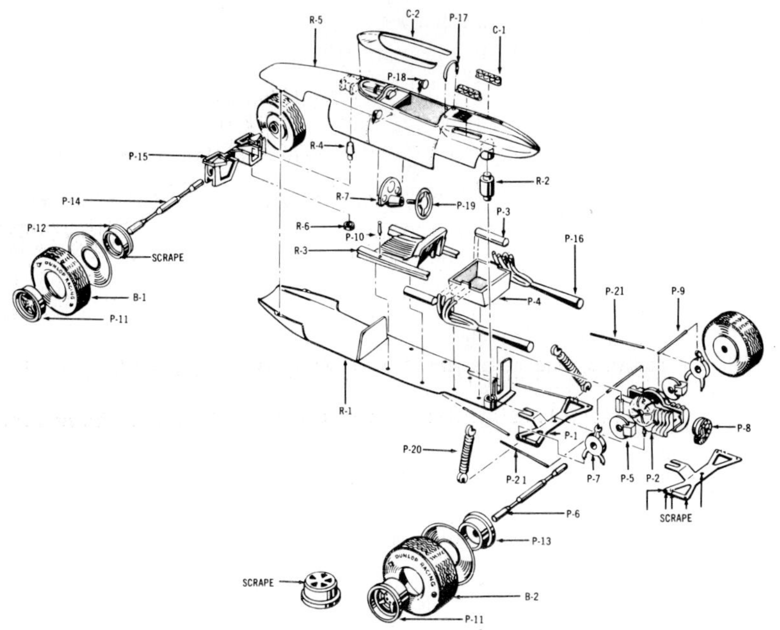

As before, the set of instructions for building this kit can be classified as an informal algorithm.

The COX 1964 Ferrari is a very simple kit: All the parts needed for its construction are shown in Figure 1.1. With more complicated kits, containing a very large number of parts, the kit-building instructions are too complex to be shown in a single diagram. In these cases the kit-building task is broken into groups of instructions for assembling components, which are then put together, producing the final model. An example of this sort, from the instruction booklet for the Tamiya 1:12-scale Lola T-70 MkIII,[4] is given in the following instructions, which refer to the diagram shown in Figure 1.2.

> Fig. 20 Assembling Engine A
>
> Study [Fig. 20] first. Then, fix Engine Parts, B25 onto Parts, H12 (13). Next, fix underside pins of Transmission, H24 and H23, into respective holes in Gear to fix the two Transmission Parts onto Parts, H20. Then

4. Reprinted with permission from TAMIYA Plastic Model Co.

FIGURE 1.2 Fragment of instructions for the Lola T-70 MkIII.

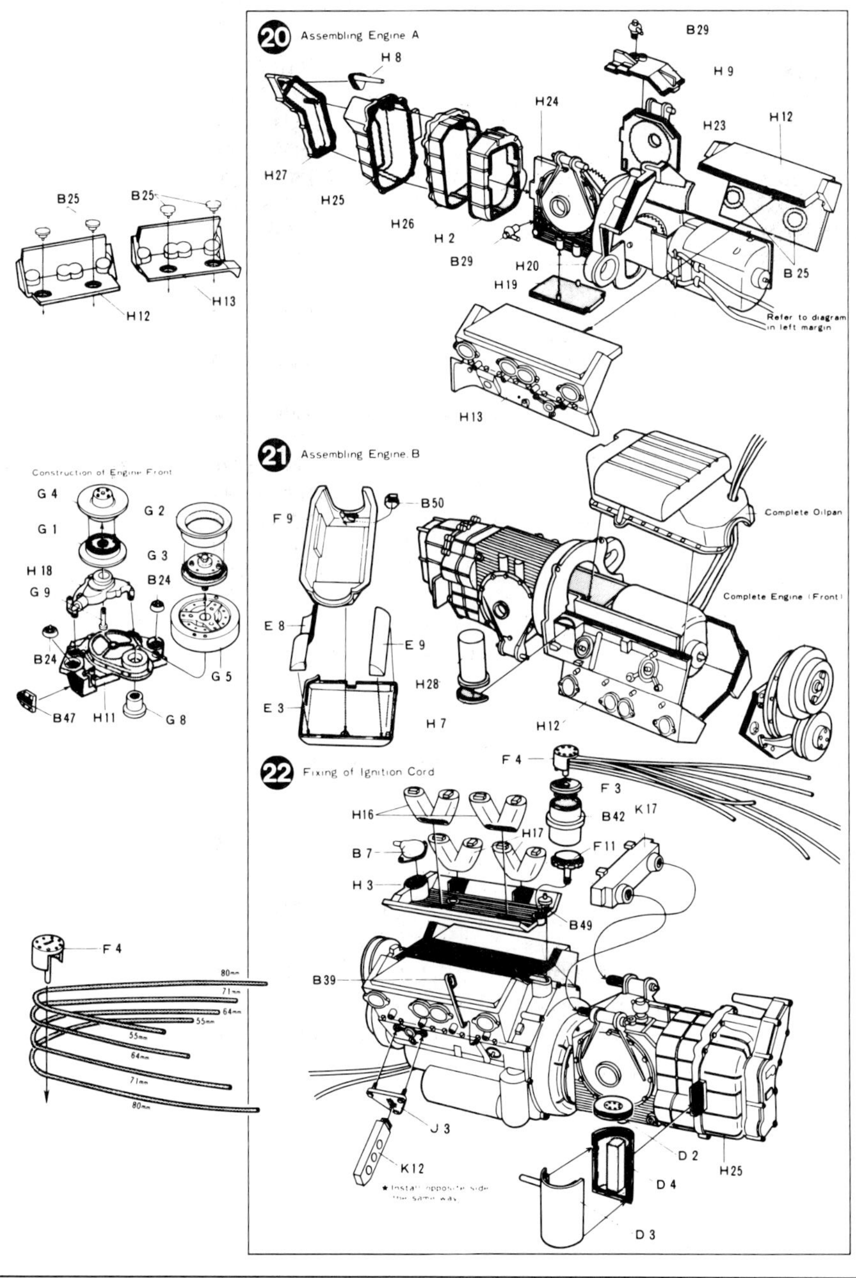

fix Parts, H19 and H9, onto the whole from above and below respectively. In so doing ensure that drive-shaft of Gearbox faces the hole of the Transmission exactly. Lastly, glue Parts, H2, H26, H25, H27, and H8.

Fig. 21 Assembling Engine B

See [Fig. 21] and construct Front Engine. Next, construct Oil Pan. In so doing, use tweezers when gluing Parts B50, as it is a very small part.

When gluing Oil Pan onto Engine pull Motor Cord out through the Hole.

Fig. 22 Fixing of Ignition Cord

Cut off four Ignition Cords 135mm each. Then, fold each of them to the same size as shown in the figure below, and Pass through Part F4. Next, fix Parts H16 and H17, onto Intake Manifold H3. In so doing, don't confuse parts H16, with the other Parts. Then, fix Parts, B7 and B49, and glue the whole onto Engine. Lastly, fix respective Parts as illustrated.

The instructions for the Lola T-70 are divided into groups; each group has a name and corresponds to a particular step in the kit-building task (for example, Fig. 20, "Assembling Engine A"). We can follow the kit-building process for the Lola T-70 by referring to each of the named steps needed for its construction. While doing this, we can forget the details involved in each one of these steps and just consider the main actions that must be carried out in the model-building task. In this way we can get a fairly good understanding of the kit-building algorithm in terms of a sequence of named steps (subproblems—which are, in turn, algorithms) in which the unnecessary detail is hidden. If, later on, we actually want to build this kit, we will have to consider each of these steps in turn and carry out the actions needed to build the component described in that step. Again, while doing so, we can forget about other instructions and concentrate only on the sequence of actions needed to assemble the desired component. The important point of this example is that we can present an overall description of a complicated task in terms of named subtasks and forget the details involved in each of them.

There are many more examples of algorithms that we use in our daily life—for example, looking for a name in a phone book or a word in a dictionary and obtaining instructions to get to some place or for making a phone call. From these examples we can see that algorithms have been used for a long time: They are finite sequences of steps that must be followed to achieve some desired goal.

The sequence of steps in an algorithm is carried out by some agent, which may be human, mechanical, electronic, or whatever. Each algorithm is associated with an agent that will carry out the instructions of the algorithm. What is an algorithm for one agent might not be an algorithm for

FIGURE 1.3 Cooking recipes are not algorithms.

another. For example, the Maracas Stitch instructions represent an algorithm for people who know how to crochet but make no sense for people who don't. However, not every sequence of steps to achieve a given goal can be considered an algorithm because an algorithm must be precise and effective and must terminate.

1. *An algorithm must be precise.* Each instruction in an algorithm must specify *exactly* what has to be done so that there is no ambiguity. The fact that an algorithm should be able to be followed mechanically requires that each of its instructions have one and only one interpretation. For example, the Meringue Layer Cake recipe is not a formal algorithm because it contains statements such as "beat the 6 egg whites" and "cover two well-buttered baking sheets with white paper or dredge them with flour," which may have several interpretations. For a person completely unaware of cooking procedures, "well-buttered baking sheet" may mean a baking sheet buttered on both sides (Figure 1.3).

   To avoid the ambiguity inherent in the languages used by human beings (called *natural languages,* such as English), special languages have been created to express algorithms in a rigorous way (called *artificial languages* or *programming languages,* such as Pascal). Programming languages were carefully crafted to avoid ambiguity and thus are useful in expressing algorithms.
2. *An algorithm must be effective.* Each instruction in the algorithm should be basic and understood well enough to be executed in a finite amount of time with a finite amount of effort. To illustrate this point, let us suppose that we are reading the instructions for Huge-Grow Plant Fertilizer and that we come across the following statement: "If the highest temperature in April was above 50°F, then use two packages of fertilizer instead of just one." Because it is not difficult to find out what the highest temperature in April was, we can easily decide whether to use two packages of fertilizer or just one. However, if the statement

reads, "If the highest temperature in the month of April of the year 1519 was above 50°F, then use two packages of fertilizer instead of just one," we certainly cannot determine the truth of the phrase "the highest temperature in the month of April of the year 1519 was above 50°F"; thus, we cannot decide whether to use one or two packages of fertilizer. This second instruction cannot be executed in a finite amount of time with a finite amount of effort and thus should not be part of an algorithm.

3. *An algorithm must terminate.*[5] An algorithm must produce a situation in which its goal has been attained and there are no more instructions to be executed. Let us consider the following procedure to raise a tire's pressure over 30 pounds: "While the pressure is less than 30 pounds, keep adding air." If the tire has a hole in it, the procedure may never terminate (depending on the size of the hole) and thus should not be classified as an algorithm.

Algorithms are fundamental in computer science; in fact, some authors—for example, Horowitz and Sahni (1984)—view computer science as the *study of algorithms:* the study of machines for executing algorithms, the study of the foundations of algorithms, and the analysis of algorithms.

1.3 Programs and algorithms

An algorithm written so that it can be executed by a computer is called a **program.** A large portion of this book is concerned with the development of algorithms and with the coding of such algorithms using a programming language (Pascal). The programs that we will develop will present aspects that resemble in some way the informal algorithms of the previous section. We discuss some of those aspects here.

1.3.1 The parts of a program

The Meringue Layer Cake recipe comprises two parts: a description of the objects to be manipulated and a description of the sequence of actions to be performed on those objects. A Pascal program has a similar structure. When writing a Pascal program, we describe at the outset the objects to

5. This last aspect is somewhat controversial. Some authors—for example, Hennie (1977, p. 8) and Hermes (1969, p. 2)—allow for an algorithm to never stop. For these authors, an algorithm presents only characteristics 1 and 2. Other authors—for example, Brainerd and Landwebber (1974, p. 2) and Hopcroft and Ullman (1969, p. 3)—distinguish between an *effective procedure*—a finite sequence of instructions that can be mechanically executed—and an *algorithm*—an effective procedure that always terminates. In this book, we take the second position.

be manipulated by the program, and then we describe, using an appropriate language, an algorithm that manipulates those objects.

In the Meringue Layer Cake recipe, the objects being manipulated include objects that exist prior to the execution of the recipe and the objects that are created during the execution of the recipe. The manipulation of these objects gives rise to the creation of an object that represents the goal of the manipulation (the Meringue Layer Cake). There is a similar behavior in a computer program. Most of the objects manipulated by a computer program are the values of variables. **Variables** are objects whose values change during the execution of the program. In a program, the values of the variables play the role of the ingredients in a cooking recipe. Typically, the computer will begin by reading some values into some variables in the program; it will then operate on these variables, possibly generating values for other variables; and, finally, the values of some variables will represent the result of the program.

1.3.2 Abstraction

The Maracas Stitch pattern contains two different kinds of symbols: symbols that represent basic operations and are known by any person who knows how to crochet (for example, "yo") and symbols that are defined for the Maracas Stitch as a combination of basic symbols (for example, "4 dc closed together") and only make sense for someone who has read the description of the Maracas Stitch.

Similarly, a computer program contains two kinds of symbols: symbols that are defined for the programming language used and are known by everyone who uses the language (for example, +, which represents the addition operation) and symbols that are defined within the program and only make sense inside the program where they are defined. These user-defined symbols are created from the basic components of the programming language, according to well-stated rules. The symbols may stand for variables, operations, or complicated sequences of actions.

One symbol defined in the Maracas Stitch pattern, "4 dc closed together," corresponds to the important programming concept of a named procedure. When we define this symbol, a sequence of actions is grouped together and given a name, the symbol itself. Afterward, the symbol is used whenever this sequence of actions is to be executed. We use the concept of named procedures every day. For example, suppose that you want someone to lock a door. You simply say, "Lock that door." In so saying, you are referring to a sequence of actions that achieves the desired goal (close the door, find the key that locks the door, insert that key in the keyhole, rotate the key in the locking direction, remove the key from the keyhole). Without the capability of naming sequences of actions, it would be impossible to communicate because we would have to explain everything in the smallest detail.

This process is called **abstraction.** The kind of abstraction that we have been describing so far is *associated with actions* to achieve desired goals; it is called procedural abstraction. **Procedural abstraction** gives a name to the sequence of actions that achieves a given goal and uses that name whenever we want to achieve the goal, without having to explicitly consider what the sequence of actions actually is.

There is another form of abstraction associated with the use of complicated objects: Whenever we manipulate complex objects, we are mostly concerned about how to *use* the objects, rather than with the details of how they are constructed. For example, suppose that you were about to learn how to use a typewriter. You would probably learn how to type characters on the sheet of paper (you must press the corresponding keys on the typewriter). In doing so, you don't care how the typewriter is constructed; that is, you are abstracting from the method of construction of the typewriter. This second form of abstraction is called data abstraction. **Data abstraction** is *associated with objects* and consists of separating the method of using an object from the details of how the object is constructed from simpler objects. In programming it is often necessary to create objects with certain characteristics. Data abstraction allows the use of such objects without concern for the method from which they are created.

The use of data and procedural abstraction in programming allows the construction of complicated programs that manipulate complex objects, without getting lost in the details of specifying the behavior of the program or the use of the objects.

1.3.3 Top-down approach

The algorithm for building the Lola T-70 may be described in terms of compound actions: assemble the engine, fix the ignition cord, and so on. We can follow the complete kit-building task without getting into the details of how each one of these compound actions is actually carried out. We already know that this is an aspect of abstraction and that this method allows us to get an overall picture of what is to be done without having to consider unnecessary details. We can get a good understanding of the advantage of this method by comparing it with the method used in the instructions for the 1964 Ferrari. To get a picture of how to build the 1964 Ferrari, we would have to read the entire set of instructions; we might get lost in details not needed for a general overview of the kit-building task. The method used in the instructions for the Lola T-70 controls the complexity of the task—it limits the amount of detail that we have to comprehend at any one time.

The topic that we describe in this section, although related to abstraction, concerns the way we approach complex problems. One of the major problems in the development of a large program is to control the complexity, to limit the amount of detail that a programmer has to consider at a given time. One method that is widely used for doing so is known as

top-down design, which consists of starting with a problem and subdividing it into smaller problems. Each of these smaller problems is given a name, and a first approximation of the algorithm is developed in terms of these subproblems. Referring to the Lola T-70 construction task, the first approximation of the algorithm would contain steps such as "assemble the engine," "fix the ignition cord," and so on. After doing this, we then consider each of these steps in turn. Note that each step is much simpler than the original problem. We keep doing this until we get to a point at which the problem to be solved can be easily expressed in terms of elementary operations.

You may be wondering what is meant by elementary operations. The operations to be performed in an algorithm should be elementary enough to be understood by the agent who executes them. They can stand for a set of simple actions to be executed in a well-defined sequence. In our examples we used as elementary actions "*beat* the 6 egg whites," "*cover* two well-buttered baking sheets," "*yarn over,*" "*single crochet,*" "*scrape* plating," and "*cement,*" although these actions may have several actions themselves. In our programs, we consider operations like addition, multiplication, division, and subtraction to be elementary actions. While performing one of these operations (for example, multiplication), the computer carries out a sequence of small steps, which are irrelevant to the person who writes the program.

1.3.4 Programming languages

We defined a **programming language** as being a language used for writing computer programs. There are many different programming languages. According to how close they are to the language humans use to solve problems, they can be classified into machine language, assembly language, and high-level languages. **Machine language** is the language that the computer understands. Machine language is composed of only 0s and 1s. Machine language is difficult for humans to use and understand; **assembly language** somewhat resembles machine language but is easier for us to use and understand; **high-level languages** are much easier to use than machine and assembly languages. Pascal is an example of a high-level language.

To enable computers to understand high-level languages (remember that machine language is the only language that the computer understands, its native tongue), there are special programs that *translate* high-level language into machine language. There are different ways of doing this, which are explained in Chapter 19. In the case of Pascal, the program that translates Pascal programs into machine language is called the **Pascal compiler.** The task of the Pascal compiler is to take a Pascal program (the source program) and to produce an equivalent program in machine language (the object program) so that the computer can understand it. Throughout this book we only consider high-level languages. At the end of the book, we will return to this topic and will give you a better idea about the differences between machine, assembly, and high-level languages and how to make a computer understand a language other than machine language.

1.4 An example from computer science

Before we end this chapter, we will develop an algorithm and a corresponding Pascal program to compute the sum of the first 1000 positive integers. To do so, we will begin by analyzing our behavior in solving this problem using a hand-held calculator. The goals of this presentation are to give you an intuitive idea about the steps and the reasoning involved in developing a program and to give you an intuitive idea of what a Pascal program looks like.

We can describe the sequence of actions to be performed in the following way:

```
set calculator's display to 0
press 1
press +
press 2
press +
press 3
press +
...
press 1000
press =
```

The symbol ... in our description of actions is very important because it indicates that there is a pattern of operations that is repeated over and over. Thus, it is not necessary to list every step that must be followed because one can easily generate and carry out the missing ones.

To describe this procedure in a more rigorous way, let us reason about what is going on in this computation. There are two quantities involved, the *running sum* (shown on the calculator's display) and the *number currently being added* to the running sum (which is kept in our head). Every time a new number is added to the running sum, we update the number inside our head (increase it by one). If we wanted to express this process in a formal way, we would need two variables, one to express the running sum (representing the current display of the calculator)—let us name it *sum*—and the other to express the number that we keep inside our head and add to the running sum—let us call it *number.* The basic steps that we perform are

```
(current value of sum) becomes (previous value of sum + number)
(current value of number) becomes (previous value of number + 1)
```

These two actions are expressed as

```
sum becomes sum + number
number becomes number + 1
```

The basic cycle that is performed to compute the sum of the first 1000 positive integers is

```
repeat
    sum becomes sum + number
    number becomes number + 1
until number > 1000
```

Remember the operations that we performed before getting into this repetitive cycle: We cleared the calculator's display (that is, we set the initial value of "sum" to be 0) and kept in mind that the first positive integer is 1 (that is, we set the initial value of "number" to be 1). With this in mind, the sequence of actions to be performed to compute the sum of the first 1000 positive integers becomes

```
sum becomes 0
number becomes 1
repeat
    sum becomes sum + number
    number becomes number + 1
until number > 1000
```

In mathematics, operations like "becomes" are usually represented by one symbol (for example, =). In programming, this operation is also represented by a symbol (=, :=, ←, and so on, depending on the programming language used). If we adopt Pascal's symbol, :=, our algorithm can be expressed as

```
sum := 0
number := 1
repeat
    sum := sum + number
    number := number + 1
until number > 1000
```

FIGURE 1.4 Sum of the first 1000 positive integers.

```
program Sum1000 (input, output);

var sum, number : integer;

begin
   sum := 0;
   number := 1;
   repeat
      sum := sum + number;
      number := number + 1
   until  number > 1000;
   writeln('The sum is: ',sum)
end. { Sum1000 }
```

This description is very close to a Pascal program to compute the sum of the first 1000 positive integers. However, to obtain a complete Pascal program, we still need to describe the variables used by the algorithm and to add some extra symbols to this description. A complete Pascal program to perform this task is shown in Figure 1.4.

There is a simple formula to compute the sum of the first 1000 positive integers, given by (in programming, * means multiplication)

sum = 1000 * (1 + 1000) / 2

and thus we could use this formula to compute the desired sum. Notice that while computing the sum using this formula, we are in fact *following* an algorithm, whose instructions are implicitly specified by the formula: Multiply by 1000 the result of adding 1 and 1000, and divide the result by 2. In general, there is not *one* single algorithm to produce the solution to a problem but rather a *collection* of algorithms (which may be very different) for achieving the desired goal.

Summary

A computer is a machine that manipulates symbols. While manipulating the symbols, the computer follows the instructions of a program, which is stored inside the computer. A computer program is an algorithm written in a programming language.

The concept of algorithm, a sequence of actions that must be followed to achieve some goal, was introduced. The characteristics that a sequence of actions has to satisfy to be considered an algorithm were defined: It has to be precise and effective and must terminate.

The parts of a Pascal program were informally described, and the concepts of procedural and data abstraction and top-down development were addressed briefly.

Suggested readings

You can explore the topics presented in this chapter more deeply by consulting the following books:

Abelson, H., Sussman, G., and Sussman, J. 1985. *Structure and Interpretation of Computer Programs.* Cambridge, MA: MIT Press.
This book deals with abstraction in programming and discusses both procedural and data abstraction.

Hayes, J. 1978. *Computer Architecture and Organization.* New York: McGraw-Hill.
The first chapter of this book traces the historical development of digital computers, providing a detailed description of a number of representative computers from each generation. It also presents an abstract model of computation—the Turing machine—and describes some theoretical limitations of computers.

Ralston, A., and Reilly, E., Jr. 1983. *Encyclopedia of Computer Science and Engineering*, 2d ed. New York: Van Nostrand Reinhold.
This book presents several interesting articles about the history of digital computers and the lives of people who helped develop them. It also describes the concept of an algorithm and its characteristics.

Exercises

1. ✓ What is a computer? What are the main characteristics of a computer?
2. ✓ What are the main technologies used in first-, second-, third-, and fourth-generation computers?
3. ✓ What is a digital computer?
4. ✓ What is an algorithm? What are its main characteristics?
5. ? The program of Figure 1.4 repeats a sequence of steps until `number` is greater than 1000. At first glance it may seem that it should repeat until `number` is *equal* to 1000. Explain what is wrong with this second approach.
6. ? Find an example of an algorithm followed in everyday life that is not considered in this chapter. Describe the steps involved.

7. ? Write an algorithm to compute the sum of the odd numbers less than or equal to 1000.
8. ? Write an algorithm that explains how to search for a person's phone number in a phone book.
9. ! Write an algorithm that explains how to make a phone call from a pay phone. (Make sure that your algorithm considers cases such as the phone booth being occupied, the line being busy, help from the operator being needed, and so forth.)
10. ? Write an algorithm that explains how to use a phone booth. Your algorithm should check the cases in which the phone booth cannot be used and should terminate when you enter the phone booth.
11. ? Write an algorithm that explains how to make a phone call from a pay phone. Assume that you are already in the phone booth and that no help from the operator is needed.
12. ? Write an algorithm that deals with the problems encountered in making a phone call and directs you to get assistance from the operator.
13. ? Rewrite the algorithm developed in Exercise 9, using the algorithm developed in Exercises 10, 11, and 12. Compare this algorithm with the algorithm you developed for Exercise 9.
14. ? A prime number is an integer that is only divisible by 1 and by itself. Write an algorithm that takes an integer number and decides whether it is prime.
15. ? Write an algorithm that takes an integer number and lists all the prime numbers less than or equal to it. (HINT: Use the algorithm that you developed for Exercise 14.)
16. ? In certain cash registers, the coins to be given to the customer as change for the cash tendered for a certain purchase are automatically computed and given to the client. Write an algorithm that takes a certain amount of cents (less than $1) and computes the number of quarters, dimes, nickels, and pennies needed to generate that amount.
17. ? Develop an algorithm that takes the price of a certain product and the cash tendered to pay for it and determines the amount of change to be given. The change should be computed in terms of the several bills and coins to be given to the client. (HINT: Use the algorithm that you developed for Exercise 16.)
18. ? Write an algorithm to represent the sequence of steps that you follow to start your car.
19. ? Write an algorithm to represent the sequence of steps that you follow to change a flat tire on your car. (NOTE: Requesting help from a garage is cheating!)

20. **?** Consider the following description of actions:

```
number1 := 5
number2 := 10
repeat
    number2 := number2 + 1
    number1 := number1 + 2
until number1 = 0
```

Can this be considered an algorithm? Why?

21. **?** Write an algorithm that takes a sequence of *unordered* numbers and tries to find whether a given number appears in the sequence.
22. **?** Write an algorithm that takes a sequence of *ordered* numbers and tries to find whether a given number appears in the sequence. What is the fundamental difference between this algorithm and the last one?
23. **!** Write an algorithm that takes a sequence of unordered numbers and places those numbers in ascending order.
24. **!** Write an algorithm that takes two sequences of ordered numbers and merges them into one single sequence of ordered numbers.
25. **!** Write an algorithm that takes two sequences of ordered numbers and merges them into one single sequence of ordered numbers, *eliminating existing duplications.*
26. **!** Write an algorithm that reads a text (assume that it can read character by character) and counts the number of characters, words, and sentences it contains.
27. **?** The following is a famous statement in mathematics, known as Fermat's Last Theorem: for $n > 2$, there are no integers x, y, z such that

$$z^n = x^n + y^n$$

This statement was made by the French mathematician Pierre de Fermat (1601–1665) and remains unproven today, even though many mathematicians over the last 300 years have devoted much effort to trying to prove it. Now consider the following instruction: "If Fermat's Last Theorem is true, then do . . ." Explain why this instruction should not be part of an algorithm. (HINT: Remember that the determination of the truth of the theorem is part of the instruction.)

CHAPTER 2

This chapter introduces the concepts of syntax and semantics. We introduce two different ways of specifying syntax: the Backus–Naur form (BNF) and syntax charts. These two formalisms are used throughout the book. The two kinds of errors that can exist in a computer program—syntactic and semantic errors—are discussed.

SYNTAX AND SEMANTICS

"Then you should say what you mean," the March Hare went on.

"I do," Alice hastily replied; "at least—at least I mean what I say—that's the same thing, you know."

"Not the same thing a bit!" said the Hatter. "You might just as well say that 'I see what I eat' is the same thing as 'I eat what I see'!"

Lewis Carroll, *Alice's Adventures in Wonderland*

To understand a language, we must understand two distinct aspects of it: the form of the language and the meaning associated with that form. These aspects are called, respectively, the syntax and the semantics of the language. When studying a programming language, it is important to understand its syntax and semantics to be able to write programs and understand what they do.

This chapter briefly introduce some topics related to the syntax and semantics of programming languages. We compare the syntax and semantics of programming languages (called **artificial languages**) with the syntax and semantics of natural languages (for example, English) that human beings use to communicate.

2.1 Syntax

The **syntax** of a language is the set of rules that define the legal relations among the components of the language, such as words, phrases, and sentences. The syntax says nothing concerning the meaning behind the components.

The syntax of a natural language is known as its grammar. In programming languages, grammars are also used to define the syntax of the language. We will draw examples of natural-language sentences from English. In English, a simple sentence is composed of a noun phrase followed by a verb phrase. For example, the sentence `The chairman lit the pipe` is composed of the noun phrase `The chairman` and the verb phrase `lit the pipe`. A noun phrase may comprise a determiner (for example, an article such as *the* or *a*) followed by a noun. In our example, the noun phrase `The chairman` is composed of the determiner `The` and the noun `chairman`. A verb phrase can be composed of a verb followed by another noun phrase. In our example, the verb phrase `lit the pipe` is composed of the verb `lit` and the noun phrase `the pipe`. Figure 2.1 shows the structure of the sentence `The chairman lit the pipe`. In this figure, S stands for sentence, NP for noun phrase, VP for verb phrase, Det for determiner, and N for noun. Note that the sentence `The pipe lit the chairman` is also syntactically correct but meaningless. This, again, stresses the idea that the syntax says nothing concerning the meaning of the sentences.

Because syntax only concerns the process of combining the symbols of a given language, it can usually be easily formalized. Linguists and mathematicians have studied syntactic properties of languages, and most of their work is applicable to programming languages.[1] To describe formally the syntax of a language, we have to present a grammar for it. A **formal grammar** has the following components:

1. A set of symbols, called **terminal symbols,** that appear in the sentences of the language. For example, in the definition of a formal grammar for English, terminal symbols are all the English words.
2. A set of symbols, called **nonterminal symbols,** that do not appear in the sentences of the language but are used to describe the components of the sentences of the language. In the definition of a formal grammar for English, the words *noun phrase* and *verb phrase* are examples of nonterminal symbols describing components of the language.

1. Of particular interest is Chomsky's work (1957, 1959) classifying languages in levels. Most of the programming languages belong to level 2, the level of *context-free languages* (Ginsburg 1966).

FIGURE 2.1 **Structure of the sentence** `The chairman lit the pipe.`

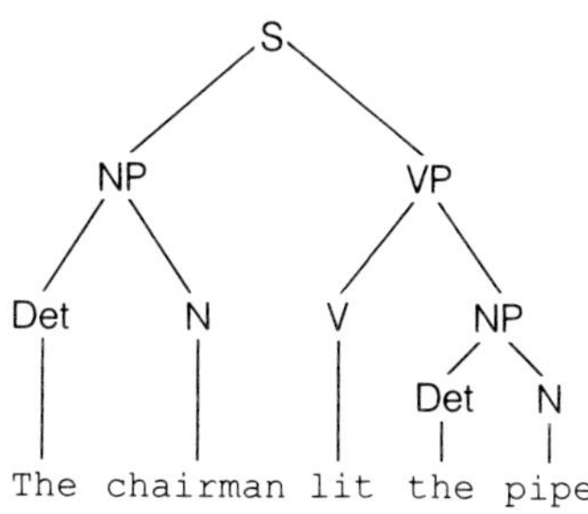

3. A special nonterminal symbol, called the **initial symbol,** that represents the main component of the language. The initial symbol for a formal grammar of English is "sentence."
4. A set of rules, called **production rules,** that describe the structure of the different components of the language. Production rules tell how to generate every possible sentence of the language from the initial symbol. As an example of a production rule for English grammar, we can say that "a sentence is a noun phrase followed by a verb phrase."

2.2 BNF notation and syntax charts

Throughout this text we will write grammars using both **BNF notation** and **syntax charts** (sometimes called **railroad charts**). BNF notation stands for **B**ackus–**N**aur **F**orm—named after John Backus and Peter Naur (1960).[2] The BNF formalism was invented by John Backus, and Peter Naur developed much of it. Its first major application was in the definition of the syntax of ALGOL 60.

The production rules of **BNF grammar** consist of a component of the language (nonterminal symbol), followed by the symbol ::=, followed by the description of that component. (Do not confuse the symbol ::= with the symbol := introduced in Chapter 1.) Nonterminal symbols are written enclosed by < and > and represent names of classes of objects. Terminal symbols are written without any enclosing symbols. The symbol | (read "or") represents possible alternatives.

2. Some authors, for example, Hopcroft and Ullman (1969) and Ginsburg (1966), use BNF to mean Backus Normal Form.

To further increase the readability of our grammars, we use two different type fonts for terminal and nonterminal symbols: `Terminal symbols` are written using a serif monospace type font (as done for "terminal symbols" above); nonterminal symbols are written using a sans serif type font (as done for "nonterminal symbols"). Notice, however, that this is just to enhance the readability of our expressions and has nothing to do with the formal properties of our grammars.

As a first example, let us consider BNF grammar for the subset of English described earlier in this chapter. We said that a sentence comprises a noun phrase followed by a verb phrase. Using S, NP, and VP to represent sentence, noun phrase, and verb phrase, respectively, the BNF rule that defines the structure of a sentence is

<S> ::= <NP> <VP>

This rule is read: "A sentence is defined to be ('is defined to be' is represented by the operator ::=) a noun phrase, followed by ('followed' is implicit when we write one nonterminal symbol after the other) a verb phrase." A noun phrase is a determiner followed by a noun, which is expressed by the rule

<NP> ::= <Det> <N>

where Det stands for determiner and N stands for noun. Finally, a verb phrase is a verb followed by a noun phrase, which can be written as

<VP> ::= <V> <NP>

where V stands for a verb. Note that there is a straightforward relationship between the rules of a BNF grammar and the structure of the sentences in the language (see Figure 2.1). In fact, each rule of the grammar can be considered as defining a structure in which the symbol at its left-hand side is immediately above the symbols at its right-hand side (we say that the symbol on the left-hand side *dominates* the symbol on the right-hand side). In Figure 2.1 S dominates both NP and VP, corresponding to the rule <S>::=<NP><VP>; NP dominates Det and N, corresponding to the rule <NP>::=<Det><N>, and so forth.

A visual interpretation of the production rules of a BNF grammar can be given by a syntax chart. A **syntax chart** defines the nonterminal symbol that appears at its upper-left corner. It comprises arrows that connect terminal and/or nonterminal symbols. Nonterminal symbols are enclosed by a box, and terminal symbols are not. To obtain a description of the nonterminal symbol defined by a syntax chart, we follow the arrows, starting at the left, as if they were railroad tracks. Whenever the road splits, we can

FIGURE 2.2 Syntax charts for S, NP, and VP.

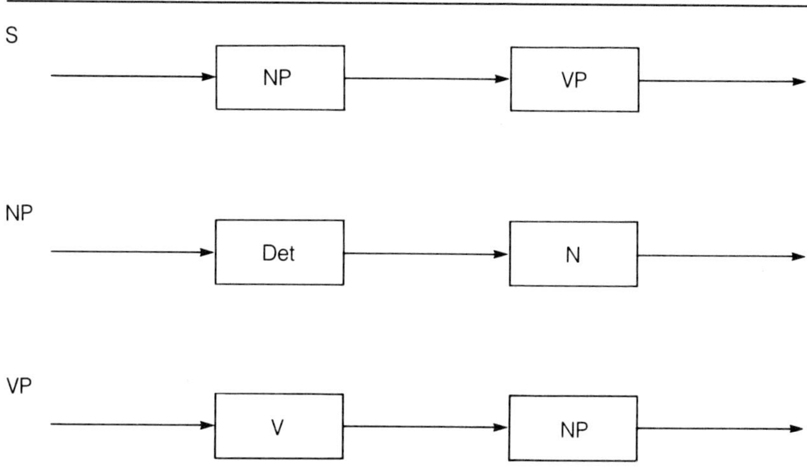

go either way. We are done when the rightmost arrow is reached. In Figure 2.2 we show syntax charts defining S, NP, and VP.

As a second example, let us consider BNF grammar to describe binary numerals. A binary numeral may have any number of the digits 0 and 1. The following BNF grammar defines binary numerals:

<binary numeral> ::= <binary digit> |
<binary digit> <binary numeral>

<binary digit> ::= 0 | 1

In this grammar, the terminal symbols are 0 and 1, and the nonterminal symbols are binary numeral (the initial symbol of the grammar) and binary digit. This grammar has two production rules. The first one defines the class of binary numerals, represented by the nonterminal symbol binary numeral, as being either a binary digit or a binary digit followed by a binary numeral.[3] The second part of this rule simply says that a binary numeral is a binary digit followed by a binary numeral. Successive uses of this rule let us conclude that in a binary numeral we can have as many binary digits as we want (that is, we can apply this rule as many times as we want). You

3. Make sure that you understand this production rule. It represents your first contact with a very important class of definitions called *recursive definitions,* in which an object is defined in terms of itself (discussed in Chapter 9).

FIGURE 2.3 Structure of `101`.

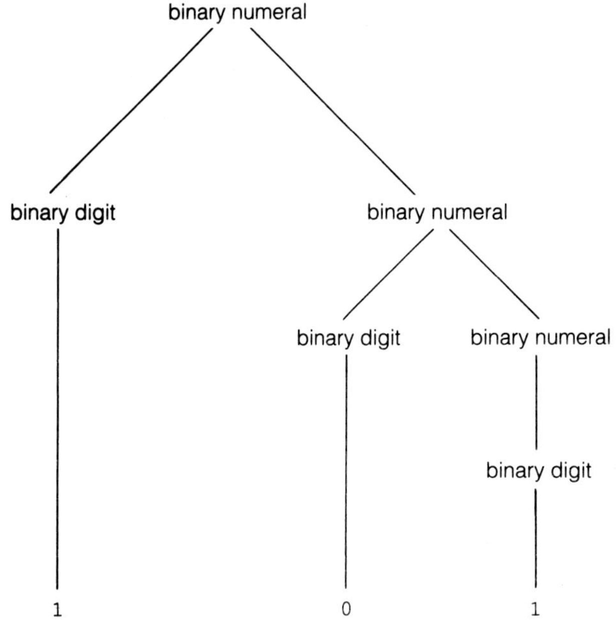

might now ask how we stop. Remember that the first part of this very same rule simply states that a binary numeral is a binary digit; so whenever we use that part, we are done. The second rule of this grammar defines a binary digit, represented by the nonterminal symbol binary digit, as being either 0 or 1. Figure 2.3 shows the structure of the binary numeral 101 according to the grammar presented, and Figure 2.4 shows syntax charts corresponding to binary numeral and binary digit.

Two aspects are worth stressing concerning this grammar: First, BNF defines a binary numeral syntactically and says nothing concerning the meaning of a binary numeral; second, this BNF is not the only grammar that defines binary numerals. Instead, we could have used the following grammar (whose syntax chart is shown in Figure 2.5):

```
<binary numeral> ::= 0 <binary numeral> |
                     1 <binary numeral> |
                     0 | 1
```

FIGURE 2.4 **Syntax charts for** binary numeral **and** binary digit.

binary numeral

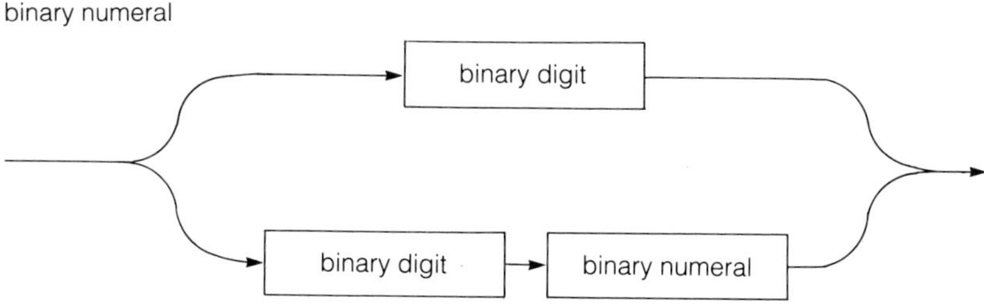

binary digit

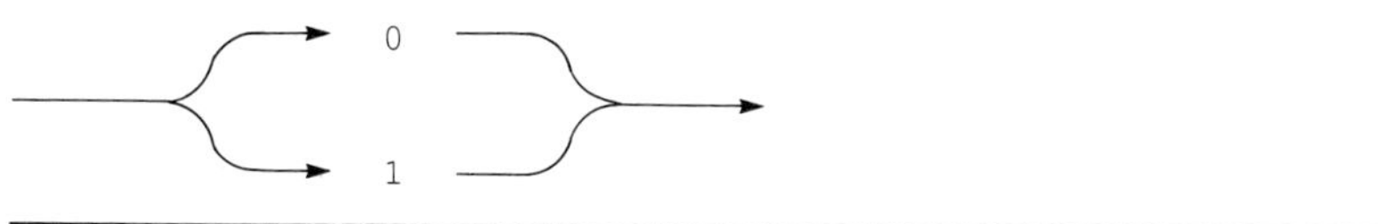

FIGURE 2.5 **Syntax chart for** binary numeral.

binary numeral

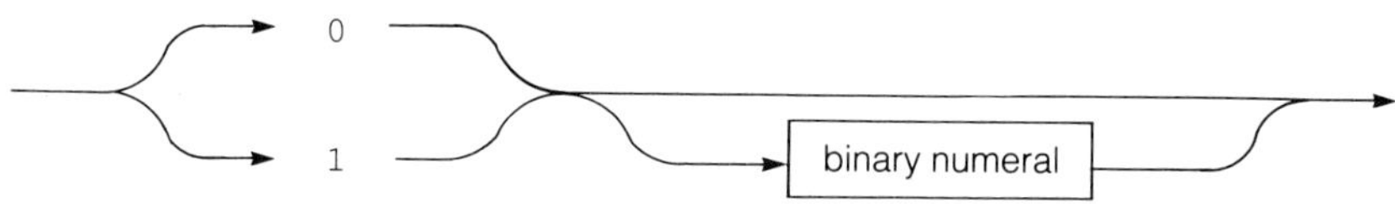

Up to now, our syntax charts have reflected the rules of our BNF grammars. One advantage of using syntax charts is that we can somewhat simplify the rules of our grammars and present the sentences generated by the grammar in an intuitive way. In Figure 2.6 another syntax chart is shown for binary numeral, which reflects the fact that a binary numeral may

FIGURE 2.6 **Alternative syntax chart for** binary numeral.

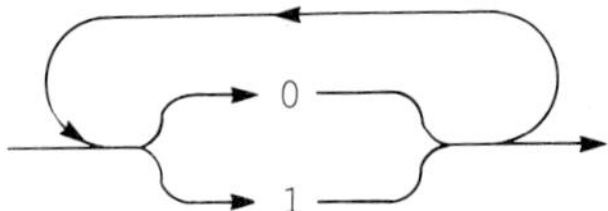

have as many 0s and 1s as we want, no matter in what order. In other words, the advantage of using syntax charts is that they give a general "picture" of what a nonterminal symbol looks like. Figure 2.6 gives an example. Syntax charts sometimes represent some simplifications, thus their usefulness; for this reason, they are not always as rigorous as BNF expressions.

The simplifications used in syntax charts sometimes may leave out the specifications of some components or fail to fully define the structure of the nonterminal symbols. For example, the syntax chart in Figure 2.6 does not say that a binary number may have two components, a binary digit and a binary numeral.

As another example, we consider the following grammar that defines the integer numerals:

<integer> ::= <numeral> | + <numeral> | - <numeral>

<numeral> ::= <digit> | <digit> <numeral>

<digit> ::= 0 | 1 | 2 | 3 | 4 | 5 | 6 | 7 | 8 | 9

The first production rule of this grammar defines an integer as being an unsigned numeral, a numeral preceded by a + sign or a numeral preceded by a − sign. The second rule defines a numeral as being either a digit or a digit followed by a numeral. The last rule defines the digits. In this grammar, the terminal symbols are 0, 1, 2, 3, 4, 5, 6, 7, 8, 9, +, and -. The nonterminal symbols are integer, numeral, and digit. The initial symbol is integer. In Figure 2.7, we show a syntax chart for integer.

Finally, let us consider the following grammar that defines a larger subset of English than our first example (in Exercise 3, you will provide syntax charts for this grammar). It should be noted that a complete grammar for English is extremely complicated and cannot be expressed with

FIGURE 2.7 **Syntax chart for** integer.

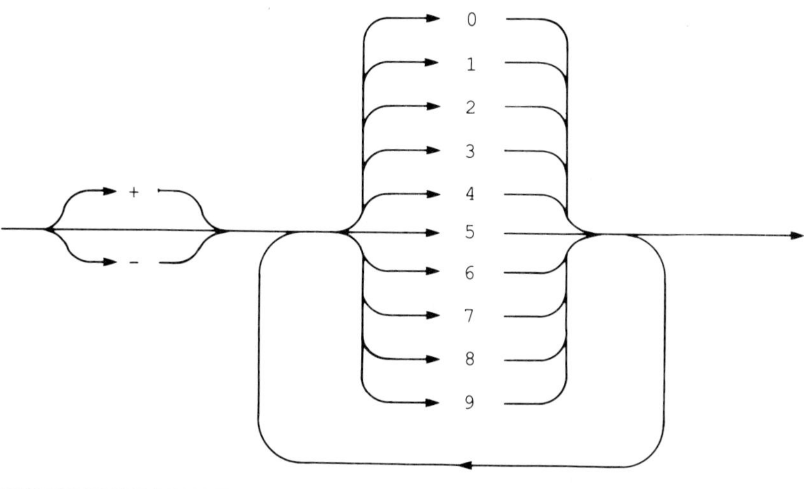

only BNF notation. (In this grammar, PP stands for prepositional phrases and Prep stands for preposition.)

<S> ::= <NP> <VP> | <NP> <VP> <PP>

<NP> ::= <N> | <Det> <N> | <N> <PP> |
<Det> <N> <PP>

<VP> ::= <V> | <V> <NP> | <V> <PP> |
<V> <NP> <PP>

<PP> ::= <Prep> <NP>

<Det> ::= `a` | `the`

<N> ::= `I` | `man` | `hill` | `telescope`

<V> ::= `saw`

<Prep> ::= `on` | `with`

FIGURE 2.8 **Possible structure of the sentence** `I saw the man on the hill with a telescope.`

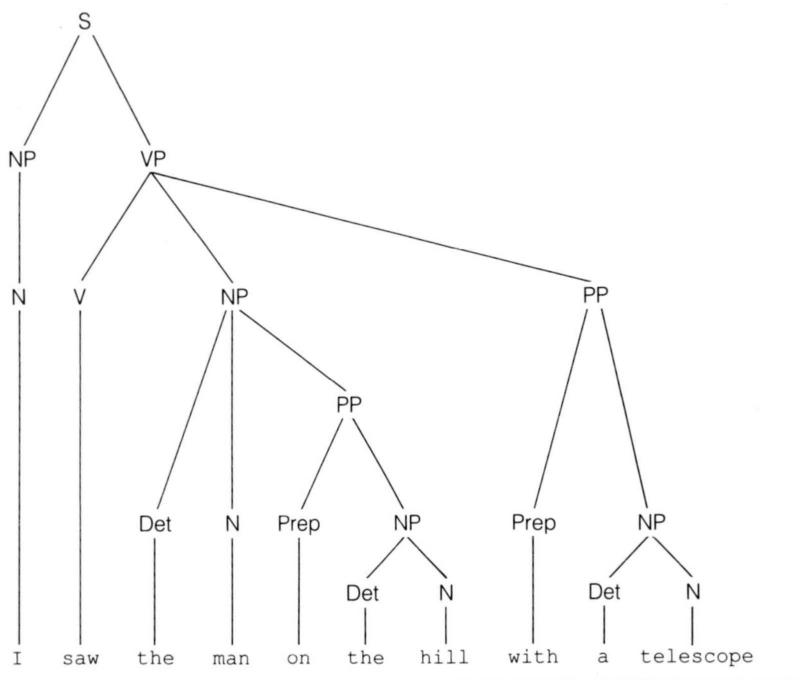

This grammar allows the construction of such sentences as `I saw the man on the hill with a telescope.`[4] This sentence can be generated in at least two different ways (Figures 2.8 and 2.9).

A grammar like this one, in which one sentence can be generated with several different structures, is said to be *ambiguous*. Grammars for natural languages are inherently ambiguous. A problem associated with ambiguous grammars is that different structures of the same sentence can have different meanings, and, thus, it is impossible to assign a unique meaning to an isolated sentence. For example, can you tell who has the telescope? Do I have it? Does the man have it? Or, is it a big telescope standing on the hill? In Figure 2.10, we show some of the possible meanings of the sentence `I saw the man on the hill with a telescope.`

In natural language, ambiguity is usually resolved by the context of the conversation. For example, the sentence `I saw the man on the`

4. This sentence represents a classical example of ambiguity in natural-language sentences. It was used by Simon (1969) and Lenhert and Ringle (1982).

FIGURE 2.9 Possible structure of the sentence `I saw the man on the hill with a telescope.`

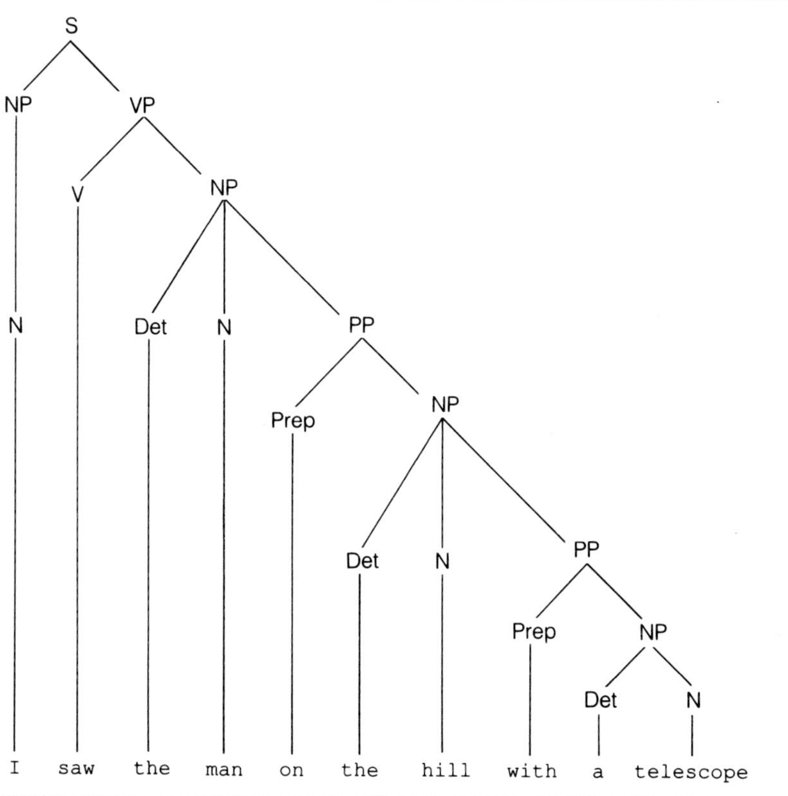

`hill with a telescope` followed by one of the sentences `I cleaned the lens to get a better view` or `We talked about astronomy` selects one of the possible interpretations of Figure 2.10 (see Figure 2.11). Syntactic ambiguity cannot be permitted in programming languages. When a language processor (for example, a compiler) analyzes a statement, it should be able to decide *exactly* what the structure of the statement is and thus what its meaning is. One of the concerns in the definition of programming languages is thus to avoid any kind of ambiguity.

The notation used to formally define a language is called a **meta-language,** which means that it is the language we use to talk *about* the language being defined. In the case of BNF grammars, the meta-language consists of the symbols <, >, |, ::=, and the nonterminal symbols. One feature of formalizing syntax in a meta-language is that the distinction between talking *in* the language and talking *about* the language becomes

FIGURE 2.10 Possible meanings of the sentence `I saw the man on the hill with a telescope.` *(Strategies for Natural Language Processing,* **1982, by W. G. Lehnert and M. H. Ringle, Figure 1.5, p. 21. Reprinted by permission of Lawrence Erlbaum Associates, Inc. and the authors.)**

perfectly clear. If such a distinction is not made, paradoxes can arise (for example, the classical sentence "This sentence is false.").

Up to now, we have been using the words *syntax* and *grammar* as synonyms. For a computational linguist, they have slightly different

FIGURE 2.11 Meaning (in context) of the sentence `I saw the man on the hill with a telescope.` (*Strategies for Natural Language Processing*, 1982, by W. G. Lehnert and M. H. Ringle, Figure 1.6, p. 22. Reprinted by permission of Lawrence Erlbaum Associates, Inc. and the authors.)

`I cleaned the lens to get a better view.`

`We talked about astronomy.`

meanings: The word *grammar* is usually used to describe the set of rules that generate the sentences of the language; the word *syntax* is usually used to describe the procedure by which we decide whether or not the sentences of the language are syntactically correct.

2.3 Semantics

"When I use a word," Humpty Dumpty said in rather a scornful tone, "it means just what I choose it to mean—neither more nor less."

"The question is," said Alice, "whether you can *make words mean so many different things."*

"The question is," said Humpty Dumpty, "which is to be the master—that's all."

Lewis Carroll, *Through the Looking Glass*

The **semantics** of a language provide the *meaning* of every sentence of the language. The semantics say nothing concerning the *process* of generating sentences of the language.

The description of the semantics of a language is usually much harder to give than the description of its syntax. One process for describing the semantics of a language consists in supplying a description in natural language (for example, English) of each of the components of the language. Although suffering from the ambiguities associated with natural language, this process has the advantage of supplying an intuitive perspective on the language.

The formal description of programming language semantics has been studied by many researchers. However, most of these descriptions still use natural language because the formal description of programming language semantics is extremely complex and thus not easily understood by a casual user of the language.

One method used in the formal specification of programming language semantics, called the **Vienna Definition Language** (Wegner 1972), consists of the creation of structures that represent the states of an abstract machine. Anther method, called the **axiomatic method** (Hoare 1969), is based on mathematic logic and associates each statement in a program with a set of logical expressions that become true after the statement is executed. A third method, called **denotational semantics** (Gordon 1979), uses functions to associate the space of the objects of the language with the space of their possible meanings. Unfortunately, these methods are too complicated to be described in an introductory text; if you are interested in pursuing this subject, you are urged to refer to the bibliographic references.

In this book natural language is used to express the semantics of Pascal statements. Whenever we present a Pascal construct, we will define its syntax using BNF and syntax charts and then will describe in English what the computer does when it encounters the construct.

2.4 Types of programming errors

From the discussions about syntax and semantics, it should now be clear that a program may contain two distinct types of errors: syntactic errors and semantic errors.

Syntactic errors occur when the statements (or instructions) of the program are not written according to the rules of the grammar of the programming language used. The detection of these errors is performed by the language processor (for example, the compiler), which supplies diagnostic messages about what is likely to be wrong. Syntactic errors must be corrected before the execution of the statements of the program; that is, the language processor cannot execute any statement that is not syntactically correct.

Semantic errors (or logical errors) are normally much harder to find than syntactic errors. These errors occur when the programmer does not properly express the sequence of actions to be executed. The programmer may have meant one thing but written another. In this book we deal with programming techniques that minimize the number of semantic errors. We also discuss methods for detecting and correcting semantic errors.

The errors in a program are called **bugs,** and the process of detection and correction of syntactic and semantic errors is called **debugging.** The expression "bug" was originated by one of the pioneers of computer science, Grace Murray Hopper. In August 1945, Hopper and some of her associates were working with an experimental computer, the Harvard Mark I, when one of its circuits stopped functioning. One of the researchers located the problem and, with the help of tweezers, removed it: a two-inch-long moth. Hopper taped the moth in her notebook and said, "From now on whenever a computer has problems I will say it has bugs." The moth still exists today, together with the records of the experiments, at the U.S. Naval Surface Weapons Center, in Dahlgren, Virginia (Taylor 1984, p. 44).

Summary

The concepts of syntax and semantics of a language were introduced, and some of the ways used to express them were presented. Two notations for describing the syntax, BNF and syntax charts, were discussed. BNF grammars are more rigorous but sometimes harder to understand than are syntax charts. We also discussed the types of errors that may arise in a program.

The concepts introduced in this chapter are used throughout the book in the definition of Pascal. They are useful to fully understand what can be written in Pascal and the meaning of what was written.

Suggested readings

You can explore the topics presented in this chapter more deeply by consulting the following publications:

Aho, A., and Ullman, J. 1977. *Principles of Compiler Design.* Reading, MA: Addison-Wesley.
This book presents one of the important applications of the syntactic formalism of programming languages: the development of compilers and interpreters. It describes in detail the process used in the syntactic analysis of a programming language and has mathematic content.

Lyons, J. 1977. *Semantics.* Cambridge, England: Cambridge University Press.
This book presents an excellent perspective on the semantics of natural languages.

Milne, R., and Strachey, C. 1976. *A Theory of Programming Language Semantics.* London: Chapmann & Hall.
This book gives an overview of the processes of semantic definition of programming languages.

Pratt, T. 1975. *Programming Languages: Design and Implementation*, 2d ed. Englewood Cliffs, NJ: Prentice-Hall.
Chapter 9 of this book presents a complete introduction to the syntactic formalism of programming languages. It also describes the syntax of several programming languages (FORTRAN, ALGOL 60, COBOL, PL/1, LISP 1.5, SNOBOL4, and APL).

Wegner, P. 1972. "The Vienna Definition Language." *Computing Surveys* 4(1): 5–63.
This article presents a good introduction to the Vienna Definition Language formalism for the semantic definition of a programming language.

Exercises

1. ✓ What are terminal symbols? What are nonterminal symbols?
2. ? Convince yourself that the syntax charts of Figures 2.4, 2.5, and 2.6 generate the same objects.
3. ? Provide syntax charts for the second version of the English grammar presented in this chapter.
4. ? Consider the following grammar in BNF notation, in which S is the initial symbol of the grammar. (NOTE: In this and in the following exercises, we purposely avoid the use of two different fonts for terminal and nonterminal symbols to stress that the distinction between them does not depend on the type font being used.)

```
<S> ::= b <B>
<B> ::= b <C> | a <B> | b
<C> ::= a
```

a. Which are the terminal symbols, and which are the nonterminal symbols of the grammar?

b. Which of the following sentences belongs to the language generated by the BNF grammar above:

baaab
aabb
bba
aab
baaaaba

c. For each of the sentences of the language, draw a diagram that shows its structure.

d. Write an equivalent grammar using syntax charts.

5. **!** Consider the following grammar in BNF notation, in which S is the initial symbol of the grammar:

<S> ::= <A> a
<A> ::= a <B>
<B> ::= <A> a | b

a. Which are the terminal symbols, and which are the nonterminal symbols of the grammar?

b. Which of the following sentences belongs to the language generated by this grammar?

a
aabaa
abc
abaa
aaaaabaaaaa

c. Informally describe the sentences that belong to the language generated by this grammar.

d. Draw a syntax chart for this grammar.

6. **?** Write a BNF grammar that generates sentences of the following form

aa...abb...b

in which the number of a's equals the number of b's. For example, ab, aabb, and aaaabbbb are sentences generated by the grammar but aab is not.

7. **?** Do Exercise 6 using a syntax chart.
8. **!** BNF notation is a syntactic formalism and, as such, can be defined using a BNF-like notation. Write a BNF-like grammar to define the syntax of BNF. (HINT: You may need to introduce some new notation.)
9. **!** Define BNF syntax using syntax charts.
10. **?** Sometimes, it may seem that BNF grammar has too many nonterminal symbols. For example, one may be tempted to give the following BNF definition for integer:

```
<integer> ::= <integer> <digit> |
              + <integer> <digit> |
              − <integer> <digit> |
              <digit>
<digit>   ::= 0 | 1 | 2 | 3 | 4 | 5 | 6 | 7 | 8 | 9
```

    Explain what is wrong with this grammar.
11. **?** Write a BNF grammar whose terminal symbols are s, a, and j. The sentences that belong to the language begin with the symbol s and are followed by any number (including zero) of pairs of characters. The first element of these pairs is the symbol a, and the second element is the symbol j. For example, s, saj, and sajajajaj are sentences of the language whereas sa and saja are not.
12. **?** Do Exercise 11 using a syntax chart.
13. **?** Write a BNF grammar whose terminal symbols are the characters c, a, d, and r. The sentences that belong to the language begin with the symbol c and end with the symbol r. Between the c and the r, there may be any number (at least one) of the symbols a and d. For example, car, cdr, caadr, and cdadar are sentences of the language whereas cr and crr are not.
14. **?** Do Exercise 13 using a syntax chart.
15. **!** Why is the sentence "This sentence is false" paradoxical?
16. **?** What are the sentences generated by the following grammar, in which the initial symbol is S?

```
<S> ::= <A> <S> | <S> <A> | b
<A> ::= a | A
```

17. **?** Write a syntax chart that is equivalent to the grammar of Exercise 16.

CHAPTER 3

This chapter describes the structure of a Pascal program and shows some examples of Pascal programs together with equivalent programs written in other programming languages. We introduce the concept of subprograms, discuss procedural abstraction, and present the syntax and semantics of Pascal's declaration and use of procedures.

STRUCTURE OF A PROGRAM

You have to have some order in a disordered world.
Frank Lloyd Wright (Green 1982)

This is the first chapter that deals with programming. Its goal is to show what a Pascal program looks like and to stress some of the great differences and similarities among high-level programming languages.

Before we start talking about Pascal programs, however, we define a concept that is used throughout the book, the concept of an identifier. An **identifier** is a name that refers to a program or to objects in a program. Just as there are standard rules for the names of people (for example, the first name of a person usually isn't A25 or xyz), there are rules for identifiers. In Pascal an identifier must begin with a letter (either uppercase or lowercase), which may be followed by any combination of letters or digits.[1] An identifier may be as long as we want (although some versions of Pascal may either restrict the maximum length of an identifier or only consider the first few characters of an identifier). As examples of identifiers, we have

```
A
A25
OvertimeWages
AVeryLongIdentifier
```

1. In nonstandard versions of Pascal, an identifier may contain other symbols. For example, for the version of Pascal for VAX-11 computers running under the VMS operating system, an identifier may also contain the characters $ and _.

FIGURE 3.1 **Syntax chart for** identifier.

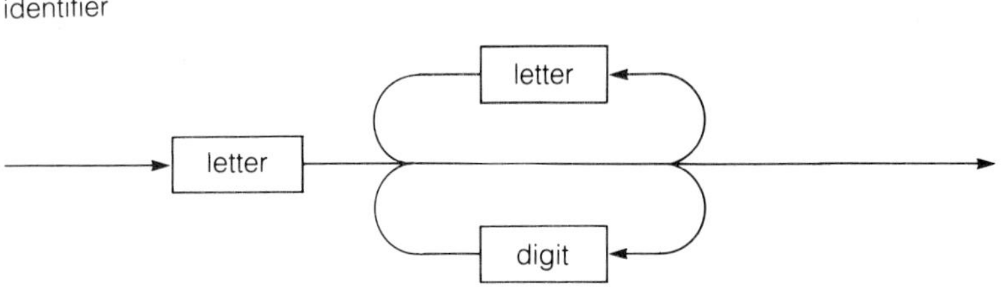

The following are not examples of identifiers: `5a` (it begins with a digit), `%2ba` (it contains a character, `%`, that is not allowed), `Computer Science` (it contains a character, " ", that is not allowed).

The legal Pascal identifiers can be formally defined by the following BNF rules (see Appendix B for the definitions of letter and digit):

<identifier> ::= <letter> |
<letter> <letters or digits>

<letters or digits> ::= <letter or digit> |
<letter or digit> <letters or digits>

<letter or digit> ::= <letter> | <digit>

Alternatively, they can be defined by the syntax chart of Figure 3.1.

3.1 Syntactic definition of a Pascal program

In Chapter 1 we said that a program is composed of two distinct parts: one part containing the description of the objects to be manipulated and the other part containing the description of the algorithm that manipulates those objects. In this section we formally describe the parts that constitute a Pascal program and briefly explain the role of each.

A Pascal program comprises a program header, followed by a block, followed by a period. Using BNF notation we can describe a Pascal program in the following way:

<Pascal program> ::= <program header> <block>.

The program header gives a name to the program and defines how it communicates with the outside world. The block contains the description of the objects used by the program and the algorithm that manipulates those objects. The program header is syntactically defined as

<program header> ::= `program` <identifier> (<file identifiers>) ;

In the program header we identify the name of the program (the program's name is given by the identifier that follows the word `program`) and the files the program uses. A **file** is a set of related information (programs or data) that is stored somewhere in the computer.

A block is syntactically defined in the following way:[2]

<block> ::= <label declaration part>
<constant definition part>
<type definition part>
<variable declaration part>
<function and procedure declaration part>
<statement part>

In a block we describe the objects that are used by the program and the algorithm that manipulates those objects. The instructions of a Pascal program are called **statements,** and they are placed in the statement part that is defined as

<statement part> ::= <compound statement>

<compound statement> ::= `begin` <statements> `end`

<statements> ::= <statements> |
<statement> ; <statements>

Figure 3.2 shows a syntax chart for Pascal program. From this chart we can see that any one of the label declaration part, constant definition part, type definition part, variable declaration part, or function and procedure declaration part might not exist in a Pascal program (this aspect is not evident from the BNF definition of block). When some optional component (nonterminal

2. The syntactic definitions of constant definition part, type definition part, and variable declaration part are given in Chapter 5. The syntactic definition of the function and procedure declaration part is given later on in this chapter. In this book we will not discuss the label declaration part, which does not exist in our programs. A description of the label declaration part can be found in Cooper (1983) or Jensen and Wirth (1974).

FIGURE 3.2 Syntax chart for Pascal program.

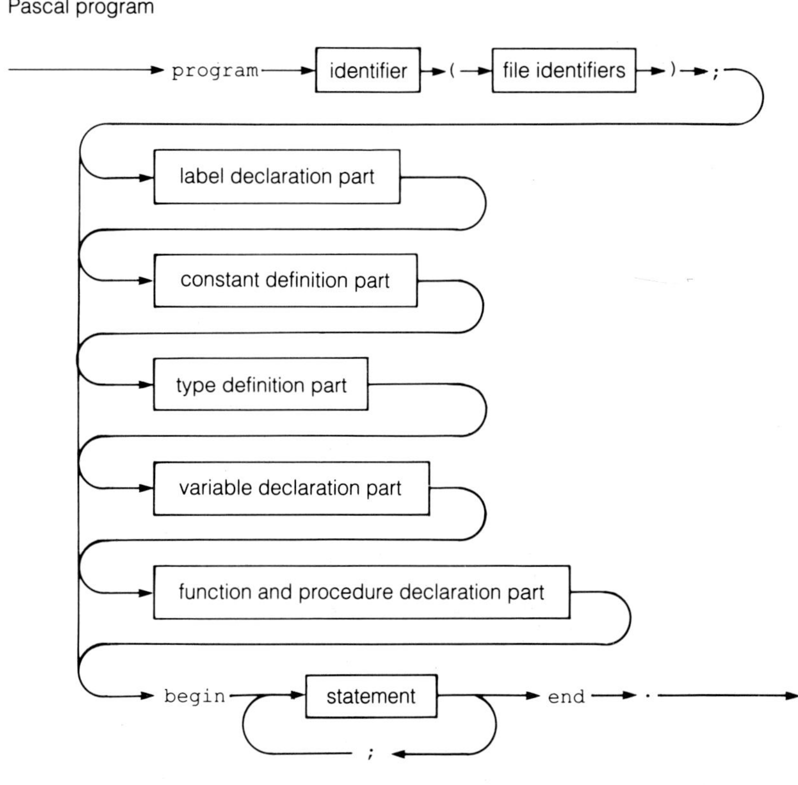

symbol) does not exist in a particular program, we say that the component is empty.

Figure 3.3 uses BNF-like notation and shows the components of a Pascal program that are used in this book. Note that the nonterminal symbol file identifiers was replaced by `input, output` (our most common use of the nonterminal symbol file identifiers) and that the label declaration part is empty. The first line in Figure 3.3 corresponds to the program header. We said that the identifier immediately following the word `program` represents the **name of the program.** The expression `input, output` identifies how the program interacts with the outside world. (This expression may sometimes be replaced by another one containing names of the files to be used by the program.)

FIGURE 3.3 Components of a Pascal program.

```
program <identifier> (input, output) ;
<constant definition part>
<type definition part>
<variable declaration part>
<function and procedure declaration part>
begin
    <statements>
end.
```

In the constant definition part, the constants that are used by the program are defined. In the type definition part, new types of objects can be defined. In the variable declaration part, *every* variable that is used by the program is declared. In the function and procedure declaration part, we define the functions and procedures used by the program.[3] The algorithm of the program is represented in Figure 3.3 by the nonterminal symbol statements. This algorithm, together with the words `begin` and `end`, belongs to the statement part.

We can insert blank lines anywhere in the program. These blank lines have no effect on the behavior of the program and are ignored by the computer. Their purpose is to separate the components of the program, thus increasing the readability of the program.

Furthermore, we can insert comments anywhere in the program. **Comments** are natural-language sentences that explain the meanings of identifiers, the goals of parts of the program, and certain aspects of the algorithm, for example. Comments may also be expressions in mathematic notation asserting or proving properties about the program. Comments increase the readability of the program. In Pascal, comments are delimited by the symbols { and }. (Some versions of Pascal also recognize the symbols `(*` and `*)` as comment delimiters.) As with blank lines, comments are ignored by the Pascal compiler. Whenever the Pascal compiler finds the symbol {, it identifies the beginning of a comment and ignores everything that is placed between this symbol and the first occurrence of the symbol }, which signals the end of the comment. Whenever you write a comment, make sure that you indicate where your comment ends. If you forget to

3. You may be wondering why some of these nonterminal symbols use the word *definition* whereas others use the word *declaration*. This is explained in Chapter 5.

signal the end of one comment (that is, if you forget to write }), the Pascal compiler will take some of the statements of your program to be part of the comment (all the statements that precede the first occurrence of either } or *)) and will therefore ignore them.

Keep in mind that what we have defined so far is the "skeleton" of a Pascal program. The next chapters will show how to flesh out this "skeleton."

3.2 Examples of programs

This section presents some programs written in Pascal and equivalent programs written in other high-level programming languages: BASIC, FORTRAN, and LISP. These other programs are equivalent in that given the same data they produce the same result. This section has two goals. On the one hand, it gives an idea of what a Pascal program looks like, and it will give you the ability to understand what a Pascal program does before you know how to write one. On the other hand, it shows the differences and the similarities that exist among high-level programming languages.

As an exercise, try to understand what each of the programs presented does. Do not be concerned about how each program was developed; rather, try to read the statements and understand their meaning.

Figure 3.4 shows a Pascal program that reads a sequence of nonnegative integers and computes their average. The amount of numbers to be read is unknown beforehand. To tell the computer that the sequence of numbers has ended, we will supply a negative number.

Figure 3.5 presents another version of the same program in Figure 3.4. Notice that the programs of Figures 3.4 and 3.5 have exactly the same words and the same punctuation marks, placed in exactly the same order. For a Pascal compiler, both programs represent *exactly* the same Pascal program. For the human reader, they don't look like the same program: The program in Figure 3.4 is neatly displayed and easy to read; the program in Figure 3.5 is a big mess.

Before proceeding with the description of this program, we should mention the usual way of writing (graphically laying out) the different components of a Pascal program. The Pascal language imposes only one restriction on the physical placement of the statements of a program: A name (identifier or string—a string is defined in Chapter 5) cannot be broken; this means that spaces and end of lines cannot appear inside a name—that is, a line cannot end in the middle of an identifier. (This contrasts with some other high-level programming languages, for example, FORTRAN, in which each statement must be written on a separate line, beginning in column 7 and not going beyond column 72.) However, to increase the readability of a program (for this effect, compare programs

FIGURE 3.4 Average computation in Pascal.

```
program Average (input, output);

{ This program reads a sequence of positive integers
  and computes their average. The end of the sequence
  is signaled with a negative number }

var number, sum, amount : integer;

{ Meaning of the variables:
   number    - number read by the computer
   sum       - sum of the numbers read so far
   amount    - amount of numbers read so far }

begin
   sum := 0;
   amount := 0;
   writeln('Please type an integer number ',
           ' followed by RETURN');
   writeln('A negative number will end the program');
   readln(number);
   while number >= 0 do { update sum and amount }
      begin
         sum := sum + number;
         amount := amount + 1;
         writeln('Please type an integer number ',
                 'followed by RETURN');
         writeln('A negative number will end the program');
         readln (number)
      end;
   if amount = 0 then
      writeln('Can''t compute the average')
   else
      writeln('The average is: ', sum/amount)
end.
```

FIGURE 3.5 Another version of the program in Figure 3.4.

```
program Average (input, output);{ This program reads a
sequence of positive integers and computes their average.
The end of the sequence is signaled with a negative number
}var number, sum, amount : integer;{ Meaning of the
variables: number  - number read by the computer sum
- sum of the numbers read so far amount  - amount of
numbers read so far }begin sum := 0;amount := 0;
writeln('Please type an integer number ','followed by RETURN');
writeln ('A negative number will end the program');readln
(number);while number >= 0 do { update sum and
amount }begin sum := sum + number;amount := amount + 1;
writeln('Please type an integer number ','followed by RETURN');
writeln('A negative number will end the program');
readln (number)end;if amount = 0 then
writeln('Can''t compute the average')else
writeln('The average is: ', sum/amount)end.
```

in Figures 3.4 and 3.5), it is usual to use the following two rules for the graphic layout of the components of a Pascal program:

1. Do not write more than one statement on a line (with the possible exception of some very short statements).
2. Statements should be indented so that every statement that belongs to a set of statements (statements that correspond to a subproblem, interrelated statements, and so on) is indented by the same amount. This second rule has the effect of laying out the statements of a program so that statements that are naturally *thought of* as a single unit are made to *look* like a unit. This aspect is described in detail throughout the book.

Let us now look at the program shown in Figure 3.4.

1. The name of this program is `Average` (the identifier that appears immediately after the word `program`).
2. Following the program header (the first line of the program), there is a comment that explains in English what the program does. This comment occupies three lines (notice that there is one single occurrence of the symbols { and }).

3. The line after the comment, beginning with the word `var`, tells the Pascal compiler the names and types of the variables used by the program. In our example, we have three variables: `number`, `sum`, and `amount`, whose meaning is explained by a comment following their declaration.
4. The word `begin` in this program signals the beginning of the algorithm.
5. In the algorithm the values of `sum` and `amount` are set to 0 (the symbol := is read "becomes"), and the computer asks the user to type an integer number. It then reads the number typed in by the user—statement `readln(number)`—and begins a repetitive loop: While the value of `number` is greater than or equal to 0—remember that a negative number signals the end of the execution of the program—the computer updates the values of the `sum` and `amount` and asks the user to type another number. It is important to understand that while the number read is greater than or equal to 0, the computer repeats the sequence of statements enclosed by the pair `begin/end`. A `begin/end` pair acts in Pascal like parentheses do in mathematics; it groups statements together. After reading a number that is less than 0, the computer then tests whether the amount of numbers read was 0. This is done in the statement that begins with the words `if amount=0 then`. If `amount` is 0, then it means that the first number typed in by the user was a negative number, and no average can be computed. In this case the computer will write `Can't compute the average`. Otherwise, the computer will tell the user the value of the average (given by `sum` divided by `amount`).

Figure 3.6 shows another Pascal program that computes the average of a sequence of positive integers. The main difference between this program and the one in Figure 3.4 is that the program in Figure 3.6 defines a new operation, `ReadNumber`, which asks the user to type a number and then reads that number. This is similar to the definition of "4 dc closed together" for the Maracas Stitch (see Chapter 1). As an exercise, carefully follow this program and compare it with the program in Figure 3.4.

Figure 3.7 presents a FORTRAN program to solve the same problem (in FORTRAN, a comment is represented by a line beginning with the character `C`). There are many similarities between this program and the Pascal program. You should have no trouble understanding what it does. The main sources of difficulty may be the expressions `NUMBER.GE.0` and `AMOUNT.EQ.0`, which should be read as "number greater than or equal to zero" and "amount equal to zero," respectively. There are fundamental differences between the Pascal and FORTRAN programs: the nonexistence of the `while` construct in FORTRAN, which has to be simulated with an explicit jump statement (statement `GO TO 1`), and the lack of punctuation

FIGURE 3.6 Average computation in Pascal with ReadNumber.

```
program Average (input, output);

{ This program reads a sequence of positive integers
  and computes their average. The end of the sequence
  is signaled with a negative number }

var number, sum, amount : integer;

{ Meaning of the variables:
   number   - number read by the computer
   sum      - sum of the numbers read so far
   amount   - amount of numbers read so far }

     procedure ReadNumber(var nbr : integer);
     begin
        writeln('Please type an integer number ',
                'followed by RETURN');
        writeln('A negative number will end the program');
        readln(nbr)
     end; { ReadNumber }

begin
   sum := 0;
   amount := 0;
   ReadNumber(number);
   while number >= 0 do { update sum and amount }
      begin
         sum := sum + number;
         amount := amount + 1;
         ReadNumber(number)
      end;
   if amount = 0 then
      writeln('Can''t compute the average')
   else
      writeln('The average is: ', sum/amount)
end.
```

FIGURE 3.7 Average computation in FORTRAN.

```
      PROGRAM AVERAGE

C THIS PROGRAM READS A SEQUENCE OF POSITIVE INTEGERS
C AND COMPUTES THEIR AVERAGE. THE END OF THE SEQUENCE
C IS SIGNALED BY A NEGATIVE NUMBER

      INTEGER NUMBER, SUM, AMOUNT

C MEANING OF THE VARIABLES:
C   NUMBER    - NUMBER READ BY THE COMPUTER
C   SUM       - SUM OF THE NUMBERS READ SO FAR
C   AMOUNT    - AMOUNT OF THE NUMBERS READ SO FAR

      SUM = 0
      AMOUNT = 0
1     PRINT*, 'Please type an integer number'
      PRINT*, '(A negative number will end the program)'
      READ*, NUMBER
      IF (NUMBER.GE.0) THEN
         SUM = SUM + NUMBER
         AMOUNT = AMOUNT + 1
         GO TO 1
      ENDIF

      IF (AMOUNT.EQ.0) THEN
         PRINT*, 'Can''t compute the average'
      ELSE
         PRINT*, 'The average is ', FLOAT(SUM)/AMOUNT
      ENDIF

      STOP
      END
```

marks in FORTRAN (there are rigid rules for displaying statements of a FORTRAN program, and thus there is no need to have a symbol that shows where one statement ends and the next begins). There are many more differences (and more important ones) between Pascal and FORTRAN than those pointed out. The comparison between the two languages, however, is beyond the scope and level of this book.

FIGURE 3.8 Average computation in BASIC.

```
100 REM THIS PROGRAM READS A SEQUENCE
110 REM OF POSITIVE INTEGERS AND
120 REM COMPUTES THEIR AVERAGE. THE
130 REM END OF THE SEQUENCE IS SIGNALED
140 REM BY A NEGATIVE NUMBER
150 SUM = 0
160 AMOUNT = 0
170 INPUT "Please type an integer number ";NUMBER
180 IF NUMBER<0 THEN GOTO 220
190 SUM = SUM + NUMBER
200 AMOUNT = AMOUNT + 1
210 GOTO 170
220 IF AMOUNT = 0 THEN GOTO 250
230 PRINT "Average = ";SUM / AMOUNT
240 GOTO 260
250 PRINT "Can't compute the average"
260 PRINT "Good bye"
```

Figure 3.8 presents a BASIC program to solve the same problem. This program is written using Applesoft BASIC for the Apple IIe Computer.[4] (In BASIC a comment is represented by a line beginning with the word REM.) One obvious difference among BASIC, Pascal, and FORTRAN programs is the number preceding each line of the BASIC program. These numbers are part of the program and are used by some of its statements (for example, the statements in lines numbered 180 and 240). Another difference in the BASIC program is that there is no explicit declaration of the variables used in the program. Besides these two features, BASIC statements presented in this program somewhat resemble statements of the Pascal and FORTRAN programs (although there are fundamental differences among those languages). As an exercise, try to understand how this program works.

As a second example, consider a program that reads an integer number and computes its factorial. The factorial of a positive integer, say n, (written $n!$) is defined to be $n! = n! * (n - 1) * ... * 2 * 1$. For example, factorial of 4 is $4 * 3 * 2 * 1 = 24$. (We will discuss this further in Chapter 9.)

4. The word *Apple* is a registered trademark of Apple Computer, Inc.

FIGURE 3.9 Factorial computation in Pascal.

```
program Factorial (input, output);

{ This program reads an integer number, computes
  its factorial, and prints the result }

var number, fact, i : integer;

{ Meaning of the variables
     number - number whose factorial we want to compute
     fact   - factorial of "number"
     i      - auxiliary variable }

begin
   repeat
      writeln('Please type a positive integer number');
      readln(number)
   until number > 0;

   fact := 1;
   for i := 1 to number do
       fact := fact * i;

   writeln('The factorial of ',number:2,' is ',fact:3)
end.
```

Figure 3.9 presents a Pascal program that computes the value of the factorial function. Let us look at the algorithm of this program: The program asks the user to type an integer number and reads that number (making sure that the number read is positive). Afterward, it will compute the factorial of the number read, using the statements

```
fact := 1;
for i := 1 to number do
    fact := fact * i;
```

The first statement sets the value of `fact` to be `1`, and the next statement begins a repetitive loop in which the value of the variable `i` varies from `1` to `number`. For each value of `i`, it executes the statement `fact := fact`

TABLE 3.1 Computing factorial for `number = 4`.

Value of `i`	*Value of* `fact` *before execution of* `fact := fact * i`	*Value of* `fact` *after execution of* `fact := fact * i`
1	1	1
2	1	2
3	2	6
4	6	24

`* i`. Table 3.1 shows the different values of the variables `fact` and `i` when `number` is 4. If we execute this program and supply the value 4, the program will print `The factorial of 4 is 24`.

Figure 3.10 presents another Pascal program that computes the value of the factorial function. The programs in Figures 3.9 and 3.10 use fundamentally different methods for the computation of the factorial function: The program in Figure 3.9 uses an **iterative process,** whereas the program in Figure 3.10 uses a **recursive process**. So that you understand how the program of Figure 3.10 works, let us discuss its method of computation. As previously stated, the value of $n!$ is defined to be $n * (n - 1) * ... * 2 * 1$. One way to look at this definition is to say that $n!$ is n times $(n - 1)!$ and to write $n! = n * (n - 1)!$. In this way, $n!$ is defined in terms of factorial itself, namely, $(n - 1)!$. The question then may be asked: When do we stop? The answer is simple: We stop at the simplest value for which we can compute its factorial, namely, 1 (because $1! = 1$). The program in Figure 3.10 is based on this way of defining factorial. This program uses a function named `factorial`, which is defined inside the program. As an exercise, try to follow what this program does.

Figure 3.11 presents a program that computes factorial using LISP language (in the Franz LISP dialect). Used here, ; is the comment indicator. The following should be noted about this program:

1. The LISP syntax is very different from Pascal's syntax. LISP uses expressions written in prefix notation: The operator is written before the operands. For example, `n - 1` is written in LISP as `(- n 1)`.

FIGURE 3.10 Factorial computation in Pascal (using recursion).

```
program Factorial2 (input, output);

{ This program reads an integer number, computes
  its factorial, and prints the result }

var number, fact : integer;

{ Meaning of the variables:
     number : number whose factorial we want to compute
     fact   : factorial of "number" }

     function factorial (n : integer) : integer;
     begin
       if n = 1 then
          factorial := 1
       else
          factorial := n * factorial(n-1)
     end; { factorial }

begin
  repeat
     writeln('Please type a positive integer');
     readln(number)
  until number > 0;

  fact := factorial(number);

  writeln('The factorial of ',number:2,' is ',fact:3)
end.
```

2. In LISP there is no explicit declaration of the variables used by the program.
3. This program can be immediately supplied a value by the user, rather than needing to read the value for which factorial is to be computed.
4. This program uses the recursive process to compute factorial.

FIGURE 3.11 Factorial computation in LISP.

```
;  This function computes factorial(n)

(defun factorial (n)
       (cond ((= n 1) 1)
             (t (* n (factorial (- n 1))))))
```

By now you should have some idea of what a Pascal program looks like even though you don't know how to write one. In the next section, we introduce a key concept in the structure of programs: subprograms.

3.3 Subprograms in Pascal: functions and procedures

In Chapter 1 when we discussed procedural abstraction, we said that the possibility of grouping pieces of information together under a given name and using the whole group by referring to its name is a fundamental aspect of knowledge acquisition and use. In this section we will study how to name groups of statements in Pascal and how to use those named groups of statements. These named groups of statements have the generic name of subprograms. **Subprograms** allow breaking a program into several modules, and each can be developed separately and independently of the others.

A subprogram performs the same actions a program does: It receives information, manipulates the information received, and produces new information. However, a subprogram is used by a program for a specific purpose. Whenever the program uses the subprogram to produce some results, we say that the subprogram is *called*. During the execution of a subprogram, it may happen that another subprogram is called, and so on.

High-level programming languages have, in general, two different types of subprograms: **functions** and **procedures** (some programming languages, for example, FORTRAN, use the word ***subroutine*** instead of procedure). In this first section on subprograms, we will present a simplified introduction to procedures. In Chapter 9 we return to this subject and introduce functions and all the capabilities of procedures.

To introduce the concept of procedure, let us consider again the Maracas Stitch pattern, which was presented in Chapter 1 and whose description is reproduced here for convenience.

MARACAS STITCH

Chain stitch: ch.

Single crochet: sc.

Double crochet: dc.

4 Double Crochet Closed Together: * yo, insert hook in 1st, yo, draw through 1 loop, yo, draw through 2 loops*. Repeat ** 3 more times, always inserting hook in the same stitch, then * yo, draw through all 5 loops on hook, ch 1*.

Instructions for Maracas Stitch:

Row 1: On a chain base: 1 sc in each ch, 1 ch to turn.

Row 2: 1 sc, * 4 dc closed together, 1 sc in each of the following 2 sc*, 1 ch to turn.

Row 3 and all odd rows: 1 sc in each stitch.

Row 4 and all even rows: Work like row 2 but stagger the 4 dc closed together by 1st toward the left.

Within the description of this stitch, another simpler stitch is defined: "4 Double Crochet Closed Together." During the description of the Maracas Stitch, whenever we want to create the pattern corresponding to the 4 dc closed together (dc is a shorthand for double crochet), we refer to its name rather than to the sequence of actions that corresponds to it. In summary, we are first "taught" what 4 dc closed together is, and then the description of the stitch makes use of this newly acquired knowledge.

Subprograms represent a method of "teaching" something to a program. Like the use of the 4-dc-closed-together pattern, the use of a subprogram requires two steps. First, we associate an algorithm with a name; in other words, we "teach" the program that the name "means" (stands for or represents) some sequence of actions (the algorithm). Second, whenever we want to execute the sequence of actions, we refer to its name rather than to its description. The two steps needed to use a procedure are the *definition of the procedure* and the *invocation of the procedure*.

In the definition of a procedure the algorithm corresponding to the procedure is given a name. In Pascal a new procedure is created through a procedure declaration. The nonterminal symbol procedure declaration is syntactically defined in the following way (a syntax chart for procedure declaration is shown in Figure 3.12):

```
<procedure declaration> ::= <procedure header> <block>

<procedure header> ::= procedure <identifier> ; |
                       procedure <identifier>
                                 (<formal parameters>) ;
```

FIGURE 3.12 Syntax chart for procedure declaration.

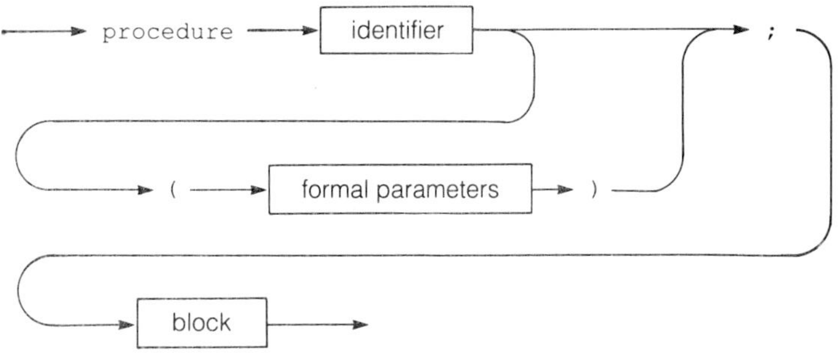

The procedure declaration has two parts: a procedure header and a block. In the procedure header we name the procedure—the name of the procedure is given by the identifier that follows the word `procedure`—and define how it communicates with the rest of the program; in the block, we define the objects used by the procedure and the sequence of actions to be executed by the procedure.

Notice the similarity between the nonterminal symbols Pascal program and procedure declaration. A Pascal program consists of a program header followed by a block, followed by a period. The program header names the block that composes the program and defines how it communicates with the outside environment by defining the files it uses. Similarly, a procedure declaration is composed of a header that names the procedure and defines how it communicates with the program followed by a block. This block, however, is not followed by a period.

By declaring a procedure, we are defining a **new statement** that will be available in the program where the procedure was declared, the statement that calls the procedure. (When a procedure is declared, the computer "learns" that the name of the procedure corresponds to the actions described in its block.) After the declaration of a procedure, the actions described in its block are executed just by naming the procedure: Whenever the computer encounters the name of the procedure in the program, it executes the algorithm associated with the procedure.

We can think of procedures as shown in Figure 3.13. The procedure has a name (represented by the nonterminal symbol proc-name) and is associated with a block (represented by a box). The block has a "door"

FIGURE 3.13 Schematic representation of procedures.

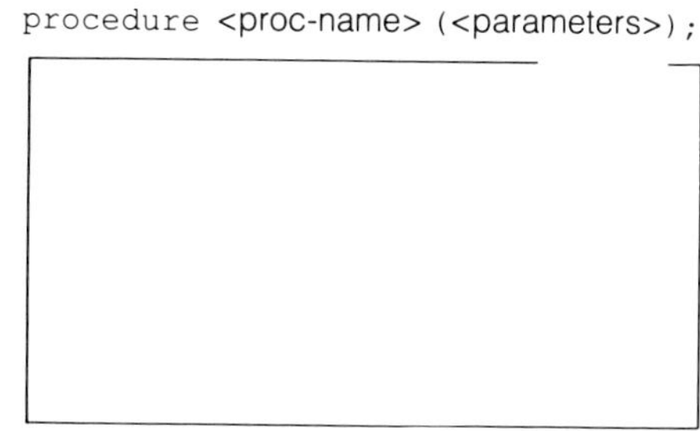

(represented by an opening near the upper-right corner of the box) that has two purposes: It may let information enter the block—the information that is given to the procedure—and thus be used by the procedure, and it may let information leave the block—the information that is produced by the procedure—and thus the outside program may know what was produced by the procedure. This communication is specified through the formal parameters, represented in Figure 3.13 by the nonterminal symbol parameters.

There are procedures that do not receive any information through their doors, and there are procedures that do not let any information come out their doors. This may seem a little strange, but, as will be discussed, there are other ways for procedures to receive and supply information.

Before we conclude this section, let us summarize the concepts introduced: We defined how procedures are created in Pascal and mentioned how they are used. After the declaration of a procedure, whenever the name of the procedure is found, the actions associated with the procedure are executed. The important aspect concerning the use of procedures is that a person looking at a program that uses procedures does not need to know *how* the procedures actually execute actions but only must know *what* the procedures do (their input/output behavior). This is **procedural abstraction**.

It is also important to remember the distinction between the *definition* (declaration) of a procedure and the *use* (invocation) of a procedure. The effect of the definition of a procedure is to teach something to the computer: The name of the procedure stands for the description of actions contained in this block. In this case no computation (action) takes place; the effect of using a procedure is the execution of a sequence of actions.

The computer does not learn anything[5] but does perform some computation. We can say that the definition of a procedure is a passive process, whereas its use is an active one.

3.4 Programs and subprograms

We have been discussing how procedures are defined and used in Pascal, and in this section we examine how to construct a complete Pascal program with procedures.

Recall that one of the components of a block is the function and procedure declaration part. This nonterminal symbol is syntactically defined by the following BNF expression and, alternatively, by the syntax chart in Figure 3.14. Notice that in this figure we don't show that the function and procedure declaration part is optional. We don't need to because this was shown in the syntax chart in Figure 3.2.

```
<function and procedure declaration part> ::=
                <declaration of procedure or function> ;
                <function and procedure declaration part> |
                <empty>

<declaration of procedure or function> ::=
                <declaration of procedure> |
                <declaration of function>
```

Subprograms are defined within the block of a program. Because subprograms are composed, in turn, by a block, they may have other subprograms defined within their blocks. In this way a Pascal program consists of a hierarchy of nested blocks: The program itself constitutes the outer block, and each one of the procedures constitutes an inner block. These inner blocks may contain, in turn, other blocks.

A family of high-level programming languages, called **block-structured languages,** is based on the definition of blocks. The first language of this family was ALGOL, developed in the 1950s, and many others have followed. Pascal is one of them. The importance of blocks in a block-

5. This is not quite true. The execution of a procedure may lead the computer to learn about other procedures that can only be used when the procedure is being executed. This aspect is first considered in the next section and is discussed in Chapter 9.

FIGURE 3.14 **Syntax chart for** function and procedure declaration part.

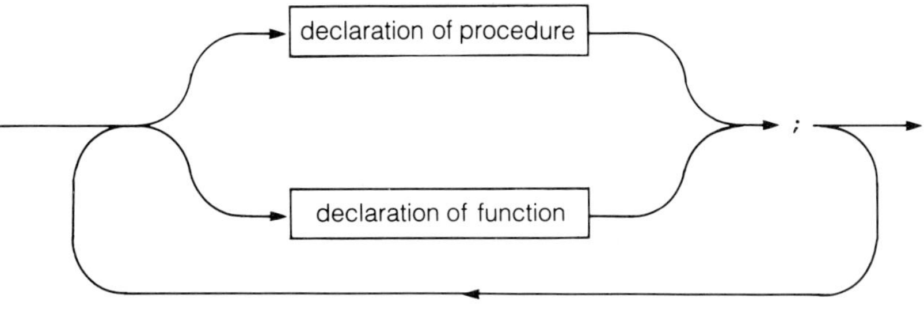

structured language stems from the following three rules that are associated with blocks:[6]

1. *Each block should correspond to a subproblem that the program has to solve.* This aspect allows the programmer to modularize the program.
2. *The algorithm used by a block is "hidden" from the rest of the program.* This allows control of the complexity of the program.
3. *Every piece of information defined within a block belongs to that block and can only be used by that block and by the blocks defined within that block.* This allows effective protection of the information defined within each block from unauthorized use by the statements of another block.

This third aspect has important consequences in Pascal and in other block-structured languages and can be simply stated as follows: Blocks are selfish, they do not allow the outer blocks to access information defined inside them. Why cannot blocks use information defined within inner blocks? Because information defined within a block may not be ready for use until some sequence of actions is applied to it. The block where that information is defined is the only one that knows about it and, consequently, the only one that can guarantee that the proper sequence of actions is applied before the information is used.

6. The rules presented here are somewhat informal and simplified. Their rigorous statements can be found in Chapter 9.

3.5 An example of subprograms

This section presents a Pascal program that uses subprograms. Besides showing the use of subprograms and the block structure of a Pascal program, a first example of the top-down design technique mentioned in Chapter 1 is given. The example allows us to illustrate the block structure of a real program and how to associate procedural abstraction with subprograms. We know *what* subprograms do, but we do not know *how* they do it.

Suppose that we want to write a program to read three positive integers, representing the lengths of the sides of a triangle, and to let the user know whether the triangle is equilateral (all its sides are of equal length), isosceles (two of its sides are of equal length), or scalene (all of its sides are of different lengths).

This program must accomplish three different tasks: Read the three values, classify the triangle, and inform the user about the nature of the triangle. Assuming that there are procedures that accomplish these three tasks, let us call them `ReadSides`, `Classify`, and `InformUser`. The desired task is accomplished by the Pascal program schematically shown in Figure 3.15. This figure also shows the communication between the program and the subprograms, done through the identifiers `side1, side2`, `side3`, and `cl`. Let us take, for example, the procedure `ReadSides`. Its formal parameters contain three integer variables, `side1`, `side2`, and `side3`. The word `var` in the formal parameters of this procedure informally means that these variables leave the "door" of the procedure; they will be transmitted back to the program that calls the procedure. Notice that in the statement part of the program `Triangles` the same variables appear. There is a one-to-one correspondence between these variables and the variables in the formal parameters of the procedure `ReadSides`. The communication between programs and subprograms is fully explained in Chapter 9.

The program in Figure 3.15 uses the procedures `ReadSides`, which reads three positive integers and assigns those values to the variables `side1`, `side2`, and `side3;` `Classify`, which takes the values read by `ReadSides` and classifies the triangle into equilateral, isosceles, or scalene (the classification is assigned to the variable `cl`); and `InformUser`, which takes the classification produced by `Classify` and tells the user whether the triangle is equilateral, isosceles, or scalene. Notice that we don't know yet how these procedures accomplish their jobs, but we know very well what they do; that's what counts for now.

The statement part of the program `Triangles` contains three statements, `ReadSides`, `Classify`, and `InformUser`, whose names trigger the execution of the corresponding procedures. Remember that after the definition of a procedure, its name becomes a *new* Pascal statement whose actions are described within the procedure's block. Thus, although we have

FIGURE 3.15 Program to classify triangles.

```
program Triangles (input, output);

   procedure ReadSides(var side1,side2,side3 : integer);

   procedure Classify(side1,side2,side3 : integer;
                      var cl : TriType);

   procedure InformUser(cl : TriType);

   begin
      ReadSides(side1,side2,side3);
      Classify(side1,side2,side3,cl);
      InformUser(cl);
   end.
```

not presented any Pascal statements yet, we know that the program `Triangles` can use three statements: `ReadSides`, `Classify`, and `InformUser`. These statements are created when we define the corresponding procedures and can only be used within this program.

We can add some further detail to the program `Triangles`. The procedure `ReadSides` should ask the user to type in the length of the sides of the triangle. Assuming that the procedure `AskUser` does this job, our program can be refined as shown in Figure 3.16. Notice that the procedure `ReadSides` uses the procedure `AskUser` three times (one for asking for each one of the sides). Notice also that the procedure `AskUser` should be used by the procedure `ReadSides` (the procedure that needs it). According to the third rule of block-structured languages, `AskUser` should only be used by the procedure `ReadSides`. The procedures `Classify` and `InformUser` should have no access to it. The third rule of block structure

FIGURE 3.16 Refinement of a program to classify triangles.

```
program Triangles (input, output);

    procedure ReadSides(var side1,side2,side3 : integer);

        procedure AskUser(var side : integer);

        begin
           AskUser(side1);
           AskUser(side2);
           AskUser(side3);
        end;

    procedure Classify(side1,side2,side3 : integer;
                       var cl : TriType);

    procedure InformUser(cl : TriType);

    begin
       ReadSides(side1,side2,side3);
       Classify(side1,side2,side3,cl);
       InformUser(cl);
    end.
```

guarantees that these two latter procedures have no access to them, even if they want it. The program in Figure 3.16 is still incomplete but gives an idea of the tasks involved in this problem and their interrelationships.

Figure 3.17 presents a complete version of the program **Triangles**. As an exercise, try to follow each statement of this program and identify the information that can be used by each one of the blocks.

The important thing to remember from this example is that we can break a program into a number of named blocks or subprograms, each

FIGURE 3.17 Program Triangles.

```
program Triangles (input, output);

type TriType = (equilateral, isosceles, scalene);
var  side1, side2, side3 : integer;
     cl : TriType;

  procedure ReadSides(var side1, side2, side3 : integer);

    procedure AskUser(var side : integer);
    begin
      writeln('Please type the length of one side');
      writeln('Followed by RETURN');
      readln(side)
    end; { AskUser }

  begin
    AskUser(side1);
    AskUser(side2);
    AskUser(side3)
  end; { ReadSides }

  procedure Classify(side1, side2, side3 : integer;
                     var cl : TriType);
  begin
    if (side1=side2) and (side2=side3) then
       cl := equilateral
    else
       if (side1=side2) or (side1=side3) or (side2=side3) then
          cl := isosceles
       else
          cl := scalene
  end; { Classify }

  procedure InformUser(cl : TriType);
  begin
    case cl of
       equilateral : writeln(' The triangle is equilateral');
       isosceles   : writeln(' The triangle is isosceles');
       scalene     : writeln(' The triangle is scalene')
    end
  end; { InformUser }
```

(continued)

FIGURE 3.17, *continued.*

```
begin
  ReadSides(side1, side2, side3);
  Classify(side1, side2, side3, cl);
  InformUser(cl)
end.
```

accomplishing some definite task, and use those subprograms without knowing how they accomplish their task. The program-development technique that we used in this example is **top-down design.** It consists of approaching the solution of a problem at the highest, most general, level. At any level we are concerned with *what* must be done and not *how* it must be done.

Summary

In this chapter, the first one dealing with Pascal, you learned that a Pascal program is composed of a program header, followed by a block, followed by a period. The program header defines the name of the program and the way it communicates with the outside world. The block contains the description of the objects used by the program and the algorithm that manipulates those objects.

Within a block, complex actions can be defined and given a name. Later on, whenever the sequence of actions is to be executed, we need only refer to their name. This corresponds to the concept of procedural abstraction, implemented in programming through subprograms.

Suggested readings

The complete syntactic description of a Pascal program can be found in many books on programming. Among those books, we strongly recommend Jensen and Wirth (1974) or Jensen, Wirth, Mickel, and Miner (1985), written by the creator of the language and which contain the complete report produced when the language was presented, and Cooper (1983), which contains a complete description of the ISO Pascal Standard as well as several interesting notes on the historical evolution of the language and comparisons between the ISO Standard and Jensen and Wirth's Pascal.

The comparative study of the syntax and semantics of high-level programming languages is fundamental for a complete understanding of programming languages. Such a study, however, should not start until considerable knowledge of a particular programming language has been acquired. If you want to study programming languages in detail, later on, we suggest the following books:

Ghezzi, C., and Jazayeri, M. 1982. *Programming Language Concepts.* New York: Wiley.
This very well-written book introduces, analyzes, and evaluates the main concepts of modern programming languages. One of the goals of this book is the analysis of the influence of the characteristics of programming languages on the process of program development.

Horowitz, E. 1983. *Fundamentals of Programming Language.* Rockville, MD: Computer Science Press.
This is a very good book on programming languages, focusing on different classes of languages. It presents the evolution of programming languages, presents criteria for programming language design, and describes the concepts of imperative, functional, data-flow, and object-oriented languages.

Organick, E., Forsythe, A., and Plummer, R. 1978. *Programming Language Structures.* New York: Academic Press.
This elementary book can be used as a first comparative study of programming languages. Presents similarities and differences among five high-level programming languages: ALGOL, FORTRAN, LISP, Pascal, and SNOBOL. Also presents an elementary discussion of the concepts of procedure and function. Chapter 10 briefly discusses the concepts for Pascal.

Pratt, T. 1984. *Programming Languages: Design and Implementation*, 2d ed. Englewood Cliffs, NJ: Prentice-Hall.
This excellent book presents the characteristics of programming languages and describes the syntax and semantics of some of them.

Wexelblat, R. 1981. *History of Programming Languages.* New York: Academic Press.
This book describes the history of several programming languages (FORTRAN, ALGOL, LISP, COBOL, APT, JOVIAL, GPSS, Simula, JOSS, BASIC, PL/1, SNOBOL, and APL). The history of each language is told by the developers of the language.

Exercises

1. ? Which of the following names do not represent Pascal identifiers? Why?

a. `1$`

b. `AwEiRdNaMeFoRaNiDeNtIfIeR`

c. `lower bound`

d. `program name`

e. `m:9`

2. **?** As we will see in this book, it is important that the name of an identifier be meaningful—that is, the names that you choose for the identifiers should indicate the exact purpose of the identifier. With this aspect in mind, choose meaningful names for the following identifiers:
   - **a.** Your grade-point average
   - **b.** Your best friend's grade-point average
   - **c.** The courses you are taking
   - **d.** Your expected year of graduation
   - **e.** Your favorite subject
3. **✓** Explain what happens if you forget to tell the Pascal compiler that a comment has ended.
4. **✓** Explain the advantages of properly displaying the statements of a Pascal program.
5. **?** Explain what the program in Figure 3.6 does. In other words, suppose that you were the computer and were supplied with the numbers 4, 3, 5, and −2. Explain, statement by statement, the behavior of the program.
6. **?** Write a line-by-line explanation of the behavior of the program shown in Figure 3.8.
7. **!** Suppose that you are the computer executing the program in Figure 3.9 and that you are supplied the number 6. Explain every operation that is performed by the program and justify its output.
8. **!** Suppose that you are the computer executing the program in Figure 3.10. Suppose furthermore that the program was supplied the number 3. Follow step by step the behavior of the program and justify its output.
9. **?** Suppose that the program `Triangles` in Figure 3.17 reads the values 5, 10, and 5. Follow step by step the behavior of the program and find out what it writes.

CHAPTER 4

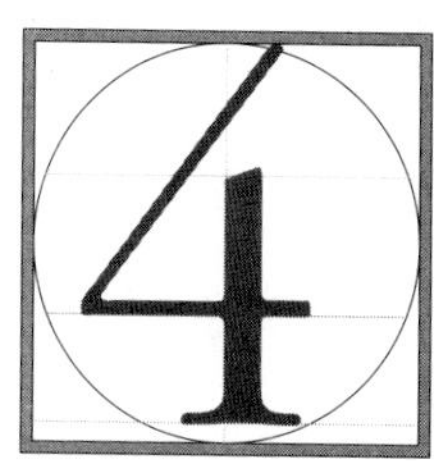

This chapter describes the steps that a programmer should take when developing a program, lists the goals for writing a good program, and describes some tools for attaining those goals. We consider top-down design technique, with an emphasis on modularization and good documentation. Approaches for debugging and testing are also discussed.

DEVELOPMENT OF PROGRAMS

I'd rather write programs to write programs than write programs.
Dick Sites (Bentley 1985)

The goal of this chapter is to present the steps that a programmer should take when developing a program and to give a global overview of programming activity. The expression "development of a program" is frequently considered a synonym for coding, that is, the production of instructions using a programming language. However, a considerable amount of preparatory work should precede the programming of any potential solution to a problem. This preparatory work consists of several steps: defining what should be done, removing uncertainties and ambiguities that could be contained in the statement of the problem, choosing an algorithm for the solution of the problem, and designing the algorithm using an adequate formal language. If this preparatory work is done properly, the programming phase, which looks like the most important phase for many people, becomes relatively easy and does not require much creativity. After program coding is finished, there is still considerable work to do before program development is complete. All errors must be detected and corrected, documentation must be developed, and the program must be maintained.

Thus, program development is a complex activity with several distinct phases, each of which is important and contributes to the solution of the problem. Program development normally goes through six distinct phases that, although executed sequentially, are interconnected. Detection of a deficiency in one of these phases can lead to the detection of deficiencies in one of the previous phases, which should then be repeated. Following are the phases of program development in order of their execution:

1. Analysis of the problem
2. Development of the solution
3. Programming the solution
4. Debugging and testing
5. Documentation
6. Maintenance

4.1 Analysis of the problem

A program is developed to satisfy the needs of a user or of a group of users. These needs are, in general, presented with gaps, imperfections, ambiguities, and sometimes even contradictions.

In this first phase the programmer meets with the users to discern exactly what must be done. This phase takes place before one starts to think about the solution to the problem. The goal is to define the specifications of the problem and to perceive exactly what goals are to be reached. This phase seems so easy that some programmers completely ignore it; they do not try to understand fully the problem at hand. As a result of disregarding this phase, they begin the development of a program that is ill-conceived and that might be an incorrect solution to the problem.

The result of this phase produces a document that clearly specifies from the computer science point of view what the program does as well as general-purpose program manuals, studies of possibilities for program development, estimated costs, and so on. This document does not specify *how* the program will solve the problem. However, it has two important goals: It serves as a written warranty for the user of what is going to be done, and it serves as a definition for the programmer of the goals to be attained.

4.2 Development of the solution

Having defined *what* must be done, the second phase is to find out *how* to do it. This is predominantly a creative phase in which an algorithm that solves the problem is developed.

This algorithm should be developed without any connection to a particular programming language: It should be developed in terms of control structures and abstract data types.[1] In general, the algorithm developed during this phase uses a language that is somewhat similar to a programming language but that allows some natural-language specifications. The goal is to formally describe how the problem will be solved without getting into the details of a particular programming language.

The methodology to be followed in this stage is **top-down design.** (This name was introduced by Mills 1971.) The goal of top-down design, introduced in Chapter 3, is to decrease the complexity of the problem, giving rise to algorithms that are more readable and easier to understand. According to the top-down technique, the first steps toward the solution of the problem are identifying the subproblems that constitute the problem at hand and determining the relationships between them. Next, a first approximation of the algorithm is developed. This first approximation of the algorithm is defined in terms of the identified subproblems and their interrelationships. In this algorithm we can use any operations and data types that are applicable to the problem at hand, even if they are sophisticated or difficult to implement. After the first approximation of the algorithm is completed, the process should be repeated for each of the subproblems. Each step in this process adds details relevant to the problem at hand. When a subproblem is found whose solution is known, then the algorithm for that subproblem should be written. When this method is followed, the solution to the problem is reached in sequenced steps, each of which corresponds to taking one problem, identifying its subproblems and their relationship, and writing the algorithm in terms of the identified subproblems. This is **step-wise refinement.**

This approach to developing an algorithm has two main advantages: It controls complexity, and it makes the solution modular. Concerning **control of complexity,** it should be said that, at any moment during the development of the algorithm, we are trying to solve a unique problem: We are not concerned about the details of its solution but only with its fundamental aspects (that is, subproblems that compose it and their relationship). Concerning the **modularity of the solution,** we can easily see that the resulting algorithm will have several modules, each of which corresponds to a subproblem and whose function is perfectly understood.

If we follow this methodology, we obtain an algorithm that is easy to understand and to modify. The algorithm is *easy to understand* because it is expressed in terms of the natural divisions of the problem being solved. If we need to change a particular aspect of the algorithm, we can easily discover in which module (that is, in which subproblem) the change

---

1. These two concepts are developed and explained later. Control structures are covered in Chapters 6–8 and abstract data types in Chapters 15–18.

should be made, and we have to consider only that module during the modification of the program. Therefore, algorithms become *easy to modify.* Similarly, if an error is detected in the algorithm, we need only consider the subproblem in which the error was detected.

The development of the solution is the most visible and most creative phase of the program-development cycle. It is in this phase that an algorithm for the problem is developed. The key concept in this phase is **abstraction.** Recall that there are two kinds of abstraction: procedural abstraction and data abstraction. **Procedural abstraction** means that subprograms are developed taking into account *what* they should do and not *how* they are implemented. **Data abstraction** means that the abstract *properties* of data are separated from the particular *implementation* of a data object. Abstraction is a key concept in this phase because it allows the problem to be divided into fairly independent modules, which can then be given to different programmers or different programming teams.

4.3 Programming the solution

The sooner you start coding your program, the longer it is going to take.
Henry Ledgard (1975)

Before beginning this section, it is important to consider the Ledgard quote. Ledgard stresses the fundamental importance of the phases that precede the programming of the solution. These phases must clearly define what has to be done and how to do it. The omission of these phases can lead to chaotic situations that require more time than would have been spent in carefully planning the algorithm. The programming phase should not begin until the problem has been clearly defined and an algorithm representing its solution has been planned.

The first problem to be solved in this third phase is the decision of which programming language to use. The choice of programming language depends on three considerations:

1. *The languages available in the computing system to be used.* This, in fact, is a fundamental limitation: We can only use the languages that are available.
2. *The nature of the problem.* Some programming languages are more adequate for numeric applications (for example, FORTRAN or Pascal), whereas other languages are more adequate for nonnumeric (or symbolic) applications (for example, LISP or PROLOG). If we have a choice among several programming languages, we should choose the language that is most suitable to our problem domain.

3. *The performance of the implementations of the languages usable on our computer.* Let us assume, for example, that for a numeric application we are undecided about using Pascal or PL/1. Let us assume, furthermore, that our PL/1 compiler does not produce very efficient machine-language code. This aspect may help us in deciding to use Pascal instead of PL/1.

Once we have decided which programming language to use and once we have a description of the algorithm, the coding of the statements of the program is fairly easy. We have to decide how to implement the abstract data types (see Chapters 15–18); then the statements in the algorithm should be translated into statements written in the chosen programming language.

4.4 Debugging and testing

Anyone who believes his or her program will run correctly the first time is either a fool, an optimist, or a novice programmer.
Michael Schneider, Steven Weingart, and David Perlman (1978)

During the debugging phase, we detect, locate, and correct errors that exist in the program that we have developed. Errors can cause the program to produce the wrong results or to produce no results at all.

Debugging can be the longest part of the development of a program. The time spent in debugging is directly related to the structure of the program. The top-down technique decreases the complexity of the program and thus makes debugging easy. Also, debugging techniques are not usually taught in the same systematic way as program-development techniques. Many programmers follow no method, make blind tries, or try anything because they do not know exactly how to do it.

As we know, errors in a program can be of two different types: syntactic errors and semantic errors. In the next two sections we focus on the debugging process for each of these types of errors.

4.4.1 Syntactic errors

Syntactic errors are the most common in programming and are the easiest to correct. A syntactic error occurs when a statement does not follow the syntactic rules specified for a given programming language. The syntactic errors can be caused by spelling errors when we write a statement or from not properly representing the structure of a statement.

FIGURE 4.1 Pascal program with syntactic errors.

```
program SumOfIntegers (input, output)

{ this program computes the sum of the
  ten first positive integers          }

var number, sum : integer;
1
%PASCAL-E-ERROR  14, (1) Syntax: ";" expected
begin
  sum := 0;
  number := 10;
  while number > 0 do
     begin
       sum ::= sum + number;
        1
%PASCAL-E-ERROR  10, (1) Syntax: type specification expected
       number := numb - 1
                 1
%PASCAL-E-ERROR 104, (1) Undeclared identifier NUMB
     end;
  witeln('The sum is: ',sum)
  1
%PASCAL-E-ERROR 104, (1) Undeclared identifier WITELN
end. { SumOfIntegers }
```

Syntactic errors are detected by the language processor, which produces error messages that tell in which statement the error was detected and, normally, what type of error it was. The current trend in high-level programming languages is to produce error messages that help the programmer as much as possible. Figure 4.1 shows a Pascal program to compute the sum of the first ten integers; it contains four syntactic errors. These errors are designated by the lines that begin with `%PASCAL-E-ERROR`[2] and contain an error code and a message describing the probable type of error. In the line preceding the error-message line, we find the character `1`, which indicates the point (on the line above it) at which the error was detected. Note that this does not necessarily mean that the point where the error

2. Notice that different language processors indicate errors differently.

FIGURE 4.2 Pascal program without syntactic errors.

```
program SumOfIntegers (input, output);

{ this program computes the sum of the
  ten first positive integers           }

var number, sum : integer;
begin
  sum := 0;
  number := 10;
  while number > 0 do
     begin
       sum := sum + number;
       number := number - 1
     end;
  writeln('The sum is: ',sum)
end. { SumOfIntegers }
```

occurs is indicated by the symbol `1`. The error might have been caused by a previous statement in the program. For example, the error message that appears immediately following line 4—`%PASCAL-E-ERROR 14, (1) Syntax: ";" expected`—was caused by a missing semicolon at the end of line 1 (we already know that the program header ends with a semicolon). Figure 4.2 presents the same program with all the syntactic errors corrected. (These programs were obtained from a VAX[3] computer running Pascal under VMS. The line numbers shown on the left of Figure 4.1 are automatically generated by this Pascal compiler.)

After detecting syntactic errors, the programmer must correct them using the text editor. Normally, correcting syntactic errors does not require major changes in the program. This cycle "identify syntactic errors→correct them→use the language processor" may have to be executed several times until all syntactic errors are corrected.

The syntactic debugging phase ends when the language processor does not find any syntactic errors in the program. The novice programmer usually is very happy when this happens, not realizing that the true debugging phase is about to begin.

3. VAX is a trademark of Digital Equipment Corporation.

4.4.2 Semantic errors

Semantic errors result when a syntactically correct program has a meaning for the computer that is different from the meaning that the programmer intended. Semantic errors can produce wrong results and infinite loops, can cause the execution of the program to be interrupted, and so on. Semantic errors are much harder to locate than syntactic errors because they are not detected by the language processor. The computer executes the syntactically correct program according to the meaning it has, which, when there are semantic errors, is different from what the programmer intended.

When a semantic error is detected, its source should be found using one or more of the following techniques:

1. *Trace the program.* Tracing the program can be done by adding temporary output statements to the program. These statements show the values of some variables of the program. The location of these statements should be carefully planned, and they should show the computer's execution of the program. When the behavior of the program does not correspond to the expected behavior, it means that an error was generated at (or just before) that point.
2. *Use debuggers.* Some language processors supply their users with special programs called debuggers. These allow automatic tracing of the program, enable the values of variables or statements to be changed, and so on.
3. *Use the bottom-up debugging technique.* This technique presupposes that the program is composed of several modules, each corresponding to a subproblem identified during the top-down design phase. The bottom-up debugging technique starts by debugging the modules that do not use any other modules. When these modules are completed, tested, and debugged, we go to the next higher-up module. In this way, when an error is found we have a guarantee that every module it uses does not have any errors; thus, the error should be located in the module where the error is detected. Suppose, then, that your program is composed of several procedures. To use the bottom-up debugging technique, you should begin with those procedures that do not use any other procedure. For each of them create a program that only uses that procedure and fully debug the procedure. Because the procedure should be small, this task is not very hard. Next, concentrate your attention on the procedures that only use the debugged procedures. Keep repeating this process until the entire program is debugged.

After detecting a semantic error, it must be corrected. The correction of a semantic error varies from simple cases that require only a trivial

FIGURE 4.3 A Pascal statement.

```
if a = b then
   a := a + 5
else
   b := b - 2
```

FIGURE 4.4 Another Pascal statement.

```
if a = b then
   a := a - 5
else
   b := b - 2
```

change (for example, having written a + 5 instead of a - 5) to extreme cases that require a complete revision of the program-development phase and, consequently, the development of a new program. Again, the correction of semantic errors follows a cycle "identify the error→correct it→run the program again."

After the program is executed and produces proper results, we can ask the question of whether the program solves the problem for which it was proposed, for every possible input value. To supply an affirmative answer to this question, you should create a series of input-data tests and test the behavior of the program for all these cases. The test data should be carefully chosen in such a way that all paths through the algorithm are tested. Consider, as an example, the Pascal statement in Figure 4.3. Suppose that you wanted to *decrease* the value of a by 5 if the variables a and b were equal and to decrease the value of b by 2, otherwise. In other words, what you had in mind was the statement in Figure 4.4. If this statement is only tested for the values of a that are different from those of b, this error will never be detected. The two cases—a being equal to b and a being different from b—correspond to the two paths through this statement. If you do not test the behavior of this statement through both paths, then your program may contain an error that is not detected.

It is not possible to test completely every path through complex programs. Thus, even if a complex program is tested in a systematic way, we always face the possibility of the existence of undetected errors. As Edsger Dijkstra said, "Program testing can be used to show the presence of bugs, but never to show their absence!" (Dahl, Dijkstra, and Hoare 1972, p. 6). Although there are methods to formally show that a program is correct (for example, Dijkstra 1976, Hoare 1969, and Wirth 1973), their practical applicability is still limited to very small and simple programs.

In summary, after developing the algorithm and having translated the algorithm into a suitable programming language—that is, after the program is written—the debugging and testing phase begins. **Debugging** begins with the first attempt to run the program (which usually uncovers several syntactic errors) and ends when the program runs successfully the first time. **Testing** immediately follows debugging. During testing we try to correct the bugs that still exist (or may exist) in the program, despite the fact that it ran correctly for a data sample.

4.5 Documentation

The job's not over until the paperwork's done.
Anon. (Bentley 1985)

Program documentation should begin simultaneously with the analysis of the problem and proceed as the solution to the program is being developed and written. Program documentation consists of two documents: documentation for the users of the program (user documentation) and documentation for the people who will maintain and change the program (technical documentation).

4.5.1 User documentation

User documentation explains how to use the program and consists of the following:

1. *A description of what the program does.* This description can include the general area of application of the program and the precise description of the behavior of the program. This description should be very similar to the description developed during the analysis of the problem.
2. *A description of how to use the program.* This should clearly describe to the user what should be done to use the program—for example, the commands that the computer must be given to start the execution of the program, the name of the file that contains the program, and how the program receives information.

3. *A description of the information needed for the execution of the program.* This part of the documentation should clearly describe what information should be supplied to the program. For example, if the program reads information from a file, how should the information be written on the file? Does the program expect the data to be placed in sharply defined fields? Or, can the data be written anywhere in the file, provided it is supplied in a preestablished order?
4. *A description of the information produced by the program.* This should include samples of all output messages and an explanation of the error messages that it may produce.
5. *A description (in nontechnical terms) of the limitations of the program.* For example, a program that computes powers of a given number may not be able to compute powers larger than a certain limit. This limit should be clearly stated in the user documentation.

4.5.2 Technical documentation

Technical documentation supplies, to the person who will modify the program, the information necessary for understanding how the program works. Technical documentation has two parts: external documentation and internal documentation.

External documentation describes the algorithm developed in phase 2—the structure of the program, the subprograms that it uses, and the interconnection between them. It should also describe the data structures used by the program, discuss their representation, and explain why they were chosen.

Internal documentation are the comments in the program itself. As we know, comments are ignored by the language processor, and their only purpose is to communicate to human beings what the meaning is of each part of the program. Comments can be extremely useful in understanding a program, and thus their placement should be very carefully considered. Comments should identify the main sections of a program and should clearly explain the goal of the section and the behavior of the algorithm that implements that part of the program. It is important not to overload a program with comments because this decreases the readability of the program. Novice programmers sometimes tend to place a comment after each statement, explaining what it does; this is usually unnecessary. Comments should be written as the program is being developed and should reflect what is in the programmer's mind as the program is developed. Comments written after the complete development of the program tend to be inadequate.

4.5.3 Summary

Good documentation is fundamental for the good use and maintenance of a program. Without user documentation, even an outstanding program is of no use because no one would know how to use it. On the other hand, good technical documentation is very important for the maintenance of the program. It is common to modify the characteristics of a program or to correct an error that is discovered long after the program is finished. For large programs these modifications are almost impossible without good technical documentation.

Finally, good documentation can have a great influence in the development of a program. When we try to develop a program for a given application, we can learn much if we study the documentation of a similar program.

4.6 Maintenance

The maintenance phase takes place after the program has been finished and has two distinct aspects. The first involves changing the program as its specifications change, and the second involves correcting errors that may be discovered during the lifetime of the program. A change in the program entails a corresponding change in documentation. A program with documentation errors can be worse than a program without documentation because it encourages the programmer to follow wrong leads.

According to Brooks (1975), the maintenance cost of a program is higher than 40 percent of the total cost of its development. This calls for careful development of an algorithm, careful testing, and good documentation, which can considerably decrease the maintenance cost.

Summary

The phases that program development goes through were presented. It is very important that these phases be followed when programs are developed. We should understand the problem, think about how to solve it, develop an algorithm for the problem, code the algorithm in a suitable programming language, and debug and test the program. Along with all these phases, we should be developing documentation for our program.

As programming activity becomes more complex, the need for the systematic study of the activity of program development becomes more important.

Suggested readings

Much has been written about program development. Most introductory computer science books dedicate a chapter to this subject. The scientific journal *Computing Surveys* (published by ACM, Association for Computing Machinery) devoted the December 1974 issue to this subject. In this issue, there are excellent papers by Brown, Wirth, and Yohe. The following books also contain good references for detailed study of program development.

Dijkstra, E. 1976. *A Discipline of Programming.* Englewood Cliffs, NJ: Prentice-Hall.
This book presents the process of program development in a formal way. It describes problems that are usually found during program development, using several examples.

Kernighan, B., and Plauger, P. 1978. *The Elements of Programming Style.* New York: McGraw-Hill.
This book presents a large number of examples that reflect good programming style. It is an excellent book that every programmer should read.

van Tassel, D. 1974. *Program Style, Design, Efficiency, Debugging, and Testing.* Englewood Cliffs, NJ: Prentice-Hall.
This book presents many rules, suggestions, and examples for an appropriate approach to the development of programs, programming style, debugging, and documentation.

Weinberg, G. 1971. *The Psychology of Computer Programming.* New York: Van Nostrand Reinhold.
This is a nontechnical book whose goal is to show the need to study the behavior of human beings during the programming phases.

CHAPTER 5

This chapter discusses what data types are and why they are important in programming languages. We introduce Pascal's elementary data types (integer, real, character, and boolean) and the notions of constant and variable, discuss the attributes of a variable (name, type, value, range, and lifetime), and explain how to define constants and declare variables in Pascal. By describing enumerated and subrange types, some user-defined types are introduced.

ELEMENTARY DATA TYPES

"The time has come," the Walrus said,
"To talk of many things:
Of shoes—and ships—and sealing wax—
Of cabbages—and kings—
And why the sea is boiling hot—
And whether pigs have wings."
Lewis Carroll. *Through the Looking Glass*

In mathematics we classify variables according to some important characteristics. There is a clear-cut distinction among real, complex, and logical variables; between variables that represent individual quantities and variables that represent sets of values; and so on. Similarly, in programming each constant, variable, or function belongs to a given type. The use of types is very important in computer science. A **type** identifies those properties common to a group of objects that distinguish it as an identifiable class. In computer science we group the information used by programs into data types. A **data type** is a set of **objects** (in this chapter it will be a set of values) together with a collection of **operations** that can be performed on those objects.

Information about the types is used by the programmer and the computer. The programmer uses information about the type to determine the possible range of values and operations to be performed with a given identifier. The computer uses information about the type at two different times:

1. During the compilation of the program, the computer verifies whether the statements of a program are legal. In other words, the computer verifies whether the information manipulation that the statement performs is possible with the types being used. For example, it would not be possible to sum a logical value with an integer value.
2. During the execution of the program, the computer uses the information regarding the type to interpret the internal representation of the value of the identifier: The information inside the computer is represented using only two symbols, 0 and 1. For example, 01101010111011 can represent the integer number 6843 or the set of characters AI (using the ASCII code—American Standard Code for Information Interchange; see Appendix A). Thus, given a sequence of 0s and 1s, how can the computer know that it represents an integer number, a real number, a logical value, or a string of characters? That is, given 01101010111011, how does the computer know whether it represents the integer 6843 or the characters AI? The computer uses the information regarding the type of the identifier associated with a given sequence of 0s and 1s to interpret its meaning. In this way, given 01101010111011, if the identifier associated with it is of type integer, it will be interpreted as 6843; if the identifier associated with it is of the type string of characters, it will be interpreted as AI.

The types of information that can be used in a program and the methods for specifying those types vary considerably from programming language to programming language. In general, we can say that the information represented in programming languages can be divided in two large groups: elementary information and structured information.

Elementary information is characterized by the fact that its elements are undecomposable. At any given moment, they represent a unique value, which cannot be further decomposed. An example of elementary information is an integer value. For example, the integer number 1966 is considered a single entity, and we are not able to access directly the digits that form it. The word *undecomposable* in this context means that we are not able to further decompose the entity. Although it may actually be composed of several elements, these elements (the digits 1, 6, and 9 in our example) are beyond our reach.

In contrast, **structured information** is characterized by the fact that it represents a collection of values (these values may, in turn, be either elementary or structured). An example of structured information is the type record. A record can contain a set of values of different types. For example, a record can be used to represent addresses. An address may have several components: a street number (an integer), a street name (a set of characters, for example, "Madison Avenue"), a city name (a set of characters), a state (a set of characters), and a ZIP code (a five-digit integer, if we consider the old-fashioned ZIP code). The information representing an address will be decomposable in that we can refer to each of its components. For example, in the case of our record, we can refer to the ZIP code. (Chapter 11 shows how to use, access, and modify each element of a record.)

Every programming language supplies certain types of elementary information and certain types of structured information. In addition, some programming languages allow a programmer to define new types of information (either elementary or structured). In general, every high-level programming language allows the following elementary data types: integer numbers, real numbers, characters, and logical values. As structured information, the array is the most common type in programming languages, being available in virtually every high-level programming language.

It is important to note that in programming languages the class of integer numbers is not contained in the class of real numbers, unlike what happens in mathematics. In programming languages these classes constitute two disjoint sets. This apparently strange separation has its foundations in the fact that integer numbers and real numbers are represented inside the computer in two different ways (Stone 1975).

In Pascal the following types are predefined as elementary information: integer, real, character, boolean, and pointer. As structured information, the types array, record, set, and file are predefined (Figure 5.1).

This chapter considers some of Pascal's elementary data types, namely, integer, real, character, boolean, subrange, and enumerated data types. (Predefined structured information is considered in Chapters 10–13.) When presenting a data type, we discuss the two aspects that characterize it: the set of values that belong to the type and the set of operations that can be performed on those objects.

5.1 Integers

Integer numerals (remember that a numeral is a *representation* of a number) are numerals with no decimal part. They can be either positive, negative, or zero. Figure 5.2 represents a syntax chart for type `integer`. For example, 4, 0, −12, and 12 are constants of type integer. As defined in Figure 5.2, the digit sequence of an integer has no restriction on its size. Each implementation of Pascal, however, puts a limit on the maximum size

FIGURE 5.1 Data types in Pascal.

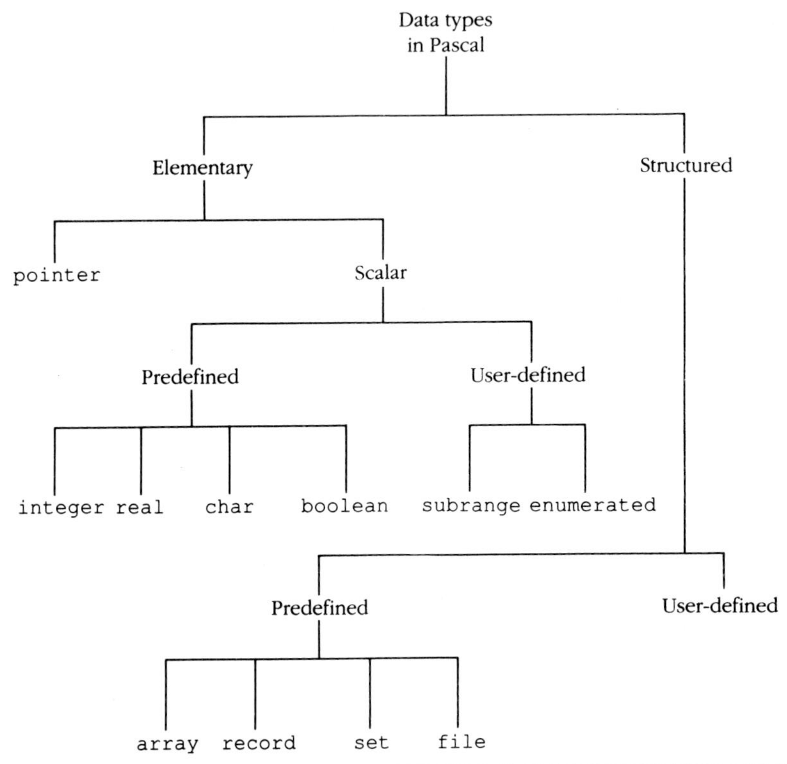

FIGURE 5.2 Syntax chart for type `integer`.

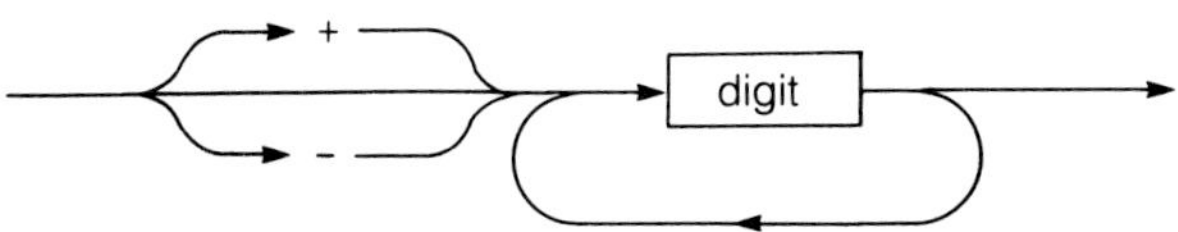

of integers. The range of the integers available in a given programming language depends on the programming language and on the computer in which the language is implemented. In Pascal an integer constant called `maxint` represents the largest (in absolute value) integer value that is representable on a given computer. The constant `maxint` exists in *every* implementation of Pascal; its value, however, varies from implementation to implementation. For example, in VAX-11 Pascal for the VMS operating system, the value of `maxint` is 2147483647. Thus, in that version of Pascal, we can represent integers between −2147483647 and +2147483647, inclusive.[1]

In Pascal we can perform the following operations with information of type `integer`: addition, subtraction, multiplication, integer division, and modulo. These operations are represented, by +, −, *, `div`, and `mod`, respectively. Operation `div` produces the integer part of the quotient of the division. Operation `mod` produces the remainder of the division. For example, `7 div 2 = 3` and `7 mod 2 = 1`. Given any two integers, `a` and `b` (`b` ≠ `0`), the following is true:

```
(a div b) * b + (a mod b) = a
```

With integer information, besides the five operations that were described, we can use relational operators (see Section 5.5) and the following predefined functions (all of which generate integer values): `abs`, `sqr`, `trunc`, and `round`.

1. The argument[2] of the function `abs` can be an integer number;[3] its value will be the absolute value of its argument. For example, `abs(3) = 3`, `abs(-3) = 3`.
2. The function `sqr` returns the square of its integer argument; for example, `sqr(5) = 25`.
3. The function `trunc` takes a real number as argument and produces the integer part of that number; for example, `trunc(3.6) = 3` and `trunc(3.1) = 3`.
4. The function `round` takes a real number as argument and produces the nearest integer; for example, `round(3.6) = 4`, `round(3.5) = 4`, and `round(3.1) = 3`.

Information about these functions is summarized in Table 5.1.

---

1. As a matter of rigor, we should say that the VAX architecture supports an additional integer value, `-maxint-1`; thus, in VMS, −2147483648 is also representable.

2. The argument of a function is the value supplied to the function.

3. It may also be a real number as we will see in the next section.

TABLE 5.1 Predefined functions producing integer values.

Function	*Type of argument*	*Result*
`abs`	`integer`	Absolute value
`sqr`	`integer`	Square
`trunc`	`real`	Integer part
`round`	`real`	Nearest integer

In this discussion it is assumed that you are acquainted with the mathematic concept of a function. The use and definition of functions is discussed further in Chapter 9.

In summary, type `integer` is composed of numerals without a decimal part, on which the following operations can be performed: +, −, *, `div`, `mod`, `abs`, and `sqr`. The functions `trunc` and `round` produce integer values. The function `ord`, discussed later on in this chapter, can also be performed on integer numbers. With the type `integer` we can use also the relational operators, discussed in Section 5.5.

5.2 Reals

Real numbers are numerals with a decimal part. In Pascal (and in most programming languages), there are two ways to represent constants of type `real`:

1. *Decimal notation,* in which a number is represented with an integer part, a period, and a decimal part. The syntax of Pascal requires that both the decimal part and the integer part of a real number have at least one digit. Figure 5.3 shows a syntax chart for real numbers in decimal notation. Examples of real numbers in decimal notation are the following: −7.236, 7.0, 0.76752. The following are not examples of real numbers in Pascal: 4. (it's missing a zero after the decimal point), .3 (it's missing a zero before the decimal point).
2. *Floating-point notation,* in which a number is represented by a fractional part and an exponent (a power of 10) that, when multiplied by the fractional part, produces the number. In Pascal the fractional part

FIGURE 5.3 **Syntax chart for type `real` (decimal notation).**

`real` (decimal notation)

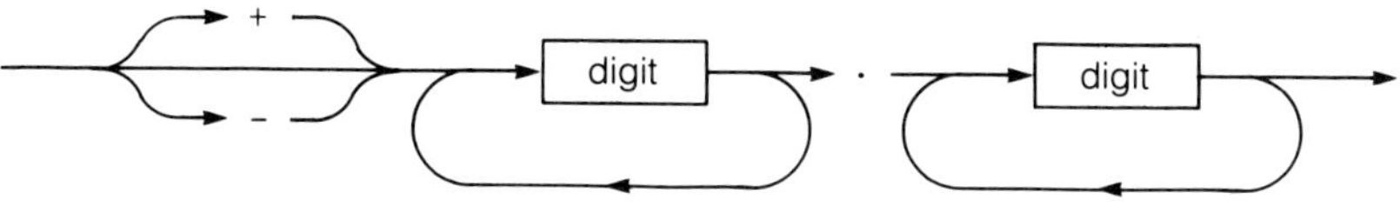

FIGURE 5.4 **Syntax chart for type `real` (floating-point notation).**

`real` (floating-point notation)

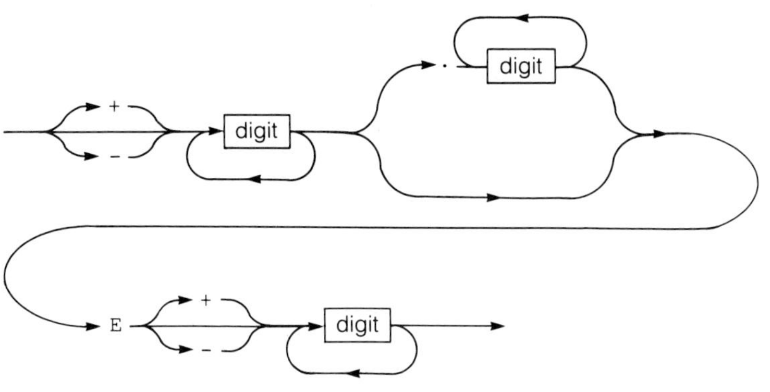

and the exponent are separated by the symbol `E`. Figure 5.4 shows a syntax chart for real numbers in floating-point notation. Notice that the exponent is an integer number. The following are examples of constants of type `real` using the floating-point notation 4.2E6 (=4200000.0), −6E−8 (= −0.00000006). Floating-point notation is used mainly to represent very large or very small numbers.

In programming languages we can only represent a subset of real numbers. Notice that a similar situation occurred with integer numbers: In Pascal, for example, we can only represent integers between `-maxint` and `+maxint`. We cannot represent very large numbers (in absolute value),

FIGURE 5.5 Real numbers representable in VAX-11 Pascal.

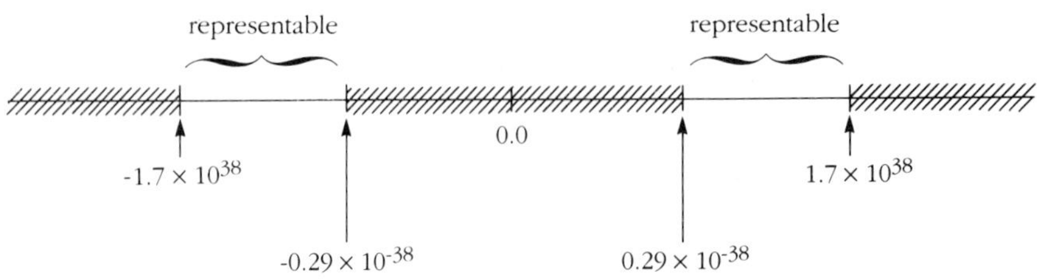

we cannot represent very small numbers (in absolute value), nor can we represent every real number between two real numbers. The range of the representable real numbers depends on the programming language and on the computer on which it is implemented. Figure 5.5 shows the representable range of real numbers in the version of Pascal for VAX-11 computers running under the VMS operating system.

Two aspects are worth noting about Figure 5.5: First, not *every* real number in the ranges denoted by "representable" can be represented in Pascal. In fact, in those ranges there are infinitely many real numbers that cannot be represented in Pascal. "Representable" means that every real number representable in VAX-11 Pascal falls within one of those ranges. Second, there is a difference between the largest representable integer (2147483647 in VAX-11 Pascal) and the largest representable real number (170000000000000000000000000000000000000 in VAX-11 Pascal).

In Pascal we can perform four arithmetic operations with real numbers: addition, subtraction, multiplication, and division. These operations are represented by `+`, `-`, `*`, and `/`, respectively. We can also use the relational operators (see Section 5.5) and the functions of real values defined in Table 5.2.

In summary, type `real` is composed of numerals with a decimal part on which the following operations can be performed: `+`, `-`, `*`, `/`, `abs`, `sqr`, `sin`, `cos`, `arctan`, `ln`, `exp`, `sqrt`. With type `real` we can use the relational operators as well.

5.3 Characters

In our programs we usually want to do more than numeric computations (remember that a computer is an information-manipulating machine, not just a huge calculator). To perform computations other than numeric, we must introduce other data types. This section presents information of type `character` that can be used for the storage and manipulation of the characters that represent a name.

TABLE 5.2 Predefined functions producing real values.

Function	*Type of argument*	*Result*
`abs`	`real`	Absolute value
`sqr`	`real`	Square
`sin`	`integer` or `real`	sine (argument in radians)
`cos`	`integer` or `real`	cosine (argument in radians)
`arctan`	`integer` or `real`	Principal value of arctangent (result in radians)
`ln`	`integer` or `real`	Natural logarithm
`exp`	`integer` or `real`	Exponential function, *e* to the power of its argument
`sqrt`	`integer` or `real` (not negative)	Square root

Information of type `character` (`char` in Pascal) is an ordered set of every character that can be represented in a given computer. The set of available characters varies from computer to computer. There is a growing trend to make the ASCII code (Appendix A) a universal standard; however, there are many machines that do not use it. ASCII code contains the following printable[4] characters:

Letters: A B C D E F G H I J K L M N O P Q R S T U V W X Y Z a b c d e f g h i j k l m n o p q r s t u v w x y z
Digits: 0 1 2 3 4 5 6 7 8 9
Special characters: ! @ # $ % ^ & * ( ) + = - [ ] { } | ; : ' " < > , . / ? ' ~
Blank character

4. These are characters that we can actually see in our printouts and terminals.

TABLE 5.3 Predefined functions for characters.

Function	*Type of argument*	*Result*
`ord`	`char`	Produces the integer that internally represents the character that is the argument of this function.
`chr`	`integer`	Produces the character that is internally represented by the integer that is the argument of the function.
`pred`	`char`	Produces the character that precedes the character that is the argument of this function; the value of this function is not defined for the first character.
`succ`	`char`	Produces the character that follows the character that is its argument; the value of this function is not defined for the last character.

The constants of type `char` are written enclosed by single quotes. Thus, `'a'`, `'9'`, and `' '` are examples of constants of type `char`. The third constant represents the blank character (or space). To represent a single quote, we must write it twice. Thus, `''` represents the character `'`.

Characters are internally represented by a sequence of 0s and 1s. If the sequences of 0s and 1s representing each of the characters are interpreted as an integer number, this interpretation defines an ordering on the set of characters. For the ASCII code, the ordering is the following:

```
"blank character" ! " # $ % & ' ( ) * + , - . / 0 1 2 3
4 5 6 7 8 9 : ; < = > ? @ A B C D E F G H I J K L
M N O P Q R S T U V W X Y Z [ ] ^ ' a b c d e f g
h i j k l m n o p q r s t u v w x y z { | } ~
```

The functions defined for information of type `char` are represented in Table 5.3. These functions make use of the internal representation of characters. For the ASCII code, we have, for example: `ord('L')` = 76, `chr(33)` = !, `chr(32)` = `' '`,[5] `pred('*')` =), `pred(''')` = &, and `succ('b')` = c. These functions are interrelated through the following

5. Notice that we used the quotes to delimit the blank character. The value of `chr(32)` is the blank character.

expressions (in which `i` represents a value of type `integer`, ranging from 0 to 127 and `c` a value of type `char`):

```
ord(chr(i)) = i
chr(ord(c)) = c
pred(c) = chr(ord(c) - 1)
succ(c) = chr(ord(c) + 1)
```

Associated with information of type `char` is a structured type called string. A **string** is a sequence of characters. The length of the string is the number of characters in the sequence. In Pascal, strings are represented by the sequence of characters enclosed in single quotes. Examples of strings are

```
'Computer Science'
'Pascal'
```

The length of these strings is, respectively, 16 characters (a blank is a character) and 5 characters. To represent a quote inside the string, we must write it twice. For example,

```
''''
'McDonald''s'
```

are strings, respectively, with 1 character (the single-quote character) and 10 characters. (Chapter 10 discusses another way to represent strings in Pascal.)

In summary, type `char` is composed of every character that can be represented in a given computer. We can perform the following operations on characters: `succ`, `pred`, and `ord`. The function `chr` generates values of type character. Again, we can use the relational operators with the values of type character as well.

5.4 Boolean

It is common to have to decide whether an expression is true or false. This is done using logical information. Logical information can have only two values: `true` and `false`. In Pascal this is represented by data of type `boolean`—named after the English mathematician George Boole (1815–1864).

In Pascal we can perform three logical operations with boolean information: negation, conjunction, and disjunction, which are represented,

TABLE 5.4 Predefined functions producing logical values.

Function	*Type of argument*	*Result*
`odd`	`integer`	The value is `true` if the integer that is the argument of this function is odd and is `false` if it is even.
`eoln`	`file`	The value is `true` if, while reading the file that is the argument of this function, an end of line is found; it is `false` otherwise (see Chapter 6).
`eof`	`file`	The value is `true` if, while reading the file that is the argument of this function, the end of file is found; it is `false` otherwise (see Chapter 6).

respectively, by `not`, `and`, and `or`. Operation `not` reverses the truth value as the word *not* does in English. Thus, "not true = false" and "not false = true." Operation `and` takes two truth values (or, better, two expressions that evaluate to a truth value), and the result of the operation is true just in case both values are true. This, again, is similar to the sense of the word *and* in English. Thus, "true and true = true," "true and false = false," "false and true = false," and "false and false = false." Operation `or`, which behaves like the English word *or,* takes two truth values, and the result of the operation is true if at least one of them is true. Thus, "true or true = true," "true or false = true," "false or true = true," and "false or false = false." Pascal also supplies other functions that return a boolean value (Table 5.4).

Besides the logical operations and logical functions described in this section, there is a class of operators—the relational operators—that take integer, real, character, or boolean values as arguments, and whose value is boolean. **Relational operators** relate the values of two expressions of the same type[6] giving, as a result, a value of type `boolean`.

The relational operators considered are: equal, different, greater than, less than, greater than or equal, and less than or equal, which are represented by =, <>, >, <, >=, and <=, respectively. For example, `5 = 5` is `true`, `27.2 < 20.5` is `false`, and `'a' = 'a'` is `true`. The expression `false = 2` is meaningless because `false` and `2` are constants of different types. There is one exception regarding the mixture of types in relational oper-

6. See Chapter 6 for a formal definition of an expression.

ators that concerns types `integer` and `real`: The mixture of these two types is allowed. For example, `5 >= 2.5` is `true`.

There is one dangerous use of the relational operator =: Never try to test directly equality between two real numbers. When directly testing the equality of two real numbers and expecting the computer to tell that they are equal, it most likely will tell that they are not. For example, `5.0 = 10/2` is likely to be false! The reason for this strange behavior stems from the representation of real numbers inside the computer. (For a detailed explanation of this see, for example, Stone 1975.) Whenever testing the equality of two real numbers, subtract them and check if the result is *small enough* so that the two numbers can be considered the same. For example,

```
abs(5.0 - 10/2) < 0.0001
```

has the value true, meaning that `5.0` and `10/2` are close enough in absolute value (their difference is less than `0.0001`) to be considered the same.

With boolean values we introduce a concept that is used extensively in this book: the concept of a condition. A **condition** is an expression whose value is of type `boolean`, that is, either `true` or `false`. This value can be directly obtained by the application of logical operators or by relational operators.

In summary, type `boolean` has two values, `true` and `false`. We can perform the operations `not`, `and`, and `or` on these values. Several other operations—namely, `odd`, `eof`, `eoln`, and the relational operators—generate values of type `boolean`.

5.5 Ordinal types

The data types `integer`, `boolean`, and `char` have one characteristic in common: We can list all their elements. Type `boolean` is easy to do because there are just two values: `false` and `true`. For type `char`, the list is slightly longer (see Section 5.3). The list is so long in type `integer` that it is not practical to list it. Nevertheless, we can list every integer representable in Pascal. In Pascal a data type whose values can be listed is called an **ordinal type.** Thus, the data types `integer`, `boolean`, and `char` are considered ordinal types. In ordinal data types, each element (except the first) has a unique predecessor, and each element (except the last) has a unique successor. For example, the predecessor of the integer constant `19` is `18`, and its successor is `20`; the predecessor of the character `'P'` is the character `'O'` and its successor is the character `'Q'`.

Do not confuse an ordinal type with a scalar type. A **scalar type** is a type whose elements are ordered. Both real and integer types are scalar types; an ordinal type is a type whose elements can be listed. `Integer` is an ordinal type but `real` is not.

The ordering of integer values is dictated by their mathematic definition. The ordering of `char` constants depends on the code being used to represent the characters; for example, for the ASCII code, the ordering is the one shown in Section 5.3. The ordering of boolean values is `false`, `true`—that is, the successor of `false` is `true`, and the predecessor of `true` is `false`.

The operations < and > can be used to test the ordering of the characters. For example, we have `19 > 2`, `'j' < 's'`, and `false < true`. What is true for the operators < and > is applicable to all the relational operators. For example, both `'j' <= 'j'` and `'j' <= 'p'` evaluate to `true`.

The only elementary data type we have studied so far that is not an ordinal type is type `real`. Although computers can only represent a finite subset of real numbers and in theory we could list every real number that is representable in a given computer, Pascal does not consider real numbers as an ordinal type. This decision is a consequence of the abstract concept of a real number that is used in mathematics. In mathematics, given any two real numbers, there are infinitely many real numbers between them, and, thus, it is not possible to list every real number.

The functions `ord`, `pred`, and `succ`, for information of type `char` described in Section 5.3, are applicable to any ordinal type. The function `ord` takes as argument an ordinal type and returns the ordinal number of its argument. By definition the ordinal number of the first element of an ordinal type is zero. For example, `ord(false) = 0`. The function `pred` takes as argument a constant of ordinal type and returns its predecessor. For example, `pred(5) = 4`. The function `pred` is undefined when its argument is the first element of the ordered set of elements. For example `pred(false)` is undefined. The function `succ` takes as argument an ordinal type and returns its successor. For example, `succ(false) = true`. The function `succ` is undefined when its argument is the last element of the ordered set of elements. For example, `succ(true)` is undefined.

5.6 Constants and variables

Having classified elementary data into four types and having defined the characteristics and the operations that are available for each of them, we now turn to the constants and variables that may exist in a Pascal program. Constants and variables are represented by identifiers. As we said in Chapter 3, **identifiers** are names that represent constants, types, variables, procedures, or functions. Syntactically, they have to begin with a letter, which can be followed by any combination of letters or digits.

To make a program readable and easy to understand, the names of the identifiers should suggest their purpose. In other words, when choosing a name for an identifier, use a mnemonic that suggests the meaning of the identifier—a well-chosen identifier emphasizes the meaning of what it represents. For example, if in a program you use a quantity that represents the pay rate, one can more easily understand what it means if it is named `PayRate` rather than `x`, and one can certainly be misled if it is named `TaxDue`. Remember that the names you choose for identifiers are to be used by you and not the computer (the computer forgets about the chosen names and translates them into an internal representation), so the names you choose should be easy to remember and should suggest what they represent.

Out of the set of possible identifiers, there are two important subsets: the set of reserved names and the set of standard names. The set of **reserved names** contains every name (identifier) used for a specific purpose by a language. For example, in Pascal the names `begin`, `end`, and `const` are reserved, as are many others. These names cannot be used by the programmer except in the context for which they are defined. The set of **standard names** contains every name that has a predefined meaning in a language (for example, the Pascal names `sin` and `cos`) but whose meanings can be changed by the programmer. In Pascal the programmer can, for example, change the meaning of the function `cos`. (Appendix C presents a complete list of the reserved names and standard names in Pascal.)

5.6.1 The constant definition part

In programming a **constant** is an object whose value does not change during the execution of a program. The use of constants in programming is common. High-level programming languages allow programmers to assign a symbolic name (identifier) to a constant and to use that name instead of the constant itself whenever they want to use its value.

Using symbolic names to refer to constants has two advantages for programmers, compared to the direct reference to the value of the constant.

1. The value of a constant does not generally supply any clue about the meaning of the constant. By using symbolic names to refer to constants, a programmer can assign a meaningful name (mnemonic) to a constant and thus increase the readability of the program. For example, suppose that in a given application we would use the constant `PrimeInterestRate`. This name is much more meaningful than the value of the constant itself, for example, 0.15.

FIGURE 5.6 **Syntax chart for** constant definition part.

constant definition part

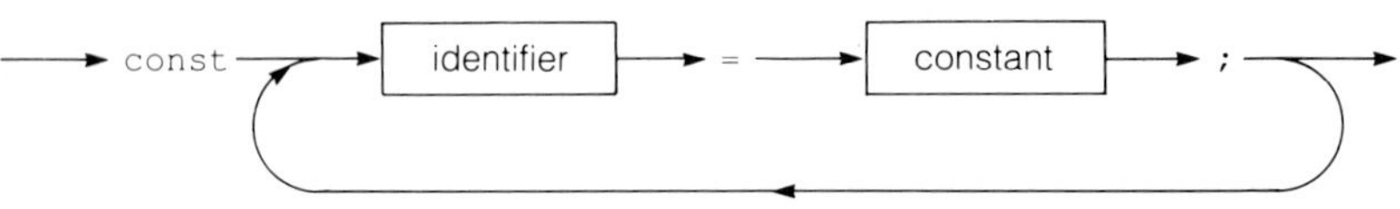

2. If symbolic names are not used for constants, modifying a program when the value of a constant has changed can be very difficult. Suppose, for example, a program makes use of the prime interest rate, and we want to change the value of this rate from 0.15 to 0.16. If the program does not use a symbolic name for this constant, we have to scan the entire program (which may have several thousand lines) looking for every occurrence of the value 0.15, verify whether each of these occurrences corresponds to the prime interest rate (as opposed to some other use of 0.15), and, if it does, change the value 0.15 to 0.16. If, on the other hand, we use a symbolic name for this constant (for example, `PrimeInterestRate`), we must modify only the statement in which this constant is defined.

In summary, the use of symbolic names for constants increases the readability of the program and makes its modification easier.

In Pascal, constant identifiers are defined in the constant definition part, which is syntactically defined by the following BNF expressions or, alternatively, by the syntax chart in Figure 5.6.

<constant definition part> ::= `const` <constants> ; | <empty>

<constants> ::= <constant definition> |
<constant definition> ; <constants>

<constant definition> ::= <identifier> = <constant>

The constant definition part (when not empty) is composed of the word `const` followed by a sequence of constant definitions, each of which is of the form <identifier> = <constant>.

FIGURE 5.7 Definition of constants with indentation.

```
const pi = 3.14159;
      e = 2.71828;
      blank = ' ';
      year = 1985;
```

FIGURE 5.8 Definition of constants without indentation.

```
const pi = 3.14159; e = 2.71828; blank = ' '; year = 1985;
```

The meaning (semantics) of the constant definition consists of the association of the value of each constant with the respective identifier. The value of the constant is used by the program whenever the corresponding identifier is referred to: The constant identifier becomes a *synonym* for the value of the constant. The constants defined in this part can be of type `integer`, `real`, `char`, or `boolean`.

To increase the readability of the program, it is usual to write each constant on a separate line, although any other graphic layout is accepted by Pascal. For example, Figure 5.7 defines two constants of type `real` (`pi` and `e`), one constant of type `char` (`blank`), and one constant of type `integer` (`year`). As far as the execution of the program is concerned, the definition of constants presented in Figure 5.7 is equivalent to the definition of constants presented in Figure 5.8.

5.6.2 The variable declaration part

The variable declaration part declares every variable that is used by the program. In programming languages a **variable** is an object whose value may change during the execution of a program. However, at any moment, a variable only has *one* value. (Our discussion only concerns variables corresponding to the elementary data types. For variables corresponding to structured data types, see Chapters 10–13.)

A variable is characterized by a name and four attributes: range, lifetime, type, and value. The **name** of a variable is an identifier that is used to select the variable. The **range** is the set of statements of a program in which the variable is known and thus usable. It is usual to say that the variable is *visible* inside its range and *invisible* outside its range. The range of a variable in Pascal is associated with the block structure of the language and with the rule that states that outer blocks cannot access information located in inner blocks. (This aspect is discussed in Chapter 9.) The **lifetime** of a variable is the interval of time when a certain location within the computer's memory is associated with the variable—that is, the interval of time when the variable exists. The lifetime of a variable in Pascal is associated with the block structure and the invocation of subprograms and is fully discussed in Chapter 9. The **type** of a variable specifies the set of values that can be associated with the variable and the set of operations that can be performed with the variable. Some programming languages (for example, Pascal, Modula-2, ALGOL, and Ada) require that every variable used in a program be declared (be given a name and a type) before the beginning of program execution. Other languages (for example, LISP, SNOBOL, and APL) do not require the declaration of the types of the variables used by the program; their type is dynamically determined during program execution. The **value** of a variable corresponds to the interpretation of the contents of the memory location that stores the value of the variable (according to the type of the variable).

The value of a variable can change during the program execution. When a variable is given a new value, its previous value is lost. The assignment of a value to a variable corresponds to the modification of the contents of the memory location that stores the value of the variable.

Following this discussion about the concept of a variable in programming languages, let us define how variables are declared in Pascal. The variable declaration part is defined by the following BNF expression and, alternatively, by the syntax in Figure 5.9.

```
<variable declaration part> ::= var <variables> ; | <empty>

<variables> ::= <variable declaration> |
                <variable declaration> ; <variables>

<variable declaration> ::= <identifiers> : <type>

<identifiers> ::= <identifier> |
                  <identifier> , <identifiers>
```

FIGURE 5.9 **Syntax chart for** variable declaration part.

variable declaration part

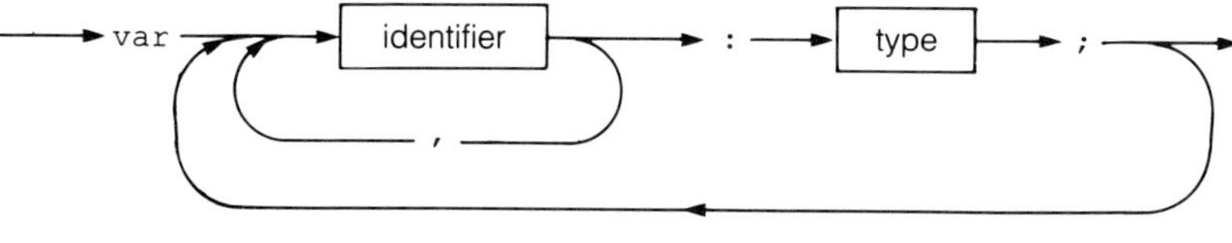

FIGURE 5.10 Declaration of variables.

```
var    number, sum : integer;
       tax : real;
       code, state : char;
       swap : boolean;
```

The variable declaration part is composed of the word `var` followed by a sequence of variable declarations. Each of these declarations consists of a set of variable names (identifiers) separated by commas, followed by a colon, followed by a description of the type to which they belong.

The meaning (semantics) of the declaration of a variable consists of the association of the name of the variable with a given type, the creation of an area in the computer's memory to store the value of the variable, and the association of the name of the variable with this storage area.

Figure 5.10 shows an example of a variable declaration. In this figure, we declare six variables: two of type `integer` (`number` and `sum`), one of type `real` (`tax`), two of type `char` (`code` and `state`), and one of type `boolean` (`swap`). Figures 3.4, 3.6, 3.9, 3.10, and 3.17 contain other examples of variable declarations in Pascal. Again, the indentation used in Figure 5.10, although highly advisable, is used only to increase the readability of the program and is not a requirement of Pascal.

It is important to distinguish between the declaration of a variable, the definition of a variable, and a reference to the value of a variable. The **declaration of a variable** is done only once in a program, and its purpose is to tell the language processor (in our case, the Pascal compiler) that there is a new variable, what its name is, what type it belongs to, and the need to associate the name of the variable with a storage location. After these operations are executed, a storage location exists in the memory to store the value of the variable; this storage area is associated with the name of the variable. The contents of this storage area, however, are *undefined.* This means that the variable exists, although without a value. Any attempt to use the value of the variable prior to the assignment of a value to the variable results in an error. The **definition of a variable** is the operation that assigns a value to a variable. This operation, which is explained in Chapter 6, can be repeated as needed during the execution of a program. Whenever the value of a variable is modified, the previous value is lost. A **reference to the value of a variable** is an operation that accesses the value of the variable. A reference to the value of a variable does not change its value. Again, a reference to the value of a variable prior to its definition gives rise to an execution error.

The difference between the declaration of a variable and the definition of a variable is the reason why the part of the program where variables are declared is called "variable declaration part" rather than "variable definition part."

Before ending this section, it should be stressed again that to make a program readable, the names of the variables should be carefully chosen. Each variable should be given a name that suggests its role in the program (that is, a mnemonic name). Names of variables such as `a1`, `a2`, `a3`, `xyz`, and so on should be avoided. In addition, it is good programming style to include a comment near the declaration of the variable that describes the meaning of the variable (for example, see Figures 3.4 and 3.9).

5.7 Extending the ordinal types

One feature of Pascal that explains its popularity is that it permits the definition of new data types. Chapters 10–18 discuss in depth how we can define new data types in Pascal. This section considers the contents of the type definition part (the part of the program in which we can define new data types) and defines new ordinal types.

FIGURE 5.11 Syntax chart for simple type.

type definition part (simple type)

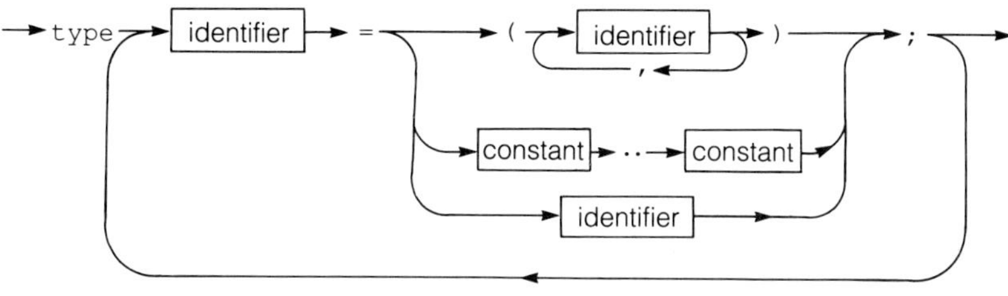

The type definition part is syntactically defined in the following way:

<type definition part> ::= `type` <types> ; | <empty>

<types> ::= <type definition> |
<type definition> ; <types>

<type definition> ::= <identifier> = <type>

<type> ::= <simple type> | <structured type> |
<pointer type>

This section considers only the simple type. The structured type is studied in Chapters 10–13, and the pointer type is studied in Chapter 14. The simple type is syntactically defined in the following way (the type definition for simple type is described by the syntax chart in Figure 5.11):

<simple type> ::= <enumerated type> | <subrange type> |
<type identifier>

<enumerated type> ::= (<identifiers>)

<subrange type> ::= <constant> .. <constant>

<type identifier> ::= <identifier>

<identifiers> ::= <identifier> |
<identifier> , <identifiers>

FIGURE 5.12 Definition of enumerated types.

```
type WeekDay = (Sunday, Monday, Tuesday, Wednesday, Thursday, Friday,
                Saturday);

     GMCars = (Cadillac, Oldsmobile, Buick, Chevrolet, Pontiac);

     StudentClass = (freshman, sophomore, junior, senior, graduate);
```

The type definition part consists of the word `type` followed by a sequence of type definitions, each of which is of the form <identifier> = <type>. The meaning (semantics) of the type definition merely says what something can look like; it does not create an area in memory to hold elements of that type. In other words, when defining *new* types, we are only defining templates that can be used to declare variables of that type; when we declare a variable as a *given* type, we are in fact creating a slot in memory that will store the value of the variable.

We said at the outset of this section that we would study processes of defining new ordinal data types. Recall that an ordinal data type is a data type in which we can list (enumerate) every one of its elements. So, the simplest way to define a new ordinal data type is just to provide a complete list of the constants of the type. This method of definition of a new data type is an **enumerated data type** (enumerated because we enumerate every possible constant of the type). This is done by defining a simple type of the enumerated type. In the definition of an enumerated type, there is a `(`, a list of identifiers, and then a `)`. The identifiers in the list of identifiers represent every possible constant of the type. For example, Figure 5.12 declares three types: `WeekDay`, `GMCars`, and `StudentClass`. In a program in which the definition of Figure 5.12 appears, if we declare a variable, `car`, by the declaration `var car : GMCars`, then the variable `car` can only take five possible values: `Cadillac`, `Oldsmobile`, `Buick`, `Chevro–let`, or `Pontiac`.

When defining a constant as being of a given enumerated type, we cannot define the same constant again as belonging to a different enumerated type. Thus, given the definition in Figure 5.12, it is illegal to define the type `WeekEnd` in a Pascal program as `WeekEnd = (Saturday, Sun–day)` because we could not determine the ordinal position of the duplicated constants. For example, is `Saturday` the last constant of type `WeekDay`, or is it the first constant of type `WeekEnd`?

Neither can we define any of Pascal's predefined ordinal types as enumerated type, that is, types `integer` (the whole numbers from `-maxint`

FIGURE 5.13 Illegal definition of types.

```
{ Illegal definitions }
SmallNumbers = (0, 1, 2, 3, 4, 5);
Vowels = ('a', 'e', 'i', 'o', 'u');
LogicalValues = (true, false);
```

FIGURE 5.14 Definition of subrange types.

```
type SmallInteger = 1..20;
     LowerCase = 'a'..'z';
     WorkDay = Monday..Friday;
     Undergraduate = freshman..senior;
```

to +`maxint`), `char` (the set of characters), and `boolean` (the values `true`, `false`). Thus, all the definitions in Figure 5.13 are *illegal*. However, the definition `Vowels = (a, e, i, o, u)` *is* legal because `a`, `e`, `i`, `o`, and `u` are not constants of type `char`.

The other method for defining new ordinal types in Pascal, the subrange type, consists of specifying a subrange of the constants of an already-defined ordinal type (either predefined or user-defined). A **subrange type** is obtained from an ordinal type by specifying two constants of that type separated by two dots. The type from which the two constants are chosen is called the **host type.** The elements of the subrange type are all the elements of the host type that fall between and include the two specified constants. A subrange is an ordinal type, and the values are ordered in the same way as in the host type. Figure 5.14 defines four subrange types: `SmallInteger`, `LowerCase`, `WorkDay`, and `Undergraduate` (this figure assumes the definition of Figure 5.12).

After the definition of a new ordinal type, the functions `ord`, `pred`, and `succ` are applicable to the constants of that type. For example, considering the definitions of Figure 5.12, we have `succ(Sunday) = Monday`, `pred(senior) = junior`, `ord(freshman) = 0`, and `ord(Saturday) = 6`. Also, `succ(Saturday)` and `pred(Cadillac)` are undefined.

Finally, we can use a **type identifier** to give another name to an existing type. For example, the definition type `MyInteger = integer` allows us to use the name `MyInteger` in place of `integer`.

Summary

This chapter introduced the concept of data type: a collection of objects together with a collection of operations that can be performed on those objects. The elementary data types that are predefined in Pascal—`integer`, `real`, `char`, and `boolean`—the operations associated with each of these types were discussed.

You learned how to define constants and declare variables in Pascal, and the method of defining your own ordinal types was introduced.

Suggested readings

You can explore the topics presented in this chapter more deeply by consulting the following books:

Organick, E., Forsythe, A., and Plummer, R. 1978. *Programming Language Structures.* New York: Academic Press.
This book presents an elementary description of several types in the programming languages ALGOL, FORTRAN, LISP, SNOBOL, and Pascal.

Pratt, T. 1984. *Programming Languages: Design and Implementation,* 2d ed. Englewood Cliffs, NJ: Prentice-Hall.
This book presents a detailed description of several elementary data types, their representation inside the computer's memory, and the possible operations that can be performed on each of them. It studies the elementary data types in the programming languages FORTRAN, COBOL, PL/1, LISP, Pascal, Ada, SNOBOL4, and APL in detail.

Wirth, N. 1976. *Algorithms + Data Structures = Programs.* Englewood Cliffs, NJ: Prentice-Hall.
The first chapter of this classic book covers fundamental data structures. It introduces the concepts of abstraction and data type and discusses primitive data types.

Exercises

1. ✓ In mathematics the set of integer numbers is contained in the set of real numbers. This does not happen in programming languages in which the set of integer constants is disjoint from the set of real constants. What is the reason for this separation?
2. ✓ Find the value of `maxint` in your particular implementation.

3. ✓ Which of the following are correctly formed Pascal constants of type `integer`?
   a. `18`
   b. `5.0`
   c. `4/1`
   d. `4 div 2`
   e. `'14'`
   f. `1,985`
4. ✓ Which of the following are correctly formed Pascal constants of type `real`?
   a. `18`
   b. `18.0`
   c. `18.`
   d. `.18`
   e. `0.18`
   f. `9/2`
   g. `'5.2'`
   h. `3,000,000`
5. ? Provide a syntax chart for real numbers in Pascal that includes both the decimal and the floating-point notation.
6. ? Write a constant definition containing the following constants: number of inches per foot, freezing temperature, number of students in your class, and year of your birth. Be sure to choose meaningful names for your constants.
7. ? Write a variable declaration for the following variables: your grade-point average, your highest grade, the balance of your checkbook, and your expected year of graduation. Make sure that you choose the right types for your variables and that you give them meaningful names.
8. ✓ Given the following identifiers, which ones are reserved names and which ones are standard names? (A full list of these names can be found in Appendix C.)
   a. `program`
   b. `prog`
   c. `successor`
   d. `succ`
   e. `myprogram`

9. ? Which of the following are valid Pascal definitions? Explain what is wrong with the invalid definitions.

a.
```
const a = 3;
      b = 124;
```
b.
```
const a := 3;
      b = 124;
```
c. `const a, b = 120`

d. `const a = 100; b = 120`

e.
```
const a = 10
      b = 20
```

10. ? Write constant definitions for the following: The number 1, the character 1. Make sure that you choose meaningful names for your constants.

11. ? What are the values of the following expressions? If an expression generates an error, explain why.

a. `succ('a')`

b. `succ(succ('a'))`

c. `chr(succ(ord('a') + 3))`

d. `chr(198/6)`

e. `chr(198 div 6)`

12. ? What a Boolean expression that decides whether, in the sequence of characters of your computer, the character `'A'` comes before the character `'a'`.

13. ? What types do each of these constants represent?

```
const a = 45;
      b = 'c';
      d = 'a';
      f = 45.32;
```

14. ? Suppose that a university has faculties of education, architecture, sciences, letters, natural sciences, engineering, and medicine. Define a type that can represent any of the faculties of this university and declare a variable of that type.

15. ? Using the definition of types of Figure 5.12, evaluate each of the following. If an expression generates an error, explain why.

a. `ord(Oldsmobile)`

b. `pred(Buick)`

c. `succ(sophomore)`

d. `succ(succ(freshman))`

e. `succ(graduate)`

f. `Buick+1`

16. Using again the definition of types of Figure 5.12, how many elements do the following subranges contain? If a subrange is illegal, explain why.

    a. `Monday..Friday`
    b. `Pontiac..Chevrolet`
    c. `0..'9'`
    d. `'a'..'3'`
    e. `Oldsmobile..Oldsmobile`
    f. `Cadillac..Buick..Chevrolet`

17. Define the type `flavors` whose constants are `chocolate`, `vanilla`, `orange`, `lemon`, and `butterscotch`.

18. Define the type `months` whose constants are the names of the months. Based on those constants, define the types `spring` and `fall`, containing the months of spring and fall, respectively.

CHAPTER 6

This is the first of three chapters that discuss control structures. Here, we cover sequencing, introduce the compound statement, and present three simple Pascal statements: the assignment statement, the input statement, and the output statement. The input and output statements are presented stressing interactive programming and user-friendly communication. Finally, some complete Pascal programs are developed using the concepts introduced.

CONTROL STRUCTURES I: SEQUENCING

The White Rabbit put on his spectacles.
"Where shall I begin, please your Majesty?" he asked.
"Begin at the beginning," the king said, very gravely,
"and go on till you come to the end; then stop."
Lewis Carroll, *Alice's Adventures in Wonderland*

This chapter discusses the mechanisms that can be used to specify the order of execution of statements in a program. Some statements that are part of a Pascal program are also presented. By the end of this chapter, you will be able to develop complete, although extremely simple, Pascal programs.

The concept of control of execution plays a fundamental role in the behavior of a program. For this reason, programming languages supply structures that enable the specification of the order of execution of the statements of a program. In machine and assembly languages, there are two kinds of control structures: sequencing and jump. **Sequencing** specifies that the statements of the program should be executed one after the other in the same order in which they are stored in memory. **Jump** specifies the transfer of execution to some point in the program.

Besides sequencing and jump, high-level languages supply other, more sophisticated, control structures—namely, selection and repetition. We discuss three types of control structures: sequencing (this chapter), selection (Chapter 7), and repetition (Chapter 8). We deliberately omit the control structure corresponding to the jump (`GO TO` statement) because the use of this control structure corresponds to a bad programming technique, which gives rise to programs that are difficult to read and modify (see, for example, Dijkstra 1968, Ghezzi and Jazayeri 1982, Knuth 1977, or Wirth 1974).

Using adequate control structures considerably increases the readability and maintainability of programs. In fact, to fully understand a program, it is very important that the program's statements be structured using simple, well-understood, and natural principles.

Besides beginning the discussion of control structures, this chapter presents three Pascal statements: the assignment statement, the input statement, and the output statement.

6.1 Sequencing

Sequencing is the simplest control structure. It corresponds to the specification that the statements of a program should be executed sequentially in the same order in which they appear in the program. If `A` and `B` represent statements, the specification that statement `B` should be executed immediately after the execution of statement `A` is represented in Pascal by

```
A ; B
```

The symbol ; represents the sequencing operator and serves as a statement separator. Note that ; is *not* a Pascal statement nor part of any Pascal statement. In languages in which each statement is written on a different line, such as FORTRAN or COBOL, the end of the line implicitly represents the sequencing operator.

In Pascal it is possible to specify that a group of statements should be considered a single statement and that the statements that are part of the group should be executed in sequence. The resulting structure is a **compound statement** and is syntactically defined by the following BNF expressions or, alternatively, by the syntax chart in Figure 6.1.

<compound statement> ::= `begin` <statements> `end`

<statements> ::= <statement> |
<statement> ; <statements>

The words `begin` and `end` are *not* Pascal statements. Their role is just to delimit the statements that comprise the compound statement. The pair `begin/end` acts like a pair of parentheses in mathematics; it groups statements together. The entire set of statements of a Pascal program constitutes a single compound statement (see Section 3.2). A compound statement

FIGURE 6.1 **Syntax chart for the** compound statement.

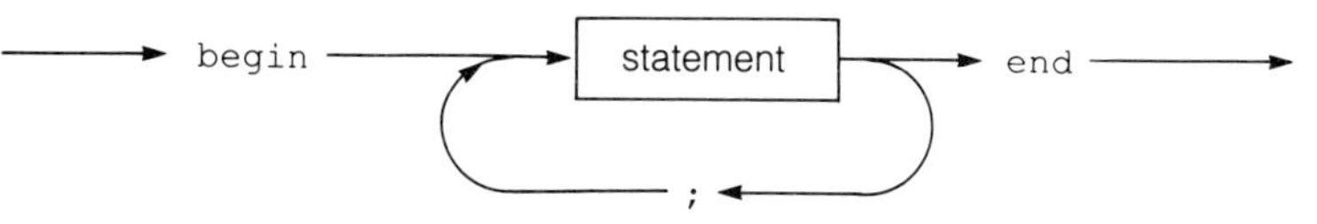

treats a sequence of statements as a single statement and simplifies the process of program development. A compound statement is, by itself, a statement (see Appendix B). Thus, the statements of a compound statement can be, themselves, compound statements.

6.2 Elementary statements

Now that we know how to specify sequencing in Pascal and know how to create new statements, we must learn some elementary, predefined, Pascal statements to be able to write complete programs. We start by discussing three types of very simple statements: the assignment statement, the input statement, and the output statement. The assignment statement assigns a value to a variable and has a fundamental importance in a class of programming languages (the imperative programming languages, an example of which is Pascal); however, in other programming languages (for example, in pure LISP, an example of a functional language), this statement may not exist. The input and output statements enable the transfer of information from the outside world into the computer and the transfer of information from the computer to the outside world. They are important in both imperative and functional programming languages. Before presenting these statements, it is convenient, however, to define formally what an expression is.

6.2.1 Expressions

An **expression** is a formula that produces a *value,* or result. An expression is composed of operands and operators. **Operands** can be constants, variables, expressions, or values generated by functions. **Operators** can be classified as *unary* operators if they take only one operand (for example, the boolean operator `not` or the operator -, representing negative) or *binary* operators if they have two operands (for example, +, * or the operator -, representing subtraction).

FIGURE 6.2 Syntax charts for expression **and** simple expression.

expression

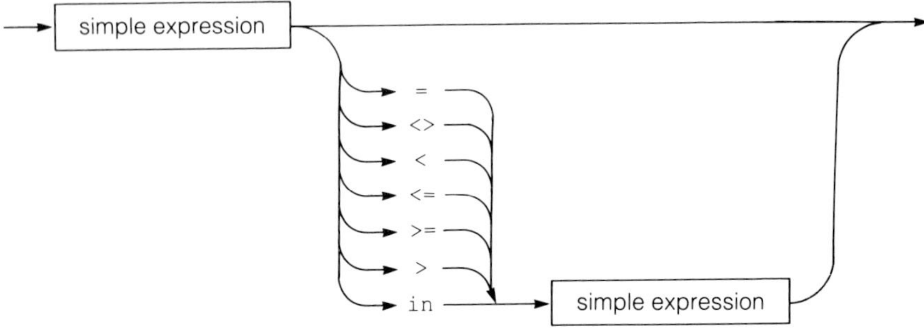

simple expression

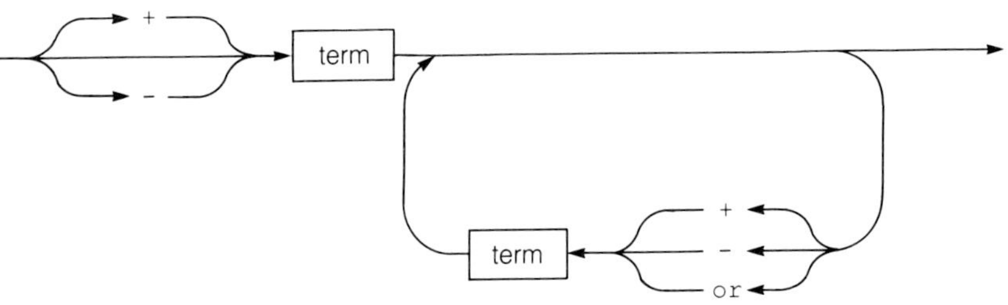

An expression is syntactically defined by the following BNF expressions or, alternatively, by the syntax charts in Figures 6.2 and 6.3:

<expression> ::=
<simple expression> |
<simple expression> <relational operator> <simple expression>

<simple expression> ::=
<term> |
<sign> <term> |
<simple expression> <adding operator> <term>

<term> ::= <factor> |
<term> <multiplying operator> <factor>

FIGURE 6.3 Syntax charts for term and factor.

term

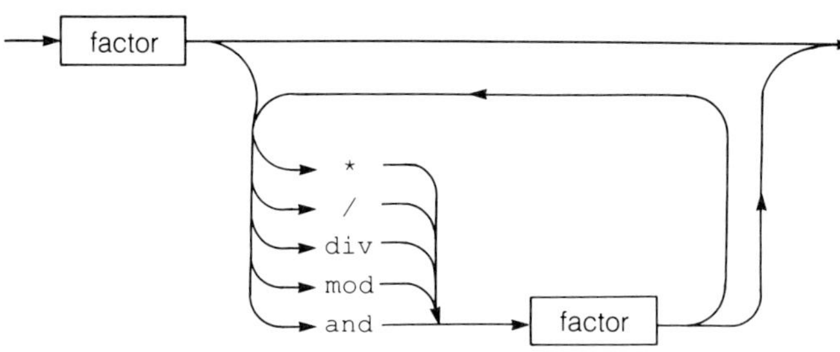

factor

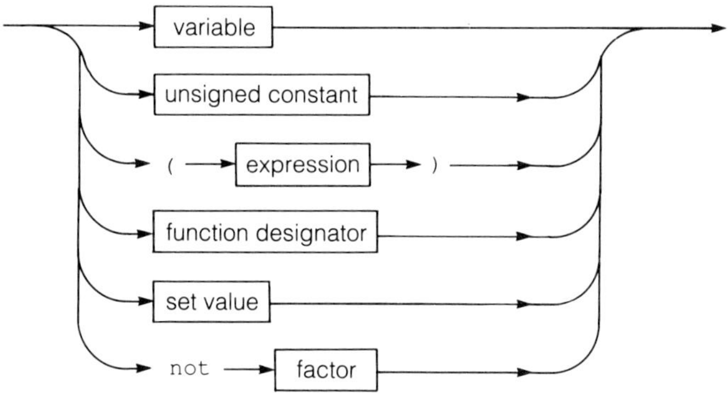

<factor> ::= <variable> |
<unsigned constant> |
(<expression>) |
<function designator> |
<set value> |
`not` <factor>

If `a`, `b`, `c`, and `d` are variables, then the following are expressions (remember that `abs` and `mod` are Pascal operators):

```
a
a + b * abs(c)
a mod b + c
a / 7 * 5 + 12.5
a / 7 * 5 + 12.5 < 49
```

TABLE 6.1 Priority of operators in Pascal.

Priority	*Operator*
Highest	Function application not, - (negative) *, /, div, mod, and +, -, or
Lowest	<, <=, =, <>, > =, >, in

A question that can be raised when considering complicated expressions concerns the order in which the operations are evaluated. For example, what are the operands of the multiplication in the last expression? 7 and 5? a/7 and 5? a/7 and 5 + 12.5? It is clear that the value of this expression is different for each of these cases.

To avoid ambiguity about the order of application of the operations in an expression, high-level programming languages specify two rules for operator application. The first rule, an operator priority list, specifies that the operators with higher priority are applied before the operators of lower priority. The second rule specifies the order of application of the operators if we find two operators with the same priority. Table 6.1 shows the priority of operators in Pascal. (The priority of operators shown in Table 6.1 is adopted, in general, in every programming language.) When two or more operators with the same priority are found, they are applied from left to right. Using parentheses—(and)—enables us to change the order of application of the operators.

For example, Figures 6.4 and 6.5 represent, respectively, the order of evaluation of the expressions 47.0 / 6.5 * 5.1 + 12.5 and 47.0 / (6.5 * 5.1 + 12.5). In these figures, two converging lines mean that the operands on top were combined to produce the value shown below.

When we defined an expression, we said that it produces a value. The value produced must belong to some type. Thus, when we write an expression, we should consider both the *types of operands* and the *type of the result* produced by their application. Using an operator with operands of different types is a **mixture of types.** Many programming languages allow using a mixture of types and automatically convert the type of one of the

FIGURE 6.4 Evaluation of the expression `47.0 / 6.5 * 5.1 + 12.5.`

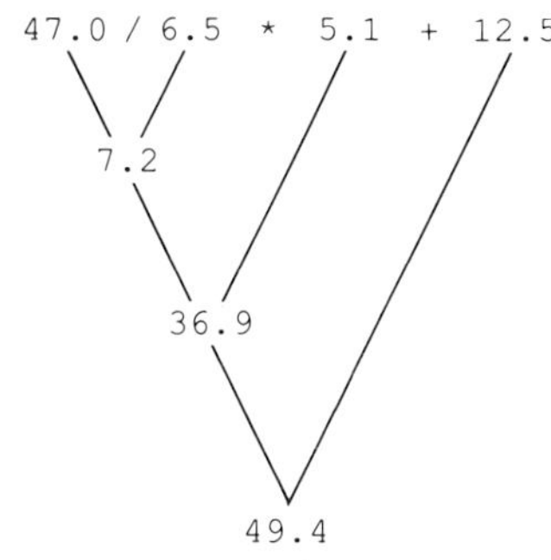

FIGURE 6.5 Evaluation of the expression `47.0 / (6.5 * 5.1 + 12.5).`

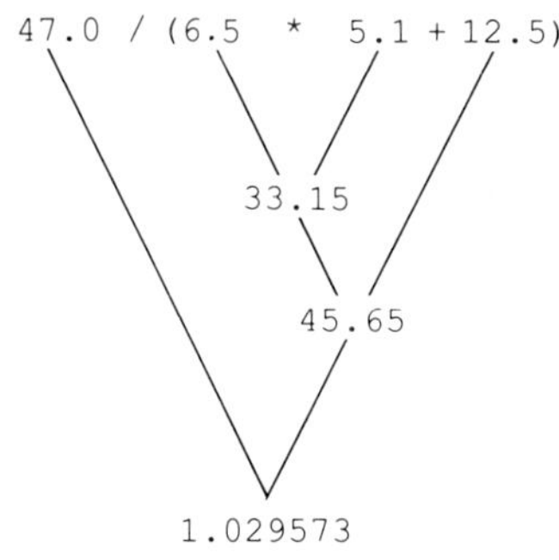

operands. In Pascal, for example, if a is a variable of type `real`, the expression `a + 5` is treated as `a + 5.0`. The result is type `real`. However, not every Pascal operator allows the automatic conversion of types. For example, the operator `div` requires that both its operands be of type `integer` and generates an error if this is not the case. For example, the operation `10 div 5.0` gives rise to an error. Good programming practice takes into account the type of the operands used in an expression and avoids mixing types, even when allowed.

If functions are used in an expression, consider not only the type of value produced by the function but also the type of its argument (or arguments). We will come back to this subject in Chapter 9.

6.2.2 Assignment statement

The **assignment statement** enables the assignment of a value to a variable. The assignment statement has the following syntax:

<assignment statement> ::= <variable> := <expression>

In this definition, variable is the symbolic name of a variable; :=, the **assignment operator,** is the symbol of the assignment statement (which should not be confused with the relational operator = or the BNF definition symbol ::=); and expression is an expression.

The semantics of the assignment statement is the following: The value of expression is determined and is assigned to the variable on the left of the assignment operator. The previous value of this variable is lost. Thus, the assignment statement *replaces* the value of the variable on the left of the assignment operator by the value of the expression on its right. Pascal requires that the value of the expression must be of a type compatible with the type defined for the variable. (Two types are compatible if they are the same type or if the variable is real and the expression is integer.)

The following are examples of assignment statements:

```
NumericGrade := 3
PriceToPay := UnitPrice * Quantity + Tax
Counter := Counter + 1
```

If `NumericGrade` is a variable of type `integer` or `real`, the assignment statement `NumericGrade := 3` assigns the value 3 to the variable `NumericGrade`. After the execution of this statement, the variable `NumericGrade` will have the value 3, no matter what value it previously had. If `NumericGrade` is not a variable of type `integer` or `real`, this statement is incorrect.

If `PriceToPay`, `UnitPrice`, `Quantity`, and `Tax` are variables of type `integer` or `real`, the assignment statement `PriceToPay := UnitPrice * Quantity + Tax` assigns the value of the expression `UnitPrice * Quantity + Tax` to the variable `PriceToPay`. To evaluate this expression, the values of the variables `UnitPrice`, `Quantity`, and `Tax` must be computed, and the operations * and + applied.

The assignment statement `Counter := Counter + 1` has the effect of assigning to the variable `Counter` (which must be of type `integer` or `real`) the previous value of `Counter` plus `1`. That is, it has the effect of incrementing the value of `Counter` by one.

An assignment statement is not a mathematic equation, but rather a *process* of assigning a value to the variable on the left of the assignment operator. Note that `Counter = Counter + 1` is not a mathematic equation. This is an advantage of the operator := used in Pascal compared with the operator = of FORTRAN or BASIC.

6.2.3 Input statement

During the execution of a program, the computer usually must obtain information from the outside. This operation is done through the **input statement,** which enables the transference of information from the outside (either from the outside world—for example, from a human being—or from elsewhere in the computer—for example, a file located on the disk) into the program. The input statement requires two types of information:

1. *The place where the input data is located.* For example, input data can be obtained through the keyboard of the terminal, can be stored in a file containing data, can be read directly from a measuring device, or can be introduced using punched cards.
2. *Which variables receive the values that are transmitted to the program.* For example, if the program has variables `a` and `b` and we supply the value `20`, we must tell the computer which variable will be assigned this value.

Pascal supplies two input statements, `read` and `readln`. The `read` statement has the following syntax (Figure 6.6 shows a syntax chart for the `read` statement):

```
read(<input information>)
```

where input information is defined as

```
<input information> ::= <file identifier>,<variable list> |
                        <variable list>

<variable list> ::= <variable> | <variable> , <variable list>
```

FIGURE 6.6 Syntax chart for the read statement.

read statement

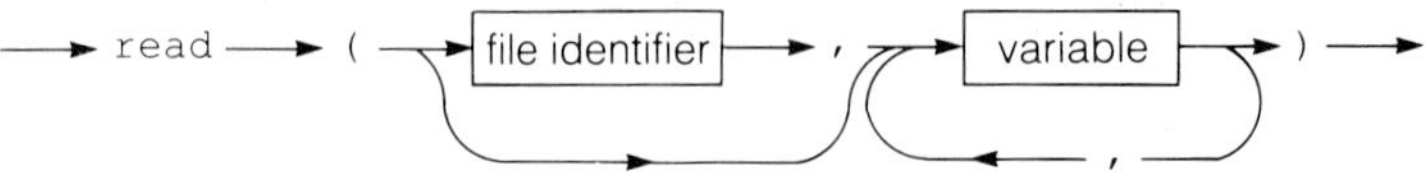

The semantics of this statement is as follows: When the computer executes the statement read(infile, var_1, ..., var_n), where infile is the identifier of a file (the file identifier in the BNF definition of input information) and var_1, ..., var_n are names of variables, the computer reads n values from the file represented by infile and assigns those values, respectively, to the variables var_1, ..., var_n. If the file identifier is the identifier `input` or if this identifier is not specified, then the input environment (that is, the place where the information that is read by the machine is located) is considered the default environment. The **default reading environment** depends on the mode of execution of the program. For example, if the program is being executed interactively, this environment is the keyboard of the terminal. Throughout this book, the input environment is referred to as the **input file.** Furthermore, the assignment of values to the variables is based on the position of the variables in the list of variables: The first value read is assigned to the first variable in the list, the second value read is assigned to the second variable in the list, and so on. The values read by a `read` statement can be scattered throughout several lines of the input file. However, the `read` statement requires that the following conditions be satisfied:

1. *The value to be read must obey Pascal syntax.* For example, if the decimal point appears in a real number, it should be preceded and followed by at least one digit.
2. *The type of value to be read must agree with the type declared by the variable that will receive it.*
3. *The values to be read must be separated by one or more spaces (or end-of-lines).* These spaces "tell" the computer where the value being read terminates. The only exception is in the case in which a value of type `char` is being read. Because this value is composed of only one character, it is not necessary (nor possible) to separate it by spaces.
4. *Each value must be completely contained on one line.* This means that each single value to be read cannot be spread across several lines.

5. *The value to be read must not belong to an enumerated type.* Unlike a value of the standard type, an enumerated value can't be read or written by a Pascal program. Also, a boolean value cannot be read by a Pascal program.

The `read` statement is somewhat similar to the assignment statement—they both assign values to variables. The difference between them is that in the assignment statement, the value assigned to the variable is computed from the value of an expression; in the `read` statement, the value assigned to the variable is received from the outside.

While reading the information, the computer maintains an "input pointer" to the next character to be read. This pointer is placed at the beginning of the file when the execution of the program begins, and, whenever an input statement is executed, it moves along the file from the beginning of the file toward the end of the file. After a `read` statement is executed, the input pointer is placed immediately after the last value read. In this book, the input pointer is represented by the symbol ↑, which is placed immediately below the character to which it points. Suppose, for example, that `a`, `b`, and `c` are integer variables and that the input file (a physical file or the keyboard of the terminal, for example) contains the following lines (the input pointer is placed at the beginning of the file):

```
  8     -3
 ↑
     47
```

Let us suppose that the statement `read(a)` is executed. This statement has the effect of assigning the value 8 to variable `a` and placing the input pointer as follows:

```
 8      -3
  ↑
     47
```

If the statement `read(b)` is executed, the value `-3` is assigned to variable `b`, and the input pointer is placed as follows:

```
 8      -3
          ↑
    47
```

If the statement `read(c)` is executed, variable `c` receives the value 47, and the input pointer is placed as follows:

```
8        -3
   47
     ↑
```

It should be stressed that if we had executed the statement `read(a,b,c)` instead of the sequence of statements `read(a); read(b); read(c)`, the result would have been *exactly* the same.

As a second example, let us assume that the input file contains the following lines:

```
  8        -3
↑
   47  4 2
```

If the statement `read(a,b,c)` is then executed, the result is exactly the same as in the previous example, and the input pointer is placed as follows:

```
8          -3
   47  4  2
     ↑
```

If the statement `read(a,b)` is executed, variable `a` is assigned the value 4, and variable `b` is assigned the value 2. The input pointer is placed as follows:

```
8          -3
   47  4  2
           ↑
```

The previous values of variables `a` and `b`, 8 and -3, respectively, are lost.

As a third example, let us assume that the input file only contains the following line:

```
  8        -3
↑
```

In this case, if the statement `read(a,b,c)` is executed, the value 8 is assigned to variable `a`, and the value -3 is assigned to variable `b`. The computer will try to read a value to variable `c` but will find the end of file, causing an execution error and terminating the execution of the program.

FIGURE 6.7 End-of-line and end-of-file characters.

```
 8                       -3[EOLN]
↑
           47    4     2[EOLN] [EOF]
```

FIGURE 6.8 Input file where all data have been read.

```
8               -3[EOLN]
     47    4    2[EOLN] [EOF]
                     ↑
```

To avoid situations in which the program tries to read values after the end of the file has been reached, Pascal supplies a function that enables a program to test whether the input pointer is placed at the end-of-file: the function `eof` of type `boolean` (mentioned in Chapter 5). The function application `eof(infile)` has the value `true` whenever the input pointer is placed at the end of the file represented by the identifier infile and has the value `false` otherwise. Another boolean function associated with the input operation is the function `eoln` (also mentioned in Chapter 5). The function application `eoln(infile)` has the value `true` whenever the input pointer is placed at the end of a line of the file represented by the identifier infile and has the value `false` otherwise. These functions use the fact that every file contains special characters (characters that are not visible when the file is inspected on the terminal screen) that indicate the end-of-line and the end-of-file. In this book these characters are represented, respectively, by `[EOLN]` and `[EOF]` (Figure 6.7). If the argument of the function `eof` or `eoln` is the identifier `input` or if this is not specified (that is, if we just write `eof` or `eoln`), the input file is taken to be the default input file.

Some care must be taken when using the functions `eof` and `eoln`: Remember that an end-of-file is *always* preceded by an end-of-line. Figure 6.8 shows a file in which all data have been read, but nevertheless the value of the function `eof` is false. In fact, the input pointer is pointing to an end-of-line, making the function `eoln` true. Because the input pointer does not point to the end-of-file, the value of `eof` is false. If our program tests for end-of-file, it will get a negative answer and may therefore try to read more data, giving rise to an error. In cases such as this, we should skip over the end-of-line mark (using the function `readln`) and then test

FIGURE 6.9 Syntax chart for the readln statement.

readln statement

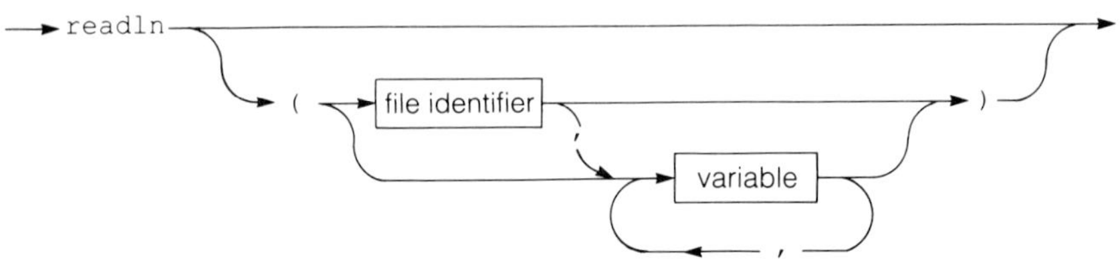

for end-of-file using the function `eof`. We will return to this problem several times in this book.

Besides the `read` statement, Pascal supplies another input statement, the statement `readln` (pronounced "read line"). The statement `readln` has the following syntax (also shown as a syntax chart in Figure 6.9):

```
readln(<input information>) |
readln(<file identifier>) |
readln
```

The semantics of the `readln` statement is very similar to the `read` statement. The difference between them concerns what happens after the input operation. Whereas the `read` statement places the input pointer immediately after the value read, the `readln` statement places the input pointer immediately after the first occurrence of the character `[EOLN]`. That is, `readln` skips a line immediately after the input operation, ignoring any information that may exist on the rest of the line, up to the end of the line.

As an example of the `readln` statement, let us consider the following file (where, for the sake of explanation, the end-of-line and end-of-file symbols are also represented):

```
 8          -3[EOLN]
↑
    47  4  2[EOLN][EOF]
```

If a and b are integer variables and if the statement readln(a) is executed, the value 8 is assigned to variable a, and the input pointer is placed as follows (immediately after the [EOLN] character):

```
8          -3[EOLN]
    47  4  2[EOLN][EOF]
↑
```

After the execution of this statement, if the statement read(b) is executed, variable b is assigned the value 47.

The execution of the statement readln(infile), where infile is the identifier of a file and where there are no variables specified, causes the input pointer to be placed in this file after the next occurrence of the character [EOLN]. The execution of the statement readln has the same effect as the execution of the statement readln(input); that is, in the default-reading environment, the input pointer is placed immediately after the next occurrence of the character [EOLN].

6.2.4 Output statement

After manipulating the information, it is important that the computer be able to communicate the results obtained. This is done using the **output statement;** it is rare to have a program without an output statement.

An output statement requires three types of information:

1. *Where the information transmitted by the computer should be placed.* For example, information can be shown on the terminal screen, can be written by a line printer, or can be stored in a file.
2. *Which values should be supplied by the program.* A program has, in general, several variables. When executing an output statement, we are only interested in the values of some of those variables or in the values of expressions containing some of those variables.
3. *How much space each of the values supplied by the computer should occupy in the output file.* It is common to neatly display the values produced by a program in tables or within certain fields. To do this, we must specify the amount of space to be occupied by the output value.

In Pascal there are two output statements, write and writeln. The write statement has the following syntax:

write(<output information>)

where output information is syntactically defined as

<output information> ::= <file identifier>, <output values> |
<output values>

<output values> ::= <write parameter> |
<write parameter>, <output values>

<write parameter> ::= <output value> |
<output value>: <field specifier>

<output value> ::= <expression>

<field specifier> ::= <expression> |
<expression> : <expression>

Figure 6.10 shows a syntax chart for the `write` statement. The semantics of this statement is the following: When the statement `write`(outfile, wp_1, ..., wp_m) is found, in which outfile is a file identifier and wp_1, ...,wp_m are objects of type write parameter, the computer evaluates output value (that is, an expression) for each wp_i ($1 \leq i \leq m$) and writes those values in the file represented by the identifier outfile, in the same order in which they are found in the `write` statement and occupying the number of columns specified by the field specifier associated with wp_i ($1 \leq i \leq m$). Remember that an object of the type write parameter may have no field specifier, or, if it has a field specifier, it can either be an expression or an expression followed by : followed by another expression. Let us now define what happens in each of these cases:

1. If the field specifier does not exist, each of the values written occupies a number of columns that depends on its type (`integer`, `real`, `boolean`, `char`, or `string`) and on the version of Pascal being used (there is no standard for these default values). For the Pascal of VAX computers running under the VMS operating system, the number of columns occupied by each one of these types is defined in Table 6.2.
2. If the field specifier is only an expression (which must be of type `integer`), the value of the expression is computed and represents the number of columns that the value written occupies in the output file. If the value of this expression is less than one, an error is generated.
3. If the field specifier is of the type <expression> : <expression>, which can only happen when a `real` value is being written, then both expressions (which must be of type `integer`) are evaluated, the value written occupies in the output file a total number of columns given by the value of the first expression, and it is printed with a total number of decimals given by the value of the second expression.

FIGURE 6.10 **Syntax chart for the** write statement.

write statement

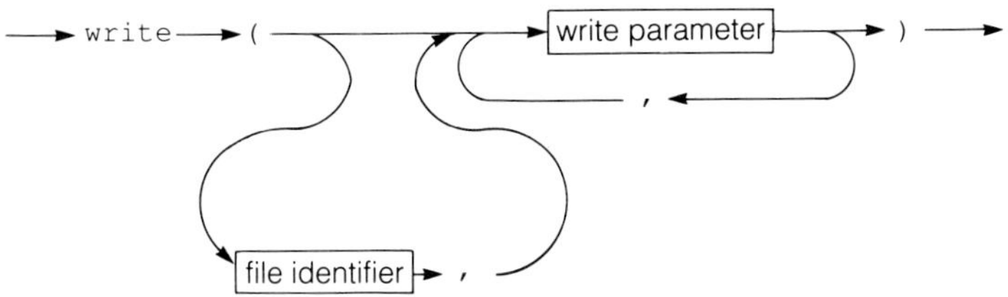

write parameter

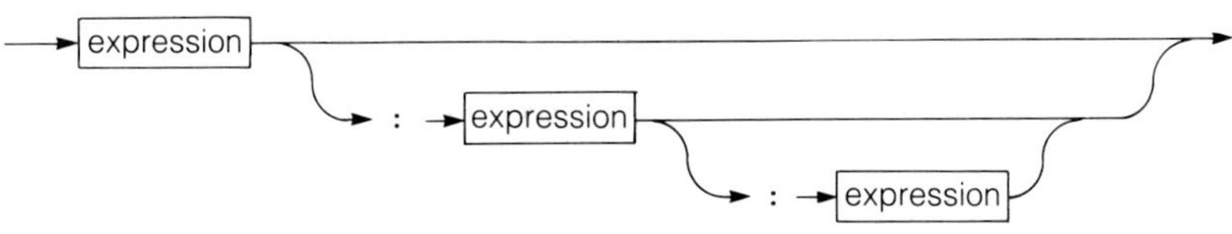

TABLE 6.2 Default values for field specifier for VAX/VMS Pascal.

Type of value written	*Number of columns occupied*
`integer`	10
`real`	12
`boolean`	6
`char`	1
`string`	Length of string

In either of these cases, if the value to be written occupies fewer positions than the specified number of positions (both implicitly or explicitly specified), then every position to the left will be occupied by a space. If the value to be written occupies more positions than the position specified then:

1. If the value to be written is a string, then the string will be written using the field specified being truncated to its right.
2. If the value to be written is a numeric variable (`integer` or `real`), then the size of the field will be automatically increased to the necessary size.

We must stress that the constants of an enumerated type cannot be written using a `write` statement. These constants do not have external character representation. Although the boolean constants `true` and `false` cannot be read by a `read` or `readln` statement, they *can* be written by `write` or `writeln` statements.

As with the input operation, the computer maintains a pointer, the **output pointer,** during output that specifies the position at which it will write next. Prior to the execution of a program, the output pointer is placed at the beginning of the output file, and whenever the computer performs an output operation, the output pointer is placed immediately after the last character written.

For example, assume that the integer variables `a` and `b` have, respectively, the values `12` and `90` and that the output file contains the following information (the output pointer is also represented):

```
23 sum =
         ↑
```

In this case, the statement `write(a,a + b)` adds to the output file the values `12` and `102` as follows:

```
23 sum =␣␣␣␣␣␣␣␣12␣␣␣␣␣␣␣102
                            ↑
```

Because the size of the field was not specified, each integer was written occupying 10 columns, and blank spaces (represented by ␣) were inserted to their left. (We are assuming the defaults shown in Table 6.2.)

Besides the `write` statement, Pascal also supplies another output statement: the `writeln` statement (pronounced "write-line"). The `writeln`

FIGURE 6.11 Syntax chart for the writeln statement.

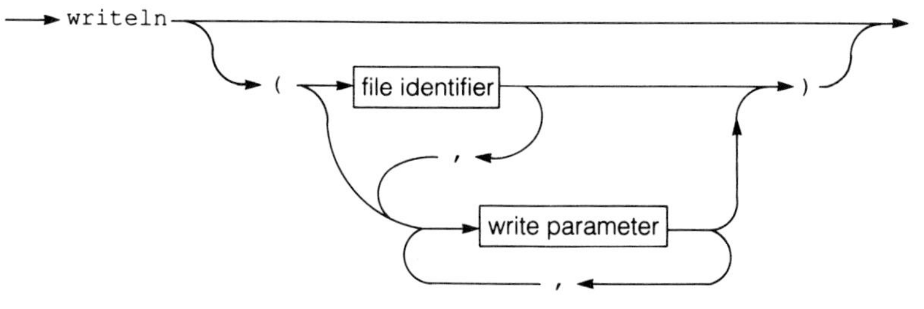

statement has a syntax defined by the following BNF expression and, alternatively, by the syntax chart in Figure 6.11.

```
writeln (<output information>) |
writeln (<file identifier>) |
writeln
```

The `writeln` statement has a semantics similar to the `write` statement. The difference between them arises after the output operation. Whereas the `write` statement places the output pointer immediately after the last character written, the `writeln` statement jumps to the beginning of the next line, and thus writes the character `[EOLN]` in the output file.

If the statement `writeln` is written without an argument—in other words, if we only write `writeln`—then its effect (semantics) is the introduction of the character `[EOLN]` in the default output file, thus causing a jump to the next line of the default output file.

With the goal of exemplifying the use of the output statement, a complete Pascal program is represented in Figure 6.12. This program has no other goal besides the explanation of the use of the statement `write` and `writeln`. The output produced by this program is represented in Figure 6.13.

Before ending this section, we should mention some programming techniques associated with the input and output statements that are helpful while developing programs. The first one is **input echo.** Sometimes, execution errors of a program are caused by input done incorrectly. During input operations, wrong values are assigned to the variables, which would

FIGURE 6.12 A Pascal program that uses the statements `write` and `writeln`.

```
program IOExample (input, output);

const
   c1 = 'a';
   c2 = 'b';
   int1 = 60202;
var
   c3 : char;
   r1, r2 : real;
   int2, int3 : integer;
   bool1, bool2 : boolean;

begin
   c3 := 'k';
   r1 := 3.776345;
   r2 := 5675.12;
   int2 := 10;
   int3 := 12;
   bool1 := true;
   bool2 := false;
   write('....+....1....+....2....+');
   writeln('....3....+....4....+....5');
   writeln('This is an example');
   write('          of Pascal''s output ');
   writeln('operations');
   write(c1, c2:3, c3);
   write(c1);
   writeln('sum= ',int1 + int2 + int3);
   writeln(' product = ',r1 * r2:10:2,' (r1*r2)');
   writeln;
   writeln('Example of field expansion:',int1:1);
   writeln('Example of truncation of a string',
           '.. this will be truncated ..':5);
   writeln('bool1':8,'bool2':8,'bool1 or bool2':16);
   writeln(bool1:8,bool2:8,bool1 or bool2:16);
   writeln(r1, r1:10,'    ',r1:10:2);
   write('....+....1....+....2....+');
   writeln('....3....+....4....+....5')
end.
```

FIGURE 6.13 Output of the program in Figure 6.12.

```
....+....1....+....2....+....3....+....4....+....5
This is an example
        of Pascal's output operations
a  bkasum=       60224
 product =    21431.21 (rl*r2)

Example of field expansion:60202
Example of truncation of a string.. th
   booll   bool2  booll or bool2
    TRUE   FALSE            TRUE
 3.77635E+00 3.776E+00         3.78
....+....1....+....2....+....3....+....4....+....5
```

FIGURE 6.14 Example of input echo.

```
read (a,b);
writeln('a= ', a, ' b= ',b);
```

then produce wrong results (this is sometimes called "garbage-in/garbage-out," or "GIGO"). To avoid this type of problem, good programming practice writes each value read immediately after reading it. This write operation shows exactly what the value of the input variable is. This allows the effective checking of which values were read by the computer. Figure 6.14 shows a fragment of a Pascal program that makes use of the input echo.

The second important technique is **variable tracing** and enables us to follow what the computer is doing. Often, our program does not do what we would like it to do. This results from semantic errors in our instructions; we meant one thing but wrote something else. One way of tracking down these errors is to write statements in our program that enable us to inspect what the values of some of the variables are and thus locate the place in the program where its behavior becomes erratic.

6.3 User friendliness

It is very important to consider the user friendliness of your program, that is, the way that the program interacts with the person using it. The interface between the program and the user is reflected in two different phases: when the program requests information from the user and when the program supplies information to the user. We consider each of these phases in turn.

The input of information is done in Pascal through a `read` or `readln` statement. When one of these statements is found and the program is being used interactively, the computer waits for the user to supply the desired information. Notice that a `read` or `readln` statement causes no prompting to the user, and, whenever one of these statements is found, the computer just patiently waits for the user to supply all information. If the user is not aware that the computer wants information (and *what* information the computer wants), then he or she may be sitting forever, looking at the terminal screen and wondering why the program is not supplying results. For clarity, your program not only should tell the user that it needs information but also should explain what kind of information the program is expecting.

Suppose, for example, that you are running a program and receive the following request:

```
Please enter the information
```

You may not know what kind of information should be supplied. What is information supposed to mean? Should it be a real number, an integer, or a character? If more than one value is to be supplied, in what order should you supply the information? On the other hand, suppose that you get the following message:

```
Please supply an integer representing a
temperature in degrees Fahrenheit, and I
will tell you its equivalent in degrees
Celsius.
```

In this case, you know exactly what to supply and what the use is of the information supplied.

The user friendliness of the output of your program is as important as the friendliness of the input. Suppose, for example, that you are running a payroll program and that you receive the following information:

```
6/21
104–60–6115     465.12     M
25.09     11.30     428.73
```

The best you could do would be to guess what the information meant. However, if the information supplied was in the following form

Pay Period	6/21
Social Security Number	104–60–6115
Current Gross Pay	$465.12
Tax Status	M
Federal Tax	$ 25.09
State Tax	$ 11.30
Net Pay	$428.73

you would know *exactly* the meaning of each piece of information supplied.

It is very important that your programs be clear. Remember always to prompt the user (using a `write` statement) whenever input is needed, explaining what information should be supplied. Whenever your program outputs information, you should explain what the information means. The user should never have to guess what to do or guess about the meaning of the output.

6.4 Examples

We now present four complete Pascal programs that use the concepts described so far.

The first program (Figure 6.15) reads the value of a temperature represented in degrees Fahrenheit and writes the corresponding value in degrees Celsius. It uses the formula $C = 5 * (F-32)/9$, in which C is the value of the temperature in degrees Celsius and F is the value of the temperature in degrees Fahrenheit. During the development of this program, we can identify three subproblems: how to read the value in degrees Fahrenheit, how to convert this value into degrees Celsius using the above formula, and how to write the value obtained.

The program uses two integer variables, `Cels` and `Fahr`, representing the value of the temperatures in degrees Celsius and Fahrenheit, respectively. It should be noted that during conversion from temperature in degrees Fahrenheit to temperature in degrees Celsius, we use the operator `/`, which produces a real value. This explains the use of the function `round` before the assignment to the integer variable `Cels`. (If we had used the expression `(5*(Fahr-32) div 9)` instead of `round(5*(Fahr-32)/9)`, the result would have been the same.)

The program in Figure 6.15 uses an input echo when the final result is produced: Instead of echoing the value read immediately after reading it, it shows the value input associated with the result produced.

FIGURE 6.15 Program to convert temperatures.

```
program TempConversion (input, output);

{ This program converts degrees Fahrenheit into degrees
  Celsius, using the formula C=5*(F-32)/9         }

var Cels, Fahr : integer;

{ Meaning of the variables:
     Cels  - temperature in degrees Celsius
     Fahr  - temperature im degrees Fahrenheit     }

begin
  writeln('What is the temperature in degrees Fahrenheit?');
  readln(Fahr);
  Cels := round(5 * (Fahr - 32) / 9);
  writeln(Fahr:4,'F = ',Cels:4,'C')
end. { TempConversion }
```

The second program (Figure 6.16) reads the Social Security number of an employee, the number of hours worked, and the hourly salary, and it computes the wages to be paid to the employee. Like the previous example, this is composed of three subproblems: the input of the information (Social Security number, number of hours worked, and hourly salary), the computation of the wages, and the output of the values computed. This program uses an integer variable `SSN`, which represents the Social Security number, and three real variables, `HoursWorked`, `PayRate`, and `Wages`, which represent, respectively, the number of hours worked, hourly salary, and the total wages to be paid.

Figure 6.17 shows another version of this program, which writes separately the amount of dollars and cents. It uses two additional integer variables, `Dollars` and `Cents`, which represent the amount of dollars and the amount of cents, respectively. As an exercise, try to understand how these values are computed.

As a final example, we develop a program that exchanges the values associated with two variables. This is a very important task in programming, and the technique explained here is used throughout the book. The program reads two values (for the sake of explanation, we assume that these values are integers; however, they could be of any other type, provided

FIGURE 6.16 Program to compute wages (version 1).

```
program Salary (input, output);

var SSN : integer;
    HoursWorked, PayRate, Wages: real;

{ Meaning of the variables:
       SSN              - Social Security number
       HoursWorked      - number of hours worked
       PayRate          - hourly salary
       Wages            - wages to be paid       }

begin
  writeln('What is the Social Security number?');
  readln(SSN);
  writeln('How many hours did the employee work?');
  readln(HoursWorked);
  writeln('What is the hourly salary?');
  readln(PayRate);
  writeln;
  writeln;
  write('The employee ',SSN:8,' worked ',
        HoursWorked:5:1,' hours');
  writeln(', receiving $',PayRate:5:2,' an hour');
  Wages := PayRate * HoursWorked;
  writeln('Wages: --> $',Wages:6:2,' <--')
end. { Salary }
```

that both values have the same type); echoes the values read, exchanges the values of the variables that store these values, and shows new values. A sample interaction using this program is shown in Figure 6.18.

The program we want to develop is composed of three subproblems: reading the values, exchanging the values read, and printing the values after the exchange. A first approximation of the program is shown in Figure 6.19. The program in this figure is not a complete Pascal program because it references one problem still to be solved (the problem of exchanging the values of variables `x` and `y`); we indicate this by using capital letters. Also, because the task for printing the values is done twice, we defined the procedure `PrintValues` to do this job—this procedure receives the values to be printed.

FIGURE 6.17 Program to compute wages (version 2).

```
program Salary2 (input, output);

var SSN, Dollars, Cents : integer;
    HoursWorked, PayRate, Wages: real;

begin
  writeln('What is the Social Security number?');
  readln(SSN);
  writeln('How many hours did the employee work?');
  readln(HoursWorked);
  writeln('What is the hourly salary?');
  readln(PayRate);
  writeln;
  writeln;
  write('The employee ',SSN:8,' worked ',
        HoursWorked:5:1,' hours');
  Dollars := trunc(PayRate);
  Cents := trunc(100 * (PayRate-Dollars));
  writeln(', receiving ',Dollars:4,' Dollars and ',
          Cents:2,' Cents an hour');
  Wages := PayRate * HoursWorked;
  Dollars := trunc(Wages);
  Cents := trunc( 100 * (Wages-Dollars));
  writeln('Wages: --> ',Dollars:6,' Dollars and ',
           Cents:2,' Cents <--')
end. { Salary2 }
```

FIGURE 6.18 Sample interaction.

```
Please write two integer values
19 33
The variable x has value 19
The variable y has value 33
... exchanging values ...
The variable x has value 33
The variable y has value 19
```

FIGURE 6.19 Fragment of program that exchanges two values.

```
program Exchange (input, output);

var x, y : integer;

   procedure PrintValues (x, y : integer);
   begin
     writeln ('The variable x has value    ', x:3);
     writeln ('The variable y has value    ', y:3)
   end; { PrintValues }

begin
    writeln ('Please write two integer values');
    readln (x, y);
    PrintValues (x ,y);
    writeln ('... exchanging values ...');

    EXCHANGE X AND Y

    PrintValues (x, y)
end.  { Exchange }
```

Let us now turn to the problem of exchanging the values associated with variables x and y. You may be tempted to write the two following statements:

```
x := y;
y := x;
```

When the first statement is executed, the value of y is assigned to variable x, destroying the previous value of x. When the second statement is executed, the (new) value of x is assigned to variable y. However, this value is *exactly* the value variable y had before the execution of this second assignment statement! Thus, the effect of the two statements is to assign the same value to both variables x and y.

To accomplish our goal, we must use an extra variable (called an *auxiliary* variable or *temporary* variable) to temporarily "remember" the value of one of the variables (x in our example). This variable, which we call temp, is assigned the value of x, thus "remembering" the initial value

FIGURE 6.20 Program that exchanges two values.

```
program Exchange (input, output);

var x, y : integer;

   procedure PrintValues (x, y : integer);
   begin
     writeln ('The variable x has value   ', x:3);
     writeln ('The variable y has value   ', y:3)
   end; { PrintValues }

begin
    writeln ('Please write two integer values');
    readln (x, y);
    PrintValues (x ,y);
    writeln ('... exchanging values ...');
    temp := x;
    x := y;
    y := temp;
    PrintValues (x, y)
end.  { Exchange }
```

of `x`. We can then execute the assignment statement `x := y`, which has the effect of assigning the value of `y` to variable `x`. Afterward, in order to assign to `y` the old value of `x`, we use the statement `y := temp`. The complete program to solve our problem is shown in Figure 6.20.

Summary

In this chapter you learned how to specify sequencing in Pascal. Five Pascal statements—the assignment statement, `read` and `readln` statements, and `write` and `writeln` statements—were given. The assignment statement allows the assignment of a value to a variable. The `read` and `readln` statements allow the transfer of information from outside into the program. The `write` and `writeln` statements allow a program to communicate the values computed to the outside world.

Both the assignment and input statements allow values to be assigned to variables. In the assignment statement, the value is computed within the program; whereas in the input statement, the value is obtained from the outside.

Two techniques useful in the debugging of programs—input echo and variable tracking—and user-friendly programming were introduced.

Suggested readings

You can explore the topics presented in this chapter more deeply by consulting the following publications:

Ghezzi, C., and Jazayeri, M. 1982. *Programming Language Concepts.* New York: Wiley.
This book discusses several control structures, pointing out their strengths and weaknesses.

Jensen, K., and Wirth, N. 1974. *Pascal User Manual and Report.* New York: Springer-Verlag.
This book presents Pascal's input and output operations in greater detail than here; namely, it presents two Pascal statements `put` and `get` that perform input and output operations. (These are discussed further in Chapter 13.)

Knuth, D. 1977. "Structured Programming with GO TO Statements." Pp. 140–194 in *Current Trends in Programming Methodology.* Edited by R. Yeh. Englewood Cliffs, NJ: Prentice-Hall.
This article presents a good discussion about whether `go to` statements should be used as a control structure.

Exercises

1. ✓ If `hours` is an integer variable, is `hours = hours + 1` a valid Pascal assignment statement? Why?
2. ? Evaluate the following expressions. Some may generate an error, in which case you should explain what is wrong.
   - **a.** `chr (ord (succ (chr (ord ('P') + 1))) + 3)`
   - **b.** `5 >= 4 and true`
   - **c.** `47.5 + 2 <= sqrt(7)`
   - **d.** `(5 <= 9) or 'true'`
   - **e.** `(not (odd (8 mod 3))) and ((5 div 4) > 2)`
   - **f.** `(5 <= 9) and true`
3. ? For each of the following expressions, give a fully parenthesized expression that shows the order of evaluation of the operators. For example, the fully parenthesized equivalent of `2 + 4/5` is `(2 + (4/5))`.
   - **a.** `a div 5 - 4 * d div b`
   - **b.** `a/sqrt(a) + c - d * e`
   - **c.** `b mod c - 2 div e - f`

4. **?** Translate into Pascal the following mathematic expressions:

   a. $\sqrt{\frac{a}{b}}$

   b. $\sin(x^2 + bx - \sqrt{c})$

   c. $\sqrt{\frac{\sin(\sqrt{b})}{\cos(x^2 - 2x)}}$

5. **✓** Explain the difference between `read` and `readln` statements.
6. **?** Suppose that `a` and `b` are integer variables.
   a. What is wrong with the statement `read(a + b)`?
   b. What about the statement `read(a:b)`?
   c. Is `write(a:b)` a valid statement? Why?
7. **?** Evaluate the following expressions. If an expression is ill-formed, explain why.
   a. `1 = 5 or 'd' > 'c'`
   b. `1 = 5 or ('d' > 'c')`
   c. `('1' = 5) and ('d' > 'c')`
   d. `not not ('a' = 'b')`
   e. `(9 > 10) and not (maxint = 45)`
8. **✓** Describe the different ways that a variable can be assigned a value.
9. **?** Suppose that a Pascal program where the following variables were declared

```
var  a, b : integer;
     c : real;
     cl, c2 : char;
```

reads information from a data file containing the following values in the following format:

```
34    a b
5.2  @
12 .. 56
```

What values would be assigned to the variables by the following statements? If a sequence of statements generates an error, explain why.
   a. `readln(a); read(c, cl, c2); read(b)`
   b. `read(a); readln(cl, c2); readln; readln(c)`
   c. `read(cl); readln(c2); readln; readln(a)`
   d. `read(a, b); readln(c2); readln; readln(a)`

10. **?** Explain why these two expressions are syntactically incorrect. (HINT: Use the diagrams in Figures 6.2 and 6.3):

```
false <= true or false <= true
```

and

```
3 <= 5 and 2 <= 10
```

11. **?** If a, b, and c are integer variables and d and e are boolean variables, which of these are valid assignment statements?
    - **a.** `a + 1 := b`
    - **b.** `a := a div c`
    - **c.** `a := b / c`
    - **d.** `a := b := c`
    - **e.** `not(d) := e`
    - **f.** `d := not e`
    - **g.** `b := (((a))) + ((c))`
    - **h.** `b := a + { } c`
    - **i.** `d := a = b`
    - **j.** `a := a { comment } div b`

12. **?** What types must the variables a, b, x, and y be for the following statement to be syntactically correct?

```
x := (2 * a = b) and (x = y)
```

13. **?** If a and b are integer variables, write equivalent expressions without using div and mod.
    - **a.** `a div b`
    - **b.** `a mod b`

14. **?** Suppose that a, b, and c are integer variables and that a = 5, b = 12, and c = 4. What is written by the following Pascal statements? Use ␣ to represent a blank. If the statement generates an error, explain why.
    - **a.** `write(a + b:2)`
    - **b.** `write(b / c)`
    - **c.** `write(a:2:1)`
    - **d.** `write(b div c)`
    - **e.** `write(sqrt(c):5:2)`
    - **f.** `write(sqrt(c):2)`

15. **✓** Give an example to show why operator precedence is necessary.

16. **?** If a is an integer variable, what is the output produced by the following sequence? (NOTE: This is a tricky question.)

```
a := 5;
read(a);
writeln('The value of a is:',a)
```

17. **?** Suppose that FullLength is a real variable and that ApprLength is an integer variable. Write a Pascal statement equivalent to

```
ApprLength := round(FullLength)
```

using the function trunc instead of the function round.

18. **?** Suppose that in a Pascal program the identifier x is declared to be a real variable. What is the output of the following set of statements?

a. `x := 2.0;`
b. `x := sqr(sqr(x) + sqr(2 * x));`
c. `x := sqrt(x + 41);`
d. `writeln(x:4:1);`

19. **?** Suppose that in a Pascal program, the identifiers a, b, and c were declared as integer variables. Is the following statement correct? Why?

```
-a := b + c
```

20. **?** What is written by the following program? Look at the comments carefully.

```
a := 0;
{here is an unclosed comment
a := a + 10;
{the above comment ends here!}
writeln (a)
```

21. **?** What is the output produced by each of the following statements? If a statement gives rise to an error, explain why. Represent blank by ␣. These statements use a variable of the type char (letter) and two integer variables (number and sum). Before the execution of the write statements, the following assignments were made:

```
letter := 'S'; number := 19; sum := 54
```

a. `writeln ('Good morning', number:4, '!')`
b. `writeln (ord(letter) - (ord(letter) - 1))`

c. `writeln ('sum' div 3)`
d. `writeln (letter, ', letter, ', letter)`
e. `writeln ('number div sum')`
f. `writeln ('letter' div sum)`

22. ✓ Explain what a compound statement is in Pascal.
23. ? Write a Pascal program that reads the price of an item and prints the sales tax (the sales tax is 8 percent) and the total amount due. Make sure that your program tells the user the price of the item, the sales tax, and the amount due.
24. ? Explain line by line the behavior of the program in Figure 6.17.
25. ? In Section 6.2.1, we said that the following are expressions:
    a. `a`
    b. `a + b * abs(c)`
    c. `a mod b + c`
    d. `a / 7 * 5 + 12.5`
    e. `a / 7 * 5 + 12.5 < 49`

    Using either the BNF or the syntax chart definition of expressions, explain why these are expressions.
26. ? If `a`, `b`, `c`, and `d` are integer variables, why is

    ```
    a <= b and c >= d
    ```

    not a valid Pascal expression? Explain.
27. ✓ Write a syntax chart for the assignment statement.
28. ? When we discussed the read statement, we said that, while reading information of the type `char`, it was not possible to separate the information being read by spaces. Explain.
29. ? Explain why the input statement does not need information about how much space the values supplied to the computer occupy in the input file.
30. ? Write the following procedures in Pascal:
    a. A procedure named `WriteG` that produces the following output:

    ```
     GGG
    G   G
    G
    G GGG
    G   G
     GGG
    ```

b. A procedure named `WriteO` that produces the following output:

```
 000
0   0
0   0
0   0
0   0
 000
```

c. A procedure named `WriteD` that produces the following output:

```
DDD
D  D
D  D
D  D
D  D
DDD
```

31. **?** Using the procedures of Exercise 30, write a Pascal program that outputs the word `Good`, written vertically.

32. **!** Write a program that reads in the time of the day (for example, 4:30 or 16:45) and prints how many seconds have elapsed since midnight.

33. **?** The `write` statements of the following program represent an example of variable tracing. What is the output of this program?

```
program Trace (input, output);
var a, b, c : integer;
begin
  a := 20;
  b := 10;
  writeln ('After first assignment:');
  writeln (' a=', a:2, ' b=', b:2);
  c:=a * sqr(b);
  writeln ('c has now the value ', c:4);
  a:=c - 64;
  c:=trunc(sqrt(a));
  writeln ('After the operation sqrt:');
  writeln (' a=', a:3, ' c=', c:3)
end.
```

34. **?** What is wrong with the following statements?

a.
```
writeln('This corresponds to a common
                      output error')
```

b.
```
writeln('Can you guess what's wrong?')
```

35. **?** Write a Pascal program that reads the speed of a car in miles per hour and writes how many seconds it will take to travel one mile.

36. **?** Write a Pascal program that reads four integer values and computes their average (a real number) and the nearest integer to the average.

37. **!** Write a Pascal program that exchanges the values of two integer variables *without using an auxiliary variable.* Can this program be used to exchange the value of two real variables? Why?

CHAPTER 7

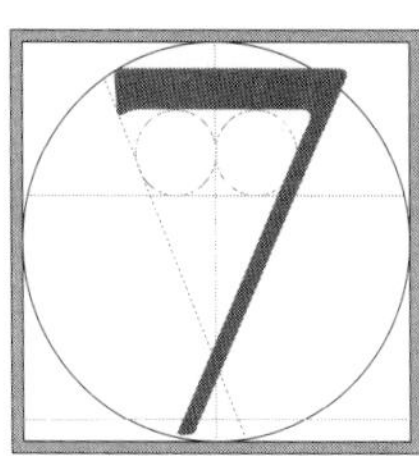

In this chapter, we show the need for making choices among the statements of a program and introduce two control structures: the `if` and `case` statements. We discuss a possible syntactic ambiguity in the `if` statement (the dangling-else problem) and how it is solved in Pascal. Finally, we present a discussion of when to use an `if` statement and when to use a `case` statement.

CONTROL STRUCTURES 2: SELECTION

"Would you tell me, please, which way I ought to go from here?"

"That depends a good deal on where you want to get to," said the Cat.

"I don't much care where—" said Alice.

"Then it doesn't matter which way you go," said the Cat.

Lewis Carroll, *Alice's Adventures in Wonderland*

After having read the previous chapter, you are now able to develop complete Pascal programs. The capabilities of your programs, however, are extremely limited: They can evaluate arithmetic or boolean expressions and show the result obtained. You don't have any control over the sequence of execution of the statements. This means that the statements are executed one after the other, starting with the first statement and ending with the last one. Each statement is executed once and only once.

To develop more complex programs, it is important to allow conditional processing of statements: It should be possible to decide if a statement or group of statements should be executed, depending on the value of an expression.

7.1 The `if` statement

The `if` statement is used to select between two alternatives: Depending on whether a particular boolean expression is true or false, we decide to execute one of two alternative instructions. The syntax of the `if` statement is defined by the following BNF expression or, alternatively, by the syntax chart in Figure 7.1.

```
<if statement> ::= if <expression> then <statement>
                   else <statement> |
                   if <expression> then <statement>
```

The semantics of the `if` statement is defined for each of its forms in the following way:

1. When the computer encounters an `if` statement of the form `if` exp `then` stmt1 `else` stmt2 (in which exp is an expression of type `boolean`, stmt1 is a statement, and stmt2 is a statement), it evaluates the expression exp, and if its value is `true`, the statement stmt1 is executed and the statement stmt2 is not executed; if its value is `false`, the statement stmt2 is executed and the statement stmt1 is not executed.
2. When the computer encounters an `if` statement of the form `if` exp `then` stmt (in which exp is an expression of type `boolean` and stmt is a statement), the expression exp is evaluated, and if its value is `true`, then the statement stmt is executed. If its value is `false`, the statement stmt is not executed. This second form of the `if` statement can be regarded as a special case of the first one, in which the statement immediately following the word `else` is the empty statement (the empty statement corresponds to no execution at all). The second form

FIGURE 7.1 **Syntax chart for the** if statement.

if statement

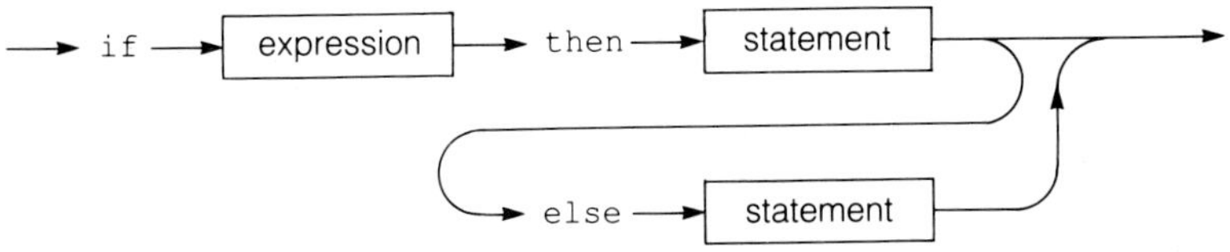

if → expression → then → statement
else → statement

FIGURE 7.2 Laying out the `if` statement.

```
if salary > 150000 then
  writeln ('You are getting rich')
else
  begin
    writeln ('You can do better');
    writeln ('Work harder')
  end
```

of the `if` statement is thus equivalent to `if` exp `then` stmt `else {do nothing};`, where the comment was used to stress the empty statement, and the `;` was used to mark the end of the statement.

To make Pascal programs easy to read, it is usual to use indentation when `if` statements are written. An `if` statement is often written like that shown in Figure 7.2. The statements of each group are indented to the right, and the words `if` and `else` appear prominently at the left, separating the two alternatives. Notice that the statement after the word `else` in Figure 7.2 is a compound statement.

For the first example of a program that uses an `if` statement, consider a program that reads the Social Security number of an employee, the number of hours worked in a given week, and the hourly salary and computes the wages to be paid to that employee. The wages are computed taking into account that, for every hour the employee works over forty hours a week, he or she will be paid double. This program is shown in Figure 7.3. It was obtained by modifying the program presented in Figure 6.16.

This program computes the wages in the following way: First, it computes the wages with every hour paid as a regular salary, statement `Wages := Payrate * HoursWorked`. Second, if the employee worked more than forty hours, it adds to the computed salary the value corresponding to the number of overtime hours. The overtime hours are computed using the regular salary, statement `OvertimeWages := (HoursWorked - 40) * Payrate`. As an exercise, verify that this is the proper result.

In the syntactic definition of the `if` statement, there is no restriction whatsoever concerning the statements that are used by the `if` statement (that is, the statements that follow the words `then` and `else`). Thus, these statements can be, in turn, other `if` statements. Figure 7.4 shows a program that converts a numeric grade into a letter grade using these conversions: 90–100 = A, 80–89 = B, 70–79 = C, 60–69 = D, and below 59 = F.

FIGURE 7.3 A program to compute wages.

```
program Salary (input, output);

{ This program computes the weekly salary of an
  employee, from the number of hours worked and the
  hourly salary. It takes into account overtime.
  Every hour worked past the 40 hours a week will
  be paid double                                }

var SSN, Dollars, Cents : integer;
    HoursWorked, Payrate, Wages, OvertimeWages: real;

begin
  writeln('What is the social security number?');
  readln(SSN);
  writeln('How many hours did the employee work?');
  readln(HoursWorked);
  writeln('What is the hourly salary?');
  readln(Payrate);
  writeln;
  writeln;

write('The employee ',SSN:8,' worked ',HoursWorked:5:1,
        ' hours');
  Dollars := trunc(Payrate);
  Cents := trunc(100 * (Payrate - Dollars));
  writeln(', receiving ',Dollars:4,' Dollars and ',
          Cents:2,' Cents an hour');

  Wages := Payrate * HoursWorked;
  if HoursWorked > 40 then { He/she worked overtime }
    begin
      OvertimeWages := (HoursWorked - 40) * Payrate;
      Wages := Wages + OvertimeWages
    end;
  Dollars := trunc(Wages);
  Cents := trunc(100 * (Wages - Dollars));
  writeln('Wages: --> ',Dollars:6,' Dollars and ',
           Cents:2,' Cents <--')
end. { Salary }
```

FIGURE 7.4 A program to convert grades (version 1).

```
program GradeConversion (input, output);

{ This program converts numeric grades into
  letter grades                              }

var Grade : integer; { numeric grade }

begin
  writeln('What is the numeric grade?');
  readln(Grade);
  if (Grade < 0) or (Grade > 100) then
    writeln('Input error ... impossible grade')
  else
    if Grade >= 90 then
       writeln('Grade is A')
    else
       if Grade >= 80 then
          writeln('Grade is B')
       else
          if Grade >= 70 then
             writeln('Grade is C')
          else
             if Grade >= 60 then
                writeln('Grade is D')
             else
                writeln('Grade is F')
end. { GradeConversion }
```

This program uses `if` statements whose statements are, in turn, `if` statements. The structure resulting from using `if` statements inside `if` statements is called a **nested if structure.**

When the nesting of the `if` statements becomes very deep, the usual indentation used for these statements tends to generate programs whose lines are longer and longer, and we may end up running out of room for writing our statements. (Look at the program of Figure 7.4 and imagine the situation where we would have several extra nested `if`s.) To avoid this problem, when there are more than three or four alternatives, one may use the indentation scheme of Figure 7.5, in which each of the nested `if`

FIGURE 7.5 A program to convert grades (version 2).

```
program GradeConversion (input, output);

{ This program converts numeric grades into
  letter grades                               }

var Grade : integer; { numeric grade }

begin
  writeln('What is the numeric grade?');
  readln(Grade);
  if (Grade < 0) or (Grade > 100) then
    writeln('Input error ... impossible grade')
  else if Grade >= 90 then
    writeln('Grade is A')
  else if Grade >= 80 then
    writeln('Grade is B')
  else if Grade >= 70 then
   writeln('Grade is C')
  else if Grade >= 60 then
   writeln('Grade is D')
  else
    writeln('Grade is F')
end. { GradeConversion }
```

statements is written immediately after the word `else` of the previous statement. Some programmers prefer this alternative, arguing that it clearly shows the several alternatives present in the structure of the `if` statements.

While converting a numeric grade into a letter grade, the program in Figure 7.4 only verifies the lower bound of each of the ranges corresponding to the letter grade, instead of the upper bound and lower bound as we may be tempted to think the first time. Figure 7.6 shows another program, whose `if` statement verifies both the upper bound and the lower bound. As an exercise, convince yourself that the additional conditions of Figure 7.6 are not necessary. The solution presented in Figure 7.4, because it is easier to read and more efficient, should be adopted over the solution presented in Figure 7.6.

FIGURE 7.6 A program to convert grades (version 3).

```
program GradeConversion (input, output);

{ This program converts numeric grades into
  letter grades                               }

var Grade : integer; { numeric grade }

begin
  writeln('What is the numeric grade?');
  read(Grade);
  if (Grade < 0) or (Grade > 100) then
    writeln('Input error ... impossible grade')
  else
    if (Grade >= 90) and (Grade <= 100) then
       writeln('Grade is A')
    else
       if (Grade >= 80) and (Grade < 90) then
          writeln('Grade is B')
       else
          if (Grade >= 70) and (Grade < 80) then
             writeln('Grade is C')
          else
             if (Grade >= 60) and (Grade < 70) then
                writeln('Grade is D')
             else
                writeln('Grade is F')
end. { GradeConversion }
```

Developing nested `if` structures must be done with some care, as shown in the following example.[1] Consider the following `if` statement, deliberately written on only one line.

```
if a > 0 then if b > 0 then b := b + 1 else a := a + 1
```

1. This example was adapted from an example in Schneider, Weingart, and Perlman (1978, pp. 141–144). (Copyright © 1978 John Wiley & Sons Inc.) Reprinted with permission of John Wiley & Sons Inc.

FIGURE 7.7 Possible meaning of the `if` statement.

```
if a > 0 then
   begin
     if b > 0 then
        b := b + 1
     else
        a := a + 1
   end
```

FIGURE 7.8 Alternative meaning of the `if` statement.

```
if a > 0 then
   begin
     if b > 0 then
        b := b + 1
   end
else
   a := a + 1
```

What is the meaning of this statement? To which `if` statement does the `else` belong? Does it have the meaning represented in Figure 7.7? Or does it have the meaning represented in Figure 7.8?

In these figures, a `begin`/`end` pair was added to *force* one of the possible meanings of the statement, and indentation was used to *stress* those meanings. The difference between these two interpretations is significant. For example, in the case of Figure 7.7, nothing happens if the value of the variable `a` is not positive. But in the case of Figure 7.8, if the value of the variable `a` is not positive, then its value is incremented by one unit. Which one is the meaning considered by the computer?

This is known as the **dangling else problem.** To solve it, Pascal and many high-level programming languages use the convention that, unless there is an indication to the contrary, an `else` is always associated with the closest unmatched `if`. Thus, the correct meaning of the statement is the one represented in Figure 7.7.

FIGURE 7.9 Alternative way to write the `if` statement.

```
if a > 0 then
   if b > 0 then
      b := b + 1
else
   a := a + 1
```

We should stress what was said in Chapter 3 about the use of indentation: If the `if` statement had been written as shown in Figure 7.9, its meaning would *still* be the one shown in Figure 7.7. Indentation is used to make programs more readable; it does not change the meaning of a program. We must be very careful using indentation so that it is not misleading. If we want to associate an `else` with an `if` that is not the last one used, we must use a `begin`/`end` pair as shown in Figure 7.8. As a final remark about this example, sometimes using a redundant `begin`/`end` pair can considerably increase the readability of a program, as the example in Figure 7.7 shows.

7.2 The `case` statement

In the previous section, we saw that a selection between several alternatives can be accomplished through the use of nested `if` statements. However, high-level nesting can produce statements that are difficult to read. As an alternative to nesting `if` statements, some programming languages supply a **multiple-selection** statement, such as the `case` statement of Pascal. However, the `case` statement is not simply a more readable version of a nested `if` statement. The nested `if` statement is appropriate for boolean conditions and tests based on continuous-range values; a `case` statement is appropriate for noncontinuous ordinal controls. This aspect is further discussed in Section 7.3.

Depending on the value of an expression, called the **selector,** the `case` statement selects one statement to be executed. The syntax of the

FIGURE 7.10 Syntax chart for the `case statement`.

case statement

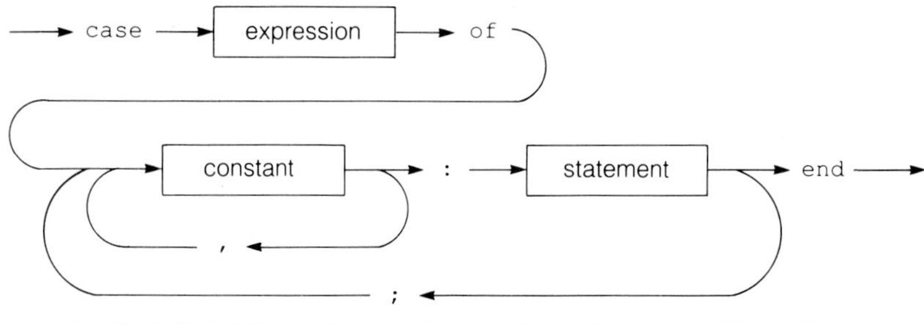

`case` statement is defined by the following BNF expression or, alternatively, by the syntax chart of Figure 7.10.

<case statement> ::= **case** <expression> **of** <body of case>
end

<body of case> ::= <case element> |
<case element> ; <body of case>

<case element> ::= <case labels> : <statement>

<case labels> ::= <case label> |
<case label> , <case labels>

<case label> ::= <constant>

The `case` statement is usually layed out as shown in Figure 7.11. The selector, `expr`, is an expression of ordinal type (it cannot be real-valued); the case label's `labelsl`, `labels2`, . . ., `labelsN` are lists containing one or more constants of the same type as `expr`. The same constant cannot be part of two different label lists. Each one of `stmt2`, `stmt2`, . . ., `stmtN` is a statement.

The semantics of the `case` statement is as follows: When a `case` statement is found, the computer finds the value of the selector (represented by `expr` in Figure 7.11) and executes the statement whose label list con-

FIGURE 7.11 Laying out a `case` statement.

```
case expr of
   labels1 : stmt1;
   labels2 : stmt2;
       .
       .
       .
   labelsN : stmtN
end {case}
```

tains the value of the selector (this explains why the same constant cannot be part of two different label lists). If the value of the selector does not equal any constant in the label lists, the execution of the program terminates, generating an error. In some Pascal implementations, if the value of `expr` does not equal any constant in the list of labels, `labels1`, `labels2`, . . ., `labelsN`, the execution of the program continues with the execution of the statement following the `case` statement. In other implementations, there is an `otherwise` clause (see below).

As an example of a `case` statement, Figure 7.12 shows a program that converts a letter grade into a numeric grade using these conventions: A = 4, B = 3, C = 2, D = 1, and F = 0. Note that this program allows the user to enter the letter grade in either upper- or lowercase letters, thus the need for the two case labels.

The `case` statement that we just described corresponds to the statement originally proposed by Jensen and Wirth (1974) and adopted by the ISO Standard Pascal (Cooper 1983). Some Pascal implementations have different versions of the `case` statement, in which it is possible to specify a statement that will be executed just in case the value of the selector does not equal any constant in the lists of labels. Because this approach has been adopted by many implementations, it is described here. Be warned, however, that this is *not* part of Standard Pascal, and, thus, before using it, check whether your implementation supports it. However, if your Pascal version does not support one of these statements, you can always handle the "out-of-range" case by combining a `case` statement with an `if` statement (see Exercise 21).

FIGURE 7.12 A program to convert letter grades into numeric grades.

```
program GradeConversion (input, output);

{ This program converts letter grades into numeric grades }

var LetterGrade : char;
    NumericGrade : integer;

begin
  writeln('What is the letter grade?');
  readln(LetterGrade);
  case LetterGrade of
    'a','A' : NumericGrade := 4;
    'b','B' : NumericGrade := 3;
    'c','C' : NumericGrade := 2;
    'd','D' : NumericGrade := 1;
    'f','F' : NumericGrade := 0
  end;
  writeln('The numeric grade is:', NumericGrade:2)
end. { GradeConversion }
```

The syntactic definition of one of these statements (the `case` statement for VAX Pascal running under the VMS operating system) is the following:

```
<case statement> ::= case <expression> of <body of case> end

<body of case> ::= <statements with labels> |
                   <statements with labels> ;
                   otherwise <statements>

<statements with labels> ::= <case element> |
                             <case element> ;
                             <statements with labels>
```

The semantics of this statement is similar to the semantics of the `case` statement of Standard Pascal with the exception of the following: If the option `otherwise` <statements> was used and the value of the selector

FIGURE 7.13 Writing enumerated types (version 1).

```
procedure WriteCar (Car : GMCars);
begin
  case Car of
    Cadillac    : write('Cadillac');
    Oldsmobile  : write('Oldsmobile');
    Buick       : write('Buick');
    Chevrolet   : write('Chevrolet');
    Pontiac     : write('Pontiac')
  end { case }
end
```

does not equal any of the constants in any of the label lists, then the statements immediately following the word `otherwise` are executed.

Before ending this section, we present a common use of the `case` statement: generating an external representation for user-defined ordinal types. Remember from Chapter 6 that because the constants of an enumerated type have no external character representation, they cannot be written using a `write` or `writeln` statement.

Suppose, for example, that in our program we define the type `GMCars` as

```
type GMCars = (Cadillac, Oldsmobile, Buick,
               Chevrolet, Pontiac);
```

and declare the variable `Car` of type `GMCars`. Most likely, at some point in the program, we would like to output the value of the variable `Car`. Because we cannot do this with the predefined output statements, we define a new statement `WriteCar` that does it. The procedure corresponding to this statement is shown in Figure 7.13. Again, this procedure receives the variable to be written—this is accomplished by the parameter `Car : GMCars`. (Parameters are discussed in Chapter 9.) Notice that the same result could have been produced using nested `if` statements (Figure 7.14). By comparing the procedures in Figures 7.13 and 7.14, we can conclude that, when we have multiple alternatives, the `case` statement has the effect of laying out these alternatives in a better way than the `if` statement.

FIGURE 7.14 Writing enumerated types (version 2).

```
procedure WriteCar (Car : GMCars);
begin
  if Car = Cadillac then
     write('Cadillac')
  else if Car = Oldsmobile then
     write('Oldsmobile')
  else if Car = Buick then
     write('Buick')
  else if Car = Chevrolet then
     write('Chevrolet')
  else
     write('Pontiac')
end
```

7.3 If versus case

A question that may be raised during the development of an algorithm that uses selection is when to use an `if` statement and when to use a `case` statement. In general, an `if` statement is used when the number of alternatives is not very large, when we want to impose an order on the evaluation of the expressions used in the selection, or when the possible alternatives correspond to subranges. Let us consider each one of these in turn.

The first possibility was already discussed in this chapter: When we have a high level of nesting of `if` statements, programs may become difficult to read because we lose track of the possible alternatives. Resorting to a `case` statement has the effect of laying out all the possible options and thus making the program more readable.

With the second possibility, be aware that there are situations in which we want to make choices based on several conditions, but we want to impose an order of evaluation on those conditions. Suppose that we have a program that uses two integer variables, say `a` and `b`, and we want to execute some statement just in case `(a div b) < 4`. We can accomplish our goal with:

```
if a div b < 4 then some-statement
```

However, if `b = 0`, this generates an execution error, and, thus, before trying to evaluate `a div b`, we may want to test whether `b = 0`. The statement

```
if (b <> 0) and (a div b < 4) then some-statement
```

does not do it, because in Pascal the order of evaluation of the components of an expression is implementation-dependent; thus, we may not know which one of the conditions is evaluated first. To solve problems of this sort, we resort to the nested `if` statement

```
if b <> 0 then
  if a div b < 4 then
    some-statement
```

In situations like this one, the `if` statement is better than the `case` statement.

Finally, when we have to select an alternative based on subranges of values, an `if` statement is clearly better than a `case` statement (for example, suppose that if a certain value was within the range 100 through 950 we want to take some action, whereas if the value was within the range 951 through 5000 we want to take another action).

Whenever possible, `case` statements should be used when selecting alternatives based on several possible values (several means more than three or four) and when all the possible values the expression may take can be easily listed.

Summary

In this chapter, two statements were presented that enable us to decide about the execution of other statements: the `if` and the `case` statements.

The `if` statement allows a decision between two alternatives (notice that even when the `if` statement is of the form `if t then s`, it still decides between two alternatives: executing the statement `s` or doing nothing), and the `case` statement allows a decision between several competing alternatives.

Suggested readings

You can explore the topics presented in this chapter more deeply by consulting the following books:

Pratt, T. 1975. *Programming Languages: Design and Implementation.* Englewood Cliffs, NJ: Prentice-Hall.
Chapter 5 of this book covers several mechanisms that can be used to specify the sequence of execution of the statements of a program. Among the structures presented, Pratt discusses several aspects of the `if` statement (in several programming languages) and considers their advantages and disadvantages.

Wirth, N. 1973. *Systematic Programming: An Introduction.* Englewood Cliffs, NJ: Prentice-Hall.
This book presents a study of the `if` and `case` statements, discussing their formal properties.

Exercises

1. ? Write a program that reads three integer numbers and prints the largest of them.
2. ✓ If a and b are integer variables, is the following a legal Pascal statement? Why?

```
if a = b then
   a := a + 1;
else
   b := b - 1
```

3. ? Write a program that converts temperatures between Celsius and Fahrenheit. The program reads an integer representing a temperature to be converted, followed by the letter *F* or the letter *C*, representing, respectively, that the temperature to be converted is in Fahrenheit or Celsius degrees. The program writes the temperature that was read and its equivalent value in the other system. For example, if the value read was `32 F`, the program should write `32 F = 0 C`.
4. ? Write a change-making program. The program reads an amount in dollars and computes the number of $100, $50, $20, $10, $5, and $1 bills and the number of 50-, 25-, 10-, 5-, and 1-cent coins needed to make up that amount.
5. ? Write a program that finds out whether a given year is a leap year. A given year is a leap year if it is divisible by 4, except if it is divisible by 100 but not 400. In other words, years divisible by 100 are not leap years unless divisible by 400 also—1900 is not; 2000 is.
6. ✓ Explain the syntax and the semantics of the `if` statement.
7. ? Suppose that the unit price of a product depends on the number of units sold, according to the following table:

Quantity ordered	*Unit price ($)*
0–99	6.00
100–199	5.50
200–299	5.00
300 or more	4.50

Write a Pascal program that reads the amount ordered and computes the total price of the order, using

a. An `if` statement.

b. A `case` statement (without using the `otherwise` nonstandard option). (HINT: You may need to combine an `if` statement with a `case` statement and find a clever way to map the ranges of quantities into integer values.)

8. ✓ Write a syntax chart that defines the syntax of the `case` statement with the `otherwise` option.

9. ? The first `if` statement of the program in Figure 7.4 may look unnecessary. Explain what could happen if we remove the test `(Grade < 0) or (Grade > 100)`.

10. ? The program in Figure 7.4 defined `Grade` to be an integer and then checked whether its value was between 0 and 100. An alternative way of doing this would be to define `Grade` to be in the subrange 0 . . . 100 and let the computer complain automatically. What is the disadvantage of this second approach?

11. ? The following version of the grade-conversion program, although producing the desired results, must be avoided by all means. Explain.

```
program GradeConversion (input, output);
var Grade : integer;
begin
  writeln('What is the numeric grade?');
  readln(Grade);
  if (Grade < 0) or (Grade > 100) then
     writeln('Input error .. impossible grade');
  if (Grade >= 90) and (Grade <= 100) then
     writeln ('Grade is A');
  if (Grade >= 80) and (Grade < 90) then
     writeln ('Grade is B');
  if (Grade >= 70) and (Grade < 80) then
     writeln ('Grade is C');
  if (Grade >= 60) and (Grade < 70) then
     writeln ('Grade is D');
  if (Grade >= 0) and (Grade < 60) then
     writeln ('Grade is F')
end.
```

12. **?** The following version of the grade-conversion program is wrong. Explain.

```
program GradeConversion (input, output);
var Grade : integer;
begin
  writeln('What is the numeric grade?');
  readln (Grade);
  if (Grade < 0) or (Grade > 100) then
     writeln('Input error .. impossible grade');
  if Grade >= 90 then
     writeln('Grade is A');
  if Grade >= 80 then
     writeln('Grade is B');
  if Grade >= 70 then
     writeln('Grade is C');
  if Grade >= 60 then
     writeln('Grade is D');
  if Grade < 60 then
     writeln('Grade is F');
end.
```

13. **✓** When should a nested `if` statement be used instead of a `case` statement?
14. **?** Assume the type definition

```
type WeekDay = (Mon, Tue, Wed, Thu, Fri, Sat, Sun)
```

and suppose that the variable `Day` is of type `WeekDay`. Write a `case` statement that prints `Go to work` if `Day` represents a working day and prints `It's the weekend` if `Day` represents a weekend day.
15. **?** Redo Exercise 14 using an `if` statement.
16. **?** Write a Pascal program that computes the roots of the equation

$$ax^2 + bx - c = 0$$

given the coefficients a, b, and c. Remember that the roots of this equation are given by

$$x_1 = \frac{-b + \sqrt{b^2 - 4ac}}{2a}$$

and

$$x_2 = \frac{-b - \sqrt{b^2 - 4ac}}{2a}$$

Make sure that your program takes the following cases into account: (a) complex roots (when $b^2 - 4ac < 0$), (b) identical roots, (c) linear equation ($a = 0$).

17. **?** A computer manufacturer builds computers that can support one to ninety-nine terminals. Depending on the number of terminals desired, a certain model should be chosen. The company uses a Pascal program that is given the number of terminals desired and decides which model should be used. Assuming that the number of terminals is represented by the integer variable `NTerminals`, write *one* (nested) `if` statement that decides which model to use, according to the following table:

Number of terminals	*Model*
`Nterminals` < 1	None—error
1 ≤ `Nterminals` < 5	Cheapomodel
5 ≤ `Nterminals` < 20	Regmodel
20 ≤ `Nterminals` < 100	Mightymodel
`Nterminals` ≥ 100	None—error

(NOTE: The boolean expressions in your `if` statement should contain *no* conjunctions.)

18. **?** Rewrite the following Pascal program using a `case` statement.

```
program TestCase (input, output);
var number : 0 .. 9;
begin
  read(number);
  if (number = 1) or (number = 5) or
     (number = 7) then
     writeln('Number in 157')
  else
     if number = 3 then
        writeln('Number is 3')
     else
        if (number = 2) or (number = 8) then
           writeln('Number in 28')
        else
           writeln('Number in 469')
end. { TestCase }
```

19. **?** Write a program that reads the number of minutes that have elapsed since midnight and outputs the time of the day in the form hours:minutes, using a twenty-four-hour clock. For example, if the number of minutes read was 1335, the value output would be 22:15; if the number of minutes read was 510, the value output would be 8:30.
20. **?** Modify the program of Exercise 19 so that it uses a twelve-hour clock. For example, if the number of minutes read was 1335, the output of your program would be 10:15 PM; if the number of minutes read was 510, the value output would be 8:30 AM.
21. **?** If the `case` statement of your Pascal version does not support the `otherwise` escape case, you can always simulate it by nesting a `case` statement inside an `if` statement that handles the out-of-range cases. Explain in detail.
22. **✓** Is the following `case` statement correct? If not, explain what is wrong.

```
program TestCase (input, output);

var Number : 0 .. 1000;

begin
  writeln('Please type a positive integer less than 1000');
  readln(Number);
  case Number of
     0 .. 100      : writeln('What a small number');
     101 .. 800    : writeln('Ok');
     801 .. 1000   : writeln('What a big number');
  end
end. { TestCase }
```

23. **?** The minimum payment and monthly interest rate on a credit card account are defined as follows:

Balance ($)	*Minimum payment*
< 100	Balance
100–199	$10
200–500	$25
> 500	6% of balance

Balance after payment ($)	*Monthly interest rate*
< 100	2
100–500	1.57
> 500	1.07

Write a Pascal program that reads in the balance on the account and prints the minimum amount due and the *amount* of interest to be paid if just the minimum is paid.

24. ? Write a Pascal program that reads two real numbers and decides whether they can be considered equal. Refer to the discussion in Section 5.4.

CHAPTER 8

This chapter introduces the concept of a loop. We discuss the advantages of using loops and the kinds of loops available in Pascal: `while`, `repeat`, **and** `for`. **We present the syntax and semantics of each of these statements and give examples of their use. The chapter ends with a comparison of the three statements and a discussion of when to use each.**

CONTROL STRUCTURES 3: REPETITION

"Then you keep moving round, I suppose?" said Alice.
"Exactly so," said the Hatter: "as the things get used up."
"But what happens when you come to the beginning again?" Alice ventured to ask.
Lewis Carroll, *Alice's Adventures in Wonderland*

The statements presented so far allow the selection of statements to be executed, but each statement is still executed only once. The execution of the program begins with the first statement and ends with the last one, each statement being executed, at most, once.

Very often it is necessary to repeat the execution of a group of statements or even to repeat the execution of the entire program for different data. In programming, a sequence of statements that is executed repeatedly is a loop. A **loop** is composed of a set of statements called the **body of the loop** and by a structure that controls the execution of those statements, describing how many times the body of the loop should be executed. Loops are very common in programming; it is very rare to find a program without a loop.

Each time the statements of the body of the loop are executed, a **pass** through the loop has been made. The statements that compose the body of the loop can be executed any number of times (or none). The number must be finite: Semantic errors may cause an interminable execution of the body of the loop: this is an **infinite loop**.

This chapter presents three statements that allow the specification of the repetitive execution of sets of statements, the `while`, `repeat`, and `for` statements. We discuss the particularities of each.

8.1 The `while` statement

The `while` statement allows the repetitive execution of a statement *while* a certain condition holds. The syntax of the `while` statement is defined by the following BNF expression or, alternatively, by the syntax chart of Figure 8.1.

<while statement> ::= `while` <expression> `do` <statement>

The semantics of the `while` statement is the following: When the statement `while` expr `do` stmt is found, in which the nonterminal symbol stmt represents the body of the loop and the nonterminal symbol expr (which must be of type `boolean`) represents the condition for terminating the execution of the loop, the computer evaluates expr. If its value is `true`, then the computer makes a pass through the loop, executing the statement stmt. Afterward, it computes the value of expr again, and this process is repeated *while* the value of the expression expr is `true`. When the value of the expression expr is found to be `false`, the execution of the loop terminates.

Clearly, the statement that constitutes the body of the loop must modify the value of the expression; otherwise, the loop may never terminate: If the value of the expression is initially `true` and if the body of the loop does not modify that expression, we will surely have an infinite loop.

As an example of using the `while` statement, consider the program shown in Figure 8.2. This program reads a sequence of positive numbers and computes its sum. The amount of numbers to be read is not known when the program begins execution. To tell the computer that the sequence of numbers has ended, we supply the program with a special value (in our example, a negative number). This value is called a **sentinel value** because it signals the end of the input. An alternative to using a sentinel value consists of testing whether the end of file is reached. Recall from Chapters 5 and 6 that the function `eof` is `true` if, during the input of the file

FIGURE 8.1 **Syntax chart for the** while statement.

while statement

→ `while` → [expression] → `do` → [statement] →

represented by its argument, the end of file is reached; it is `false` otherwise. If the values to be read end with the file, this function can be used. Figure 8.3 shows another version of the program in Figure 8.2, in which the function `eof` is used. Note that the `eof` function can be used interactively. During an interactive session, it is possible to specify the end of file; however, the method of doing so varies from implementation to implementation. (For example, in the Pascal version for VAX computers running under the VMS operating system, this is achieved by typing `control Z`.)

FIGURE 8.2 A program to sum integers (version 1).

```
program SumOfIntegers (input, output);

{ This program computes the sum of a sequence
  of positive integers }

var Sum, Number : integer;

{ Meaning of the variables:
  Sum    - running sum
  Number - number to be added to the running sum }

   Procedure AskUser;
   begin
     writeln('Please type an integer number');
     writeln('Any negative number terminates execution')
   end; { AskUser }

begin
  Sum := 0;
  AskUser;
  readln(Number);
  while Number >= 0 do
    begin
      Sum := Sum + Number;
      AskUser;
      readln(Number)
    end;
  writeln('The sum is ', Sum:3)
end. { SumOfIntegers }
```

FIGURE 8.3 A program to sum integers (version 2).

```
program SumOfIntegers (input, output);

{ This program computes the sum of a sequence
  of positive integers }

var Sum, Number : integer;

{ Meaning of the variables:
  Sum    - running sum
  Number - number to be added to the running sum }

   Procedure AskUser;
   begin
     writeln('Please type an integer number');
     writeln('End of file terminates execution')
   end; { AskUser }

begin
  Sum := 0;
  AskUser;
  while not eof do
    begin
      readln(Number);
      Sum := Sum + Number;
      AskUser
    end;
  writeln('The sum is ', Sum:3)
end. { SumOfIntegers }
```

As a second example, consider the program shown in Figure 8.4. This program counts the number of words on a text and the number of lines it contains. It assumes that two words are separated by one or more blanks, the first word can begin anywhere in the line, and the line may be empty. This program uses the functions `eof` and `eoln`.

There are two important points to remember about the `while` statement:

1. In general, the number of times that the body of the loop will be executed cannot be known beforehand: The condition that ends the execution of the loop is tested during the execution of the loop itself, and we may not know beforehand how its execution will proceed.

FIGURE 8.4 A program to compute number of words and lines.

```
program WordCounter (input,output);

{ Counts the number of words on a text and the
  number of lines it contains }

const Blank = ' ';

var  Character, LastChar : char;
     WordCounter, LineCounter : integer;

{ Meaning of the variables:
  Character   - current character
  LastChar    - previous character read
  WordCounter - number of words read
  LineCounter - number of lines read }

begin
   WordCounter := 0;
   LineCounter := 0;
   LastChar := Blank;
   while not eof do { process the whole text }
     begin
       while not eoln do { process a line }
         begin
           read(Character);
           if (Character <> Blank) and (LastChar = Blank) then
              WordCounter := WordCounter + 1;
           LastChar := Character
         end;
       readln;
       LineCounter := LineCounter + 1;
       LastChar := Blank; { end-of-line is equivalent to Blank }
     end;

   writeln('The number of words is: ',WordCounter:3);
   writeln('The number of lines is: ',LineCounter:3)
end. { WordCounter }
```

2. It may happen that the body of the loop is not executed at all. In fact, the semantics of the `while` statement states that the value of the condition that ends the execution of the loop is tested before the execution of the loop begins. If the initial value of this condition is `false`, the statements that constitute the body of the loop will not be executed.

8.2 The `repeat` statement

"That's enough about lessons," the Gryphon interrupted in a very decided tone. "Tell her something about the games now."
Lewis Carroll, *Alice's Adventures in Wonderland*

The `repeat` statement allows the repetitive execution of a sequence of statements *until* certain conditions hold. The syntax of the `repeat` statement is defined by the following BNF expressions or, alternatively, by the syntax chart in Figure 8.5.

<repeat statement> ::= `repeat` <statements> `until` <expression>

<statements> ::= <statement> |
<statement> ; <statements>

As opposed to the `while` statement, the syntax of the `repeat` statement allows the specification of a *sequence* of statements to be executed. Thus, it is not necessary to resort to a compound statement when the body of the loop has more than one statement. This stems from the fact that the body of the loop in the `repeat` statement is delimited by the reserved words `repeat` and `until`; thus, there is no ambiguity about which statements should be repeated.

The semantics of this statement is the following: When the statement `repeat` stmts `until` expr is found, where expr must be of type `boolean`, the computer repeatedly executes the statements stmts until the value of expr is `true`. The computer begins by executing the statements that constitute the body of the loop (stmts). Afterward, it computes the value of expr. If this value is `false`, then it executes the body of the loop again, and so on. As soon as the value of expr is `true`, the execution of the loop terminates. Notice, however, that the loop only terminates after a complete pass. In other words, if the condition that terminates the loop becomes `true` after the execution of the first statement in the body of the loop, its value will be computed only after the complete execution of the body of the loop.

FIGURE 8.5 **Syntax chart for the** repeat statement.

repeat statement

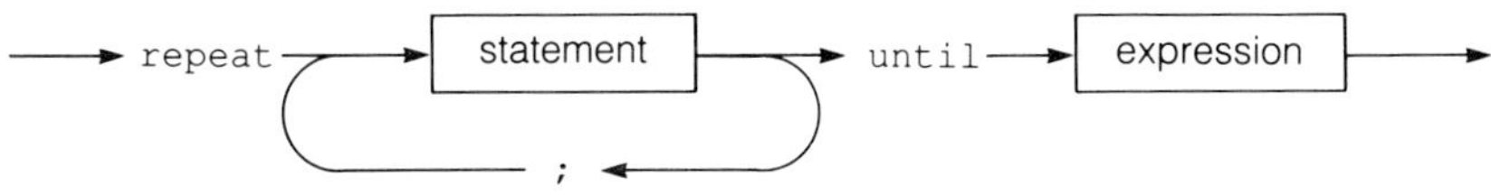

As with the `while` statement, in general, the number of times the body of a `repeat` statement is repeated cannot be computed beforehand. However, as opposed to what happens with the `while` statement, the body of a `repeat` statement is always executed at least once (because the condition is evaluated at the end of the loop).

As an example, consider the program shown in Figure 8.6. This program plays a game with the user. It starts out by "thinking" about a number between 0 and 100. Afterward, it asks the user to guess which number it thought of. Following the user's guess, the program tells whether the number guessed is bigger or smaller than the number the computer thought of. The game ends when the user discovers the number. The number that computer "thinks" of is generated by the function `random(100)`. This function is not a predefined Pascal function and is discussed in Chapter 9. The program in Figure 8.6 is incomplete: It is missing the definition of the `random` function (although we show a box, inside which the computation of `random` takes place). For the sake of the presentation of the `repeat` statement, it is enough to say that the function `random` randomly generates an integer number between 0 and 100.

The program in Figure 8.6 uses three `repeat` statements. The first one successively begins a new game until the user wants to quit playing. The second `repeat` statement corresponds to the part of the game in which the program interacts with the user while the user is trying to guess the number thought of by the computer. Finally, the last `repeat` statement asks the user to supply the answer `Y` or `N`, indicating whether he or she wants to continue playing. This last `repeat` statement shows an interesting technique to ensure that the user supplies one of the possible answers. A question is asked and then a loop begins, being executed until the user supplies one of the alternative answers. Every time the computer goes through this loop, it indicates the possible answers to the user, asking for one of them. As soon as a legal answer is supplied, the loop terminates.

FIGURE 8.6 A program to play guessing games.

```
program GuessWhich (input, output);

var Number, Guess : integer;
    MoreGames : char;

{ Meaning of the variables:
   Number      - number "thought of" by the computer
   Guess       - user's guess
   MoreGames   - user's answer concerning whether he/she wants to
                 continue playing         }
 function random (x:integer) : integer;


begin
  repeat
    writeln('I am thinking about a number.');
    writeln('Why don''t you try to guess it..');
    Number := random(100); { note that this is not defined }
    repeat
      writeln('What number am I thinking of?');
      readln(Guess);
      if (Guess < 0) or (Guess > 100) then
         writeln('The number should be between 0 and 100')
      else
         if Guess < Number then
            writeln('Your guess is too low')
         else
            if Guess > Number then
               writeln('Your guess is too high')
    until Guess = Number;
    writeln('That''s it!');
    writeln('Do you want to play again?');
    repeat
       writeln('Please answer Y or N');
       readln(MoreGames)
    until (MoreGames = 'Y') or (MoreGames = 'N')
  until  MoreGames = 'N'
end. { GuessWhich }
```

8.3 The for statement

The for statement has a nature very different from the while and repeat statements. The for statement gives rise to a **counted loop.** Execution of this loop is controlled by a variable called the **control variable** (which *must* be of ordinal type). The loop will be executed for a sequence of the values of this variable. Before the beginning of the execution of the loop, this variable is assigned a value; the loop is then executed. After each pass through the loop, this value is incremented (or decremented) by a constant amount, and the execution of the loop is repeated. When the value of the control variable reaches a certain limit (which is specified before the beginning of the execution of the loop), the execution of the body of the loop terminates. In a for loop, it is thus possible to know beforehand the number of times the loop will be executed, which contrasts with both the while and the repeat statements.

Assume that we want to compute the sum of the first *n* positive integers, where the value of *n* is supplied to the machine. This problem can be solved using the while statement, as shown in Figure 8.7. This program solves our problem, but we have to specify statements for the following: (a) initializing the first integer value to be added, (b) increasing the value of the integer to be added to the running sum, and (c) testing whether the value of the integer has reached the limit. Note that, for this problem, we knew beforehand (after reading the value of the variable Limit) how many times the loop should be repeated and the amount of the increment to the variable after each pass through the loop. The for statement allows the solution of the same problem without needing to explicitly write the statements for the actions corresponding to (a), (b), and (c).

The syntax of the for statement is defined by the following BNF expression or, alternatively, by the syntax chart of Figure 8.8.

```
<for statement> ::= for <control variable> := <for list>
                    do <statement>

<control variable> ::= <identifier>

<for list> ::= <initial value> to <final value> |
               <initial value> downto <final value>

<initial value> ::= <expression>

<final value> ::= <expression>
```

In a for statement, the control variable *must* be of ordinal type, and initial value and final value must be expressions of the same type as the control

FIGURE 8.7 A program to compute the sum of integers (version 1).

```
program SumOfIntegers (input, output);

{ This program computes the sum of the first "n"
  integers, where "n" is given by the value of
  the variable "Limit" }

var Sum, Limit, Number : integer;

{ Meaning of the variables:
    Sum       - running sum
    Limit     - limit of the integers to be added
    Number    - integer being added to the sum  }

begin
  writeln('What is the limit of the integers ',
          'being added?');
  readln(Limit);
  Sum := 0;
  Number := 1;
  while Number <= Limit do
    begin
      Sum := Sum + Number;
      Number := Number + 1
    end;
  writeln('The sum of the integers less than or ',
          'equal to ',Limit:2,' is ',Sum:2)
end. { SumOfIntegers }
```

variable. In addition, the statement that constitutes the body of the loop must not modify the value of the control variable (this contrasts with other languages, for example, BASIC).

The semantics of this statement is the following: When a `for` statement is found, the computer evaluates the expressions representing initial value and final value. According to the values computed, and for each of the forms of the `for` statement, it takes one of the following actions.

1. If the `for` statement is of the form `for` iv `to` fv `do` stmt, then if the value of iv is less than or equal to the value of fv, the body of the loop stmt is executed successively for the values of the control variable given by iv, `succ(`iv`)`, `succ(succ(`iv`))`, ..., fv. If the value of iv is greater

FIGURE 8.8 Syntax chart for the for statement.

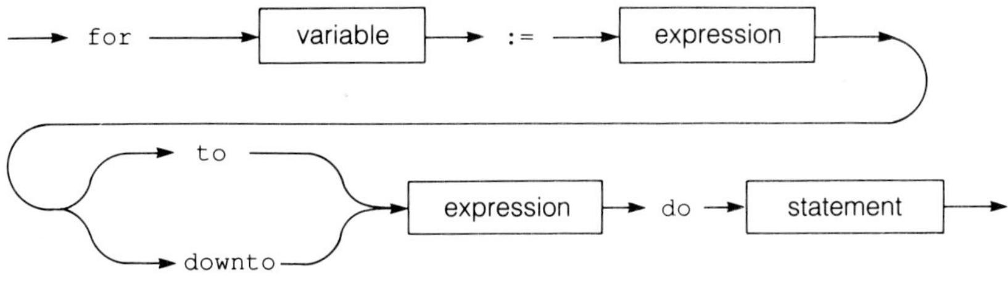

than the value of fv, then the statement that constitutes the body of the loop is not executed. If the control variable is of not of type `integer` (remember, it has to be an ordinal type), the words *less than* and *greater than* refer to the preestablished order for the constants of its type.

2. If the `for` statement is of the form `for` iv `downto` fv `do` stmt, then if the value of iv is greater than or equal to the value of fv, the body of the loop stmt is executed successively for the values of the control variable given by iv, `pred(`iv`)`, `pred(pred(`iv`))`, . . ., fv. If the value of iv is less than the value of fv, then the body of the loop is not executed. Again, for control variables not of type `integer`, the words *less than* and *greater than* refer to the preestablished order for the constants of its type.

Note that the values of initial value and final value are calculated only once, *before the execution of the loop begins.* Those values define how many times the loop will be executed.

After normal termination of a `for` loop[1], the control variable is undefined (this means that we cannot rely on the fact that the control variable has had values assigned to it); thus, it should not be used afterward unless a new value is assigned to it.

As a first example of a `for` statement, consider the program shown in Figure 8.9, which computes the sum of the first n positive integers. This program solves the same problem as the program in Figure 8.7 but with the difference that it uses a `for` statement instead of a `repeat` statement.

1. By **normal termination,** we mean termination not caused by a `go to` statement.

FIGURE 8.9 A program to compute the sum of integers (version 2).

```
program SumOfIntegers (input, output);

{ This program computes the sum of the first "n"
  positive integers, where "n" is given by the
  value of "Limit" }

var Sum, Limit, Number : integer;

{ Meaning of the variables:
    Sum       - running sum
    Limit     - limit of the integers to be added
    Number    - integer being added to the sum  }

begin
  writeln('What is the limit of the integers ',
          'being added?');
  readln(Limit);
  Sum := 0;
  for Number := 1 to Limit do
      Sum := Sum + Number;
  writeln('The sum of the integers less than or ',
          'equal ',Limit:2,' is ',Sum:2)
end. { SumOfIntegers }
```

The program in Figure 8.10 computes the sum of the even numbers less than or equal to 1000. The `for` statement for a problem of this type would need to increase the control variable by two after each pass through the loop. Because the Pascal `for` statement does not allow the specification of an increment to the control variable, in this program we use an auxiliary variable `OrdEven` that tells which is the ordinal order of the even number that we are about to add to the running sum (the first even number, the second even number, and so on). The actual even number to be added to the running sum, `EvenNumb`, is computed from the variable `OrdEven`. A similar trick should be used whenever you need a `for` loop whose control variable must be increased or decreased by more than one.

FIGURE 8.10 A program to compute the sum of even integers.

```
program SumOfEven (input, output);

{ This program computes the sum of the first 500
  even numbers }

var Sum, OrdEven, EvenNumb : integer;

{ Meaning of the variables:
    Sum      - running sum
    OrdEven  - ordinal order of the even
                 number being added
    EvenNumb - even number being added to the sum  }

begin
  Sum := 0;
  for OrdEven := 1 to 500 do { we are adding 500
                                 even numbers      }
     begin
        EvenNumb := OrdEven * 2;
        Sum := Sum + EvenNumb
     end;

  writeln('The sum of the even numbers less than or ',
          'equal 1000 is ',Sum:2)
end. { SumOfEven }
```

As a last example, consider a `for` loop that uses a noninteger variable. Suppose that in a Pascal program the variable `Letter` has been defined as being of type `char` and that the statement

```
for Letter := 'P' downto 'J' do write(Letter)
```

occurs in this program. Convince yourself that this statement causes the output of `PONMLKJ`.

8.4 Choosing repetition statements

When deciding which of these structures to use, you should analyze the problem to find out which of these statements is better adapted to the given situation. The following questions should be asked in order to decide which one to use.

Should the statements be repeated *until* a certain condition holds? If so, use a `repeat` statement.

Should the statements be repeated *while* a certain condition holds? If so, use a `while` statement.

Are the statements being repeated for several known values of the given variable? If so, use a `for` statement.

Can we find out beforehand how many times the loop is going to be repeated? If so, use a `for` statement.

The use of a repetition control structure that is not the proper one for a given situation can give rise to programs that are difficult to develop, read, and modify.

Another point to remember when choosing a repetition structure concerns the efficiency of the program. The `for` statement is, in most cases, more efficient than an equivalent `while` or `repeat` statement and thus should be used whenever appropriate.

Summary

This chapter discussed three repetitive control structures: the `repeat`, `while`, and `for` statements. Before concluding this chapter, we summarize the properties of these control mechanisms.

The `while` construct repeats a statement *while* a certain condition is true. It may be that the body of the loop is never executed.

The `repeat` construct repeats a set of statements *until* a certain condition is true. The body of the loop must be executed at least once.

The `for` construct executes one statement a fixed number of times (including none). The number of times the loop is repeated is computed before the beginning of the loop.

Suggested readings

You can explore the topics presented in this chapter more deeply by consulting the following publications:

Friedmann, D., and Shapiro, S. C. 1974. "A Case for While-Until." *SIGPLAN Notices* (July 1974): 7–14.
This article presents a control structure, the `while-until`, which is a combination of the `while` and `until` statements. Through examples, the authors show that this control structure gives rise to programs that are easier to understand and to develop than those that do not use it. This structure has been successfully used in functional languages, namely, some of the dialects of LISP.

Ghezzi, C., and Jazayeri, M. 1982. *Programming Language Concepts.* New York: Wiley.
Chapter 5 of this book is devoted to the study of control mechanisms. It presents detailed descriptions of several repetition mechanisms and evaluates the advantages and disadvantages of each of the structures presented. It also describes the process of creation by the user of new control structures.

Pratt, T. 1975. *Programming Languages: Design and Implementation.* Englewood Cliffs, NJ: Prentice-Hall.
Chapter 5 of this book is devoted to the study of control mechanisms and presents a good discussion comparing several repetition mechanisms and their use in different programming languages.

Exercises

1. ✓ Explain the difference between a `repeat` and a `while` loop.
2. ? Write a program that counts how many times each of the vowels appears in a text. The program should compute the total number of vowel appearances, and for each vowel, it should print out how many times it appears.
3. ? If `Letter` is a variable of type `char`, what is the output of the following statement?

```
for Letter := 'P' downto 'J' do
    writeln (Letter);
```

   Notice that this is different from the statement in Section 8.3.
4. ? Write a program that reads an expression containing parentheses and tells whether the expression has the parentheses properly placed. An expression has parentheses properly placed if the following conditions hold:
   a. The number of opening parentheses should be the same as the number of closing parentheses.

b. If you read the expression from left to right, the number of closing parentheses should never exceed the number of opening parentheses. For example, `(())` has parentheses properly placed but `())(` does not.

5. **?** Write a program that writes the first *n* terms of the Fibonacci sequence. The value of *n* is supplied to the program. The Fibonacci sequence is defined in the following way:

$F(1) = 1$

$F(2) = 1$

$F(i + 2) = F(i + 1) + F(i) \qquad (\text{for } i = 1, 2, 3, \ldots,)$

For example, the first six terms of the Fibonacci sequence are 1, 1, 2, 3, 5, and 8.

6. **?** What is the output produced by the following Pascal program?

```
program TestLoop (input, output);
var x, i, j : integer;
begin
  x := 0;
  for i:= 1 to 12 do
     for j := 1 to 24 do
        if j mod 5 = 0 then x := x + 1;
  writeln(x)
end. {  TestLoop }
```

7. **?** What is the output produced by the following statements?

a.
```
x := 2;
for i := 1 to 20 do x := x + 1;
writeln (x:2);
```

b.
```
x := 2;
for i := 1 to 20 do; x := x + 1;
writeln (x:2);
```

8. **?** How many times is the following loop executed? (Be careful; this is a tricky question.)

```
a := 5;
while a > 0 do;
    a := a - 1;
```

9. **?** Is the following statement syntactically correct?

```
while a > a do;
```

10. **?** Is the following statement syntactically correct?

```
repeat
   begin begin ; ;
      a := a + 1
   end end ; ;
until a = a
```

11. **?** What is the output produced by the following program?

```
program Mystery (input, output);
var pv, cv, temp : integer;
begin
  pv := 1;
  writeln(pv);
  cv := 1;
  writeln(cv);
  repeat
     temp := cv;
     cv := pv + cv;
     pv := temp;
     writeln(cv)
  until cv > 20
end. { Mystery }
```

12. **?** Write a program that reads a sequence of integer numbers and computes

a. The average of the numbers read.

b. The largest number read and its position in the sequence of the numbers read.

c. The smallest number read and its position in the sequence of the numbers read.

Your program should begin by asking the user the amount of integers in the sequence and then reading that amount. For example, for the sequence of ten integers `4 10 2 45 -2 5 9 9 100 3`, the output of your program will be:

```
average:  18.5
largest number:  100; position:  9
smallest number:  -2; position:  5
```

13. Write a program that reads a positive integer (making sure that the value read is positive) and then computes the largest even number such that the sum of all even numbers less than or equal to it is smaller than the number read. For example, if the value read is `57`, then the result printed by the program will be `14`, because (2 + 4 + 6 + 8 + 10 + 12 + 14 = 56).

14. Suppose that the `while` loop of Figure 8.7 was replaced by the following:

```
Sum := 0;
Number := 0;
repeat
  Number := Number + 1;
  Sum := Sum + Number
until Number > Limit;
```

What is wrong with this loop? What should you do to fix the bug? There is a very important lesson to be learned from this exercise: Whenever you write a loop, *make sure that you check the terminating condition.*

15. Suppose that the `while` loop of Figure 8.7 was replaced by the following:

```
Sum := 0;
Number := 0;
repeat
  Sum := Sum + Number
  Number := Number + 1;
until Number > Limit;
```

Is there anything wrong with this loop? Explain.

16. Write a program that uses a `for` statement to print the following triangle:

```
    *
   ***
  *****
 *******
*********
```

Your `for` loop should have only one `write` statement. (HINT: Use variables as field specifiers.)

17. **?** How many times is the following `while` statement executed? Consider it very carefully because it contains a common type of error associated with `while` loops.

```
x := 10;
while x > 0 do
   writeln(x:2);
   x := x - 1 ;
```

18. **?** Write a Pascal program to write out a ten-by-ten multiplication table. Make sure that your table comes out neatly displayed.
19. **?** Write a program that reads a sequence of characters and counts the number of odd and even digits that appeared in the sequence. All other characters in the sequence other than the digits should be ignored.
20. **?** Can you generate an infinite loop using a `for` statement? Explain.
21. **?** Consider the following statement (where `r` is a `real` variable):

```
r := 0.0;
repeat
  writeln(r:5:2);
  r := r + 0.2
until r = 2.0
```

This statement is likely to produce an infinite loop. Explain.

22. **?** What is written by the following program?

```
program TestLoop (input, output);
var count : integer;
begin
  for count := 10 downto 1 do
      writeln (count);
  writeln('Go!');
end. { TestLoop }
```

23. **!** Write a Pascal program that converts integer numbers written in Arabic numerals into Roman numerals.
24. **!** Write a Pascal program that converts from Roman numerals into Arabic numerals.
25. **!** Write a Pascal program that asks the user to type a real number, verifies whether the number typed by the user obeys Pascal's syntax for real numbers, and prints how many digits the number has to the left and to the right of the decimal point. (HINT: Read the number character by character. Make sure that you test for the end of the number.)

26. ❗ Write a program that reads a positive integer number (as an integer) and reverses the order of its digits. For example, if the input is 34204, the output will be 40243. (HINT: Remove the digits from the number by successive division by 10. Be careful to handle the case where the number ends with 0s. This is, the reverse of 4300 is 0034.)
27. ❓ Write a program that reads an integer number (as an integer) and decides whether it is a palindrome (that is, it reads the same backward as forward). For example, 457754 is a palindrome.

CHAPTER 9

This chapter returns to the concept of subprogram and discusses parameters in detail. We discuss the two types of subprograms one can define in Pascal: procedures and functions. We return to the block structure of Pascal, discussing the distinction between local and nonlocal variables. We present methods of parameter passing and give examples for each of them. Finally, we present complete programs illustrating the concepts introduced. Our discussion of subprograms, although drawing examples from Pascal, is, in general, applicable to most high-level programming languages.

SUBPROGRAMS REVISITED

Never write a large program!
Schneider, Weingart, and Perlman (1978, p. 320)

Chapter 3 gave an introduction to subprograms through the use of procedures, told how to define procedures in Pascal, and explained one of the great advantages of procedures, *procedural abstraction*. When looking at a procedure, we can forget *how* the procedure actually carries out the actions and just concentrate on *what* the procedure does (its input/output behavior). Although functions were mentioned in Chapter 3, we did not learn how to define new functions.

This chapter is concerned with the communication between programs and subprograms, the effect that the block-structure of Pascal has on that communication, and the definition and use of functions. We also take a detailed look at recursive subprograms.

9.1 Procedures and parameters

As you read Chapters 5–8 you learned some Pascal statements—for example, the `read` and `write` statements. What you were not told then is that `read` and `write` are nothing more than **predefined Pascal procedures.** Recall that, although they look like predefined functions, they do not return a value as functions do but cause some action to be taken. The procedure `read` has the effect of changing the values of some variables; the procedure `write` does not change values of variables but causes actions to take place. Again, notice the advantage of procedural abstraction: You know what these procedures do, you know how to work with them, but you don't know (and don't even need to know) how they do their job. The procedures `read` and `write` present a characteristic that we have mentioned but haven't used yet: They allow the communication of information between the program and the procedure. In fact, the procedure `write` receives the values that we want to write and outputs them; the procedure `read` receives the names of the variables whose values will be read and changes the values of those variables. The communication between programs and subprograms is discussed here.

Recall that a procedure is created through a procedure declaration whose syntactic definition is given by the following BNF expressions:

```
<procedure declaration> ::= <procedure header> <block>

<procedure header> ::=
              procedure <identifier> ; |
              procedure <identifier> ( <formal parameters> ) ;
```

The nonterminal symbol formal parameters is defined as

```
<formal parameters> ::=
              <formal parameter section> |
              <formal parameter section> ; <formal parameters>

<formal parameter section> ::=
                     <parameters group> |
                     var <parameters group>

<parameters group> ::= <identifiers> : <type identifier>

<identifiers> ::= <identifier> |
                  <identifier> , <identifiers>

<type identifier> ::= <identifier>
```

Figure 9.1 shows a syntax chart for procedure declaration, together with formal parameters.

We already know that the identifier immediately following the word `procedure` represents the name of the procedure, that the nonterminal symbol formal parameters describes the name and type of the arguments, and that the statements in the block (the **body of the procedure**) represent the algorithm to be followed during the execution of the procedure. We also know that when we define a procedure, we are also defining a **new statement,** the statement that calls the procedure.

FIGURE 9.1 Syntax chart for procedure declaration.

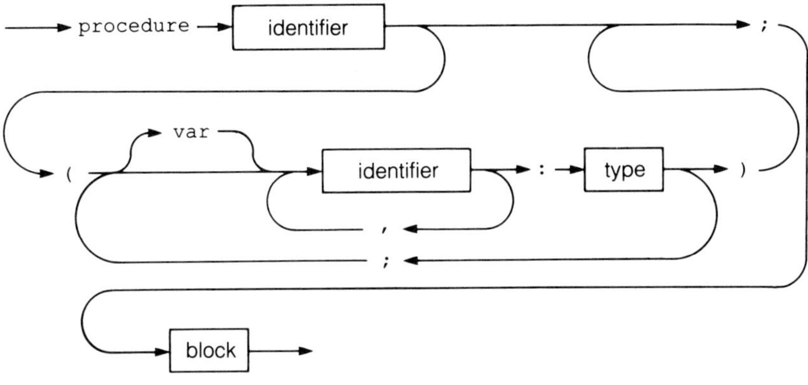

After the declaration of a procedure, the statement in its body is executed when the name of the procedure, followed by the appropriate number of arguments, called **actual parameters,** is found by the computer. This statement is called the **procedure-call statement** and is the only way to call the procedure.

When a procedure is called, the values of the actual parameters are assigned to the formal parameters (in a way to be discussed later), and the body of the procedure is executed. For the purposes of this section, it is enough to say that this association is based on the position that the parameters occupy in the parameter list: The first actual parameter is associated with the first formal parameter, the second actual parameter is associated with the second formal parameter, and so on. (Section 9.6 discusses exactly how this is done.)

To motivate the use of parameters in procedures, suppose that we want to write a procedure to exchange the values of two integer variables. The problem of exchanging the values of two variables was discussed in Chapter 6, and, based on the program of Figure 6.20, we might be tempted to write the procedure shown in Figure 9.2. Notice, however, that the procedure in Figure 9.2 can only exchange the values of integer variables `x` and `y`. If we want to exchange the values of other variables, we would have to write a new procedure. This is clearly *not* the way to go. What we really want is a procedure to which we will supply two variables and that exchanges the values of the variables received: We need to specify a method of communication between programs and subprograms. This can be done through the use of parameters.

FIGURE 9.2 A procedure to exchange two values.

```
procedure Exchange;
var temp : integer;
begin
  temp := x;
  x := y;
  y := temp
end
```

FIGURE 9.3 A procedure that exchanges the values of two variables.

```
procedure Exchange (var x, y : integer);
var temp : integer;
begin
   temp := x;
   x := y;
   y := temp;
end
```

Figure 9.3 shows a revised version of the procedure `Exchange` that makes use of parameters. In this procedure, the formal parameters are preceded by the word `var`. As a first approximation, we can say that they represent the values that the procedure modifies in the calling program: The variables in the actual parameters are assigned the values that the corresponding formal parameters had when the execution of the procedure terminates. The difference between a formal parameter preceded by the word `var` and a formal parameter not preceded by the word `var` is actually more complicated than what we have just described and will be discussed in Section 9.6.

Consider the program in Figure 9.4, which uses the procedure `Exchange` in Figure 9.3. We trace the execution of the program when the values assigned to `v1`, `v2`, and `v3` are `9`, `8`, and `3`, respectively. (Figure 9.5 represents a diagram showing the trace of the execution of the program `sort` for these values.) The expression in the first `if` statement—`v1 > v2`—has the value `true`, and thus the procedure `Exchange` is called with actual parameters `v1` and `v2` (Figure 9.5). When this happens, the actual param-

FIGURE 9.4 A program to sort three values.

```
program Sort (input, output);
var v1, v2, v3 : integer;

{ This program reads three integer values and exchanges
  the values of the variables v1, v2, and v3 so that
  v1 <= v2 <= v3                  }

  procedure Exchange (var x,y : integer);
  var temp : integer;
  begin
    temp := x;
    x := y;
    y := temp
  end; { Exchange }

begin
   writeln('Please write three integer values');
   readln(v1,v2,v3);
   if v1 > v2 then Exchange (v1, v2);
   if v2 > v3 then Exchange (v2, v3);
   if v1 > v2 then Exchange (v1, v2);
   writeln('The sorted values are: ');
   writeln(v1,v2,v3)
end. { Sort }
```

eters are associated with the formal parameters (variables x and y of the procedure Exchange), and the statements in the body of the procedure are executed. These statements exchange the values of variables x and y. After the execution of the procedure, control returns to the point of the function call, with the values of variables x and y (8 and 9, respectively) assigned to the actual parameters (variables v1 and v2, respectively). Thus, in the program the values of v1, v2, and v3 are now 8, 9, and 3, respectively (Figure 9.5). The expression in the second if statement—v2 > v3—also has the value true, and thus the procedure Exchange is called again, which has the effect of assigning the values 3 and 9, respectively, to variables v2 and v3. Thus, in the program the values of v1, v2, and v3 are now 8, 3, and 9, respectively (Figure 9.5). Finally, the expression in the

FIGURE 9.5 Execution of the program `Sort`.

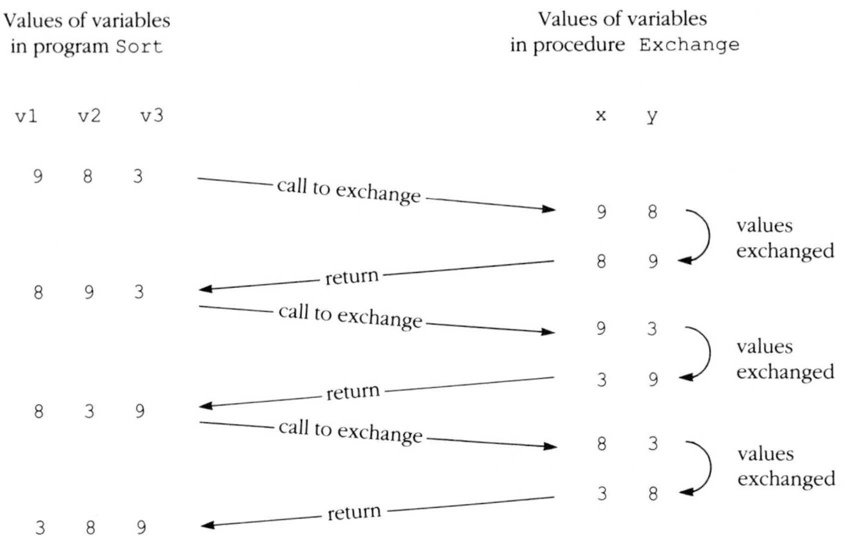

last `if` statement—`v1 > v2`—also has the value `true`, and the procedure `Exchange` is called again, assigning the values 3 and 8 to variables `v1` and `v2`, respectively. Therefore, the values of `v1`, `v2`, and `v3` become 3, 8, and 9, respectively.

In this section we took a first look at procedures with parameters and followed an example of the use of parameters. We now turn to another important kind of subprograms: functions.

9.2 Functions

Chapter 5 described some functions that are associated with each one of the predefined data types and said that the value of each of these functions is computed when we supply the name of the function together with the appropriate number and type of arguments. For example, if `sqrt` is the name of the function that computes square roots, `sqrt(4)` evaluates to 2.0. ("Has the value 2.0," "produces the value 2.0," and "returns the value 2.0" are different ways to say that it evaluates to 2.0.)

High-level languages supply their users with a set of **predefined functions** (or **built-in functions**) that can be used directly in the programs. However, during the development of a program, it is frequently necessary to use functions that are not predefined in the language. High-level languages allow programmers to define their own functions and to use them as if they had been predefined in the language.

To motivate the usefulness of user-defined functions, suppose that we want to write a Pascal program to compute the number of r-combinations of n objects (n and r being supplied to the program). By r-combinations of n objects, we mean the different ways of forming groups containing r objects from a set containing n objects, with no regard to the order of the objects in each group. For example, given `A`, `B`, and `C`, the 2-combinations of these objects are `{A,B}`, `{A,C}`, and `{B,C}`. The number of r-combinations of n objects is given by the formula $n!/r!*(n - r)!$, in which ! represents the factorial function (see Chapter 3).

Figure 9.6 shows a Pascal program to compute the number of r combinations of n objects. This program would be much easier to read and write if the factorial function were predefined in Pascal. In this case, we would not need variables `Nfact`, `Rfact`, or `NminusRfact`, nor the auxiliary variable `i`. Besides, the three `for` loops used to compute each one of these values would be unnecessary. If `Factorial` were a predefined Pascal function, the program in Figure 9.6 could be written as shown in Figure 9.7.

This example clearly shows that, similarly to what happened with procedures, the introduction of user-defined functions can significantly improve the ease of development and the readability of programs.

Before discussing how you can define your own functions in Pascal, we look at the mathematical definition of a function and the use of functions in mathematics. The word *function* is used broadly to mean any determinate correspondence (or mapping) between two classes of objects. By definition, a **function** is a set of ordered pairs that does not contain two pairs with the same first component. The set of the first components of the pairs is the **domain** of the function, and the set of the second components of the pairs is the **range** of the function.

To define a function it is not common to list every pair that belongs to the function (in most cases, this is not even possible—for example, if the domain is infinite). In general, to define a function we supply the domain of the function and some algorithm that takes an element of the domain (the **argument** of the function) and computes the corresponding element of its range (the **value** of the function).

We can describe the way of computing the elements of the domain of a function by supplying an expression, such as $f(x) = x + 3$, in which the

FIGURE 9.6 A program to compute the number of combinations.

```
program Combinations (input, output);

{ This program computes the number of r-combinations of n
  objects. The values of n and r are supplied by the
  user. }

var N, R, Nfact, Rfact, NminusRfact, Comb, i : integer;

{ Meaning of the variables:
   N            - number of objects
   R            - number of objects in each group
   Nfact        - N!
   Rfact        - R!
   NminusRfact  - (N - R)!
   Comb         - number of combinations
   i            - auxiliary variable                        }

begin
  writeln('What are the values of ''n'' and ''r''?');
  read(N,R);

  Nfact := 1;
  for i := 1 to N do Nfact := Nfact * i;

  Rfact := 1;
  for i := 1 to R do Rfact := Rfact * i;

  NminusRfact := 1;
  for i := 1 to (N - R) do NminusRfact := NminusRfact * i;

  Comb := Nfact div (Rfact * NminusRfact);
  writeln('The number of combinations is ',Comb:8)
end. { Combinations }
```

variables that appear on the right-hand side also appear on the left-hand side. To compute the value of the function for a given value of its domain, replace the variable in this expression by its value. For example, if we define a function f whose range is the set of positive integers by the expression $f(x) = x + 3$, we are defining the following set of ordered pairs: {(1,4), (2,5), (3,6), ...}. To compute the value of the function for the argu-

FIGURE 9.7 Fragment of program.

```
program Combinations (input, output);

{ This program would compute the number of r-combinations of
  n objects, if Factorial were a predefined function.
  The values of n and r are supplied by the user.   }

var N, R, Comb : integer;

{ Meaning of the variables:
   N          - number of objects
   R          - number of objects in each group
   Comb       - number of combinations              }


begin
  writeln('What are the values of ''n'' and ''r''?');
  read(N,R);
  Comb := Factorial(N) div (Factorial(R) * Factorial(N - R));
  writeln('The number of combinations is ',Comb:8)
end. { Combinations }
```

ment 1 (that is, to compute the second component of the pair whose first component is 1), replace x by 1 in $x + 3$ to obtain 4. It should be noted that $f(y) = y + 3$ and $f(z) = z + 3$ define the same function (that is, the same set of ordered pairs) as $f(x) = x + 3$. The variables, such as x, y, and z, that, when replaced everywhere in one expression yield an equivalent expression, are called **dummy variables.**

here are two steps involved in providing user-defined functions in a programming language: the **function definition,** which, as in mathematics, provides a specification of an algorithm for computing the values of the function, and the **reference** to the value of the function for a given value of its argument.

In Pascal a function is created through a function declaration, whose syntactic definition is given by the following BNF expressions or, alternatively, by the syntax chart of Figure 9.8, where the formal parameters also are shown.

FIGURE 9.8 Syntax chart for function declaration.

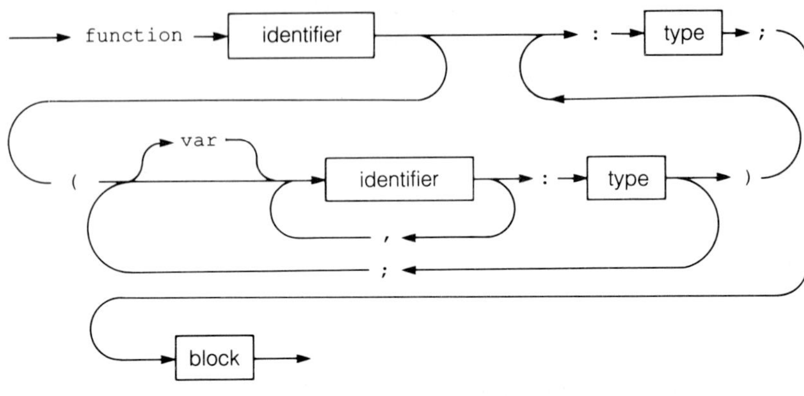

<function declaration> ::= <function header> <block>

<function header> ::=
`function` <identifier> : <result type> ; |
`function` <identifier> (<formal parameters>) :
<result type> ;

<result type> ::= `integer` |
`real` |
`char` |
`boolean` |
<simple type> |
<pointer type>

In the function declaration, the identifier immediately following the terminal symbol `function` represents the name of the function. The formal parameters describe the name and type of the arguments of the function (that is, the domain of the function). These arguments are **formal parameters,** and, as in the mathematic definition of a function, they are dummy variables. The result type represents the type of the result returned by the function (that is, the range of the function);[1] that is, it defines the range of the function and *must* be an elementary data type (scalar or pointer

FIGURE 9.9 Declaration of `Factorial`.

```
function Factorial (x : integer) : integer;

{ Computes x!  }

var f, i : integer;
begin
  f := 1;
  for i := 1 to x do f := f * i;
  Factorial := f
end
```

type). The statements in the block (the body of the function) represent the algorithm for computing the values of the function for a given value of its argument(s). The body of the function *must* contain at least one statement of the form <name> := <expression>, in which the nonterminal symbol name represents the name of the function and the expression should be of the same type as result type.

After the declaration of a function, its value is computed whenever the name of the function, followed by the appropriate number of arguments **(actual parameters),** appears in an expression being evaluated. When this happens, we say that the function has been **called.** During the execution of the body of a function, when the end of the block is reached, the last value assigned to the identifier that represents the name of the function is considered to be the value of the function. The value of the function is returned to the point where the function was called, and execution resumes from that point.

Functions represent another form of **procedural abstraction:** Whenever the name of the function, together with the appropriate number of arguments, appears in an expression being evaluated, the value of the function is returned, and we don't have to think about *how* it was computed.

As a first example, consider the factorial function,[2] whose declaration is shown in Figure 9.9. In this figure we declare a function whose name is `Factorial`, with only one argument of type `integer`, represented by the

1. The type in the function declaration must be an existing type (either predefined or user-defined). It cannot be defined on the spot.

2. Recall the definition of `Factorial` from Chapter 3.

identifier `x`, and whose range is also of type `integer`. The function uses two integer variables, `f` and `i`. The body of the function contains three statements, two assignment statements and one `for` loop. Although the need for variable `i` should be evident, the need for variable `f` may raise some questions at this point. The need for this variable is fully explained in Section 9.3.

It should be stressed that, like the declaration of a procedure, the declaration of a function does not start any computation *by itself*. It just "teaches" the computer that some symbol (in our example, `Factorial`) stands for a function and how to compute its value. Execution of the statements that constitute the body of the function takes place *when and only when* the name of the function (followed by the appropriate arguments) appears in an expression being evaluated. When this happens (when the function is called), the actual parameters are associated with the formal parameters, and the body of the function is executed.

Assume that the function presented in Figure 9.9 had been defined in the program of Figure 9.7 (the way this is done was discussed in Chapter 3). Assume further that the program of Figure 9.7 receives the values `4` and `2` for variables `N` and `R`, respectively. When the computer finds the statement `Comb := Factorial(N) div (Factorial(R) * Factorial(N - R))`, it starts by calculating `Factorial(N)`. To do this, the value of variable `N` in the program (namely, `4`) is associated with variable `x` in the function, and the body of the function is executed, returning the value `24`,[3] which becomes the value of `Factorial(N)`. Next, the value of `Factorial(R)` is computed; to do this, the value of variable `R` (namely, `2`) is associated with variable `x` in the function, and the body of the function is executed again, returning the value `2`, which becomes the value of `Factorial(R)`. Finally, to compute the value of `Factorial(N - R)`, the value of `N - R` is computed (yielding the value `2`), and the function is called again, returning the value `2`. Now the value of the expression `Factorial(N) div (Factorial(R) * Factorial(N - R))` can be computed, and its result (`6`) is assigned to `Comb`.

The declaration of the function `Factorial` has the effect of extending the vocabulary of the Pascal language. After the declaration of this function, the computer "knows" not only the predefined functions in Pascal but also "knows" how to compute `Factorial`.

---

3. As an exercise, convince yourself that when `x = 4` the value `24` is assigned to the variable `Factorial` in the function shown in Figure 9.9.

9.3 Recursive subprograms

Once she remembered trying to box her own ears for having cheated herself in a game of croquet she was playing against herself.
Lewis Carroll, *Alice's Adventures in Wonderland*

This section considers a technique of defining subprograms—recursive definition. A given object is **recursive** if it is defined in terms of itself. Recursive definitions are frequently used in mathematics. Throughout this book, we have been using recursive BNF definitions; see, for example, Section 2.2.

As an example of a recursive definition, the set of natural numbers can be defined in the following way: 1 is a natural number; the successor of a natural number is a natural number.[4] The second clause of this definition is recursive because it uses one natural number to define another one: 2 is a natural number because it is the successor of the natural number 1 (and we know that 1 is a natural number by the first clause).

Another typical example of a recursive definition is the following definition of factorial:

$$x! = \begin{cases} 1 & \text{if } x = 1 \\ x * (x - 1)! & \text{if } x > 1 \end{cases}$$

This definition should be read in the following way: The factorial of 1 ($x = 1$) is 1; if x is greater than one then the factorial of x is given by x times the factorial of $x - 1$. The recursive definition of factorial is more suggestive and more rigorous than the following (more familiar) definition:

$$x! = x * (x - 1) * (x - 2) * \ldots * 2 * 1$$

In the nonrecursive definition, ... means that there is a repeated pattern in the expression and that pattern should be discovered by whomever is computing the value of the function; however, in the recursive definition, the process of computation is completely specified.

The power of recursive definitions is based on the possibility of specifying an infinite set using a finite sentence. Likewise, a long computation may be specified through a recursive subprogram, even if this program does not explicitly contain repetitive statements.

Assume that we want to define *factorial* in Pascal. We now have two alternatives: We can use either the nonrecursive definition, giving rise to

4. To be precise, we also must say that nothing else is a natural number.

FIGURE 9.10 **Recursive declaration of** `Factorial`.

```
function Factorial ( x : integer ) : integer;
{ This function computes x!              }

begin
  if x = 1 then
    Factorial := 1
  else
    Factorial := x * Factorial(x - 1)
end
```

FIGURE 9.11 **First call to** `Factorial`.

```
function Factorial
value of x: 3
value returned: 3 * Factorial(2)
```

the function in Figure 9.9, or the recursive definition, giving rise to the function of Figure 9.10.

As an exercise, we will trace the execution of the function of Figure 9.10 to compute 3!. Assume that in a Pascal program, in which the function of Figure 9.10 has been defined, there is an expression containing `Factorial(3)`. When this expression is evaluated, the value 3 is associated with variable `x` in the `Factorial` function, and the body of the function is evaluated. Because the expression `3 = 1` has the value `false`, the value of `Factorial(3)` is `3 * Factorial(2)` (Figure 9.11).

Here is another expression that uses the `Factorial` function, and this initiates the computation of `Factorial(2)`. Remember, however, that a computation is waiting for the result of `Factorial(3)`. To compute `Factorial(2)`, the value 2 is associated with variable `x` in the `Factorial` function, and the body of the function is evaluated. Because the expression `2 = 1` has the value `false`, the value of `Factorial(2)` is `2 * Factorial(1)` (Figure 9.12), which initiates the computation of `Factorial(1)`. Two computations are waiting for the result of factorial: `Factorial(3)` and `Factorial(2)`.

FIGURE 9.12 Second call to `Factorial`.

```
function Factorial
value of x: 3
val
    function Factorial
    value of x: 2
    value returned: 2 * Factorial(1)
```

FIGURE 9.13 Third call to `Factorial`.

```
function Factorial
value of x: 3
val
    function Factorial
    value of x: 2
    val
        function Factorial
        value of x: 1
        value returned: 1
```

Again, to compute `Factorial(1)`, the value `1` is associated with variable `x` in the factorial function, and the body of the function is evaluated. Because the expression `1 = 1` has the value `true`, the value of `Factorial(1)` is `1` (Figure 9.13). Now we can continue the computation of `Factorial(2)`, whose value is `2 * Factorial(1) = 2 * 1 = 2` (Figure 9.14). This, in turn, allows us to finish the computation of `Factorial(3)`, whose value is `3 * Factorial(2) = 3 * 2 = 6` (Figure 9.15).

Figure 9.16 shows a diagram with several calls to function `Factorial` during the computation of `Factorial(3)`. According to this diagram, we have `Factorial(3) = 3 * Factorial(2) = 3 * (2 * Factorial(1)) = 3 * (2 * 1) = 3 * 2 = 6.`

FIGURE 9.14 Factorial(2) resumes.

```
function Factorial
value of x: 3
val
    function Factorial
    value of x: 2
    value returned: 2 * 1
```

FIGURE 9.15 Factorial(3) resumes.

```
function Factorial
value of x: 3
value returned: 3 * 2
```

FIGURE 9.16 Computation of Factorial(3).

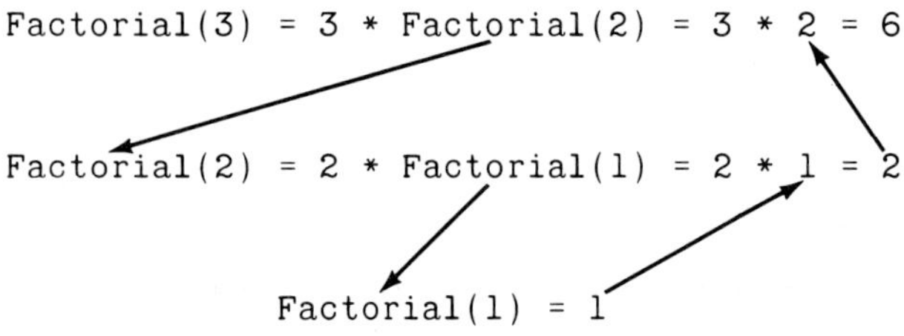

At this point, let us return to the function of Figure 9.9 and explain why we must introduce variable f during the computation of the nonrecursive version of Factorial. Suppose that we had written the function without the variable f, using the variable Factorial instead. The for loop would then become for i := 1 to n do Factorial := Factorial * i. During the evaluation of the expression in the assignment statement, the computer would take Factorial to represent a call to the function Factorial (remember that the identifier of the function appears in an expression being evaluated) and would generate an execution error because the argument of the function is missing. Thus, this is the need for auxiliary variable `f`, whose value is then assigned to the value of the function. Let us note further that for the reason pointed out, the statement `Factorial := Factorial * i` is syntactically incorrect.

As defined earlier, a subprogram is recursive if it is defined in terms of itself. The fundamental concept behind a recursive subprogram is defining a problem in terms of a simpler version of itself. In fact, when we define $x!$ to be $x * (x - 1)!$, we are defining factorial in terms of a simpler version of itself—the number for which we want to compute factorial is smaller. This definition is repeated successively until a version of the problem is reached for which the solution is known. That solution is then used to compute the solution of each of the subprograms generated and to produce the desired answer. Recursive definitions and recursive subprograms have two distinct parts:

A **base case,** also called a **termination case,** which constitutes the simplest version of the problem for which the solution is known. In the `Factorial` function, this corresponds to the case where `x = 1`.

A **recursive case,** also called a **general case,** in which the problem is defined in terms of a simpler version of itself. In the `Factorial` function, this corresponds to the case where `x > 1`.

There are two types of recursive subprograms, corresponding to two possible cases of recursive definitions: proper recursion and mutual recursion. When a program calls itself, we have **proper recursion** (or **direct recursion**). The other kind of recursion, **mutual recursion** (or **indirect recursion**), is obtained when, for example, program `A` calls program `B`, which, in turn (directly or indirectly) calls `A`.[5] Both of these cases are allowed in Pascal; however, in most Pascal implementations, the use of mutual recursion requires some additional statements, which are discussed in the next section.

9.4 The block structure of Pascal

This section returns to the block structure of a Pascal program that was introduced in Chapter 3. Recall that, in Pascal, a block is a set of declarations and statements associated with a program or subprogram. An interesting feature of the block structure of programs is that it allows effective protection of the information corresponding to each block from unauthorized use by the statements of another block. This aspect is obtained by the

5. In this case, recursion may not correspond to defining a problem in terms of a simpler version of itself.

FIGURE 9.17 A schematic representation of a Pascal program.

```
program BlockExample (input, output);
var p1, p2, p3 : integer;

    procedure Proc1 ;
    var b11, b12 : real;
        b13 : integer;
    begin
      <statements of Proc1>
    end; { Proc1 }

    procedure Proc2 ;
    var b21, b22 : integer;

      procedure Proc3 ;
      var b31, b32 : integer;
      begin
        <statements of Proc3>
      end; { Proc3 }

    begin
      <statements of Proc2>
    end; { Proc2 }

begin
  <statements of BlockExample>
end. { BlockExample }
```

following rule (introduced in Chapter 3): Every piece of information (for example, constants, variables, procedures, and functions) declared within a block belongs to that block and can be used only by the statements and declarations of that block, including procedures and functions declared within that block. To illustrate this, consider the program schematically shown in Figure 9.17. In this program there are four blocks and ten variables.

1. Variables `p1`, `p2`, and `p3` are declared in the outer block (the block of the program `BlockExample`) and can be used by every statement of the program.
2. Variables `b11`, `b12`, and `b13` are declared in the block of procedure `Proc1` and thus can be used only by the statements of its block, the

statements represented by the nonterminal symbol `statements of Proc1`.

3. Variables `b21` and `b22` are declared within the block of procedure `Proc2` and can be used only within its block. This means that they can be used by the statements represented by the nonterminal symbols `statements of Proc2` and `statements of Proc3` (note that procedure `Proc3` is declared within procedure `Proc2`).
4. Variables `b31` and `b32` are declared in the block of procedure `Proc3` and can be used only by the statements represented by the nonterminal symbol `statements of Proc3`.
5. Procedures `Proc1` and `Proc2` are declared in the outer block and thus can be used by every statement of the program.[6]
6. Procedure `Proc3` is declared within the block of procedure `Proc2` and consequently can be used only by the statements enclosed within the block of `Proc2` (the statements represented by the nonterminal symbols `statements of Proc2` and `statements of Proc3`).

Although procedures `Proc1` and `Proc2` are declared within the outer block and thus can use each other, most Pascal implementations require that a procedure or a function be physically declared in a program before the occurrence of the first statement that calls it. This restriction would rule out mutual recursion. To avoid this limitation, most Pascal implementations supply a special declaration that precedes the declaration of the procedure or function and that tells that the procedure or function will be declared later on in the program. This special declaration should precede the first statement call to that procedure or function and has the following syntax (for procedures and functions, respectively):

<procedure header> ; `forward` ;

<function header> ; `forward` ;

For example, in the program schematically presented in Figure 9.18, the statements of `Proc1` may call the procedure `Proc2`.

Finally, note that in Figures 9.17 and 9.18 indentation is used to stress the block structure of the programs. This is good programming practice.

---

6. This is not absolutely true—refer to the discussion of the `forward` declaration that follows.

FIGURE 9.18 A Pascal program allowing mutual recursion.

```
program BlockExample (input, output);
var p1, p2, p3 : integer;

    procedure Proc2 ; forward;

    procedure Proc1 ;
    var b11, b12 : real;
        b13 : integer;
    begin
      <statements of Proc1>
    end; { Proc1 }

    procedure Proc2 ;
    var b21, b22 : integer;

      procedure Proc3 ;
      var b31, b32 : integer;
      begin
        <statements of Proc3>
      end; { Proc3 }

    begin
      <statements of Proc2>
    end; { Proc2 }

begin
  <statements of BlockExample>
end. { BlockExample }
```

9.5 Local and nonlocal variables

In Chapter 5 we said that a variable has a name and four attributes: scope, lifetime, type, and value. Up to now, we have been considering only the type and the value of a variable. This section discusses the attributes scope and lifetime. The **scope** of a variable is the *range of statements* in which the variable is known (and thus in which the values of the variable can be accessed and modified). The **lifetime** of a variable is the *interval of time* in which a given area within the computer's memory is associated with the variable's name.

FIGURE 9.19 Classification of variables in a block.

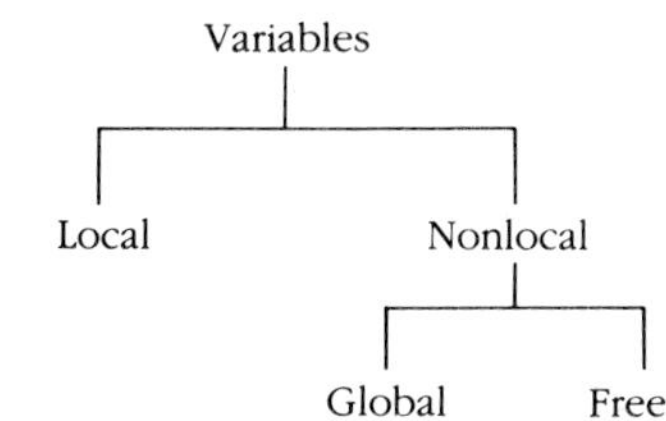

The discussion is applicable to every identifier declared within a block (for example, constants, variables, procedures, and functions). However, because the largest application of these concepts pertains to variables, throughout the discussion we use the word *variable* instead of *identifier*. It should be understood that what we say can be applied to any identifier.

9.5.1 Scope

When we introduced the concept of block, we said that the variables declared within a block could be used only inside that block. The variables declared within a given block are **local variables** (with respect to that block) because they can only be used locally. Every variable that can be used in a block and that has not been declared within that block is a **nonlocal variable** (with respect to that block). Nonlocal variables can be further divided into two groups: the variables that are defined in the outer block and thus can be used by every block in the program—**global variables**—and the variables that, although not global, can be used inside a given block—**free variables** (Figure 9.19).

Consider the program of Figure 9.17: Variables that can be used by the statements of procedure `Proc3` are `p1`, `p2`, `p3`, `b21`, `b22`, `b31`, and `b32`, where `b31` and `b32` are local variables and the remaining are nonlocal. Among the nonlocal variables, `p1`, `p2`, and `p3` are global variables, and `b21` and `b22` are free variables.

The exclusive use of local variables allows the independence of subprograms to be maintained because communication among them is limited to the association between actual parameters and formal parameters. When this is the only type of communication between subprograms, we only have to know *what* a subprogram does and not *how* it was implemented in order to use it. We already know that this is called procedural abstraction and presents multiple advantages to programmers. Another advantage of local variables, to be discussed later, is related to the amount of memory a program needs.

Although the use of local variables should be encouraged, it is sometimes (but rarely) useful to access and modify nonlocal variables (an example of such a case is presented in Section 9.7.2). The fact that a variable is nonlocal means that the information that it represents can be shared by several blocks, which can access and modify that information.

The modification of a nonlocal variable is called a **side effect.** It is very dangerous to use side effects because whenever we are side-effecting the value of a variable, we are located within one block but modifying a variable that belongs to some other block, and such a modification will last even after the execution of the current block terminates. When deciding to use side effects, be very careful while developing the program, and the statements that perform the side effects should be properly commented. Remember that semantic errors caused by side effects are very difficult to detect.

As an example of a bad use of nonlocal variables and side effects, consider the program of Figure 9.20.[7] This program pretends to compute the number of lines in a text and the number of characters on each line. But the procedure `ProcessLine` uses the global variable `Counter`, unwittingly destroying the count of the number of lines. For this program to work properly, a local variable `Counter` should have been declared in procedure `ProcessLine`. Finally, notice that variable `c` is only used in procedure `ProcessLine`; thus, it should be a variable local to this procedure and *not* a variable of the outer block.

In Pascal and other block-structured languages, the scope of a variable is the block in which the variable is declared and every block contained within that block in which a variable with the same name is not declared. To be precise, for constants, variables, and types, the scope is from the end of their definition to the end of the block in which the definition appears unless overridden by an interior definition. For procedures and functions, the scope is from the beginning of the definition to the end of the block in which the definition appears, unless overridden by another definition.

To clarify what we mean by "in which a variable with the same name is not declared," consider the program of Figure 9.21. In this program there are two variables represented by the same identifier—`x`. What is the relationship between them? Are they the same variable? The answer to this last question is NO! The two identifiers named `x` in the program of Figure 9.21 represent *two different variables.* The fact that they have the same name is just a coincidence. We are all used to dealing with different people who happen to have the same name. The fact that they have the same name

7. Adapted from an example of Dale and Orshalick (1983, pp. 186–187). (Reprinted with permission from D.C. Heath & Co.)

FIGURE 9.20 Bad use of side effects.

```
program Trouble (input, output);

var Counter : integer;
    C : char;

  procedure ProcessLine;
  { Counts the number of characters in one line  }
  begin
    Counter := 0; { Reinitializes the Counter -  notice
                    that we are modifying a global
                    variable     }
    while not eoln do
      begin
        read(C); {  Another side effect because C is
                    global }
        Counter := Counter + 1 { another one }
      end;
    readln;
    writeln('The number of characters in the line is: ',
            Counter:2)
  end; { ProcessLine }

begin
  Counter := 0;
  while not eof do
    begin
      Counter := Counter + 1;
      ProcessLine;
    end;
  writeln('The number of lines is: ',Counter:2)
end. { Trouble }
```

does not impose any relationship or similarities between them. The exact thing happens with variables with the same name. The scope of a variable is limited to the block in which it is defined. In case of a conflict between the name of a local variable and the name of a nonlocal variable, the local variable takes precedence over the nonlocal one, and the nonlocal one cannot then be used in the block. Any reference to variable `x` within procedure `ExProc` is to the variable declared within that procedure.

FIGURE 9.21 Different variables with the same name.

```
program MyProg (input, output);
var x : integer;

   procedure ExProc ;
   var x : integer;
   begin
     <statements of ExProc>
   end; { ExProc }

begin
  <statements of MyProg>
end. { MyProg }
```

We should stress further that the formal parameters of a subprogram and the names of the functions represent, in the corresponding block, local variables; their status, as identifiers, is the same as if they had been defined inside the block.

The kind of scoping of Pascal is called **static scoping:** The scope of a variable is defined in terms of the structure of the program (the nesting of its blocks) and has nothing to do with the way the execution of the program proceeds. In other languages—for example, LISP—there exists another kind of scoping, **dynamic scoping,** in which the scope of a variable is independent of the structure of the program and depends exclusively on the execution of the program. This means that the same variable, inside the same procedure, may have different scopes depending on the way the procedure was called.

9.5.2 Lifetime

One question can now be raised: What happens to a variable when the block in which it is declared stops being executed? The answer is extremely simple: The variable disappears.

When the execution of a block begins, the computer associates storage locations with the variables that are defined at the beginning of the block, and this association is maintained as long as the block is being executed. Upon termination of the execution of the block, the association between the variables and the memory locations ends, and the memory locations are freed for further usage. In Pascal, the *lifetime* of a variable corresponds to the execution of the block in which it is declared.

FIGURE 9.22 Possible savings in memory.

```
program MyProg (input, output);
var p1, p2 : integer;

   procedure Proc1 ;
   var p11, ..., p110000 : integer;
   begin
     <statements of Proc1>
   end; { Proc1 }

   procedure Proc2 ;
   var p21, ..., p210000 : integer;
   begin
     <statements of Proc2>
   end { Proc2 }

begin
  <statements of MyProg>
end. { MyProg }
```

The concept of lifetime of a variable, together with the use of local variables, allows the amount of memory needed for the execution of a program to be decreased in a large number of applications. To illustrate this, consider the program fragment outlined in Figure 9.22. This program uses two procedures, `Proc1` and `Proc2`, each of which uses 10,000 integer variables. If these variables had been declared as global variables, we would need 20,000 integer variables that would not be used simultaneously.[8] If, on the other hand, the variables are declared as local variables (as is done in Figure 9.22), then, when one of the procedures `Proc1` or `Proc2` is being executed, we only have space allocated for 10,000 integer variables, considerably decreasing the amount of storage needed.

The concepts of lifetime and scope of a variable increase the reliability of programs and guarantee the independence of programs and subprograms. Some high-level languages—for example, COBOL and some implementations of BASIC—define the scope of a variable to be the whole set of statements in a program and define the lifetime of a variable to be the entire period of execution of a program. This represents a serious drawback of these languages.

8. We are excluding the possibility of mutual recursion with `Proc1` and `Proc2`.

9.6 Parameter transmission techniques

Earlier, we said that when a subprogram is called an association was made between the actual parameters and the formal parameters. This section discusses the techniques of establishing such an association. The several ways to establish the correspondence between the actual and formal parameters are **parameter transmission techniques.**

There are two basic ways to establish the correspondence between actual and formal parameters: call by value and call by reference. Each programming language uses one or more of these methods. For example, Pascal uses both call by value and call by reference; FORTRAN only uses call by reference.

9.6.1 Call by value

When a parameter is transmitted **by value,** the actual parameter is evaluated; that is, its value is computed, and assigned to the corresponding formal parameter, independently of whether the actual parameter is a constant, a variable, or an expression. When call by value is used, the formal parameter receives the *value* of the corresponding actual parameter and no other information. The only connection between the actual parameter and the formal parameter is a one-directional association of values (*from* the point of call *to* the subprogram). The values are *not* transmitted from the subprogram to the program. Call by value is one of the parameter transmission techniques used in Pascal. In Pascal, call by value is used for every actual parameter whose corresponding formal parameter is not preceded by the word `var`.

As an example of call by value, consider the function `Largest` (Figure 9.23), which takes two integer values and returns the largest of its arguments. The formal parameters of this function are not preceded by the word `var`; thus, whenever this function is called, call by value is used. When the call to function `Largest` is found in the program `ExCallByValue` (Figure 9.23), the expressions `sqr(a)` and `b` are evaluated, and their values (`9` and `50`) are assigned, respectively, to variables `x` and `y`. The body of the function is then executed, and the function returns the value `50`.

Call by value is a simple parameter passing technique that has the disadvantage of being a one-directional communication process. That is, the only connection between the point of call and the subprogram is made through the *value* that is transmitted *from* the actual parameters *to* the formal parameters: There is no connection whatsoever between the actual and the formal parameters themselves. This means that the actual parameters cannot be modified by modifying the formal parameters, and thus it may not be very useful for procedure calls.

FIGURE 9.23 An example of call by value.

```
program ExCallByValue (input, output);
var a, b : integer;

   function Largest (x, y : integer) : integer;
   { Returns the largest of its arguments }
   begin
     if x > y then
       Largest := x
     else
       Largest := y
   end; { Largest }

begin
  a := 3;
  b := 50;
  writeln(Largest(sqr(a), b))
end. { ExCallByValue }
```

9.6.2 Call by reference

When a parameter is transmitted **by reference** (sometimes known as **by address**), what is supplied to the corresponding formal parameter is not the value of the actual parameter but rather its *memory location*. When call by reference is used, the actual parameter and the formal parameter *share* the same memory storage area, and thus any change made to the formal parameter is reflected in the actual parameter.

Call by reference is the other parameter transmission technique used in Pascal. In Pascal, to specify that call by reference is to be used for one (or several) parameters, its declaration in the subprogram (procedure or function)[9] must be preceded by the word `var`. As an example of call by reference, let us consider procedure `MaxMin` (Figure 9.24). As an exercise, convince yourself that after the execution of this procedure the actual parameters will be in decreasing order (remember that it uses call by reference). When procedure `MaxMin` is called in the program `ExCallByRef`, communication between the program and the procedure is made through reference to the memory cells that store the values of variables `A` and `B`, and not directly through the values of these variables. When the procedure is called, variables `A` and `Max` will *share* the same

9. As discussed later in this chapter, call by reference should be avoided in functions.

FIGURE 9.24 An example of call by reference.

```
program ExCallByRef (input, output);
var a, b : integer;

   procedure MaxMin (var Max, Min : integer);
   { The variables Max and Min will be assigned,
     respectively, the biggest and the smallest
     values of the arguments  }
   var Temp : integer;
   begin
     if Max < Min then
        begin
          Temp := Max;
          Max := Min;
          Min := Temp
        end
   end; { MaxMin }

begin
  a := 3;
  b := 5;
  MaxMin (a, b);
  write(a, b)
end. { ExCallByRef }
```

memory location, and variables B and Min will *share* the same memory location. In this case, if the values of variables Min and Max are changed in the procedure (which happens in our example), the values of variables A and B also will be changed. After the execution of the procedure, the values of variables A and B will be 5 and 3, respectively.

In Pascal, a subprogram may simultaneously have some parameters that are passed by reference and other parameters that are passed by value. As an example, the program in Figure 9.25 converts a sequence of real values representing quantities in meters to the equivalent values in feet and inches. The procedure FeetAndInches in this figure takes a quantity representing meters and produces two quantities representing the equivalent in feet and inches. In this procedure, variable M represents the value supplied to the procedure, which remains unchanged throughout the execution of the procedure and thus is transmitted by value. This is not compulsory but, rather, a good programming technique. The values of variables

FIGURE 9.25 A program to convert meters to feet and inches.

```
program UnitConversion (input, output);

{ This program reads a sequence of values in meters and
  converts them to equivalent values in feet and inches }

var Meters : real;
    Feet, Inches, Numb, i : integer;

   procedure FeetAndInches (M : real;
                            var F, I : integer);

   { This procedure takes a value representing meters
     (variable M), computes the total number of inches
     corresponding to it, and from that value it computes
     the number of feet (F) and inches (I) corresponding
     to M }

   var : TotalInches : integer;

   begin
     TotalInches := round(M * 39.39);
     F := TotalInches div 12;
     I := TotalInches mod 12
   end; {  FeetAndInches }

begin
  writeln('How many values to convert?');
  readln(Numb);
  for i := 1 to Numb do
    begin
      writeln('What is the value to be converted?');
      readln(Meters);
      FeetAndInches(Meters,Feet,Inches);
      writeln(Meters:6:2,'m = ',Feet:2,'feet and',
              Inches:2,'inches')
    end
end. { UnitConversion }
```

F and I are computed by the procedure and are transmitted back to the calling program; thus, for these variables, call by reference is used.

Pascal requires that when we use call by reference, the actual parameter *must be* a variable. This apparently strange requirement is imposed to avoid some problems that arise in other programming languages that use call by reference. In FORTRAN, for instance, the only way of communicating between programs and subprograms is through call by reference; FORTRAN allows, as actual parameters, constants, variables, and expressions.[10] When an expression is passed by reference, the computer evaluates it and stores its value in a new memory cell whose location is then passed to the subprogram. The subprogram can manipulate the contents of this location but has no way of passing its value back to the calling program. In this case, there is no communication between the subprogram and the calling program.

However, serious problems may show up when *constants* are passed by reference. Consider the hypothetical program presented in Figure 9.26. It is *hypothetical* because it uses Pascal syntax but also uses call by reference with a constant, which is not allowed in Pascal. To stress that this is not a Pascal program, we use uppercase in the statements, so that it looks different from the other programs we present. When the procedure MAXMIN is called by the statement MAXMIN(2,B), what is transmitted to the procedure is the memory location that stores the constant 2 and the memory location that stores variable B. Procedure MAXMIN exchanges the values stored in these locations, and thus the value of variable B becomes 2 and the value of constant 2 becomes 7. When the statement WRITE(A + 2) is executed, the value written is 10 (3 + 7) instead of 5 as would be expected (remember, the value of A is 3, and the value of 2 is 7). This error is prevalent in many implementations of FORTRAN.

As a final remark, it is not good programming practice to transmit parameters to functions by reference. (There is an exception, however, concerning the transmission of large arrays—see Chapter 10.) The reason for this is that the only action that a function should take is to return a value (as the value of the function). A function is a mapping from the elements in its domain to the elements in its range; it *should not* modify any of its parameters.

In summary, we presented two methods of transmitting parameters to procedures: call by value and call by reference. Call by value is a one-directional communication process, from the point of call to the subprogram, and has the advantage of being simple and allowing the protection

10. It should be stressed that FORTRAN was designed and implemented in the mid-1950s. Since then knowledge about programming languages has increased considerably. There are now some implementations of FORTRAN that allow both call by value and call by reference.

FIGURE 9.26 Using call by reference with constants.

```
PROGRAM HYPOTHETICAL (INPUT,OUTPUT);
VAR A,B : INTEGER;

   PROCEDURE MAXMIN (VAR MAX, MIN : INTEGER);
   VAR TEMP : INTEGER;
   BEGIN
     IF MAX < MIN THEN
       BEGIN
         TEMP := MAX;
         MAX := MIN;
         MIN := TEMP
       END
   END; { MAXMIN }

BEGIN
  A := 3;
  B := 7;
  MAXMIN(2, B);
  WRITELN(A + 2)
END. { HYPOTHETICAL }
```

of the information in the calling program. Call by reference is a two-way communication process, allowing the information in a program to be modified by a subprogram. It represents the most common way of communication between programs and procedures.

There is a third parameter-passing technique, call by name. When a parameter is transmitted by **name,** what is supplied to the corresponding formal parameter is the actual parameter itself (unevaluated). When call by name is used, what is transmitted is a *process of computing* the value of the actual parameter rather than the *value* of the parameter. If the actual parameter is a constant or a variable, call by name has the same behavior as call by reference; this means that the procedure for computing the formal parameter consists of supplying the memory location of the parameter itself. When the actual parameter is an expression, the subprogram receives a *procedure* to compute the formal parameter,[11] and that procedure is executed whenever the formal parameter is used. The basic idea behind call by name is to leave the formal parameter unevaluated until its

11. This procedure is sometimes called a **thunk** (Ingerman 1961).

value is needed. Call by name is used in both ALGOL and LISP but not in Pascal. A behavior similar to call by name can be simulated in Pascal through the function and procedure parameters. This aspect is not considered in this book but can be found, for example, in Cooper (1983, pp. 83–86).

9.7 Final examples

This section presents two complete programs that use functions and procedures. The first example shows the solution to a puzzle. The goal of its presentation is to show that recursive subprograms can, in some cases, considerably simplify the solution of a problem. The second program discusses the generation of random numbers, a problem that was mentioned in Chapter 8.

9.7.1 The Towers of Hanoi

We present a program that solves a puzzle called the *Towers of Hanoi*. The Towers of Hanoi consists of three vertical pegs, on which hollowed disks of different diameters can be placed (the number of disks varies from puzzle to puzzle). In the beginning of the puzzle, all disks are on the left peg in increasing size from top to bottom. The goal is to move all the disks to the right peg according to the following rules:

1. Move only one disk at a time.
2. Move only the topmost disk on any peg.
3. Never place a bigger disk on a smaller disk.

Figure 9.27 shows the initial and final configurations of the Towers of Hanoi with three disks. As an exercise, and before reading further, try to solve this puzzle. Furthermore, try to express its solution recursively.

Suppose that we want to write a Pascal program to solve the Towers of Hanoi with n disks (the value of n will be supplied to the program). To solve the puzzle with n disks ($n > 1$), perform the following three steps:

1. Move $n - 1$ disks from the left peg to the central peg (used as an auxiliary peg).
2. Move the disk on the left peg to the right peg.
3. Move the $n - 1$ disks from the central peg to the right peg.

These steps are shown in Figure 9.28 for the case of $n = 3$. Notice that we reduced the problem of moving n disks to the problem of moving $n - 1$ disks; that is, the problem of moving n disks was described in terms of the same problem with one fewer disk (and thus we have a recursive solution). When $n = 1$, the problem is trivially solved by moving the disk from the left peg to the right peg.

FIGURE 9.27 Towers of Hanoi with three disks.

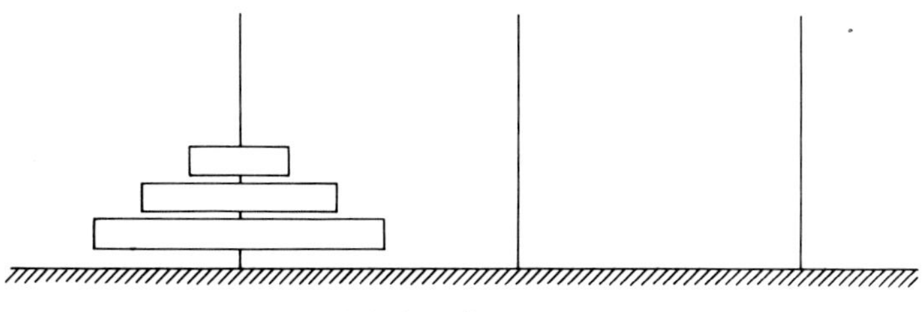

Initial configuration

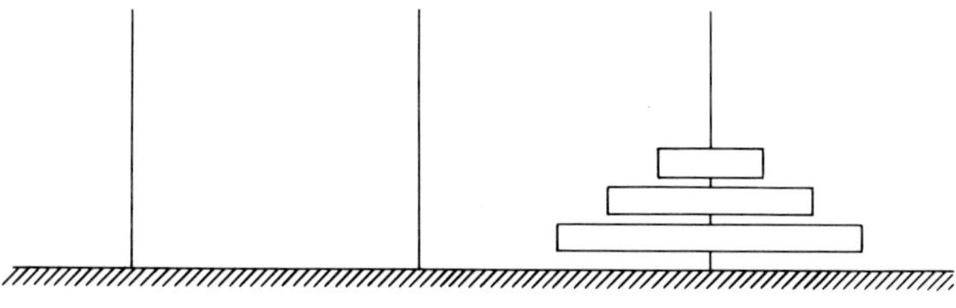

Final configuration

FIGURE 9.28 Solution of the Towers of Hanoi for $n = 3$.

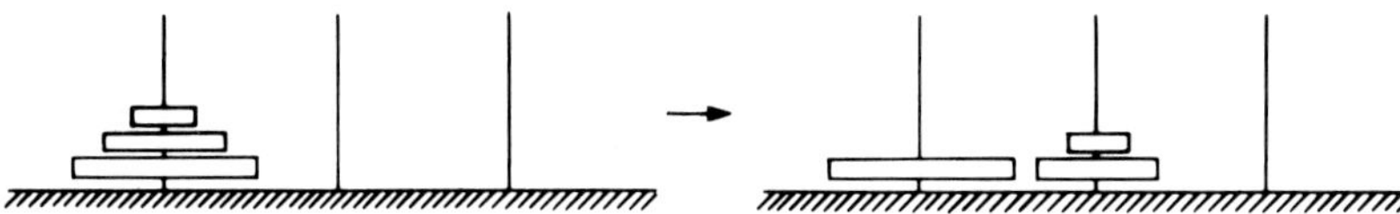

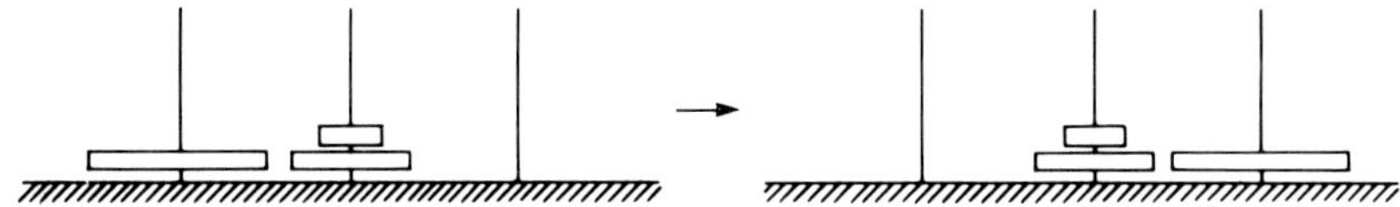

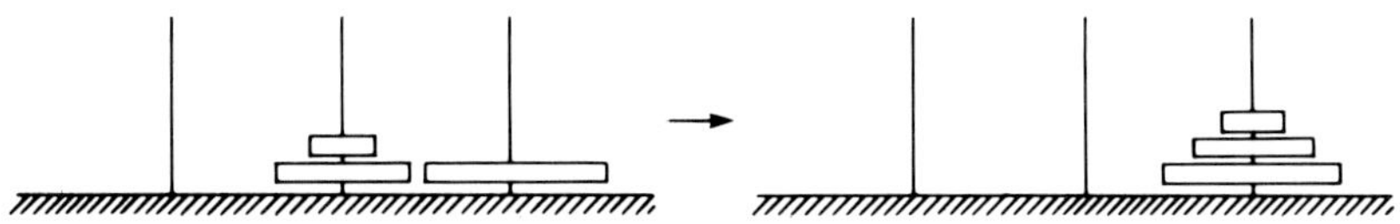

FIGURE 9.29 A procedure to solve the Towers of Hanoi.

```
procedure Move(N : integer;
               Source, Aux, Destination : Peg);

{ Moves N disks from the Source peg to the Destination
  peg, using the Aux peg as an auxiliary peg.                  }

begin
  if N = 1 then
   MOVE DISK FROM THE SOURCE TO THE DESTINATION
  else
    begin

      { Moves N - 1 disks from the Source peg to the Aux peg,
        using the Destination peg as auxiliary }
      move(N - 1, Source, Destination, Aux);

      { Moves the disk from the Source peg to the
        Destination peg                                 }
      MOVE DISK FROM THE SOURCE TO THE DESTINATION

      { Moves the N - 1 disks in the Aux peg to the
        Destination peg, using the Source peg as an
        auxiliary peg                                          }
      move(N - 1, Aux, Source, Destination)

    end
end { Move }
```

As a first approximation, we write the procedure `Move` (Figure 9.29). This procedure moves `N` disks. An important aspect shown by this procedure is the top-down design technique. The first step toward solving a problem consists in identifying the main subproblems that compose the problem being solved and their interrelation and writing a first approximation to the solution in terms of these subproblems. In our example, the problem of moving the disks was described in terms of two subproblems: the problem of moving the disks itself (and thus the recursive solution) and the problem of moving one disk. These are the two problems referenced by the procedure of Figure 9.29. In this procedure, the problem of moving one disk is still specified in English (and thus the use of capitals).

We can now complete the procedure of Figure 9.29 by writing the procedure to move one disk from the source to the destination. We call this procedure `MoveDisk`. We can use procedure `Move` in a Pascal program that asks the user how many disks should be considered and solves the puzzle for that many disks (Figure 9.30). Figure 9.31 presents an interaction with the program of Figure 9.30 for $n = 3$.

FIGURE 9.30 A program to solve the Towers of Hanoi.

```
program TowersOfHanoi (input, output);
type Peg = (left, center, right);
var Ndisks : integer;

   procedure Move(N : integer;
                  Source, Aux, Destination : Peg) ;

      procedure MoveDisk (From, To : Peg) ;
      { Tells the user to move one disk }

         procedure WritePeg (P : Peg) ;
         begin
           case P of
             left   : write('left');
             center : write('center');
             right  : write('right')
           end
         end; { WritePeg }

      begin
        write('Move the top disk from the ');
        WritePeg(From);
        write(' to the ');
        WritePeg(To);
        writeln(' peg')
      end; { MoveDisk }
```

(continued)

FIGURE 9.30, *continued.*

```
   begin
     if N = 1 then
       MoveDisk(Source, Destination)
     else
       begin
         Move(N - 1, Source, Destination, Aux);
         MoveDisk(Source, Destination);
         Move(N - 1, Aux, Source, Destination)
       end
    end; { Move }

begin
  writeln('How many disks do you want to consider? );
  read(Ndisks);
  writeln('Towers of Hanoi with ',Ndisks:2,' disks');
  writeln;
  writeln('Move the following disks:');
  writeln;
  Move(Ndisks, left, center, right)
end. { TowersOfHanoi }
```

FIGURE 9.31 Solution for the Towers of Hanoi with three disks.

```
How many disks do you want to consider?
3
Towers of Hanoi with  3 disks

Move the following disks:

Move the top disk from the left peg to the right peg
Move the top disk from the left peg to the center peg
Move the top disk from the right peg to the center  peg
Move the top disk from the left peg to the right peg
Move the top disk from the center peg to the left peg
Move the top disk from the center peg to the right peg
Move the top disk from the left peg to the right peg
```

9.7.2 Random-number generation

Very often in computer science, we must generate random numbers in a given interval. We saw an example of this in Chapter 8. This section presents a Pascal program that generates a sequence of random numbers.

Random-number sequences produced by a program are not "random" in the true sense of the word because it is possible, in theory, to predict what the generated sequence will be. After all, they are generated by an algorithm. Thus, they are called **pseudorandom.** However, the numbers generated can be considered random numbers because the chances of any number being generated are equal. These random-number sequences are repeated whenever the program is executed. This fact should not be considered as a drawback of the program but rather as an interesting feature because it allows the exact duplication of the execution of a program, which is crucial to debugging.

Assume that we want to generate integer random numbers in the interval $[1, n]$.[12] The idea behind the generation of random numbers in the interval $[1, n]$ is to generate real numbers uniformly distributed in the interval $[0, 1)$, multiply the number generated by n, to obtain a real number in the interval $[0, n)$, and, finally, to truncate the decimal part and add 1 to the result, obtaining an integer number in the interval $[1, n]$.

To generate numbers randomly in the interval $[0, 1)$ we begin with an arbitrary number (the **seed**), multiply it by a constant, add another constant to the result, and remove the integer part of the number generated, giving rise to the new value for the seed—the seed is in the interval $[0, 1)$. Next, we multiply the number generated by n and use the function `trunc` (generating an integer number in the interval $[0, n)$). The last step consists of adding one to this number. If we had started with a different seed, the sequence generated would have been different.

This is the method used in the program in Figure 9.32. [Other techniques to generate random numbers can be found in Dromey (1982) and Knuth (1969). The chapter in Knuth's book discusses methods for choosing the constants used in the generation of the numbers.]

As a last remark concerning program `RandomNumbers`, note that the variable `Seed` is a global variable that is modified by the function `Random`. As an exercise, verify that if the variable `Seed` had been declared as a variable local to the function `Random`, the number generated would always be the same.

---

12. $[a,b]$ represents the set of numbers between a and b, including a and b; $[a,b)$ represents the set of numbers between a and b, including a but excluding b.

FIGURE 9.32 Random-number generation.

```
program RandomNumbers (input, output);
var Seed : real;
    UpperBound, N, I : integer;

   function Random (Limit : integer) : integer;
   begin
     Seed := Seed * 66.4582376 + 65.8723454;
     Seed := Seed - trunc(Seed);
     Random := trunc(Seed * Limit) + 1
   end; { Random }

begin
  Seed := 0.526255;
  writeln('How many numbers do you want to generate?');
  read(N);
  writeln('What is the upper bound for those numbers?');
  read(UpperBound);
  for I := 1 to N do writeln(Random(UpperBound))
end. { RandomNumbers }
```

Summary

Some of the advantages of using subprograms are as follows:

Programs are easier to write. When developing a program, we can express the main problem in terms of subproblems that constitute it and thus free the program from the specification of the details of each of those subproblems. In this way, we can follow the *top-down design* technique.

Programs are easier to read. When reading a program, we find references to the *results* of operations (whose details are not important for understanding the program), and we can avoid looking into the details of how these results were computed. This is *procedural abstraction.*

Programs are generally shorter. If we need to perform the same action in several places in the program, we just reference a name of the subprogram that corresponds to that action rather than list every statement that belongs to the subprogram.

Programs are easier to modify. If we want to modify a certain aspect of a program, we do it in the function or procedure that implements this aspect, and we know that we are globally affecting the rest of the program.

Suggested readings

You can explore topics presented in this chapter more deeply by consulting the following books:

Abelson, H., Sussman, G., and Sussman, J. 1985. *Structure and Implementation of Computer Programs.* Cambridge, MA: MIT Press.
This is an excellent book with a chapter devoted to procedures and procedural abstraction. It treats recursion very well and draws a distinction between the syntactic definition of a recursive procedure and a recursive computation.

Dijkstra, E. 1976. *A Discipline of Programming.* Englewood Cliffs, NJ: Prentice-Hall.
Chapter 10 of this book, entitled "An Essay on the Notion: The Scope of Variables," presents an excellent discussion of the scope of variables.

Ghezzi, C., and Jazayeri, M. 1982. *Programming Language Concepts.* New York: Wiley.
This book compares the use of functions and procedures in three high-level languages—Pascal, SIMULA67, and Ada (Chapter 7)—and presents a good discussion of the scope and lifetime of a variable (Chapter 3) and on the dangers of using nonlocal variables (Chapter 6).

Knuth, D. 1969. *The Art of Computer Programming, Vol. 2, Seminumerical Algorithms.* Reading, MA: Addison-Wesley.
The first part of this book (pp. 1–157) discusses in great detail several techniques for random-number generation, criteria for the choice of the constants used during the generation, and criteria for evaluating the sequence generated.

Organick, E., Forsythe, A., and Plummer, R. 1978. *Programming Language Structures.* New York: Academic Press.
This book presents an elementary discussion of the concepts of procedure and function, parameter transmission techniques, local and nonlocal variables, and recursive subprograms. Chapter 10 briefly discusses the concepts for Pascal.

Pratt, T. 1975. *Programming Language: Design and Implementation.* Englewood Cliffs, NJ: Prentice-Hall.
This book discusses subprograms, parameter transmission techniques, local and nonlocal variables, and memory management in great detail. It is extremely well-written and complete.

Rohl, J. S. 1984. *Recursion via Pascal.* Cambridge, England: Cambridge University Press.
This is a book on recursion. It explains how recursion works, the storage and time cost of recursion, and the several types of recursion. It presents several applications of recursion and explains how to eliminate recursion. The examples presented use Pascal.

Wirth, N. 1976. *Algorithms + Data Structures = Programs.* Englewood Cliffs, NJ: Prentice-Hall.
Chapter 3 presents a good discussion of the concept of recursive subprograms, discusses when we should (and should not) use recursion, and presents several examples of recursive subprograms.

Exercises

1. ✓ What is the difference between a local and a global variable?
2. ✓ What is the scope of an identifier?
3. ✓ What is a side effect? Give an example. Why is it undesirable?
4. ✓ What is the difference between a function and a procedure? When should a function be used? When should a procedure be used?
5. ✓ Explain what happens when a parameter is transmitted
   a. By value.
   b. By reference.
6. ? Explain why the exclusive use of local variables allows the independence of subprograms to be maintained.
7. ? Compare the procedure declaration with the function declaration. List their similarities and differences. Explain the reasons for the differences.
8. ✓ What is wrong with the following function declaration?

```
function WrongSyntax (x, y : integer);
begin
  x := x + 2;
  WrongSyntax := x * y
end; { WrongSyntax }
```

9. ✓ What is wrong with the following procedure declaration?

```
procedure WrongSyntax (x, y : integer);
begin
  x := x + 2;
  WrongSyntax := x * y
end; { WrongSyntax }
```

10. ✓ What is wrong with the following procedure declaration?

```
procedure WrongSyntax (var x, y : integer);
var x : real;
begin
  x := x + 2;
  y := x * y
end; { WrongSyntax }
```

11. **?** Consider the function G defined for nonnegative numbers as follows:

$$G(n) = \begin{cases} 0 & \text{if } n = 0 \\ n - G(G(n-1)) & \text{if } n > 0 \end{cases}$$

a. What is the value of $G(5)$?

b. Write a recursive function in Pascal that computes the value of $G(n)$.

12. **!** Consider the Ackermann function, defined for nonnegative integers as follows:

$$A(m, n) = \begin{cases} n + 1 & \text{if } m = 0 \\ A(m - 1, 1) & \text{if } n = 0 \\ A(m - 1, A(m, \mathrm{n} - 1)) & \text{if } m > 0 \text{ and } n > 0 \end{cases}$$

a. Write a recursive function in Pascal to compute the value of the Ackermann function.

b. Concerning the execution time, is the recursive method the best one to compute the value of the Ackermann function? Why? (HINT: Consider the amount of times the recursive version computes the same values.)

13. **?** The binomial coefficients $B(n,i)$ are defined for $n > 0$ and $0 < i < n$ in the following way:

$$B(n, i) = \begin{cases} 1 & \text{if } i = 0 \\ 1 & \text{if } n = 1 \\ B(n - 1, i - 1) + B(n - 1, i) & \text{if } 0 < i < n \end{cases}$$

Write a Pascal function to compute the binomial coefficients.

14. **?** What is the output of the following Pascal program?

```
program Unexpected (input, output);
var global : integer;

  function Side (n : integer) : integer;
  begin
    global := global + 1;
    side := global + n
  end; { Side }

begin
  global := 0;
  writeln(Side(0), Side(0), Side(0))
end. { Unexpected }
```

Explain the reason for the unexpected behavior of the function `Side`.

15. **?** What is the output produced by the following Pascal program? If a variable to be written has an undefined value, write ? and proceed.

```
program ScopeTest (input, output);
var x, y, z : integer;

   procedure Scope (x : integer;
                    var z : integer);
   var y : integer;
   begin
     writeln('Entering scope, x, y, z are:');
     writeln(x:3, y:3, z:3);
     x := 15;
     y := 25;
     z := 5;
     writeln('Leaving scope, x, y, z are:');
     writeln(x:3, y:3, z:3)
   end; { Scope }

begin
  x : = 25;
  y : = 0;
  z : = 13;
  Scope(z, y);
  writeln(x:3, y:3, z:3)
end. { ScopeTest }
```

16. **?** Write a Pascal function to implement Euclid's algorithm to compute the greatest common divisor (gcd) between two integer numbers: the gcd between a number and one is the number itself; the gcd between two numbers is the same as the gcd between the smallest number and the remainder of the division of the largest by the smallest.

17. **?** Consider the following Pascal program:

```
program Test (input, output);
var a, b : integer;

   procedure p3 ; forward;

   procedure pl;
   var b, c : integer;

      procedure p2;
      var d, e : integer;
```

```
      begin
        <statements of p2>
      end; { p2 }

   begin
     <statements of p1>
   end; { p1 }

   procedure p3;
   var e : integer;
   begin
     <statements of p3>
   end; { p3 }

begin
  <statements of test>
end. { Test }
```

a. What are the variables that the statement represented by `statements of p2` can modify? Which of these are global, free, and local variables?
b. Which procedures can the statements represented by `statements of p2` use?
c. Which procedures can the statements represented by `statements of p3` use?
d. Which variables can be modified by the statements represented by `statements of test`?

18. ? What is the output produced by the following program?

```
program Mystery (input, output);
var x, y : integer;

   function p(x, y : integer) : integer;
   begin
      if x = 0 then
         p := 0
      else
         p := y + p(x - 1, y)
   end; { p }

begin
  x := 3;
  y := 4;
  writeln('The value of mystery is: ',p(x, y):4)
end. { Mystery }
```

19. **?** Consider the following function:

```
function p(x, y : integer) : integer;
begin
  if x = 0 then p := 0
  else p := y + p(x - 1, y)
end
```

a. What is the value of `p(4, 5)`? Explain.
b. What is the value of `p(-4, 5)`? Explain.
c. What does this function do?

20. **?** Write a recursive function, `power`, that takes two positive integers (`b` and `c`) and returns `b` to the power of `c`. For example,

```
power(3, 2) = 9
power(2, 10) = 1024
```

21. **?** Write a boolean-valued function, `multiple`, that receives two positive integers and returns `true` just in case one of them is multiple of the other. For example:

```
multiple(2, 4) = true
multiple(4, 2) = true
multiple(3, 2) = false
```

22. **?** What is the output produced by the following program?

```
program TestExecution (input, output);
var a, b, c : integer;

   procedure Proc1(c, a, b : integer);

       procedure Proc2(a, b, c : integer);
       begin
         writeln('Entering Proc2');
         writeln(' a=',a:3,', b=',b:3,', c=',c:3);
         if b <> 0 then
           Proc1(b div 2, a + b + c, c);
         writeln('Leaving Proc2');
         writeln(' a=', a:3,', b=', b:3,', c=',c:3)
       end; { Proc2 }
```

```
  begin
    writeln('Entering Procl');
    writeln(' a=',a:3,', b=',b:3,', c=',c:3);
    if odd(a) then
      Procl(c, a - 1, b)
    else
      Proc2(a, b, c);
    writeln('Leaving Procl');
    writeln(' a=',a:3,', b=',b:3,', c=',c:3)
  end; { Procl }

begin
  a := 2;
  b := 12;
  c := 1;
  writeln('I am about to begin ...');
  writeln(' a=',a:3,', b=',b:3,', c=',c:3);
  Procl(a, b, c);
  writeln('I am about to end ...');
  writeln(' a=',a:3,', b=',b:3,', c=',c:3)
end. { TestExecution }
```

23. **?** Consider the definition of the following two procedures:

```
procedure Timesl (var x : integer; y : integer);
begin
  x := x * y
end; { Timesl }

procedure Times2 (x : integer; y : integer);
begin
  x := x * y
end; { Times2 }
```

a. What is the output produced by the following statements?

```
a := 5;
b := 2;
Timesl(a, b);
writeln('a=',a:3,',b=',b:3);
```

b. What is the output produced by the following statements?

```
a := 5;
b := 2;
Times2(a, b);
writeln('a=',a:3,',b=',b:3);
```

c. Is the following correct? Why or why not?

```
Times1(a * b, b)?
```

d. Is the following correct? Why or why not?

```
Times2(a * b, b)?
```

24. **?** Consider the following program:

```
program TestCalls (input, output);
var a, b, c : integer;

   procedure Example (x, y, z, w : integer);
    begin
      z := x + y;
      writeln(x:5, y:5, z:5, w:5);
      w := x * y;
      writeln(x:5, y:5, z:5, w:5)
    end; { Example }

begin
  a := 5;
  b := 2;
  c := 3;
  Example(a, a + c, c, b);
  writeln(a:5, b:5, c:5)
end.  { TestCalls }
```

Show the output it produces when the variables in the procedure `Example` receive the values

a. By value.

b. By reference (all except y, which is transmitted by value).

25. **!** Addition can be defined in terms of successor and/or predecessor. Write two recursive functions (`Sum1` and `Sum2`) that receive as arguments two integer numbers and return their sum, using the following ideas:

a. The function `Sum1` should work in the following way:

```
Sum1(3,4) = Sum1(2,5) = Sum1(1,6) = Sum1(0,7) = 7
```

b. The function `Sum2` should work in the following way:

```
Sum2(3,4) = Sum2(2,4) + 1 = Sum2(1,4) + 1 + 1 =
Sum2(0,4) + 1 + 1 + 1 = 4 + 1 + 1 + 1 = 7
```

Although these functions are not efficient, they would be useful if the operator + was not defined in Pascal. For this reason, your functions should not use +. (HINT: Use `pred` and/or `succ`.)

26. ? Give a natural-language explanation of the behavior of the following function. Be careful regarding the possible values that `i` and `j` may have.

```
function Mystery (i, j : integer) : integer;
begin
  if i = j then
     Mystery := 0
  else
     Mystery := Mystery (i, j + 1) + 1
end
```

27. ! What does the following procedure do?

```
procedure Mystery (x : integer);
begin
  if x = 0 then
     writeln
  else
     begin
       Mystery(x div 10);
       write(x mod 10)
     end
end
```

(HINT: Trace the execution of this procedure with some integers. Then, admire the power of recursive definitions.)

28. ? We said that if the variable `Seed` in the program of Figure 9.32 had been declared as a local variable to the function `Random`, the numbers generated would always be the same. Explain.

CHAPTER 10

This is the first of a sequence of chapters where we discuss structured data types. We start by showing the severe limitations of the exclusive use of elementary data types and introducing the concept of structured data type or data structure. As an example of a structured data type, we define arrays and describe the methods for manipulating arrays along with a discussion of programs that use arrays. We present some applications of arrays, namely, the representation and manipulation of character strings, sorting, and searching. Finally, we discuss some issues related to the efficiency of sorting and searching algorithms.

STRUCTURED DATA TYPES I: ARRAYS

"Get your data structures correct first, and the rest of the program will write itself."
David Jones (Bentley 1985)

Suppose that we want to write an interactive program that asks a user to type the student number and the numeric grade for every student in a class. Afterward, the program tells the user which students had a grade above average. Assume further that the class has 100 students.

This program must manipulate information concerning the grades of a large number of students (100) in order to compute the class average. Afterward, the program must consider again the grade of every student in the class in order to compare it with the class average. In other words, this program must process a large number of elements twice: First, it computes the average of the grades in the class; second, it compares the grade of each student with the computed average. Furthermore, these two steps must be done in sequence.

To write a program that performs this task, with the concepts developed so far, we have two alternatives. The first one uses a program that reads the grade of every student and computes the class average; after doing this, the program reads again the student number and the grade for every student; it then compares the grade of the student with the grade average and outputs the student's number if he or she obtained a grade above average. A program using this type of approach is shown in Figure 10.1. The drawback of this approach is that the user has to type the information twice, once to compute the class average and again for the program to decide if the student had a grade above average. This approach places an extra burden on the user, although the program is very simple.

FIGURE 10.1 Students with grade above average (version 1).

```
program AboveAverage1 (input, output);
{ This program outputs the student number of the
  students whose grade is above average  }

const NbOfStudents = 100;

type  StudentGrade = 0..100;

var Average : real;
    SumOfGrades, StudNo : integer;
    Grade : StudentGrade;

begin
  SumOfGrades := 0;

  for i := 1 to NbOfStudents do
     begin
       writeln('Enter the student''s Grade');
       readln(Grade);
       SumOfGrades := SumOfGrades + Grade
     end;

  Average := SumOfGrades / NbOfStudents;

  for i := 1 to NbOfStudents do
     begin
       writeln('Enter the student''s number);
       readln(StudNo);
       writeln('Enter the student''s Grade');
       readln(Grade);
       if Grade > Average then
         writeln('Student ',StudNo,
                 ' had a Grade above Average')
     end
end. { AboveAverage1 }
```

The second approach, shown in Figure 10.2, consists of using a variable to store the student number of every student in the class and a variable to store the grade of every student in the class. Because we have 100 students in the class, we need 200 variables. The program in Figure 10.2 uses the variables `Sn1,Sn2, ..., Sn100` to store the student number of every student in the class and uses the variables `Grade1, Grade2, ..., Grade100` to store the numeric grade of the students. For any value of *i* ($1 \leq i \leq 100$), `Sn`*i* represents the student number of the student whose numeric grade is stored in the variable `Grade`*i*. This approach frees the user from typing the information twice but places an extra burden on the program (and on the programmer). The program of Figure 10.2 has much repetition.

We can easily imagine a program that has to perform similar kinds of computation over thousands or even millions of values. Suppose, for example, that instead of processing the grades of the students in a class, we want to process the grades of the students in a university.

For problems of this sort, either one of these approaches is not practical. The difficulty is because a simple variable can store only *one value:* a unique number (either integer or real), a unique boolean value, a unique character, or a unique identifier (in the case of user-defined enumerated types).

This and following chapters present methods that allow variables to store a set of values and some of the ways of structuring those values. We also study how to access each value of the set of values. The data types resulting from bundling together sets of elements[1] are **nonelementary data types, structured data types,** or simply **data structures.** This contrasts with the kind of information that we have studied so far, which are **elementary data types.** Whenever a structured data type is considered, it is necessary to consider how to add new elements to the structure, how to access its elements, and the types of the elements that it can have.

This chapter presents one of the most simple and widely used data structures—arrays—and presents some programs that represent typical applications of arrays.

We can draw a parallel between what we will do with *data* from now on and what we have done with *statements* up to now. Chapters 6–8 presented *how to structure statements* and provided much more powerful ways of expressing actions. We now turn to the *structure of data* and thus

---

1. We deliberately avoided the use of the word *value* because the elements can either be values or structured data.

FIGURE 10.2 Students with grade above average (version 2).

```
program AboveAverage2 (input, output);
{ This program outputs the student number of the
  students whose grade is above average  }

const NbOfStudents = 100;

type StudentGrade = 0..100;

var Grade1, Grade2, ..., Grade100 : StudentGrade;
    Sn1, Sn2, ..., Sn100 : integer;
    SumOfGrades : integer;
    Average : real;
begin
  SumOfGrades := 0;

  writeln('Please type a student''s number',
          ' and the corresponding grade');
  readln(Sn1, Grade1);
  SumOfGrades := SumOfGrades + Grade1;

  writeln('Please type a student''s number',
          ' and the corresponding grade');
  readln(Sn2, Grade2);
  SumOfGrades := SumOfGrades + Grade2;

      ...

  writeln('Please type a student''s number',
          ' and the corresponding grade');
  readln(Sn100, Grade100);
  SumOfGrades := SumOfGrades + Grade100;

  Average := SumOfGrades / NbOfStudents;

  if Grade1 > Average then
    writeln('The student ',Sn1,' had Grade above Average');

  if Grade2 > Average then
    writeln('The student ',Sn2,' had Grade above Average');

     ...

  if Grade100 > Average then
    writeln('The student ',Sn100,' had Grade above Average');
end. { AboveAverage2 }
```

introduce another dimension to the complexity and power of our programs. In Chapters 3 and 9 we studied how to name sequences of actions; in Chapters 14–18 we will study how to name new structured types and how to use those types as if they were predefined in the language.

10.1 Characteristics of arrays

An **array** can be defined as an ordered set of elements, *all of the same type*. The elements stored in an array are accessed by giving the position that the element occupies in the array. Figures 10.3–10.5 show three arrays: one-dimensional, two-dimensional, and three-dimensional, respectively.

FIGURE 10.3 One-dimensional array.

23	2	12	34	0	12	4	87

FIGURE 10.4 Two-dimensional array.

2	4	12	5
14	45	0	13
67	35	78	1

FIGURE 10.5 Three-dimensional array.

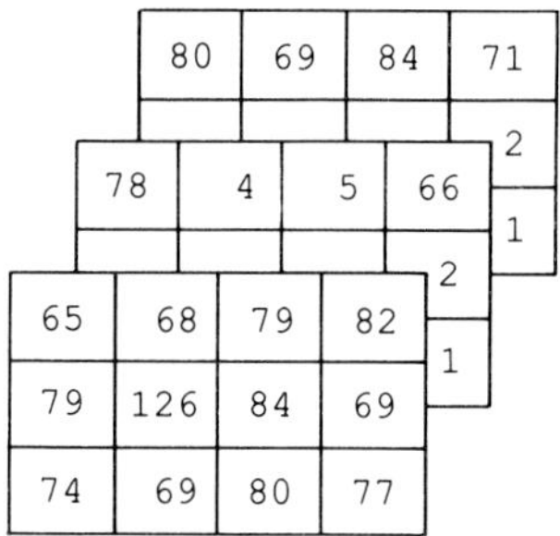

The **dimensions** of an array represent, by definition, the number of values that we must specify to completely define the position of an element in the array. For example, to reference an element of the array shown in Figure 10.3, we only have to specify one value: the position of the element in the line. Thus, the array of Figure 10.3 is a **one-dimensional** array. To reference an element of the array of Figure 10.4, we need to supply two values, the row and the column in which the element is located. Thus, the array of Figure 10.4 is a **two-dimensional** array.

Arrays have their origin in the mathematic notions of vector and matrix. In mathematics, to refer to the elements of a vector or matrix, we use subscripts that uniquely characterize each one of its elements. So, if x is a vector with three elements, we can characterize each one of its elements as x_1, x_2, and x_3. Likewise, in computer science, each array has a name (identifier) that refers to the array (set of elements) as a whole. The elements of the array are accessed (or referenced) by giving the name of the array and the position of the element inside the array. In computer science, we use an index, which acts like a subscript, to represent each of the elements of an array. These indexes are written on the same line as the name of the array. To distinguish the indexes from the name of the array, it is usual to enclose the indexes in brackets. Thus, if the array of Figure 10.3 is represented by the identifier `Averages`, then `Averages[1]` represents the first element of this array, that is, 23. If the array of Figure 10.4 is represented by the identifier `Matrix`, then `Matrix[2,3]` represents the element that can be found in the second row, third column of the array `Matrix`, that is, 0. It should be stressed that `Averages[1]` (as well as any other reference to an element of an array) is the *name of a variable* and thus can be subjected to any operation that can be performed on variables.

10.2 Definition of arrays in Pascal

Almost every high-level programming language requires that the data type `array` be declared prior to its use in a program. This decision was taken even in languages in which it is not necessary to declare variables (for example, LISP). The reason for such a requirement is related to the way arrays are stored in main memory and with the way of accessing the elements of an array.

To define an array, we have to specify the following: its name, the type of its elements, the number of dimensions of the array, and the upper and lower bound of each dimension.

If we want to use an array in a Pascal program we have two alternatives: We can define a type `array` and then declare a variable as being of that type, or we can declare a variable as being of a type that is defined as an array, on the spot, in the variable declaration part.

To define an identifier as being of type `array`, we must define it as being of structured type. A structured type is syntactically defined in the following way:

<structured type> ::= <unpacked structured type> |
    `packed` <unpacked structured type>

<unpacked structured type> ::= <array type> |
    <record type> |
    <set type> |
    <file type>

For the array type we have the following definition (Figure 10.6 shows a syntax chart for the array type):[2]

<array type> ::= `array [` <index types> `] of` <component type>

<index types> ::= <index type> |
    <index type>`,` <index types>

<index type> ::= <near-ordinal type>

<near-ordinal type> ::= <char> |
    <boolean> |
    <enumerated type> |
    <subrange type>

<component type> ::= <type>

Here, index types defines the dimensions of the array and is, usually, of the form `lb1..ub1, lb2..ub2,...,lb`*n*`..ub`*n* (which defines an n-dimensional array). In this definition, `lb`*j* represents the lower bound of the jth index ($1 \leq j \leq n$), `ub`*j* represents the upper bound of the jth index ($1 \leq j \leq n$), and component type represents the type of the elements of the array. The semantics of this definition is the creation of a type `array` whose dimensions are specified by index types and whose elements are of component type.

Figure 10.7 defines four identifiers of type `array` (represented by `Grades`, `InfoClass`, `Bars`, and `Letters`), and, using these types, declares five variables, `NbGrades` (an array of type `Grades`, that is, a one-dimensional array with four integer elements), `NbStudents` and `GreatSum` (two

2. Note that near-ordinal type excludes the type `integer`.

FIGURE 10.6 **Syntax chart for** array type.

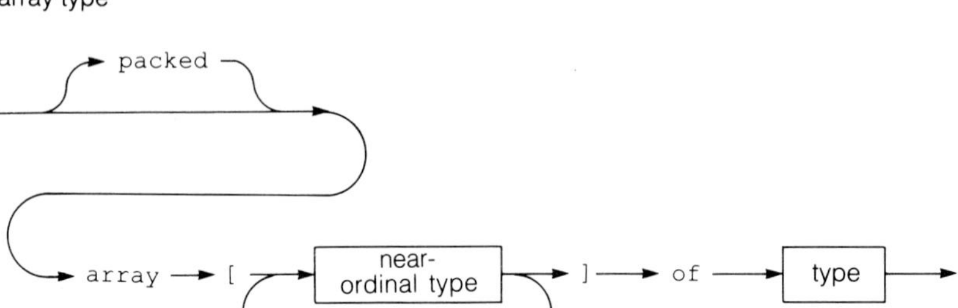

FIGURE 10.7 **Definition of arrays.**

```
type Grades = array ['A'..'D'] of integer;
     InfoClass = array [15..22] of integer;
     Bars = array [0..20,0..50] of char;
     Letters = array [char] of integer;

var  NbGrades : Grades;
     NbStudents, GreatSum : InfoClass;
     Graph: Bars;
     LetterCount : Letters;
```

arrays of type `InfoClass`), `Graph` (an array of type `Bars`), and `LetterCount` (an array of type `Letters`).

Figure 10.8 declares five arrays: `Averages`, `NbGrades`, `Truths`, `Matrix`, and `Counter`, of, respectively, one dimension (and eight elements of type `integer`), one dimension (and four elements of type `integer`), one dimension (and three elements of type `boolean`), two dimensions (and twelve elements of type `integer`), and one dimension (and twenty-six elements of type `integer`).

There is a sharp difference between declaring an array exclusively in the variable declaration part and declaring the same array using both the type definition part and the variable declaration part: Figure 10.7 defines a type `Grades` as being an array with four integers and declares an identifier `NbGrades` as being of the type `Grades`. Figure 10.8 declares the array

FIGURE 10.8 Declaration of arrays.

```
var  Averages : array [1..8] of integer;
     NbGrades: array ['A'..'D'] of integer;
     Truths: array [3..5] of boolean;
     Matrix: array [1..4, 1..3] of integer;
     Counter: array ['A'..'Z'] of integer;
```

NbGrades as being an array with four integers. The difference between these two approaches is that whereas in the first one we define a *type* and an *object*, in the second one we just define an *object*. Having defined a type, we can now define as many objects of that type as necessary, without needing to specify the structure of the objects in each definition. Besides, if we declare two objects of type array only in the variable declaration part, they are of the same type only if they are declared by the same statement. This is related to the process by which new types are stored inside the computer. Remember that in Chapter 5 we said that when we define new types we are creating templates that tell what something looks like. The computer considers that two identifiers are of the same type *only* if they refer to the *same* template. If, in two different declarations, we declare two templates that look exactly alike, the computer considers them as two different types. For this reason, the first approach is far better and is adopted in this book.

After the declaration of a variable as an array, we can reference any of its elements by referring to the name of the array and the position that the element occupies in the array. The values used to reference an element of an array are **subscripts.** Subscripts may be constants, variables, or expressions of the same type as the corresponding index type. For example, for the arrays declared in Figure 10.7, suppose variables `i` and `j` are of type `integer` and variable `ch` of type `char`; suppose further that `i = 3`, `j = 5`, and `ch = 'D'`. Then, `NbStudents[sqr(i) + 2 * j - 2]` references `NbStudents[17]` and `NbGrades[pred(pred(ch))]` references `NbGrades['B']`. The array `NbStudents` may correspond to the array shown in Figure 10.3. It contains eight elements of type `integer`; the first element is referenced by `NbStudents[15]`, the second element by `NbStudents[16]`, and so on.

If you look carefully at the syntactic definition of array type, notice that there is no restriction concerning the type that the elements of an array might have. The elements of an array can be, in turn, other arrays.[3] Consider, for example, the definition of types and declaration of variables

3. They can also be other structured types, as we will see later.

FIGURE 10.9 Definitions of arrays.

```
type Sexes = (Male, Female);
     AgeCount = array [15..35] of integer;
     AgeSexCount = array [Sexes] of AgeCount;

var  Counter : AgeSexCount;
```

shown in Figure 10.9. This figure defines an array `AgeCount` with twenty-one elements of type `integer`. It also defines an array `AgeSexCount` with two elements (whose indexes are `Male` and `Female`) of type `AgeCount`! In other words, each element of an array of type `AgeSexCount` is itself another array. Figure 10.9 also declares the variable `Counter` as being of type `AgeSexCount`. The variable `Counter[Female]` represents an array of type `AgeCount`. Because `Counter[Female]` is an array, to reference one of its elements, we write the name of the array followed by an index. For example, `Counter[Female][20]` represents a variable of type `integer`.

As was said, the reference to an element of an array (the name of the array followed by the corresponding subscripts enclosed by brackets) is considered to be a reference to a variable and thus can be subjected to any operation that can be performed on a variable. This variable is of the type defined for the elements of the array.

Be warned, right from the beginning, that when we define the upper and lower bounds of an index of an array we are, in fact, defining a type subrange for that index. If our program violates that definition—that is, if an index falls outside of the specified bounds—the computer generates an execution error.

10.3 Examples of usage of arrays

Arrays are very useful when we want to process in a similar way each member of a collection of objects that are simultaneously stored in memory. As a first example, consider again the problem presented at the beginning of this chapter: to write the student number of every student whose grade in a given exam was above average. We want a program that reads each student's number and the numeric grade that he or she received on a given exam. After reading the information concerning every student in the class, it writes the student number of every student whose grade was above average. The problem entails reading the information concerning the complete set of students in order to compute the class average. Afterward, we must compare the grade of each student with the class average

FIGURE 10.10 **Students with grade above average.**

```
program AboveAverage3 (input,output);
{ This program outputs the student number of
  the students whose grade is above average }

const NbOfStudents = 100;

type StudentInfo = array [1..NbOfStudents] of integer;
     StudentGrade = 0..100;
     GradeArray = array [1..NbOfStudents] of StudentGrade;

var  StNumber : StudentInfo;
     Grade : GradeArray;
     SumOfGrades, i : integer;
     Average : real;

begin
  SumOfGrades:=0;
  for i := 1 to NbOfStudents do
    begin
      writeln('Please type the student number',
              ' and the corresponding grade');
      readln(StNumber[i],Grade[i]);
      SumOfGrades := SumOfGrades + Grade[i]
    end;

  Average := SumOfGrades / NbOfStudents;

  writeln('Students with grade above average:');
  for i := 1 to NbofStudents do
      if Grade[i] > Average then writeln(StNumber[i])
end. { AboveAverage3 }
```

and decide if the student number should be printed. We have to process a set of values, "remember" each of the values processed, and then perform another operation with each one of those values. Problems of this kind are very well-suited for arrays.

The program in Figure 10.10 uses two arrays, `StNumber` and `Grade`, containing, respectively, the student numbers and the grades of the students. The student number of each student is located in the array `StNumber` in the same position that the grade of the student is located in the array

FIGURE 10.11 Counting the number of characters in a text.

```
program CharCounter (input, output);
{ This program counts the number of occurrences
  of each of the characters in a text }

type CharArray = array ['!'..'~'] of integer;

var CharCount : CharArray;
    Chr, i : char; { auxiliary variables }

begin
  { Initialize the array CharCount }
  for i := '!' to '~' do CharCount[i] := 0;

  while not eof do
      begin
        read(Chr);
        if (Chr >= '!') and (Chr <= '~') then
          CharCount[Chr] := CharCount[Chr] + 1
      end;

  writeln('Number of occurrences of each character:');
  writeln;
  for i := '!' to '~' do
     writeln('The character ',i,' occurred ',
             CharCount[i]:3,' times')
end. { CharCounter }
```

Grade; that is, the first element of the array StNumber (StNumber[1]) contains the student number of a student whose grade can be found as the first element of the array Grade (Grade[1]), the second element of the array StNumber (StNumber[2]) contains the student number of the student whose grade can be found in the second position of the array Grade (Grade[2]), and so on. Such arrays are **parallel arrays.** As an exercise, compare this program with the programs of Figures 10.1 and 10.2.

As a second example, we present a program that uses one array whose subscript is of type char. Assume that we want to compute the number of occurrences of every nonblank character in a given text. The characters that we consider are the visible ASCII characters—that is, from ! to ~. The program shown in Figure 10.11 uses a one-dimensional array, CharCount, whose index varies between ! and ~. (Remember that ! is the character in the lowest position and that ~ is the character in the highest position.) Each one of the elements of this array contains the number of times that the character represented by its index appeared in the text. For example, `CharCount['A']` represents the number of times character `A` appeared in the text. There is one aspect that is worthwhile noticing about this program. Recall that whenever we have variables that represent counters we always have to initialize them to 0. In this case, array `CharCount` contains ninety-four counters (one for each character) that must be initialized. This is done in the first `for` loop of the program.

Our third example uses a one-dimensional and a two-dimensional array. Suppose that we want to write a Pascal program that reads the age of every student in a class and plots a graph of the ages of the students who are between fifteen and thirty-five years old. This program, shown in Figure 10.12, is composed of four distinct parts: The first part uses the procedure `Initialize` to initialize the arrays `Age` and `Graph`; the second part uses the procedure `FillAges` that reads the ages of the students and computes the number of students whose ages are between fifteen and thirty-five years old. To do that, it uses an array `Age` containing the number of students with a given age. The index of this array goes from fifteen through thirty-five, and, for a given value of the index, it contains the number of students whose age equals that index. For example, `Age[19]` contains the number of students who are nineteen years old. After reading the ages of every student and thus having filled the array `Age`, the program begins its third part, using the procedure `FillGraph` that fills a two-dimensional array, `Graph`, which contains the graph of the ages of the students. Each column of this two-dimensional array corresponds to a given age. The array has ten rows (and thus we assume that there are no more than ten students with a given age). The array `Graph` is filled from the bottom to the top; that is, the first line filled will be line ten (corresponding to the value ten as second index), the next one will be line nine, and so on. Finally, using the procedure `PlotGraph`, the program writes the two-dimensional array `Graph`. Figure 10.13 shows the output produced by this program for some sample data.

When using two-dimensional arrays, it is irrelevant whether the first index represents the row or the column. When defining an array, decide whether the first index represents the row and the second one the column, or the first index represents the column and the second one the row. However, *after this decision is taken,* your program must be written taking into account the meaning of each of the indexes. In the array `Graph` in Figure 10.12, the first index represents the row and the second index the column. Clearly, this remark should be applicable to arrays with more than two dimensions.

FIGURE 10.12 A program to plot a graph.

```
program PlotAges (input, output);
{ This program plots the ages of the students
  in a class }

const Blank = ' ';

type TyGraph = array [1..10, 15..35] of char;
     TyAge = array [15..35] of integer;

var  Age : TyAge;
     Graph : TyGraph;

   procedure Initialize (var Age : TyAge;
                         var Graph : TyGraph);
   var i, j : integer;
   begin
     for i := 15 to 35 do
        begin
          Age[i] := 0;
          for j := 1 to 10 do
              Graph[j,i] := Blank
        end
   end; { Initialize }

   procedure FillAges(var Age : TyAge);
   var StudentAge : integer;
   { Loop to compute how many students are 15 years old,
     16 years old, ...                                 }
   begin
      while not eof do
         begin
           writeln('Please enter the age of the next',
                   'student');
           readln(StudentAge);
           if (StudentAge >= 15) and (StudentAge <= 35) then
              Age[StudentAge] := Age[StudentAge] + 1
         end
   end; { FillAges }
```

(continued)

FIGURE 10.12, *continued.*

```
   procedure FillGraph(var Age : TyAge; var Graph : TyGraph);
   { The array "Graph" is now filled with #s }
   var i, j : integer;
   begin
     for i := 15 to 35 do
         for j := 1 to Age[i] do
             Graph[10 - (j - 1), i] := '#'
   end; { FillGraph }

   procedure PlotGraph (var Graph : TyGraph);
   var i, j : integer;

      procedure PlotLine;
      var i : integer;
      begin
        write('+');
        for i := 15 to 35 do
        write('-');
        writeln('+')
      end; { PlotLine }

   begin
     PlotLine;
     for j := 1 to 10 do
         begin
           write('|');
           for i := 15 to 35 do write(Graph[j,i]);
           writeln('|')
         end;
     PlotLine
   end; { PlotGraph }

begin
  Initialize(Age, Graph);
  FillAges(Age);
  FillGraph(Age, Graph);
  PlotGraph(Graph)
end. { PlotAges }
```

FIGURE 10.13 Output of the program in Figure 10.12.

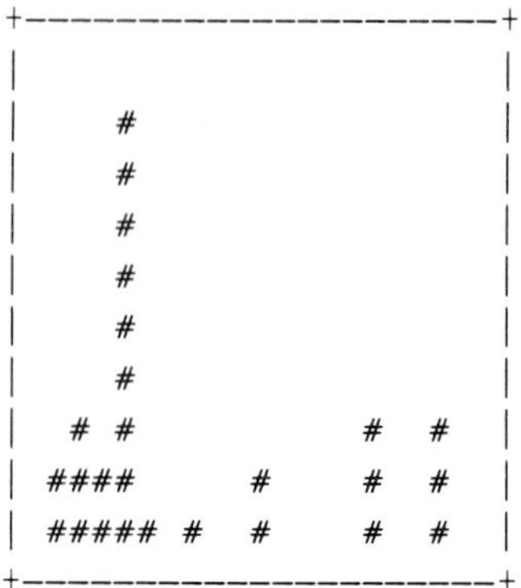

10.4 Representation of strings

You may have noticed that we have avoided representing names in the programs presented so far. In programs where the use of names would have been natural (for example, the name of a student or the name of an employee), names have been replaced by numbers (for example, student number or Social Security number). The reason for this is that we had no way of representing names. This section introduces a structure that allows us to represent names: the string.

A **string** is a structured data type composed of an ordered sequence of characters. The typical operations that can be performed on strings are:

Comparison of strings to find out whether they are equal or to sort them in alphabetic order
Concatenation of two strings into a unique string
Breaking of a string into several substrings
Search for patterns (substrings) in a given string

Some programming languages have the data structure `string` predefined, for example, SNOBOL4 [a string-oriented language, see Griswold, Poage, and Polonsky (1971)], BASIC, and UCSD Pascal.[4] In Standard Pascal, strings can be represented using one-dimensional arrays. To define a string using arrays, we should define an array whose elements are of type `char` and whose number of elements represents the maximum length of the

4. UCSD Pascal is a trademark of the Regents of the University of California.

string. For example, to define a string with a maximum length of eighty characters, we can use the following:

```
type String = array [1..80] of char;
var  Line   : String;
```

This declaration creates an array (named `Line`) of eighty elements, each of which contains one character. Each element of this array (for example, `Line[66]`) represents the name of a variable and thus occupies one memory location. In general, one character does not fully occupy one memory location, and this technique for string representation generates a large amount of wasted space in memory. To save memory in string representation, Pascal supplies a special type of arrays—**packed arrays**—that stores the maximum possible number of characters in each memory location. To define an array as a packed array, the word `packed` should precede the word `array` in the declaration of the array (refer to the definition of structured type in Section 10.1). For example, the following declaration

```
type String = packed array [1..80] of char;
var  Line   : String;
```

defines a string represented by a packed array. A one-dimensional packed array whose components are of type `char`, whose index is an `integer` subrange with lower bound one and upper bound greater than one, is called a `string-type`. Although a `string-type` is not a type in Standard Pascal, an array that is of `string-type` has certain special properties:

1. A variable of `string-type` can have a string constant assigned to it all at once, not just one element at a time. The restriction to this rule is that the string constant being assigned to the variable must be of the same length as the `string-type`. Suppose, for example, that in a program we have the following (as an exercise, convince yourself that `Names` is a `string-type`):

```
type Names = packed array [1..18] of char;
var  Course, FirstName, LastName : Names;
```

In this program, we could use the following assignments:

```
Course    := 'Computer Science  ';
LastName  := 'Wirth             ';
FirstName := LastName;
```

However, we could *not* use the assignment

```
LastName := 'Wirth';
```

because LastName has length eighteen and the string 'Wirth' has length five.

2. Variables of string-type and constants can be compared using the relational operators. Returning to the previous example, after the three assignment statements, Course < LastName is true, LastName < 'Dijkstra   ' is false, and LastName < FirstName is false. Again, the expression LastName < 'Dijkstra' is illegal because the constant 'Dijkstra' does not have the same length as LastName.
3. Variables of string-type may be written as a whole using write or writeln statements, rather than having to write one character at a time. Using the variable Course of our example, the statement

```
writeln('The course is ',Course,'.')
```

writes

```
The course is Computer Science
```

Notice that the variables of string-type can also be inspected one element at a time like ordinary arrays. This is the method to use to input variables of string-type: The statements read and readln *cannot* be used for this purpose.

The next sections present examples of programs that use packed arrays.

10.5 Search algorithms

Searching for information is one of our everyday activities. We search for words in dictionaries or phone numbers in phone books. With the constant increase in the amount of information stored inside computers, it is natural that searching for information is one of the main activities in a computing system. Although the problem of finding a given element among a set of elements looks at first sight to be very simple, the development of efficient search algorithms raises several problems.

Searches in computer science are very often carried out using arrays. This section presents two methods for searching for an element in an array: sequential search and binary search. Other searching methods can be found, for example, in Knuth (1973b) or Tremblay and Sorenson (1976).

Figure 10.14 presents a fragment of a Pascal program that reads the names and phone numbers of a group of 1000 people, after which it

FIGURE 10.14 A program to search for phone numbers.

```
program SearchFor(input,output);

const Arrsize = 1000; { Number of people considered }
      NameLen = 25;   { Maximum length of a name    }
      Finished = 'end                      ';

type RepName = packed array [1..NameLen] of char;
     TpNames = array [1..ArrSize] of RepName;
     TpPhoneNumbers = array [1..ArrSize] of integer;

var  Name : TpNames;
     PhoneNumber : TpPhoneNumbers;
     DesiredName : RepName;
     Phone : integer;

  procedure ReadName (var Name : RepName);
  var i, j : integer;
  begin
    i := 1;
    while not(eoln) and (i <= NameLen) do
      begin
        read(Name[i]);
        i := i + 1
      end;
    for j := i to NameLen do Name[j] := ' '
  end; { ReadName }

  procedure Initialize (var Name : TpNames;
                        var PhoneNumber : TpPhoneNumbers);
  var i : integer;

     procedure NameAndNumber (var Name : RepName;
                              var Num : integer);
     begin
       writeln('Please type the name',
               ' - end the line with RETURN');
       ReadName(Name);
       writeln('Please type the phone number');
       readln(Num)
     end; { NameAndNumber }
```

(continued)

FIGURE 10.14, *continued.*

```
  begin
     for i := 1 to ArrSize do
         NameAndNumber(Name[i],PhoneNumber[i]);
  end; { Initialize }

  procedure AskName (var WhichName : RepName);
  begin
    writeln('Please type the name of the person whose',
           ' phone you want');
    writeln('(type "end" to terminate execution)');
    ReadName(WhichName);
    readln;
  end; { AskName }

  function Search(Key : RepName ;
                 var Names : TpNames;
                 var Nums : TpPhoneNumbers) : integer;
```

```
begin
  Initialize(Name, PhoneNumber);
  AskName(DesiredName);
  while DesiredName <> Finished do
    begin
      Phone := Search(DesiredName, Name, PhoneNumber);
      if Phone <> -1 then
        begin
          write('The phone number of ',DesiredName);
          writeln(' is ',Phone);
        end
      else
        writeln('Unknown telephone number...');
      AskName(DesiredName)
    end
end. { SearchFor }
```

interacts with a user, supplying the phone number of a person whose name is supplied by the user. This interaction is repeated until the user supplies, as a "dummy" name, the word `end`. In the program in Figure 10.14, the array `Name` contains names of people, and the array `PhoneNumber` contains their respective phone numbers. It is assumed that `Name` and `PhoneNumber` are parallel arrays. We also assume that each person has at most one phone number.

The program of Figure 10.14 uses the function `Search`, which receives as input parameter the desired name (corresponding to the formal parameter `Key`) and returns the phone number of the person whose name is represented by `Key`.[5] This function returns `-1` if the name cannot be found among the list of names. Note, again, the use of procedural abstraction: We know what this function does, but we don't know how it does it.

We will now present two alternatives for writing the function `Search`: the sequential search technique and the binary search technique.

10.5.1 Sequential search

One of the simplest ways to search for the element (or elements) of an array with a given value consists of beginning with the first element and successively comparing each element of the array with the value for which we are searching. This process continues until either the end of the array is found or the element is found. This search process is **sequential search** (or **linear search**). Figure 10.15 presents the function `Search` needed for the program in Figure 10.14, using the sequential search method.

The function of the program in Figure 10.15, while conducting the search—statement `while (Names[i] <> Key) and (i < ArrSize) do i := i + 1`—must perform two tests: to check whether the desired name has been found—condition `Names[i] <> Key`—and to check whether the end of the array being searched has been reached—condition `i < ArrSize`. Note that the second test is only necessary because we are not sure whether the name being searched exists in the array. One technique normally used to get rid of this second test (and thus to improve the efficiency of the algorithm) consists of using a sentinel value.

A **sentinel value** is a special value that we insert into the array to ensure that the search is successful. In this case, we need an extra element in the array (to hold the sentinel value), and the first operation that we perform is to insert the sentinel in the array. At the end of the search, we must test whether the value found is the sentinel or the real value. Figure 10.16 illustrates this feature, and Figure 10.17 shows the changes needed

5. It also receives as input the list of the names and the corresponding phone numbers.

FIGURE 10.15 Sequential search.

```
function Search(Key : RepName ;
                var Names : TpNames;
                var Nums : TpPhoneNumbers) : integer;
{ This function performs a sequential search on the
  array Names, looking for the value of Key }
var i : integer;

begin
  i:=1;
  while (Names[i] <> Key) and (i < ArrSize) do i := i + 1;
  if Names[i] = Key then
    Search := Nums[i]
  else
    Search := -1
end; { Search }
```

FIGURE 10.16 Sequential search using a sentinel.

```
function Search(Key : RepName ;
                var Names : TpNames;
                var Nums : TpPhoneNumbers) : integer;
{ This function performs a sequential search on the
  array Names for the value of the variable Key. It
  uses a sentinel value    }
var i : integer;

begin
  Names[ArrSize + 1] := Key; { The sentinel is placed }

  i := 1;
  while Names[i] <> Key do i := i + 1;
  if i <> ArrSize + 1 then
    Search := Nums[i]
  else
    Search := -1
end; { Search }
```

FIGURE 10.17 Changes needed for using a sentinel.

```
const ArrSize = 100;
      ExtArrSize = 101;
      NameLen = 25;
      Finished = 'end

type RepName = packed array [1..NameLen] of char;
     TpNames = array [1..ExtArrSize] of RepName;
     TpPhoneNumbers = array [1..ExtArrSize] of integer;
```

in the type definition of the program `SearchFor` in case a sentinel value is used.

As an exercise, convince yourself that the technique that uses a sentinel is more efficient (it requires less time to produce the result) than the technique that doesn't.

10.5.2 Binary search

Sequential search is very simple, but it may require the inspection of every element of the array. This certainly happens if the value we are searching for cannot be found in the array. **Binary search,** an alternative to sequential search, assumes that the elements of the array are sorted. Using binary search, we first consider the element in the middle of the array. If the middle element is bigger than the value for which we are searching (by "bigger" we mean "comes after"), then we can guarantee that the value we are searching for cannot be found in the *second* half of the array, and we repeat the binary search process for the *first* half of the array. If the middle element is smaller than the value we are searching for (by "smaller" we mean "comes before"), then we can guarantee that the value we are searching for cannot be found in the *first* half of the array, and we repeat the binary search process with the *second* half of the array. If the middle element equals the value for which we are searching, then we are done. At every step, binary search disregards half of the elements being considered.

Figure 10.18 shows the function `Search` needed for the program of Figure 10.14, using the binary search technique. This function assumes that the array `Name` is sorted in alphabetic order.

The binary search technique requires that we keep a sorted list of elements. Thus, the cost of the insertion of a new element using this method is higher than if we use sequential search. However, because generally searches are much more frequent than insertions, it is preferable to keep the sorted list.

FIGURE 10.18 Binary search.

```
function Search(Key : RepName ;
                var Names : TpNames;
                var Nums : TpPhoneNumbers) : integer;
{ This function performs a binary search on the array
  Names looking for the value of the variable Key }

var LowerBound, UpperBound, HalfWay : integer;

begin
  LowerBound := 1;
  UpperBound := ArraySize;

  repeat
     HalfWay := (LowerBound + UpperBound) div 2;
     if Key < Names[HalfWay] then
        UpperBound := HalfWay - 1
     else
        LowerBound := HalfWay + 1
  until (Key = Names[HalfWay]) or (LowerBound > UpperBound);
  if Key = Names[HalfWay]  then
    Search := Nums[HalfWay]
  else
    Search := -1
end; { Search }
```

If you look carefully at the different versions of the function `Search` that we have been discussing, you may be surprised that two of its parameters are transmitted by reference rather than by value. This somewhat clashes with what we have been saying about passing parameters to functions. However, there is a perfectly good explanation for our decision, which we now discuss. When a parameter is transmitted by value, what is passed to the subprogram is a copy of its value. Whenever we pass arrays by value to subprograms, the computer must copy the entire array, which generates an overhead both in time (the time required to copy the array) and in space (the memory space needed to hold the copy of the array). On the other hand, when we pass parameters by reference, we just pass the location in memory where the actual parameter is stored. Whenever we pass arrays by reference, we are just passing one memory location, and so we gain both in processing time and in amount of storage needed. It is thus advisable to use call by reference whenever we pass arrays, independently of whether we are passing them to procedures or to functions.

10.6 Sorting algorithms

A set of elements is generally sorted to make a search easier; we sort because we want to make search easier, not because we are neat. To stress how helpful a sorted list of elements can be to a human when searching for a given element, suppose what it would be like if phone books were not sorted. In programs the use of a sorted list allows the writing of more efficient searching algorithms (for example, binary search instead of sequential search).

Sorting algorithms can be classified into two large groups, internal sorting algorithms and external sorting algorithms. **Internal sorting algorithms** sort a set of elements that are *all* stored in main memory. **External sorting algorithms** sort elements that, due to their large number, cannot all fit in main memory, and, thus, some of them are stored elsewhere in the computer (in an auxiliary memory device in form of a file, to be precise). In this case, at any moment, we only have in memory some of the elements to be sorted.

This section considers internal sorting algorithms. External sorting algorithms can be found in Knuth (1973b). Two internal sorting programs corresponding to two sorting methods are presented: bubble sort and selection sort.

In our discussion of sorting algorithms, we assume that we want to sort a sequence of integer numbers that may contain a maximum of 1000 elements. Our sorting program reads the number of elements to be sorted, followed by the elements themselves; stores the elements in an array; sorts them; and writes the sorted elements. The sorting is done using the procedure `Sort` that returns an array containing the sorted elements. The program that uses the sorting procedure is presented in Figure 10.19. Notice that, although this is a simple-minded example, it is enough for us to consider the sorting techniques.

We now focus on the development of the procedure `Sort`. The several versions for this procedure receive as parameters the number of elements to be sorted and a one-dimensional array with those elements, and they return as a parameter the sorted array.

10.6.1 Bubble sort

The first sorting procedure that we will consider is **bubble sort.** The basic idea behind the bubble-sort algorithm consists of scanning the elements to be sorted, comparing adjacent elements, and exchanging those pairs

FIGURE 10.19 A sorting program.

```
program SortedNumbers (input, output);

type TpNumbers = array [1..1000] of integer;

var  Numbers : TpNumbers;
     NumbElements, i : integer;

   procedure Sort (Size : integer; var Numbers : TpNumbers);



begin
  writeln ('How many elements to Sort?');
  readln (NumbElements);

  writeln('Please type ',NumbElements,' integers');
  for i := 1 to NumbElements do read(Numbers[i]);

  Sort(NumbElements, Numbers);

  writeln('The Sorted Numbers are:');
  for i := 1 to NumbElements do writeln(Numbers[i])
end. { SortedNumbers }
```

that are out of order (that is, unsorted). A single pass does not generally sort the array, and normally it is necessary to perform several passes through the array. The array is sorted when a pass is made in which no exchange of elements is performed. The reason this method is called "bubble" sort is that the elements of the array move up the way bubbles move up in water. Figure 10.20 presents the bubble-sort procedure. The bubble-sort algorithm uses the boolean variable `NoExchange` whose value is `false` if, during a pass through the array, an exchange of elements is performed, and is `true` otherwise.

The procedure in Figure 10.20 contains one statement (`repeat ... until NoExchange`) that may seem odd at first. You probably would expect to find the condition `NoExchange = true`. Notice, however, that the value of this expression is *exactly* the value of the variable `NoExchange`!

FIGURE 10.20 A program using bubble sort.

```
procedure Sort (Size : integer; var Numbers : TpNumbers);
{ This procedure sorts the array Numbers using bubble sort }

var i : integer;
    NoExchange : boolean;

        procedure Exchange(var x, y : integer);
        var temp : integer;
        begin
          temp := x;
          x := y;
          y := temp
        end; { Exchange }

begin
  repeat
    NoExchange := true;

    for i := 1 to Size - 1 do
      if Numbers[i] > Numbers[i + 1] then
        begin
          Exchange(Numbers[i], Numbers[i + 1]);
          NoExchange := false
        end
  until NoExchange
end; { Sort }
```

Bubble sort is very simple but not very efficient. One of the reasons for its lack of efficiency is because we exchange only adjacent elements; thus, if an element is far away from its final position, it is necessary to perform several passes in order to place that element in its final position.

A modification of the bubble sort, the **Shell sort**—named after its creator, Donald Shell (Shell 1959)—consists of comparing and exchanging not the adjacent elements but the elements that are separated by a certain interval. After a complete sort procedure of type bubble sort with a given interval, the interval is divided in half and the process is repeated with the new interval. This process is repeated until the interval is one. As the initial interval, it is usual to take half of the number of elements to be sorted. Shell sort is more efficient than bubble sort because the first pass through

FIGURE 10.21 Shell sort.

```
procedure Sort (Size : integer;
                var Numbers : TpNumbers);
{ This procedure sorts the array Numbers using
  Shell sort }

var Interval, i : integer;
    NoExchange : boolean;

       procedure Exchange(var x, y : integer);
       var temp : integer;
       begin
         temp := x;
         x := y;
         y := temp
       end; { Exchange }

begin
  Interval := Size div 2;
  repeat
      repeat
         NoExchange := true;
         for i := 1 to Size - Interval do
            if Numbers[i] > Numbers[i + Interval] then
               begin
                 Exchange(Numbers[i], Numbers[i + Interval]);
                 NoExchange := false
               end
      until NoExchange;
      Interval := Interval div 2
  until Interval = 0
end; { Sort }
```

the array considers only a subset of the elements to be sorted, and later passes that consider every element of the array find these elements partially sorted. The procedure for Shell sort is presented in Figure 10.21.

10.6.2 Selection sort

The third sorting procedure that we consider, **selection sort,** consists of scanning the elements to be sorted and, in every pass through those elements, placing one element in its final position. In the first pass through the array, we place the smallest element in its final position; in the second

FIGURE 10.22 Selection sort.

```
procedure Sort (Size : integer;
                var Numbers:TpNumbers);
{ This procedure sorts the array Numbers using
  selection sort }

var Smallest, i, j : integer;

       procedure Exchange(var x, y : integer);
       var temp : integer;
       begin
         temp := x;
         x := y;
         y := temp
       end; { Exchange }

begin
  for i := 1 to Size - 1 do
    begin
      Smallest := i;
      for j := i + 1 to Size do { Find the position of
                                  the smallest number }
          if Numbers[j] < Numbers[Smallest] then
             Smallest := j;
      Exchange(Numbers[i], Numbers[Smallest])
    end
end; { Sort }
```

pass through the array, we place the second smallest element in its final position; and so on. The selection-sort procedure is presented in Figure 10.22.

10.7 Efficiency considerations

We said that binary search performs better than sequential search and that Shell sort is more efficient than bubble sort. In this section we discuss methods for comparing the efficiency of algorithms. The efficiency of algorithms is an important issue in computer science because it gives us a rough measure of the work involved in executing the algorithm.

One way to determine the work involved in executing an algorithm is to get up some sample data and trace the execution of the algorithm for that data. This is illustrated in Tables 10.1–10.3 where we show the sorting pattern when an array of six elements containing the values `a[1] = 4`, `a[2] = 8`, `a[3] = 17`, `a[4] = 3`, `a[5] = 11`, and `a[6] = 2` is sorted using the three described methods. (As an exercise, trace through the procedures of Figures 10.20–10.22 with the sample data provided and compare the results obtained with the results shown in Tables 10.1–10.3.)

This approach, however, has the drawback that the work involved in the execution of an algorithm may vary drastically from sample data to sample data (for example, if the sample data was already sorted, bubble sort would need just one pass); therefore, we want to find a measure of the work involved in the execution of the algorithm independently of the particular values that we supply for the data.

One convenient way to describe the work involved in an algorithm is to use the notion of *order of growth* to obtain a gross measure of the resources required by the algorithm as the size of the data manipulated becomes larger. The idea behind this approach is to isolate a particular operation fundamental to the algorithm and to count the number of times this operation is performed. In the case of sorting and searching algorithms, this operation is comparison (of two elements, which one is bigger?). In our study of the efficiency of searching and sorting algorithms, we will use the number of comparisons as a measure of the efficiency of the algorithms. Thus, given two sorting (or searching) algorithms, we will say that the algorithm that requires fewer comparisons is the most efficient.

10.7.1 Efficiency of bubble sort

In the bubble sort (Figure 10.20), we exchange adjacent pairs of elements. The overall sort process consists of a number of passes over the data. The bubble-sort algorithm shown in Figure 10.20 is implemented with two nested loops. The outer loop is a `repeat` statement and the inner one a `for` statement. Every time the inner loop is executed there are `Size - 1` comparisons. The outer loop is executed until all the elements are sorted. In the best case it can be executed just once (and thus the number of comparisons will be `Size - 1`); in the worst case it will be executed `Size` times (and thus the number of comparisons will be `Size * (Size - 1)`). The average case will fall between the two extremes; thus the average number of comparisons required by bubble sort is

```
1/2 Size * (Size - 1)
```

where `Size` is the number of elements being sorted.

10.7.2 Efficiency of selection sort

In the selection sort (Figure 10.22), the basic operation is the selection of the smallest (or largest) element from a sequence of elements. The selec-

TABLE 10.1 Sorting pattern using bubble sort.

a[1]	a[2]	a[3]	a[4]	a[5]	a[6]	*Comment*
4	8	17	3	11	2	Original array
4	8	3	17	11	2	First pass
4	8	3	11	17	2	First pass
4	8	3	11	2	17	First pass
4	3	8	11	2	17	Second pass
4	3	8	2	11	17	Second pass
3	4	8	2	11	17	Third pass
3	4	2	8	11	17	Third pass
3	2	4	8	11	17	Fourth pass
2	3	4	8	11	17	Fifth pass

TABLE 10.2 Sorting pattern using Shell sort.

a[1]	a[2]	a[3]	a[4]	a[5]	a[6]	*Comment*
4	8	17	3	11	2	Original array
3	8	17	4	11	2	Interval = 3
3	8	2	4	11	17	Interval = 3
3	2	8	4	11	17	Interval = 1
3	2	4	8	11	17	Interval = 1
2	3	4	8	11	17	Interval = 1

TABLE 10.3 Sorting pattern using selection sort.

a[1]	a[2]	a[3]	a[4]	a[5]	a[6]	*Comment*
4	8	17	3	11	2	Original array
2	8	17	3	11	4	First pass
2	3	17	8	11	4	Second pass
2	3	4	8	11	17	Third pass

tion-sort algorithm shown in Figure 10.22 is implemented with two nested `for` loops. The outer loop is executed `Size - 1` times; the number of times the inner loop is executed depends on the value of the variable `i` of the outer loop: the first time it will be executed `Size - 1` times; the second time it will be executed `Size - 2` times; the last time it will be executed only once. Thus, the number of comparisons required by selection sort is:

```
(Size - 1) + (Size - 2) + ... + 2 + 1
```

with some simple algebra this can be proved to be equal to

```
1/2 Size * (Size - 1)
```

10.7.3 Efficiency of sequential search

In the sequential search, we sequentially search the sequence of elements until we find the desired one. In the sequential-search algorithms shown in Figure 10.15, every time we make a pass through the `while` loop we have to perform two comparisons (we must check whether we have found the desired element, and we must check whether we reached the end of the array). As with the analysis of bubble sort, we may require just one pass through the loop (if the element we are searching for is the first one), or we may have to scan the entire array. Thus, the average number of comparisons required by sequential search is

```
1/2 * 2 * ArrSize = ArrSize
```

where `ArrSize` is the size of the array being searched.

Using a sentinel (see Figure 10.16), we cut down the number of comparisons in each pass to just one but increase the `ArrSize` by one. Thus, using a sentinel, the average number of comparisons required is

```
1/2 (ArrSize + 1)
```

10.7.4 Efficiency of binary search

In the binary search we are able to halve the number of elements being considered every time we make a comparison (see Figure 10.18). So if we start with `ArrSize` elements, the number of elements after one pass through the loop is `ArrSize/2`; the number of elements after two passes is `ArrSize/4`, and so on. In general, after `m` passes, the number of elements left to check is $\texttt{ArrSize}/2^{m}$. The algorithm terminates when the number of elements left is less than one; that is, we stop after `m` steps if

$$\frac{\texttt{ArrSize}}{2^{m}} < 1$$

or

```
ArrSize < 2^m
```

or

```
Log₂ ArrSize < m
```

Thus, for an array of size `ArrSize`, binary search will require no more than `1 + (log₂ ArrSize)` steps. In each step we perform three comparisons (one in the `if` statement and two to evaluate the expression of the loop—see Figure 10.18); thus the number of comparisons required by binary search is no more than

```
3 * (1 + log₂ ArrSize)
```

10.7.5 Big-O notation

Our concern with efficiency is related to solving a problem with a large size. If we are searching or sorting an array of five elements, then even the less efficient algorithm will do. However, as the number of elements being considered grows, the work required becomes very different from algorithm to algorithm. For example, if we were searching an array of 100,000,000 elements, sequential search would require an average of 100,000,000 comparisons, whereas binary search would require no more than 61 comparisons!

We can express an approximation of the relationship between the amount of work required and the number of elements involved using a mathematical notation called *order of magnitude,* or Big-O notation (read "big-oh"). The order of magnitude of a function is the same as the order of the term that increases fastest relative to the argument of the function. For example, the order of magnitude of $f(N) = N^2 + N$ is N^2 since for large values of N, N^2 will dominate the value of the function (it will be so important in the overall value of f that we can almost forget about the other term). In Big-O notation we say that the order of magnitude of $N^2 + N$ is $O(N^2)$.

From the previous discussion we can say that binary search is of order $O(\log_2 N)$; sequential search is of order $O(N)$; and both selection and bubble sort are of order $O(N^2)$. In Table 10.4 we show a comparison between the values of N, $\log_2 N$ and N^2 as the value of N increases, to give you a feeling of the order of growth of the algorithms that we have been discussing.

TABLE 10.4 Comparison of order of growth of some functions.

N	$\log_2 N$	N^2
1	0	1
2	1	4
4	2	16
8	3	64
16	4	256
32	5	1,024
64	6	4,096
128	7	16,384
256	8	65,536
512	9	262,144
1,024	10	1,048,576

Summary

This chapter discussed arrays. An array is an ordered collection of elements, all of the same type, that are accessed by supplying the position of the element inside the array. All elements of the array have the same name; the index (or indexes) that follows the name differentiates them and makes them distinct.

Arrays are useful when we want to store large amounts of data and want to process in a similar way all the elements stored. Arrays are also useful to store names and perform manipulations on the names.

This chapter also discussed two searching techniques—sequential and binary search—and three sorting techniques—bubble sort, Shell sort, and selection sort.

Suggested readings

You can explore the topics presented in this chapter more deeply by consulting the following publications:

Bentley, J. 1984. "Programming Pearls: How to Sort." *Communications of the ACM* 27(4): 287–291.
This book presents an elementary description of some of the sorting methods and compares the efficiency of the methods described.

Dromey, R. 1982. *How to Solve It by Computer.* Englewood Cliffs, NJ: Prentice-Hall.
This book presents many Pascal programs that use arrays, namely, for partitioning arrays, inverting arrays, and searching and sorting using arrays. Each program presented is followed by a detailed description of its development.

Knuth, D. 1973b. *The Art of Computer Programming, Vol. 3, Sorting and Searching.* Reading, MA: Addison-Wesley.
This is a book on searching and sorting techniques. It exhaustively studies the various searching and sorting techniques and analyzes the efficiency and complexity of the algorithms corresponding to each of the methods presented.

Pratt, T. 1975. *Programming Languages: Design and Implementation.* Englewood Cliffs, NJ: Prentice-Hall.
Chapter 3 of this book discusses nonelementary data structures and how they are used by several programming languages.

Tremblay, J., and Sorenson, P. 1976. *An Introduction to Data Structures with Applications.* New York: McGraw-Hill.
This book presents a good discussion of the concept of an array and its storage process. It also describes many searching and sorting algorithms.

Exercises

1. ? Explain why the two steps involved in the program in Figure 10.1—that is, computing the class average and finding out which students had a numeric grade above the class average—cannot be done simultaneously.
2. ? Explain why we need the statement

```
if (c >= '!') and (c <= '~') then ...
```

   in the program of Figure 10.11.
3. ? Write a Pascal program that reads ten characters into an array and outputs them in reverse order.
4. ? Write a Pascal program that takes as input a text and computes the number of times that each of the visible ASCII characters (from ! to ~) appears in the text. The output of the program is a series of lines, each line containing an ASCII character, the number of times it appeared in the text, and the percentage of occurrences of the character in the text.
5. ✓ Out of the following definitions of arrays, which are illegal? Why?

```
type Colors = (Red, Yellow, Blue);
     FebruaryDays = 1..29;
     Counter = array [FebruaryDays] of Colors;
     Counter1 = array [integer, Colors] of integer;
     Counter2 = array [Colors, Colors] of Colors;
     Counter3 = array [1..2, 1..2.0] of real;
```

6. **?** Consider the following declarations of variables:

```
type Faculties = (Math, CompSci, Engin, Law);
     Divisions = (Und, Grad);
     Grades = array ['A'..'D'] of integer;
     StGrades = array [1..100] of Grades;
     DepGrades = array [Faculties] of StGrades;
     SchoolGrades = array [Faculties] of DepGrades;
var  OurGrades : SchoolGrades;
```

What are the types of the following variables? If one of these variables is ill-formed, explain why.

a. `OurGrades[Und][Math][4]`
b. `OurGrades[CompSci]`
c. `OurGrades[CompSci][Grad][50][A]`
d. `OurGrades[Law][Engin]`
e. `OurGrades[Law,Und]`

7. **?** Write a Pascal program that reads a line of text (up to eighty characters) and tells whether the line read corresponds to a palindrome. For example, `Radar` is a palindrome, `Radar or ro radar` is also a palindrome. Be prepared to handle a mixture of uppercase and lowercase characters.

8. **?** Modify the program of Figure 10.12 so that it plots the ages in the form of a histogram with one # per student. For example,

```
15 | ###
16 | ####
17 | #####
18 | #########
19 | ####
20 | ##########
21 | ####
22 | ###
23 | ####
24 | #####
25 | #########
26 | ####
27 | ##########
28 | ####
29 |
30 | #
31 | ####
32 | ###
```

```
33 | ####
34 | #####
35 | #########
```

9. ✓ Suppose that the array `Arr` is declared in the following way:

```
var Arr : array [1..50, 1..50, 1..50] of integer
```

   a. How many dimensions does the array `Arr` have?
   b. How many elements does the array `Arr` have?
   c. Suppose that `Arr` is passed to a procedure. Which of the following techniques corresponds to greater efficiency in execution time: call by value or call by reference? Why?

10. ? Write a Pascal program that uses an integer array with ten rows and ten columns and fills in the value for each element of the array in such a way that the value stored is 1 if the row index is greater than the column index and is 0 otherwise.

11. ? Write a Pascal function that takes as argument an array whose type is defined as

```
type rectangle = array [1..10, 11..30] of integer
```

   and returns the largest value in the array.

12. ? Write a Pascal program that reads fifty integer numbers and sorts them in decreasing order using
   a. Bubble sort
   b. Shell sort
   c. Selection sort

13. ? We defined binary search in terms of binary search itself. However, the function shown in Figure 10.18 is not recursive. Rewrite the function of Figure 10.18 using recursion.

14. ? Write a program that reads a sequence of names and outputs every name that occurs more than once. (HINT: Keep a sorted list of the names read in.)

15. ! Write a Pascal procedure that takes two sorted arrays (each one with 100 integer values) and produces a new sorted array obtained by merging the two arrays received. Your procedure should use no sorting techniques, and the resulting array should not contain duplicate elements.

16. ! Modify the program of Figure 10.14 to handle the case where one person can have several phone numbers. Present a complete program, including the search procedure to handle this case.

17. **!** A very efficient sorting procedure, **Quick Sort,** consists of a series of steps, each of which takes an array and partitions it into three disjoint arrays. One of these arrays contains only one element, the key element, and the other two arrays satisfy the following properties: every element of one of the arrays is smaller than the key element, and every element of the other array is greater than the key element. Furthermore, the key element is placed in its final position in the sorted array. The key element is usually taken to be the first element of the array. For example, the array containing the elements

```
14   23   34   10   9   2   29   11   90
```

would be partitioned in the following way:

```
[10   9   2   11]   {14}   [23   34   29   90]
```

in which brackets delimit the arrays generated and the key element is enclosed in curly brackets. Each of the arrays generated is then recursively sorted using Quick Sort. In our example, we would have

```
[9   2]   {10}   [11]   14   {23}   [34   29   90]
[2]   {9}   10   {11}   14   23   [29]   {34}   [90]
{2}   9   10   11   14   23   {29}   34   {90}
```

Write a recursive procedure in Pascal that implements Quick Sort.

18. **?** Write a program that reads a two-dimensional array of integers, with n rows and n columns. The value of n is supplied by the user. Your program then computes whether the array read satisfies any of the following conditions:
    a. The array is *symmetric*. This would be the case if, for all `i` and `j`, we have `a[i,j] = a[j,i]`, where `a` denotes the name of the array.
    b. The array is *diagonal*. This would be the case if, whenever `i` ≠ `j`, we have `a[i,j] = 0`, where `a` denotes the name of the array.
    c. The array is *upper triangular*. This would be the case if, for all `i` and `j`, if `i > j`, then `a[i,j] = 0`.

19. **?** Write a program that reads in a two-dimensional array of integers with n rows and n columns and interchanges the rows and columns of the array. For example, if the array read is

```
4  3  2  1
5  7  4  9
0  5  6  2
8  8  0  4
```

it becomes

```
4  5  0  8
3  7  5  8
2  4  6  0
1  9  2  4
```

(HINT: Be careful not to interchange the array twice; in other words, if you are not careful, you may get back the original array.)

20. **!** Arrays can be used to represent mazes. One such maze is shown below, in which a + represents a wall and a blank represents a pathway.

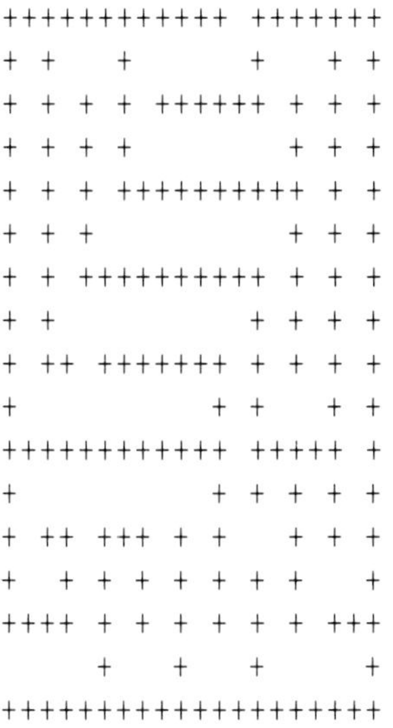

Write a program that reads in an array representing a maze and a starting point and finds its way through the maze. (HINT: Whenever the road divides, use the same process to select your way—for example, always take the rightmost way—when you get stuck, backtrack to the last crossroad and take the other way.)

21. **?** In Chapter 6, there is an exercise to output the wood `Good` written vertically. The normal way to print large characters is horizontally, rather than vertically (for example, this is used for generating banner headlines). Write a Pascal program that reads a string and outputs it using large characters. HINTS: Store each letter to be output in an array, for example,

```
DDD
D  D
D  D
D  D
DDD
```

and output the several letters, line by line; be careful with the length of the output produced.

22. ? Write a Pascal program that uses an array to keep track of unoccupied rooms in a hotel (assume that the rooms are numbered sequentially from 1 to `NbRooms`). The program interacts with a user and accepts the following commands:

`F`

This command lists the number of every available room.

`I <n>`

The nonterminal n represents a positive integer. This command checks a guest into room n. If room n is already taken, it prints a message stating so; if n does not correspond to a room number, it warns the user about it.

`O <n>`

The nonterminal symbol n represents a positive integer. This command checks a guest out of room n. If room n is available, it prints a message stating so; if n does not correspond to a room number, it warns the user about it.

`N`

This command tells the user how many rooms are available.

`H`

This command helps the user, explaining what the possible commands are and what they do.

`E`

This command terminates execution.

23. **!** Write a Pascal program that takes as input a syntactically correct Pascal program and produces an equivalent Pascal program with proper indentation of the statements.

24. **!** The Ackermann function presented in Exercise 12 of Chapter 9 is very inefficient because during its execution it computes the same values many times. One technique to avoid this problem, called **memoization**—see, for example, Abelson, Sussman, and Sussman (1985)—consists of recording in an array the values that previously have been computed. Write a Pascal function that computes the Ackermann function using the memoization technique.

25. **!** Discuss the advantages and disadvantages of making the array used by the function of the previous exercise a global variable.

CHAPTER 11

This chapter presents the need for another structured data type, the record, by showing some limitations of arrays. We discuss the characteristics of records and show some examples using records and arrays of records.

STRUCTURED DATA TYPES 2: RECORDS

He spoke on a quick succession of subjects—on miracle plays, on mediaeval pottery, on Stradivarius violins, on the Buddhism of Ceylon, and on the warships of the future—handling each as though he had made a special study of it.
Sir Arthur Conan Doyle, *The Sign of Four*

In the previous chapter, we studied the data type `array`, and we considered some typical algorithms that use arrays. We said that the elements of an array had to be all of the same type and that each element is accessed by indicating its position in the array.

To show some of the limitations of arrays, suppose that we want to write a program to keep track of the students in a given class. Each student is represented by a student number, name, address, phone number, grade-point average, and major. Because these pieces of information are of different kinds—for example, the student number is represented by an integer and the name by a string—we cannot store all the information concerning a student in the same array. To store the student information in arrays, we can use parallel arrays, as described in Chapter 10 and shown in Figure 11.1. Although the types shown in this figure are enough to represent the information we need, a program using this information could be hard to write. If, for example, we want to sort all the students by student number, we would need to exchange the values stored in six parallel arrays several times. This is because there is no single identifier that represents a student: The information concerning a student is spread across six arrays.

This chapter presents a data type, the record, that enables the storage of information of different types. The main differences between records

FIGURE 11.1 Student information using parallel arrays.

```
const   MaxStudents   = 200;
        MaxWord       = 12;
        FullWord      = 24;

type    Word          = packed array [1..MaxWord] of char;
        DoubleWord    = packed array [1..FullWord] of char;

        StNumbers     = array [1..MaxStudents] of integer;
        StNames       = array [1..MaxStudents] of Word;
        StAddress     = array [1..MaxStudents] of DoubleWord;
        StPhones      = array [1..MaxStudents] of integer;
        StGPAs        = array [1..MaxStudents] of real;
        StMajors      = array [1..MaxStudents] of Word;
```

and arrays concern the type of the elements that can belong to the structure and the way the elements are accessed.

A **record** is an association of elements that can be of different types and thus processed using different techniques. Each element of a record has a name, and the element is accessed by supplying its name. Records are similar to arrays in the sense that they can store a set of elements. However, they differ from arrays by the fact that their elements can be of different types and by the process of accessing each element.

A record is composed of several parts, called **fields.** Each field has a name that identifies the field, a type that identifies the type of element stored in the field, and a value. In the example concerning the student, we need six fields: one field containing the student number, one field containing the student's name, one field containing the student's address, one field containing the phone number, one field containing the grade-point average, and one field containing the major. Figure 11.2 schematically represents the information about one student.

11.1 Definition of records in Pascal

To define a record, we must supply the name of the record, the name of each of the fields, and the types of the elements of each of its fields. Like arrays, in Pascal a record can be defined either in the variable declaration part or in the type definition part. Because the declaration of records in the type definition part is far better, this is the only alternative that we consider.

FIGURE 11.2 Information contained in the record for one student.

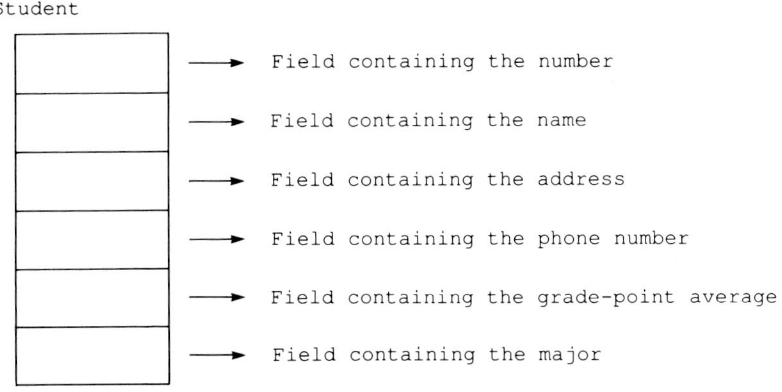

FIGURE 11.3 Syntax chart for record type.

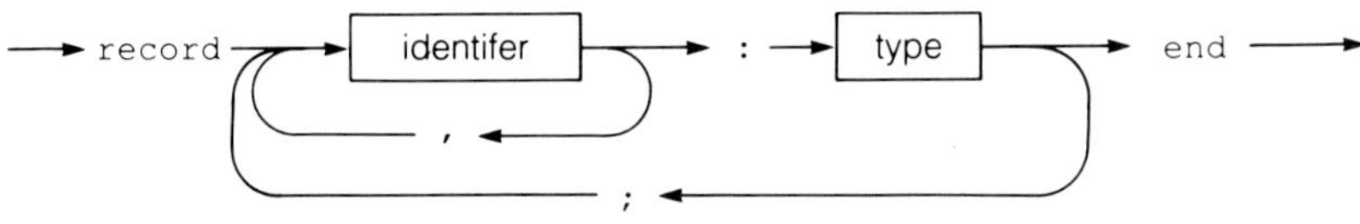

To define a record, we must define an identifier as being of record type. A record type is syntactically defined by the following BNF expressions, or, alternatively, by the syntax chart of Figure 11.3.[1]

<record type> ::= `record` <records> `end`

<records> ::= <record part> | <record part> ; <records>

<record part> ::= <identifiers> : <type> | <empty>

---

1. This is a limited definition of record type. It leaves out the variant part. For a complete treatment of records, refer to Cooper (1983); Jensen, Wirth, Mickel, and Miner (1985); or Wirth (1976).

FIGURE 11.4 A student record.

```
type RepName = packed array [1..14] of char;
     RepAddress = packed array [1..30] of char;
     RepMajor = packed array [1..16] of char
     StInfo = record
                Number   : integer;
                Name     : RepName;
                Address  : RepAddress;
                Phone    : integer;
                GPA      : real;
                Major    : RepMajor
              end; { StInfo }

var Student : StInfo;
```

FIGURE 11.5 The tree corresponding to the student record.

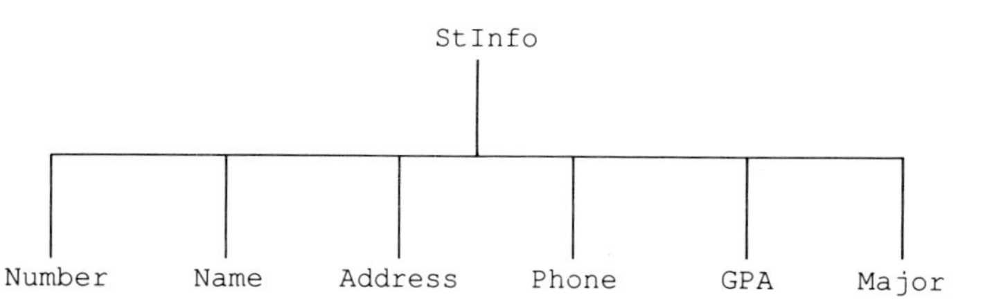

As an example, consider the record containing information about a student. Figure 11.4 presents the definition of the student record `StInfo` and the declaration of the variable `Student` of that type. Notice the comment that follows the complete definition of the record, which warns the programmer that the definition of the record has ended. This is a good programming practice. When we define a record, we are implicitly defining a structure called a **tree.** The tree corresponding to the student record is shown in Figure 11.5.

In the syntactic definition of a record, there is no restriction whatsoever concerning the type of each of its fields. This means that each field of a record can be, in turn, another record. Figure 11.6 presents an alter-

FIGURE 11.6 An alternative definition of a student record.

```
type Word = packed array [1..25] of char;
     RepStreet = packed array [1..50] of char;

     StInfo = record
                 Number : integer;
                 Name : record
                          FirstName : Word;
                          LastName  : Word
                        end; { Name }
                 Address : record
                             IDStreet : record
                                          Street : RepStreet;
                                          No     : integer;
                                          Apt    : chr
                                        end; { IDStreet }
                             City    : Word;
                             ZIPCode : integer;
                             State   : Word
                           end; { Address }
                 Phone : integer;
                 GPA   : real;
                 Major : word
               end; { StInfo }
```

native definition of the student record in which both the student's name and address are represented by records. Figure 11.7 represents the tree corresponding to the record of Figure 11.6.

11.2 Accessing the components of a record

To access a field of a record, we supply the name of the record and the name of the field, *separated by a period.* For example, considering the record defined in Figure 11.4, assume that the variable `Student` contains the information about the student whose student number is `12345`, whose name is `Humpty Dumpty`, whose address is `15 Main Street, Somewhere, USA`, whose phone number is `8756166`, whose GPA is `3.5`,

FIGURE 11.7 The tree corresponding to the student record in Figure 11.6.

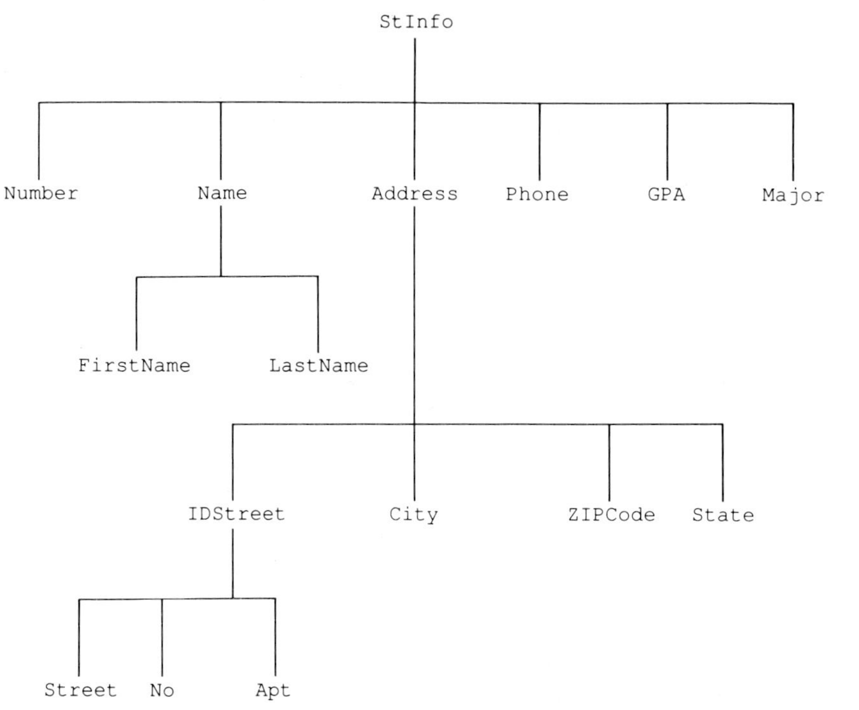

and whose major is `Computer Science`. This information can be assigned to the record `Student` by the following assignment statements:

```
Student.Number  := 12345
Student.Name    := 'Humpty Dumpty '
Student.Address := '15 Main Street, Somewhere, USA'
Student.Phone   := 8756166
Student.GPA     := 3.5
Student.Major   := 'Computer Science'
```

Like arrays, the symbolic name that references one element of the record—for example, `Student.Name`—is a variable, and therefore can be subjected to any operation that can be performed on a variable of its type.

If we have a record whose fields include, in turn, other records, the process of reference to the values of the fields is similar. For example, suppose that using the definition in Figure 11.6, we declared the variable

Student as a record of type StInfo. If we want to assign the value 14217 to the ZIP code, we can use the following assignment statement:

```
Student.Address.ZIPCode := 14217
```

11.3 Arrays of records

Although a single record can be useful, many applications require collections of records. Arrays are the ideal structure to represent a collection of similar objects. Thus, many programs use arrays of records.

Suppose, for example, that a company must store the following information about each employee: Social Security number, name, address, phone number, department where the employee works, and salary. Suppose further that the company must process information about the employee—for example, computing the weekly wage. Assuming that each employee receives a fixed amount of money every week, this processing would entail getting the information concerning each employee, retrieving the salary to be paid, and writing a paycheck, which would be sent to the department of the employee. Information in this paycheck should contain the Social Security number, the name, the salary, and the department where the employee works. The natural data structure to be used for this kind of processing is an array (or a file). We can define an array, `Employees`, whose elements are of type `Employee` (Figure 11.8). Each element of the array `Employees` is a record. For example, `Employees[5]` represents a record of type `Employee`. It is important to realize that `Employees[5]` is the name of a record, and thus it makes sense to access each element of the record. For example,

1. `Employees[5].SSN` represents the Social Security number of the employee whose information is stored in the fifth position of the array `Employees`.
2. `Employees[5].Name.LastName` represents the last name of the employee whose information is stored in the fifth position of the array `Employees`.
3. `Employees[5].Name.LastName[1]` represents the first character of the last name of the employee whose information is stored in the fifth position of the array `Employees`.

Most applications that use records store them as elements of arrays and thus the structure: Array of records is very useful. In the next section, we develop a complete example that uses arrays of records.

FIGURE 11.8 An array of records.

```
const NbEmpl = 100;

type Word = packed array [1..20] of char;
     DoubleWord = packed array [1..40] of char;

     Employee = record
                  SSN : packed array [1..11] of char;
                  Name : record
                           FirstName : Word;
                           LastName  : Word
                         end; { Name }
                  Address : record
                              Street  : DoubleWord;
                              City    : Word;
                              ZIPCode : integer;
                              State   : Word
                            end; { Address }
                  PhoneNum   : Word;
                  Department : Word;
                  Salary     : real
                end; { Employee }
     AllEmployees = array [1..NbEmpl] of Employees;

var  Employees : AllEmployees;
```

11.4 Case Study: flight information at an airport

Suppose that the information concerning the flights that arrive and depart at a given airport is stored in a computer. Suppose further that we want to take the information concerning the departing flights and write it sorted by departure time. Each departing flight contains the following information: flight number, name of the airline, city of destination, departure time, and gate number. Because the several pieces of information concerning the departing flights are of a different nature (for example, the gate number is represented by an integer, and the airline is represented by a string), the ideal structure to store this information is a record. Because we have several objects of this type, we should store them in an array. In this case, we have an array of records, each record representing a departing flight.

This program is used by airport personnel whenever they update the information concerning the departing flights. When the program is executed, it reads the information concerning the departing flights within a

FIGURE 11.9 Main subproblems.

```
program Airport (input, output);

    ...

begin
  ReadInfo(NbFlights, Departures);
  SortFlights(NbFlights, Departures, SortedFlights);
  WriteFlights(NbFlights, Departures, SortedFlights)
end. { Airport }
```

given interval, sorts the flights by departure time, and outputs a sorted list of all these flights. The number of flights that depart in a given interval of time may change, depending on the time when the information is read. For this reason, the number of flights that the program considers will not be fixed beforehand but, rather, calculated during program execution. The program reads information concerning every departing flight and stores the number of departing flights in an integer variable called `NbFlights`. Furthermore, our program needs two other variables: `Departures`, which contains the information concerning the departing flights (array of records), and `SortedFlights`, which contains the information about the sorted flights. The main subproblems to be solved are shown in Figure 11.9.

The procedure `ReadInfo` reads the information about the departing flights and returns by reference the number of flights read and the array `Departures`. The procedure `SortFlights` receives as parameters the number of flights and the array of departing flights and returns by reference an array containing information about the sorted flights. The procedure `WriteFlights` receives as parameters the number of flights, the array of departing flights, and the array that contains information about the sorted order of flights and outputs the flights sorted by departure time. Again, notice the advantage of procedural abstraction: We know what our procedures will do, we can write a program that uses them (the program in Figure 11.9), but we don't yet know how they will do their job.

Before we start working on these procedures, let us define the information about a given flight. The information concerning each flight contains the flight number (`FlightNb`, represented by a string), the name of the airline (`Airline`, represented by a string), the city of destination (`Destination`, represented by a string), the departure time (`DepTime`, represented by hours and minutes), and the gate number (`Gate`, represented by an integer). This information is stored in the record `FlightInfo`,

FIGURE 11.10 Information concerning one flight.

```
type FlightID = packed array [1..FIDLimit] of char;
     Word = packed array [1..WLimit] of char;

     FlightInfo = record
                      FlightNb    : FlightID;
                      Airline     : Word;
                      Destination : Word;
                      DepTime     : Time;
                      Gate        : integer
                  end; { FlightInfo }

     FlightList = array [1..FLimit] of FlightInfo;
```

shown in Figure 11.10. The information concerning the departing flights is stored in an array, `Departures` (of type `FlightList`), whose elements are of type `FlightInfo`.

The procedure `ReadInfo` reads the information concerning every departing flight and returns (by reference) the number of flights read and the array `Departures`. This procedure, shown in Figure 11.11, assumes that the information concerning several flights is supplied in the following way: Each flight is represented in a single line; in the first five positions of this line, we find the flight number; the airline is separated from the flight number by a single blank (thus the statement `read(blank)` of procedure `ReadFlight`) and occupies twelve characters; the destination city, separated from the airline by a single blank, occupies twelve characters; finally, we have two integer numbers that represent the departure time (the departure time is supplied as an integer containing the hours and minutes of the departing time—for example, 2345 represents 23 hours and 45 minutes, that is, 11:45 PM) and the gate number, respectively. Figure 11.12 shows an example of information concerning departing flights.

The flights are sorted by the procedure `SortFlights` (Figure 11.13). To sort the flights, we use the selection sort. The selection-sort procedure used by this program is different from the selection-sort procedure presented in Chapter 10 in two respects: It is recursive; it does not change the position of the elements to be sorted. Rather, it returns another array, `SortedFlights`, containing an indication of the sorted order of the elements in the original array. The first element of the array `SortedFlights` contains the position (index) in the array `Departures` of the earliest departing flight, the second element of the array `SortedFlights` contains the index of the second earliest departing flight in the array `Departures`, and so on.

FIGURE 11.11 A procedure that reads airline departures.

```
procedure ReadInfo (var NbFlights : integer;
                    var Departures : FlightList);
{ This procedure reads all the departing flights.
  It returns by reference the number of departing
  flights (NbFlights) and an array containing the
  departing flights (Departures) }

   procedure ReadFlight (N : integer);
   var Gt, DepTime, i : integer;
       Airl, Dest : Word;
       FlightNb : FlightID;
       blank : char;
   begin
     for i := 1 to FIDLimit do read(FlightNb[i]);
     read(blank);
     for i := 1 to WLimit do read(Airl[i]);
     read(blank);
     for i := 1 to WLimit do read(Dest[i]);
     readln(DepTime,Gt);

     Departures[N].FlightNb := FlightNb;
     Departures[N].Airline := Airl;
     Departures[N].Destination := Dest;
     Departures[N].DepTime.Hours := DepTime div 100;
     Departures[N].DepTime.Min := DepTime mod 100;
     Departures[N].Gate := Gt
   end; { ReadFlight }

begin { ReadInfo }
  NbFlights := 0;
  while not eof do
    begin
      NbFlights := NbFlights + 1;
      ReadFlight(NbFlights)
    end
end; { ReadInfo }
```

FIGURE 11.12 Information concerning departing flights.

```
QT714 QANTAS       SYDNEY      1225 3
TP312 TAP          NEW YORK    1330 4
TP450 TAP          LONDON      1745 22
AZ123 ALITALIA     ROME        1112 19
TP402 TAP          PARIS       1024 12
TP572 TAP          FRANKFURT   1215  7
TW901 TRANS WORLD  NEW YORK     935 22
AF127 AIR FRANCE   PARIS/ORLY  1420 8
BA425 BRITISH AIR  LONDON      2112 25
BA712 BRITISH AIR  LONDON      2009 5
RG757 VARIG        SAO PAULO   020 22
TP397 TAP          RIO DE JANEI 102 16
CP277 CP AIR       TORONTO     1045 10
SA221 SAS          STOCKHOLM    930 1
TP304 TAP          MONTREAL    1400 12
IB351 IBERIA       MADRID      1735 35
SR234 SWISSAIR     ZURICH      1200 12
SN703 SABENA       BRUSSELS    1230  4
```

FIGURE 11.13 Procedure to sort departing flights.

```
procedure SortFlights (NbFl : integer;
                       var Departures : FlightList;
                       var SortedFlights : FlightOrder);
{ This procedure sorts by departure time the flights in
  the array Departures and returns by reference an
  array containing an indication of the sorted order of
  the elements in the original array }

var i : integer;

   procedure Sort (First, Last : integer;
                   var Departures : FlightList;
                   var SortedFlights : FlightOrder);
```

(continued)

FIGURE 11.13, *continued.*

```
   var Smallest, i : integer;

      function DepTime(F : FlightInfo) : integer;
      begin
        DepTime := F.DepTime.Hours * 100 + F.DepTime.Min
      end; { DepTime }

      procedure Exchange (var x, y : integer);

   begin { Recursive Selection Sort }
     if First < Last then
       begin
         Smallest := First;
         for i := First + 1 to Last do
           if DepTime(Departures[SortedFlights[i]]) <
              DepTime(Departures[SortedFlights[Smallest]]) then
              Smallest := i;
         Exchange(SortedFlights[First],
                  SortedFlights[Smallest]);
         Sort(First + 1, Last, Departures, SortedFlights)
       end
   end; { Sort }

begin { SortFlights }
  { Initialize the array SortFlights }
  for i := 1 to NbFl do SortedFlights[i] := i;
  { Sort the flights }
  Sort(1, NbFl, Departures, SortedFlights)
end; { SortFlights }
```

Again, the procedure `SortFlights` receives the argument `Departures` by reference for efficiency reasons: Passing arrays by reference is much more efficient than passing arrays by value.

Finally, the procedure `WriteFlights` takes as a parameter the number of departing flights, the array containing the departing flights, and the information concerning the sorted order of the departing flights and outputs the flights sorted by departure time. This procedure, shown in Figure 11.14, uses the fact that the array `SortedFlights` contains the ordering

FIGURE 11.14 Procedure to output the sorted flights.

```
procedure WriteFlights (NbFlights : integer;
                        var Departures : FlightList;
                        var SortedFlights : FlightOrder);
{ This procedure outputs the departing flights sorted by
  departure time. It uses the information contained in the
  array SortedFlights }

var i, j : integer;
begin
  writeln('Flight  Airline        Destination',
          '     Hours   Gate');
  writeln;
  for i := 1 to NbFlights do
    begin
      for j := 1 to FIDLimit do
        write(Departures[SortedFlights[i]].FlightNb[j]);
      write('   ');
      for j := 1 to WLimit do
        write(Departures[SortedFlights[i]].Airline[j]);
      write('   ');
      for j := 1 to WLimit do
        write(Departures[SortedFlights[i]].Destination[j]);
      write('   ');

      write(Departures[SortedFlights[i]].DepTime.Hours:2,':');
      if Departures[SortedFlights[i]].DepTime.Min < 10 then
        write('0',Departures[SortedFlights[i]].DepTime.Min:1)
      else
        write(Departures[SortedFlights[i]].DepTime.Min:2);
      writeln('     ',Departures[SortedFlights[i]].Gate:2)
    end
end; { WriteFlights }
```

of the sorted flights. The `for` loop used by the procedure `WriteFlights` considers every flight. (Notice that `i` goes from `1` to `NbFlights`.) For each flight, it uses the array `SortedFlight` to find out the position in the array `Departures` on which the flight to be written is located and then outputs that flight. It is a good programming principle to keep the input and output in modular procedures, distinct from the data manipulation.

Figure 11.15 presents the complete program that we have been discussing, and Figure 11.16 shows the results produced by this program when it receives the information of Figure 11.12.

FIGURE 11.15 A program to sort flights.

```
program Airport (input, output);

{ This program reads information about the departing flights
  from a given airport and outputs those flights sorted by
  departure time }

const FIDLimit = 5;
      WLimit   = 12;
      FLimit   = 200;

type FlightID = packed array [1..FIDLimit] of char;
     Word = packed array [1..WLimit] of char;

     Time = record
              Hours : integer;
              Min   : integer
            end; { Time }

     FlightInfo = record
                    FlightNb    : FlightID;
                    Airline     : Word;
                    Destination : Word;
                    DepTime     : Time;
                    Gate        : integer
                  end; { FlightInfo }

     FlightList = array [1..FLimit] of FlightInfo;
     FlightOrder = array [1..FLimit] of integer;

var NbFlights : integer;
    Departures : FlightList;
    SortedFlights : FlightOrder;

    { Meaning of the variables:
      NbFlights     - number of departing flights
      Departures    - array of records containing the
                      departing flights
      SortedFlights - array containing the sorted order of the
                      flights in Departures}
```

(continued)

FIGURE 11.15, *continued.*

```
procedure ReadInfo (var NbFlights : integer;
                    var Departures : FlightList);
{ This procedure reads all the departing flights.
  It returns by reference the number of departing
  flights (NbFlights) and an array containing the
  departing flights (Departures) }

   procedure ReadFlight (N : integer);
   var Gt, DepTime, i : integer;
       Airl, Dest : Word;
       FlightNb : FlightID;
       blank : char;
   begin
     for i := 1 to FIDLimit do read(FlightNb[i]);
     read(blank);
     for i := 1 to WLimit do read(Airl[i]);
     read(blank);
     for i := 1 to WLimit do read(Dest[i]);
     readln(DepTime,Gt);

     Departures[N].FlightNb := FlightNb;
     Departures[N].Airline := Airl;
     Departures[N].Destination := Dest;
     Departures[N].DepTime.Hours := DepTime div 100;
     Departures[N].DepTime.Min := DepTime mod 100;
     Departures[N].Gate := Gt
   end; { ReadFlight }

begin { ReadInfo }
  NbFlights := 0;
  while not eof do
    begin
      NbFlights := NbFlights + 1;
      ReadFlight(NbFlights)
    end
end; { ReadInfo }
```

(continued)

FIGURE 11.15, *continued.*

```
procedure SortFlights (NbFl : integer;
                       var Departures : FlightList;
                       var SortedFlights : FlightOrder);
{ This procedure sorts by departure time the flights in
  the array Departures and returns by reference an
  array containing an indication of the sorted order of
  the elements in the original array }
var i : integer;

   procedure Sort (First, Last : integer;
                   var Departures : FlightList;
                   var SortedFlights : FlightOrder);
   var Smallest, i : integer;

      function DepTime(F : FlightInfo) : integer;
      begin
        DepTime := F.DepTime.Hours * 100 + F.DepTime.Min
      end; { DepTime }

      procedure Exchange (var x, y : integer);
      var temp : integer;
      begin
        temp := x;
        x := y;
        y := temp
      end; { Exchange }

  begin { Recursive Selection Sort }
    if First < Last then
      begin
        Smallest := First;
        for i := First + 1 to Last do
          if DepTime(Departures[SortedFlights[i]]) <
             DepTime(Departures[SortedFlights[Smallest]]) then
             Smallest := i;
        Exchange(SortedFlights[First],
                 SortedFlights[Smallest]);
        Sort(First + 1, Last, Departures, SortedFlights)
      end
  end; { Sort }
```

(continued)

FIGURE 11.15, *continued.*

```
begin { SortFlights }
  { Initialize the array SortFlights }
  for i := 1 to NbFl do SortedFlights[i] := i;
  { Sort the flights }
  Sort(1, NbFl, Departures, SortedFlights)
end; { SortFlights }

procedure WriteFlights (NbFlights : integer;
                        var Departures : FlightList;
                        var SortedFlights : FlightOrder);
{ This procedure outputs the departing flights sorted by
  departure time. It uses the information contained in the
  array SortedFlights }

var i, j : integer;
begin
  writeln('Flight  Airline        Destination',
          '     Hours   Gate');
  writeln;
  for i := 1 to NbFlights do
    begin
      for j := 1 to FIDLimit do
        write(Departures[SortedFlights[i]].FlightNb[j]);
      write('   ');
      for j := 1 to WLimit do
        write(Departures[SortedFlights[i]].Airline[j]);
      write('   ');
      for j := 1 to WLimit do
        write(Departures[SortedFlights[i]].Destination[j]);
      write('   ');
      write(Departures[SortedFlights[i]].DepTime.Hours:2,':');
      if Departures[SortedFlights[i]].DepTime.Min < 10 then
        write('0',Departures[SortedFlights[i]].DepTime.Min:1)
      else
        write(Departures[SortedFlights[i]].DepTime.Min:2);
      writeln('     ',Departures[SortedFlights[i]].Gate:2)
    end
end; { WriteFlights }
```

(continued)

FIGURE 11.15, *continued.*

```
begin
  ReadInfo(NbFlights, Departures);
  SortFlights(NbFlights, Departures, SortedFlights);
  WriteFlights(NbFlights, Departures, SortedFlights)
end. { Airport }
```

FIGURE 11.16 Output produced by the program in Figure 11.15.

```
Flight  Airline        Destination     Hours   Gate

RG757   VARIG          SAO PAULO        0:20    22
TP397   TAP            RIO DE JANEI     1:02    16
SA221   SAS            STOCKHOLM        9:30     1
TW901   TRANS WORLD    NEW YORK         9:35    22
TP402   TAP            PARIS           10:24    12
CP277   CP AIR         TORONTO         10:45    10
AZ123   ALITALIA       ROME            11:12    19
SR234   SWISSAIR       ZURICH          12:00    12
TP572   TAP            FRANKFURT       12:15     7
QT714   QANTAS         SYDNEY          12:25     3
SN703   SABENA         BRUSSELS        12:30     4
TP312   TAP            NEW YORK        13:30     4
TP304   TAP            MONTREAL        14:00    12
AF127   AIR FRANCE     PARIS/ORLY      14:20     8
IB351   IBERIA         MADRID          17:35    35
TP450   TAP            LONDON          17:45    22
BA712   BRITISH AIR    LONDON          20:09     5
BA425   BRITISH AIR    LONDON          21:12    25
```

11.5 The `with` statement

The reference to a record element may become extremely long. To compensate for this fact, Pascal supplies a special statement that allows easy access to several fields of a given record: the `with` statement. The syntax of the with statement is defined by the following BNF expressions or, alternatively, by the syntax chart in Figure 11.17.

<with statement> ::= `with` <record variables> `do` <statement>

<record variables> ::= <record variable> |
<record variable> , <record variables>

<record variable> ::= <variable>

The `with` statement allows a reference to a field of a record by mentioning only the name of the field; the name of the record will be taken as the record variable, specified immediately following the word `with`. For example, the procedure `WriteFlights` of Figure 11.14 could have been written using the `with` statement (Figure 11.18).

The specification of more than one variable of record type in a `with` statement has the same effect as the use of nested `with` statements. So, the procedure `WriteFlights` could have been written using a `with` statement with two records (Figure 11.19).

FIGURE 11.17 Syntax chart for the with statement.

with statement

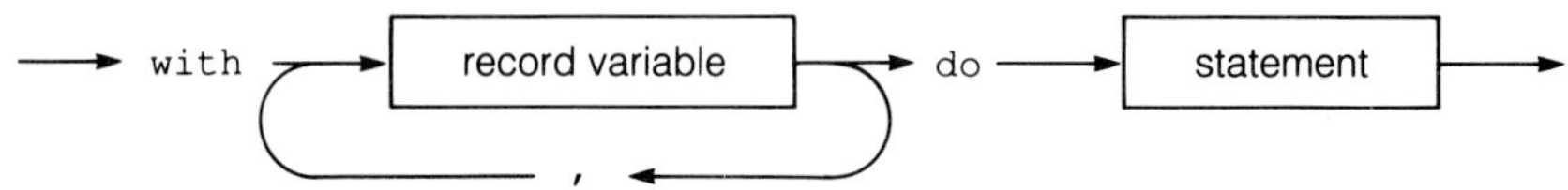

FIGURE 11.18 An example of `with` statements.

```
procedure WriteFlights (NbFlights : integer;
                        var Departures : FlightList;
                        var SortedFlights : FlightOrder);
{ This procedure outputs the departing flights sorted by
  departure time. It uses the information contained in the
  array SortedFlights }

var i, j : integer;
begin
  writeln('Flight  Airline        Destination',
          '     Hours   Gate');
  writeln;
  for i := 1 to NbFlights do

      with Departures[SortedFlights[i]] do
      { All the field names in this "with" statement
        refer to the record Departures[SortedFlights[i]] }

           with DepTime do
           { All the filed names in this "with" statement
             refer to the record Departures[SortedFlights[i]].DepTime }

              begin
                for j := 1 to FIDLimit do write(FlightNb[j]);
                write('   ');
                for j := 1 to WLimit do write(Airline[j]);
                write('   ');
                for j := 1 to WLimit do write(Destination[j]);
                write('   ');
                write(Hours:2,':');
                if Min < 10 then
                   write('0',Min:1)
                else
                   write(Min:2);
                writeln('      ',Gate:2)
              end
end; { WriteFlights }
```

FIGURE 11.19 `with` statement with two records.

```
procedure WriteFlights (NbFlights : integer;
                        var Departures : FlightList;
                        var SortedFlights : FlightOrder);
{ This procedure outputs the departing flights sorted by
  departure time. It uses the information contained in the
  array SortedFlights }

var i, j : integer;
begin
  writeln('Flight  Airline        Destination',
          '     Hours   Gate');
  writeln;
  for i := 1 to NbFlights do
      with Departures[SortedFlights[i]], DepTime do
           begin
             for j := 1 to FIDLimit do write(FlightNb[j]);
             write('    ');
             for j := 1 to WLimit do write(Airline[j]);
             write('    ');
             for j := 1 to WLimit do write(Destination[j]);
             write('    ');
             write(Hours:2,':');
             if Min < 10 then
                write('0',Min:1)
             else
                write(Min:2);
             writeln('      ',Gate:2)
           end
end; { WriteFlights }
```

Summary

This chapter introduced the data structure `record`. A record is a collection of elements that may be of different types, which are accessed by supplying the name of the record and the name of the field that stores the desired element. All elements of the record are stored under the same name; the field that follows the name is what differentiates them and makes them distinct.

We saw that a single record is usually not very useful and that an important structure consists of having arrays of records. We developed a complete application that uses arrays of records and introduced the `with` statement.

Suggested readings

You can explore the topics presented in this chapter more deeply by consulting the following books:

Pratt, T. 1975. *Programming Languages: Design and Implementation.* Englewood Cliffs, NJ: Prentice-Hall.
This book presents a good discussion of the concept of a record, how it is used in several programming languages, and how records are stored in memory.

Wirth, N. 1976. *Algorithms + Data Structures = Programs.* Englewood Cliffs, NJ: Prentice-Hall.
This book describes in great detail the concept of a record and its representation in main memory.

Exercises

1. ? Write a Pascal program that reads a text and produces an alphabetized list of every word in the text, followed by the number of times that that word appeared in the text. HINT: Use the record

```
WordRep  = packed array [1..20] of char;
WordInfo = record
               word  : WordRep;
               count : integer
           end; { WordInfo }
```

to store information about the occurrence of words and to create an array of `WordInfo`. Decide whether this array should contain the words already sorted. Both approaches have advantages and disadvantages. Try to see what they are.

2. ✓ Consider the following declaration in a Pascal program:

```
type    Word        =  array [1..50] of char;
        Line        =  packed array [1..132] of char;
        Numbers     =  array [1..30] of integer;
        IndexEntry  =  record
                             Key  : Word;
                             Occs : integer;
                             Pags : Numbers
                         end; { IndexEntry }
         IndexRep    =   array [1..100] of IndexEntry;
         BookRep     =   record
                             Title : Line;
                             Index : IndexRep
                         end; { BookRep }
         ClassRep    =   array [1..400] of BookRep;
         LibRep      =   array [1..10000] of ClassRep;

var      Index       :   IndexRep;
         Lib         :   LibRep;
```

For each of the following Pascal identifiers, either list its type or explain why the identifier does not make sense.

a. `Index [4]`
b. `Index [4].Pags`
c. `Index.Title`
d. `Index[45].Occs`
e. `Lib [500]`
f. `Lib [500].Title`
g. `Lib [500][200]`
h. `Lib [500,200]`
i. `Lib [500,200].Title[50]`
j. `Lib [500][200].Title[50]`

3. ! Define a record called `CarInfo` containing the following information about cars: `make` (a string containing up to fifteen characters), `model` (a string containing up to fifteen characters), and `year` (an integer between 1900 and 1987). Declare `car` to be an array variable of up to thirty records of type `CarInfo`. Write a Pascal program that does the following:

a. It reads information about thirty cars.

b. It sorts the information, concerning the cars read, by year of manufacture. If there are more than two cars built in the same year, they are sorted by their manufacturer; if there is more than one car with the same year and built by the same manufacturer, they are sorted by their model. (HINT: Use bubble sort.)
c. It prints a list of the cars read, sorted by year, make, and model.

4. **?** Define a record to represent a chessboard. A chessboard is an eight-by-eight board in which the following pieces can be placed: pawn, knight, bishop, rook, queen, and king. Remember, also, that a given square can either have a piece or be empty.
5. **?** Consider the following definition of a record:

```
type     PartRep = packed array [1..20] of char;
         PartInfo = record
                      PartNumber : integer;
                      PartName   : PartRep;
                      Price      : real;
                      Quantity   : integer
                    end; {PartInfo}
         Parts = array [1..10000] of PartInfo;
var      Inventory : Parts;
```

Write statements that assign the `PartNumber`, `PartName`, `Price`, and `Quantity` to the tenth item of `Inventory`
a. Without the `with` statement.
b. Using the `with` statement.

6. **?** Using Pascal, define a standard deck of cards. A card may be represented as a record containing the suit (spades, hearts, diamonds, clubs) and a face value (A, 2, 3, 4, 5, 6, 7, 8, 9, 10, J, Q, K). A deck of cards is an array of cards. Write a Pascal program using your representation of a deck of cards that initializes the deck—that is, assigns a suit and a face value to every card of the deck.
7. **!** Using the deck of cards of the previous exercise and the function `random` of Chapter 9, write a Pascal program that shuffles the cards in the deck and gives five cards to each one of a group of poker players. The number of players is read by the program.
8. **?** Suppose that you are asked to write a Pascal program to manipulate information concerning the books in a library. Each book in the library is represented by the following information: ISBN (a thirteen-character code), a title, a list of authors (decide on the maximum number of authors recorded per book), publisher, year of publication, edition, room where the book can be found, and shelf location. Define the type `Book` in Pascal and declare a variable to represent a library.

9. **?** Using the data structure of the previous exercise, write a Pascal program that interacts with a user of the library. The user may ask for a book by title or by author (decide what the interaction between the user and the program should be). The program supplies the room and shelf location where the book (or books—suppose that an author writes more than one book) can be found or an appropriate message if the book does not exist in the library.

10. **!** In Pascal we can implement character strings using the following record:

```
SRep = array [1..MaxLen] of char;
String = record
            Length : integer;
            S      : SRep
         end; { String }
```

in which `Length` contains the length of the string, `MaxLen` represents the length of the largest string, and `S` is an array that stores the string. Based on this representation write the following procedures:

a. `Concat`: This procedure takes two strings and computes the string obtained by concatenating them. For example, the result of concatenating `Air` and `port` is `Airport`. Make sure that your procedure handles overflow.

b. `Substring`: This procedure takes a string and two integers (say, `i` and `j`) and computes another string contained between positions `i` and `j`. For example, if the string is `Airport`, `i = 2`, and `j = 4`, then the result would be the string `irp`. Make sure that your procedure produces appropriate error messages.

c. `Match`: This function takes two strings and returns the starting position of the first string where a match can be found for the record string. For example, if the first string is `Airplane` and the second string is `Plane`, then `Match` will return 4; if the first string is `Computer Science` and the second string is `Sci`, then `Match` will return `10`; if the first string is `Computer Science` and the second string is `Computers`, then `Match` will return `0`, meaning that no match was found.

CHAPTER 12

This chapter discusses the data structure set, presents the operations associated with it, and shows some examples of programs using sets, stressing the advantages of this data structure.

STRUCTURED DATA TYPES 3: SETS

As they were lying on their faces, and the pattern on their backs was the same as the rest of the pack, she could not tell whether they were gardners, or soldiers, or courtiers, or three of her own children.
Lewis Carroll, *Alice's Adventures in Wonderland*

So far, we have studied two structured data types: arrays and records. These data types share a common characteristic: We work with them by manipulating the individual elements of the structure; we never work with the entire structure at one time or with a single operation (with the exception of packed arrays).[1] Notice that this is a limitation of Pascal rather than a limitation of the data types themselves; for example, the language APL works with entire arrays with a single operation.

This chapter introduces a new structured data type, the set. A **set** is a data type that contains a collection of elements. By itself, this does not make it very different from records or arrays. However, the novelty of sets stems from the operations that we can perform on them. We do not index or access specific elements that belong to a set; rather, we work with the entire set as a single structure. Pascal is one of the few high-level languages that supply the set as a predefined data type.

The set concept is a fundamental concept in mathematics. Sets were introduced in the late nineteenth century by Georg Cantor (1845–1918). Set theory has grown as a fundamental branch of mathematics and has

---

1. This is not quite true. We can use assignment in whole arrays and records provided that we assign variables of the same type.

influenced most mathematic concepts. A set is any collection of distinct objects. The objects that belong to the set are **elements of the set.** The mathematic concept of set does not impose any restriction on the number of elements a set may have: It may have no elements at all, or it may have an infinite number of elements. The operations that we can perform with sets are the following:

1. Test whether a given element belongs to (or is a *member* of) a set
2. Test whether a set has any elements (a set with no elements is an *empty set*)
3. Given any two sets, create a new set that contains every element in either of them (this operation is *set union*)
4. Given any two sets, create a new set that contains every element in both of them (this operation is *set intersection*)
5. Given any two sets, create a new set that contains every element that is in the first set but not in the second (this operation is *set difference*)
6. Given any two sets, test whether every element of the first set is also an element of the second set (if this is the case, the first set is *contained in* the second set or is a *subset of* the second set)
7. Given any two sets, test whether they have the same elements (two sets with the same elements are *equal*)
8. Given any two sets, test whether they have no elements in common (in this case, they are *disjoint*)

In mathematics, sets are represented by enclosing their elements in braces— { and } . For example, {a, b, c}, {c, d}, and {d} represent three sets, with three, two, and one elements, respectively; { } represents the empty set. We say that b is a *member* of the set {a, b, c} but is not a member of the set {d}. The *union* of {a, b, c} with {d} is the set {a, b, c, d}. The *intersection* of {a, b, c} with {c, d} is the set {c}. The *set difference* of the sets {a, b, c} and {c, d} is the set {a, b} ({a,b} contains every element of the first set that is not an element of the second set); the set difference of {c,d} and {a, b, c}, however, is {d}. The set {d} is a *subset* of the set {c, d}. The sets {a, b, c}, {c, a, b}, and {a, a, b, b, c, c} are *equal.* The sets {a, b, c} and {d} are *disjoint.*

This chapter presents how sets are defined and used in Pascal. The data type `set` does not seem very important compared to the data types `array` and `record`. As you read this chapter, you may wonder why sets are needed because every operation that we can do with sets can be done without them. However, once you get used to using sets, you may wonder how you could ever have programmed without them.

12.1 Definition of sets in Pascal

Although in mathematics the members of a set can be of any type, in Pascal the elements of a set must belong to a given ordinal type. To define a set in Pascal, we must supply the ordinal type to which the members of the set belong. The definition of a set can be given using only the variable declaration part or using both the type definition part and the variable declaration part. (This book only considers the second approach.) To define a set, we must define a new type as being of set type. A set type is defined by the following BNF expressions or, alternatively, by the syntax chart in Figure 12.1.

<set type> ::= `set of` <base type>

<base type> ::= <simple type>

Once a set type is defined we can declare any variable as being of that type. Figure 12.2 shows the definition of two ordinal types, `Operations` and `Countries`, and based on them, we define the set types `Set-Operation` and `CountrySet`. We also define three other sets (`LetterSet`, `NumberSet`, and `DigitSet`), based on subrange types. Furthermore, Figure 12.2 declares the variables `NewWorld`, `EECCountries`, and `Latin-Countries`, which are of type `CountrySet`. These sets may contain any number—or none—of the countries listed under `Countries`. The variables `FirstOp` and `SecondOp`, which are of type `DigitSet` (sets that may contain any number of digits), are also declared in Figure 12.2.

For implementation reasons, Pascal limits the maximum number of elements that may belong to a set. This number is implementation-dependent. (For example, in Pascal for VAX computers running under the VMS operating system, the maximum number of elements a set may have is 256.) Traditionally, the maximum set size has been equal to the size of the memory cells of the computer where the version of Pascal was implemented. This situation is changing, and the current trend is to define it as the size of available memory (Cooper 1983, p. 121).

FIGURE 12.1 Syntax chart for set type.

set type

→ `set of` → [simple type] →

FIGURE 12.2 Definition of sets.

```
type Operations = (A, S, M, D, R, C);
     Countries = (Austria, Belgium, Bulgaria, Denmark, Finland,
                  France, GreatBritain, Greece, Iceland, Ireland,
                  Italy, Luxembourg, Netherlands, Norway,
                  Portugal, Spain, Sweden, Switzerland,
                  WestGermany, UnitedStates, Canada, Mexico,
                  Brazil, Venezuela);

     SetOperation = set of Operations;
     CountrySet = set of Countries;
     LetterSet = set of 'a' .. 'z';
     NumberSet = set of 1 .. 100;
     DigitSet = set of 0 .. 9;

var  NewWorld, EECCountries, LatinCountries : CountrySet;
     FirstOp, SecondOp : DigitSet;
```

12.2 Using sets in Pascal

Once a set type has been defined, variables of that type may be declared and used in a Pascal program. This section considers how to use variables of set type. In Pascal, we denote a set value using notation borrowed from mathematics, replacing the { and } with [and]. A constant of set type is syntactically defined by the following BNF expressions or, alternatively, by the syntax chart in Figure 12.3.

<set> ::= [<member designator>]

<member designator> ::= <empty> | <elements>

<elements> ::= <element> | <element> , <elements>

<element> ::= <expression> | <expression> . . <expression>

All expressions appearing as elements of a set *must* be of the type defined as the base type of the set. The specification of set elements can either be a single expression whose value determines the corresponding

FIGURE 12.3 Syntax chart for set.

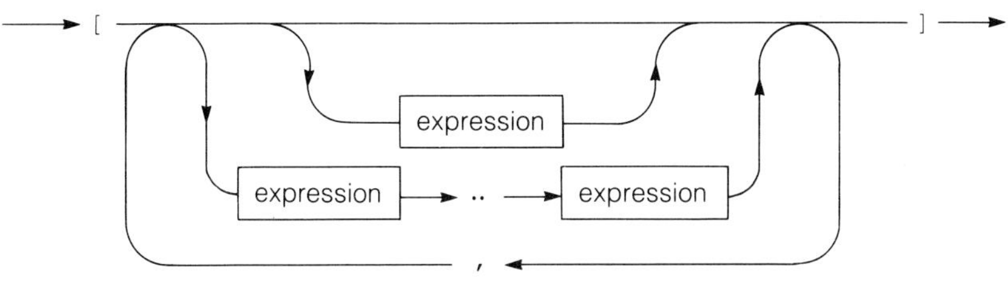

element of the set, or two expressions separated by `..`, which determines a consecutive range of elements for the set. Standard Pascal states that the specification of an element of a set of the form `x .. y` in which `x` > `y` (> should be interpreted as comes after) is illegal. Most implementations, however, take this to represent the empty set. Here are some examples, referring to the definitions shown in Figure 12.2:

1. `[UnitedStates, Canada]` and `[Portugal, West Germany, Italy]` are constants of the type `CountrySet` and have two and three elements, respectively.
2. `[0, 1, 2, 9]` is a set of four elements of type `DigitSet`.
3. `[A]` is a set of one element (also called a **singleton set**) of type `SetOperation`.
4. [] is a set of no elements (the empty set), which may belong to any set type.
5. `[Austria..Finland]` is a set equal to `[Austria, Belgium, Bulgaria, Denmark, Finland]`.
6. `[A..A]` is a set of one element `A`, and thus this set is equal to `[A]`.
7. `[pred (Belgium) .. succ(Denmark)]` is equal to `[Austria .. Finland]`.

Given a variable of type set, we can use the assignment operation to assign any set value to that variable. For example, Figure 12.4 represents possible assignment statements of a Pascal program that uses the declaration shown in Figure 12.2.

FIGURE 12.4 Assigning values to set variables.

```
EECCountries := [Belgium, Denmark, GreatBritain, France,
                 Greece, Ireland, Italy, Luxembourg, Netherlands,
                 Portugal, Spain, WestGermany];

LatinCountries := [France, Italy, Portugal, Spain];

NewWorld := [UnitedStates, Canada, Brazil, Mexico, Venezuela]
```

12.3 Operations on sets

With sets, like any data type, we want to be able to perform more complex operations than simply assigning a value to a variable. In Pascal there are several operators that can be used to manipulate sets. They can be grouped into three different classes:

1. An operator that tests whether a given element belongs to a set. The operator `in` takes as operands an element of a set and a set; it returns `true` if the element belongs to the set and returns `false` otherwise. For example, considering the assignments of Figure 12.4, the expression `Italy in EECCountries` evaluates to `true`, and the expression `Austria in NewWorld` evaluates to `false`.
2. Operators that take as operands two sets and generate a new set. Pascal operators are summarized in Table 12.1. For example, considering the sets defined in Figure 12.4, we have:

```
NewWorld + LatinCountries = [UnitedStates, Canada,
           Brazil, Mexico, Venezuela, France, Italy,
           Portugal, Spain]

EECCountries * LatinCountries = [France, Italy,
               Portugal, Spain]

EECCountries * NewWorld = []

NewWorld - [Brazil, Mexico, Venezuela] =
           [UnitedStates, Canada].
```

TABLE 12.1 Set operators that take as operands two sets and generate a new set.

Operator	*Name*	*Result*
+	Set union	Returns a set whose elements belong to either one of the operands
*	Set intersection	Returns a set whose elements belong to both of the operands
-	Set difference	Returns a set whose elements belong to the first argument of the operator *and* do not belong to the second argument

3. Operators that take as arguments two sets and produce a boolean value. Pascal operators are summarized in Table 12.2. For example, considering the sets defined in Figure 12.4, we have

```
EECCountries = LatinCountries is false;

LatinCountries <= EECCountries is true;

[UnitedStates] >= NewWorld is false.
```

As an application of the set operations, Figure 12.5 shows a program that reads an integer number and outputs how many distinct digits it has. The program makes use of a set called `DigitsInNumber` that contains all the digits found in the number so far. It also keeps an integer variable `DigitCount` that counts the number of different digits found. As an exercise, try to write this program without resorting to sets.

12.4 Case Study: implementation of a calculator

In this section we develop a complete Pascal program that uses sets. This program implements a simple calculator. Our calculator only executes four arithmetic operations on integer numbers, producing integer numbers as a result. It has a set of seventeen keys (with the symbols `1`, `2`, `3`, `4`, `5`, `6`, `7`, `8`, `9`, `0`, `+`, `-`, `x`, `:`, `=`, `C`, and `E`), with which a person communicates with the calculator, and a display, with which the calculator communicates with the

TABLE 12.2 Set operators that take as arguments two sets and produce a boolean value.

Operator	*Name*	*Result*
=	Set equality	Returns `true` if its arguments represent the same set; returns `false` otherwise
<>	Set inequality	Returns `true` if its arguments do not represent the same set; returns `false` otherwise
<=	Subset operator	Returns `true` if its first argument is a subset of its second argument; returns `false` otherwise
>=	Superset operator	Returns `true` if its second argument is a subset of its first argument (that is, the first argument is a *superset* of the second argument); returns `false` otherwise

person. The calculator shows in the display the number that the person is inputting and the result of the operation executed. The calculator has two memories, one to store the first operand of the arithmetic operation and the other to store the operation that is to be performed. When the calculator is turned on, both memories are cleared, and the display shows nothing. The following is a description of the behavior of the calculator for each of the keys pressed:

1. If we press one of the keys `1`, `2`, `3`, `4`, `5`, `6`, `7`, `8`, `9`, or `0`, the digit corresponding to the key pressed is appended to the right of the number being introduced, and the resulting number is shown in the calculator's display.
2. If we press one of the keys `+`, `-`, `x`, or `:`, the calculator memorizes (in the memory containing the first operand) the number shown in the display, memorizes (in the memory containing the operation) the

FIGURE 12.5 A program to count the number of distinct digits.

```
program DigitCounter (input, output);

{ This program computes the number of distinct digits
  in an integer number }

type DigitSet = set of 0 .. 9;

var DigitsInNumber : DigitSet;
    DigitCount, Digit, Number : integer;

    { Meaning of the variables:
      DigitsInNumber  - set that contains the distinct
                        digits that we have seen so far
      DigitCount      - number of distinct digits found
                        so far
      Number          - number whose distinct digits we
                        want to count
      Digit           - digit being considered       }

begin
  writeln('Please write an integer number.');
  writeln('I will tell you how many distinct digits it has');
  readln(Number);

  DigitCount := 0;
  DigitsInNumber := [];
  repeat
    Digit := Number mod 10; { rightmost digit of Number}
    Number := Number div 10; { Number without its rightmost
                               digit                      }
    if not (Digit in DigitsInNumber) then
      begin
        DigitCount := DigitCount + 1;
        DigitsInNumber := [Digit] + DigitsInNumber
      end
  until Number = 0;

  writeln('The number of distinct digits is:',DigitCount:3)
end. { DigitCounter }
```

operation corresponding to the key pressed, and gets ready to accept a new number, showing nothing on the display. If there is already a memorized operation, it shows an indication of an error, the display and both memories are cleared, and the calculator gets ready to accept a new number.

3. If we press key =, the calculator executes the memorized operation on the memorized number (first operand) and the number in the calculator's display (second operand), shows in the display the result of the operation in the display, clears both memories, and is ready to accept new information. If there is no memorized number (and thus no memorized operation), it shows an indication of an error, the display and both memories are cleared, and the calculator gets ready to accept a new number. If the memorized operation is : and the number in the display is 0, then it shows an indication of an error, the display and both memories are cleared, and the calculator gets ready to accept a new number.
4. If we press key `C`, the calculator clears the display, the memorized operation, and the memorized number and gets ready to accept a new number, showing nothing in the display.
5. If we press key `E`, the calculator terminates the execution.

When our calculator is turned on, it clears the display and both memories and shows nothing on the display. Then it goes into a loop in which it accepts information from the keyboard and executes the action corresponding to the key pressed. This loop is repeated until the calculator is turned off, that is, when key `E` is pressed.

Let us first turn our attention to the representation of the information needed by the calculator: the calculator's memories and display. The memory that stores the first operand of the arithmetic operations should contain information about whether there is anything stored in the memory and, if so, the value stored. The memory that stores the operation to be performed should contain information about whether there is any operation stored and, if so, the operation to be performed. The display should contain information about whether a number is being entered and, if so, the number being entered. The display and the memory that stores the operand need the same kind of information. They are represented as a record called `Register`, with two fields: The field labeled `HasValue` contains information about whether there is anything stored in the register; the field labeled `Value` contains the value stored in the register (Figure 12.6). The memory that stores the operation to be performed is represented in a similar way, except that the value stored is of type `char` (the representation

FIGURE 12.6 Representation of the display and memory.

```
Register = record
             HasValue : boolean;
             Value    : integer
           end; { Register }
```

FIGURE 12.7 Memory that stores the operation.

```
OpRegister = record
               HasValue : boolean;
               Value    : char
             end; { OpRegister }
```

FIGURE 12.8 Information needed by the calculator.

```
RepCalculator = record
                  Display   : Register;
                  Memory    : Register;
                  Operation : OpRegister;
                  Error     : boolean;
                  ErrMsg    : RepMsg
                end; { RepCalculator }
```

of an operation) instead of type `integer`. Such a record, named `OpRegister`, is shown in Figure 12.7.

There are two other pieces of information needed by our calculator: the information about whether an error occurred and, if so, the appropriate error message to be shown in the display (this latter is of type `RepMsg`, a packed array of fifteen characters). The information in our calculator is represented by a record of type `RepCalculator` (Figure 12.8).

FIGURE 12.9 The calculator's loop.

```
begin
  ClearCalculator;
  DisplayInformation;
  repeat
    WaitFor(Key);
    ExecuteAction(Key)
  until Key = 'E'
end
```

FIGURE 12.10 Waiting for a key to be pressed.

```
procedure WaitFor (var Key : char);
begin
  repeat
    write('? ');
    readln(Key)
  until Key in (Digits + OpKeys)
end; { WaitFor }
```

Figure 12.9 shows a fragment of a Pascal program that simulates the behavior of our calculator. The procedure `ClearCalculator` has the effect of clearing the calculator's display and its two memories. The procedure `DisplayInformation` has the effect of showing the information in the calculator's display and memories. To enhance our understanding of the functioning of the calculator, our program not only shows the calculator's display but also the contents of the calculator's memories.

After clearing the calculator and showing the user the contents of the display and memories (in this case, all are empty), the program goes into a loop that waits for a key to be pressed and executes the action corresponding to that key. This loop is executed until key `E` is pressed.

Let us now turn our attention to the procedure `WaitFor` that waits for the user to press a key. This procedure relies on the existence of two sets: `Digits` and `OpKeys` (Figure 12.10). The set `Digits` contains the digits 0 through 9; the set `OpKeys` contains characters corresponding to every key the machine has except the digits—that is, it contains the characters +, -, x, :, =, C, and E. The procedure WaitFor simply waits for the user to press one of the calculator's keys. We made the decision of displaying a prompt (a question mark) to tell the user that the program is waiting for something. This procedure prompts the user with a question mark and then waits for the user to press a key. After this is done, it checks whether the key pressed is one of the calculator's keys (whether it is in the union of sets Digits and OpKeys). If it is not, the loop is repeated until this condition is satisfied. If the key pressed is in the union of the sets Digits and OpKeys, the procedure WaitFor has completed its work, and the character corresponding to the key pressed is returned (notice that this procedure uses call by reference).

This procedure shows how useful the in operator is in contexts where we have to express an equality test with several alternatives. Thus, writing Key in (Digits + OpKeys) is clearer and, for most implementations, more efficient than the clumsy

```
(Key = '0') or (Key = '1') or (Key = '2') or (Key = '3') or
(Key = '4') or (Key = '5') or (Key = '6') or (Key = '7') or
(Key = '8') or (Key = '9') or (Key = '+') or (Key = '-') or
(Key = 'x') or (Key = ':') or (Key = '=') or (Key = 'C') or
(Key = 'E').
```

The procedure ExecuteAction (Figure 12.11) takes a character corresponding to one of the keys pressed (remember that the procedure WaitFor guarantees that this character does correspond to one of the calculator's keys) and decides what to do with it. If the key pressed was a digit, then this digit is added to the display—procedure call Add(Key, Display). If the key pressed was one of the operators (that is, if it was +, -, x, or :), then it memorizes the operation pressed and memorizes the number in the display. This is achieved through the procedure call MemOpNDisplay. If the key pressed was the equals sign, it performs the memorized operation on the memorized number and the number in the display—procedure call PerformOperation. If the key pressed was C, then it clears the calculator—procedure call ResetCalculator. If the key pressed was E, then it does nothing (this is emphasized by the comment in the program). Again, this procedure shows that, when membership has to be tested, the use of sets greatly simplifies our programs.

Figure 12.12 shows the complete Pascal program that implements the calculator; Figure 12.13 shows a sample interaction using the program in Figure 12.12.

FIGURE 12.11 Executing the action corresponding to the key pressed.

```
procedure ExecuteAction (Key : char);

  procedure Add (Key : char; var Reg : Register);



  procedure MemOpNDisplay (Key : char);



  procedure PerformOperation;



  procedure ResetCalculator;



begin
  if Key in digits then
    Add(Key, display)
  else
    if Key in ['+', '-', 'x', ':'] then
      MemOpNDisplay(Key)
    else
      case Key of
        '=' : PerformOperation;
        'C' : ResetCalculator;
        'E' : {Do nothing}
      end
end; { ExecuteAction }
```

FIGURE 12.12 A program that implements the calculator.

```
program Calculator (input, output);

{ This program implements a simple calculator that
  performs arithmetic operations }

const Digits = ['0' .. '9'];
      OpKeys = ['+', '-', 'x', ':', '=', 'C', 'E'];

type  RepMsg = packed array [1..15] of char;
      Register = record
                   HasValue : boolean;
                   Value    : integer
                 end; { Register }
      OpRegister = record
                     HasValue : boolean;
                     Value    : char
                   end; { OpRegister }
      RepCalculator = record
                        Display   : Register;
                        Memory    : Register;
                        Operation : OpRegister;
                        Error     : boolean;
                        ErrMsg    : RepMsg
                      end; { RepCalculator }

var   Key : char;
      Calc : RepCalculator;

      { Meaning of the variables:
        Key  - character corresponding to the key pressed
        Calc - calculator }

   procedure ClearRegister (var Reg : Register);
   { This procedure deletes the value of the register "Reg" }
   begin
     Reg.HasValue := false
   end; { ClearRegister }

   procedure ClearMemory;
   { This procedure clears the calculator's memory }
   begin
     Calc.Operation.HasValue := false
   end; { ClearMemory }
```

(continued)

FIGURE 12.12, *continued.*

```
procedure ClearCalculator;
{ This procedure resets the calculator }
begin
  ClearRegister (Calc.Display);
  ClearRegister (Calc.Memory);
  ClearMemory;
  Calc.Error := false
end; { ClearCalculator }

procedure DisplayInformation;
{ This procedure displays the information in the
  calculator }
var i : integer;

  procedure WriteSeparator;
  var i : integer;
  begin
    for i := 1 to 25 do write('-');
    writeln
  end; { WriteSeparator }

  procedure WriteRegister (Reg : Register);
  var i : integer;
  begin
    if Reg.HasValue then write(Reg.Value:13)
  end; { WriteRegister }

begin
  WriteSeparator;
  write(' Memory :  ');
  WriteRegister(Calc.Memory);
  writeln;
  write(' Operation: ');
  if Calc.Operation.HasValue then write(Calc.Operation.Value);
  writeln;
  write(' Display:  ');
  if Calc.Error then for i := 1 to 15 do write(Calc.ErrMsg[i])
  else WriteRegister(Calc.Display);
  writeln;
  WriteSeparator;
  writeln
end; { DisplayInformation }
```

(continued)

FIGURE 12.12, *continued.*

```
procedure HandleError (Msg : RepMsg);
{ This procedure displays the error message represented
  by "Msg" and resets the calculator }
begin
  Calc.Error := true;
  Calc.ErrMsg := Msg;
  DisplayInformation;
  ClearCalculator
end; { HandleError }

procedure WaitFor (var Key : char);
{ This procedure waits for a key to be pressed }
begin
  repeat
    write('? ');
    readln(Key)
  until Key in (Digits + OpKeys)
end; { WaitFor }

procedure ExecuteAction (Key : char);
{ This procedure executes the action corresponding
  to a key pressed }

  procedure Add (Key : char; var Reg : Register);

    function Digit (c:char) : integer;
    { This function is given a character representing a digit
      and returns the "Value" of that digit.                  }
    begin
      Digit := ord(c) - ord('0')
    end; { Digit }

begin { Add }
  if Reg.HasValue then
     Reg.Value := 10 * Reg.Value + Digit(Key)
  else
     begin
       Reg.HasValue := true;
       Reg.Value := Digit(Key)
     end;
  DisplayInformation
end; { Add }
```

(continued)

FIGURE 12.12, *continued.*

```
procedure MemOpNDisplay (Key : char);
{ This procedure memorizes the operation
  corresponding to the key pressed and the
  number in the display }
begin
  if Calc.Operation.HasValue then
    HandleError('Duplicated op. ')
  else
    begin
      Calc.Memory := Calc.Display;
      Calc.Operation.HasValue := true;
      Calc.Operation.Value := Key;
      ClearRegister(Calc.Display);
      DisplayInformation
    end
end; { MemOpNDisplay }

procedure PerformOperation;
var result : integer;
begin
  if Calc.Memory.HasValue then
    if (Calc.Operation.Value = ':') and
       (Calc.Display.Value = 0) then
       HandleError('Division by 0   ')
    else
      begin
        case Calc.Operation.Value of
         '+' : result := Calc.Memory.Value +
                         Calc.Display.Value;
         '-' : result := Calc.Memory.Value -
                         Calc.Display.Value;
         'x' : result := Calc.Memory.Value *
                         Calc.Display.Value;
         ':' : result := Calc.Memory.Value div
                         Calc.Display.Value;
        end;
        ClearCalculator;
        Calc.Display.HasValue := true;
        Calc.Display.Value := result;
        DisplayInformation
      end
  else
    HandleError('No Operation    ')
end; { PerformOperation }
```

(continued)

FIGURE 12.12, *continued.*

```
  procedure ResetCalculator;
  begin
    ClearCalculator;
    DisplayInformation
  end; { ResetCalculator }

  begin { ExecuteAction }
    if Key in Digits then Add(Key, Calc.Display)
    else
      if Key in ['+', '-', 'x', ':'] then
        MemOpNDisplay(Key)
      else
        case Key of
          '=' : PerformOperation;
          'C' : ResetCalculator;
          'E' : {Do nothing}
        end
  end; { ExecuteAction }

begin { Calculator }
  ClearCalculator;
  DisplayInformation;
  repeat
    WaitFor(Key);
    ExecuteAction(Key)
  until Key = 'E'
end. { Calculator }
```

FIGURE 12.13 A sample interaction using the program in Figure 12.12.

```
Memory:
Operation:
Display:

? 3

Memory:
Operation:
Display:          3

? 2

Memory:
Operation:
Display:         32

? +

Memory:         32
Operation: +
Display:

? 1

Memory:         32
Operation: +
Display:          1

? =

Memory:
Operation:
Display:         33
```

Summary

This chapter discussed the data type `set` and presented the operations that can be performed on sets. Sets differ from arrays and records in the sense that we work with the entire structure at one time and with a single operation. We presented an example that uses sets and pointed out the advantages of operations with sets.

Suggested readings

You can explore the topics presented in this chapter more deeply by consulting the following publications:

Kennedy, K., and Schwartz, J. 1975. "An Introduction to the Set Theoretical Language SETL." *Journal of Computer and Math with Applications* 1:97–119.
This article discusses the computer language SETL, which is based on set theory.

Pratt, T. 1975. *Programming Languages: Design and Implementation.* Englewood Cliffs, NJ: Prentice-Hall.
Section 3.11 of this book describes sets and discusses their implementation in high-level programming languages. In particular, it explains why we have to limit the number of elements of a set.

Wirth, N. 1976. *Algorithms + Data Structures = Programs.* Englewood Cliffs, NJ: Prentice-Hall.
This book presents the data structure set, shows some examples that use sets, and discusses how sets are implemented in programming languages.

Exercises

1. ? What are the values of the following expressions? If any of them produces an error, explain what is wrong.
   a. `[] - [3, 4, 5]`
   b. `[3, 4] * [3, 4, 5]`
   c. `[3, 4] + [2, 3]`
   d. `([3, 4] - []) * [3]`
   e. `[3] in [3]`
2. ? Write a program that prints all the consonants in a text that are followed by a vowel. The program should use two sets, the set of characters `'A' .. 'Z', 'a' .. 'z'` and the set of vowels.

3. **?** Given these sets

```
S1 := ['a', 'b', 'c']
S2 := ['x', 'y', 'z']
S3 := ['b'..'z']
S4 := ['j'..'s']
```

what are the values of

a. `S1 + S2`
b. `S1 * S3`
c. `S1 - S3`
d. `'b' in (S3 + S4)`
e. `S3 <= S4`
f. `(S1 - ['a']) + S4`
g. `S1 + S2 * S3`
h. `S1 - S2 - S3`
i. `((S1 * S2) + (S3 * S4)) + S3`

4. **!** Write a procedure that receives as parameter a set containing uppercase letters and prints every element of the set. (This is an important exercise because it shows how to perform the same operation over all the elements of a set. Remember that we cannot "pick" individual elements from a set. Instead, for each element of the base domain, we have to test its presence in the set, and, if present, do something with it.)

5. **?** Let `S1` be a set of lowercase letters. Which of the following is (or are) not valid. Why?

```
S1 := S1 + 'a'
S1 := S1 + ['a']
S1 := S1 + {'a'}
```

6. **?** Rewrite the following expressions using set notation:

a. `(i > 5) and (i <= 25)`
b. `(i >= 15) and (i < 30) or (i > 75) and (i <= 80)`
c. `(ch = 'L') or (ch = 'J') or (ch = 'M') or (ch = 'S')`

7. **?** Write the program in Figure 12.5 without using sets. Admire the power of sets.

8. **?** Is the following a legal Pascal expression? Why?

```
17 not in [18, 19, 20]
```

9. **!** Write a function called `SetSize` that takes as argument a set and returns the number of elements of the set.

10. **?** Suppose that you define a set S with the following declaration:

```
S: set of 'a' .. 'c'
```

How many distinct values exist for the set S? List them.

11. **?** Consider the following definitions:

```
type States = (Alabama, Alaska, Arizona, Arkansas,
               California, Colorado, Connecticut,
               Delaware, Florida, Georgia, Hawaii, Idaho,
               Illinois, Indiana, Iowa, Kansas, Kentucky,
               Louisiana, Maine, Maryland, Massachusetts,
               Michigan, Minnesota, Mississippi, Missouri,
               Montana, Nebraska, Nevada, NewHampshire,
               NewJersey, NewMexico, NewYork, NorthCarolina,
               NorthDakota, Ohio, Oklahoma, Oregon,
               Pennsylvania, RhodeIsland, SouthCarolina,
               SouthDakota, Tennessee, Texas, Utah, Vermont,
               Virginia, Washington, WestVirginia,
               Wisconsin, Wyoming);

     US     = set of States;
```

And consider the following declaration of variables:

```
var       AtlanticStates, PacificStates, NorthernStates,
          SouthernStates, AtlanticTimeStates,
          CentralTimeStates, MountainTimeStates, PacificTimeStates,
          CanadianBorderStates, MexicanBorderStates,
          GreatLakesStates : US;
```

Assume that appropriate assignment statements were made in a program, assigning to each variable the corresponding states suggested by the name of the variable. Write expressions whose values are the following:

a. The states in the Pacific time zone that share a border with Canada.
b. The Atlantic states except New York.
c. The states that share a border with either Mexico or Canada.
d. The states that share a border with the Atlantic or the Pacific oceans.
e. The Great Lakes states that share a border with Canada and are located in the Central time zone.
f. The Great Lakes states that share a border with Canada and are *not* located in the Central time zone.

g. Write a procedure (named `WriteStates`) whose argument is a variable of type `US` and that outputs all the states in the set defined by the variable. For example, if `MyFavoriteStates` is a variable of type `US` with the value `[New York, Massachusetts]`, the procedure call `WriteStates(MyFavoriteStates)` produces `[New York, Massachusetts]`. Make sure that your procedure encloses the elements of the set by [and] and separates them by commas.

CHAPTER 13

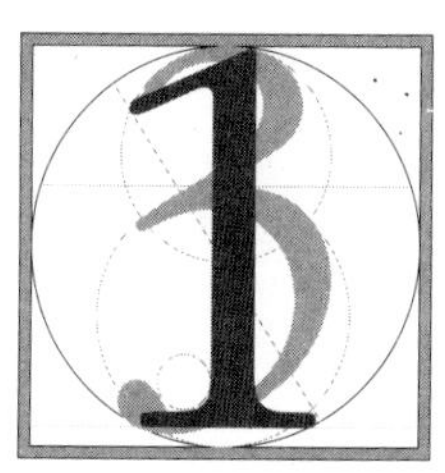

This chapter introduces the concept of a file, discusses the operations that a Pascal program can perform on files, and presents an example of file usage. A file is a structured data type that exists independently of the execution of a program. For this reason, files are used to save the results of the execution of programs.

STRUCTURED DATA TYPES 4: FILES

"They're putting down their names," the Gryphon whispered in reply, "for fear they forget them before the end of the trial."
Lewis Carroll, *Alice's Adventures in Wonderland*

The programs that we developed so far have a single source of input and a single destination for output. Most real-world programs, however, have multiple sources of input and multiple destinations for output. Some of these sources and destinations may need to be saved somewhere in the computer to be used by another program or by the same program at some later time. The typical structure to store this information is called a file. A **file** is a structured data type consisting of a sequence of components all of the same type. In standard Pascal the elements of a file are accessed sequentially—that is, to access the nth element of a file we must first access the $n - 1$ elements that precede it. (In some versions of Pascal, nonsequential file access is also allowed, but these files will not be discussed further here.)

The variables of type `file` are different from the variables that we considered up to now in the sense that their value may exist independently of any program: A file may exist before the execution of a program begins and may remain in existence after the program terminates execution. Files share with arrays the aspect that their elements must be all of the same type; however, they differ from arrays in the method of access to their elements—by position in the case of arrays, and sequentially in the case of files. Files also differ from arrays in the sense that their size may grow and shrink at will during program execution. The main use of files is to record a collection of related information so that it can be used later by another program.

13.1 The `file` type

In Pascal a `file` is defined as an ordered sequence of elements all of the same type. The file type is a structured type defined by the following BNF expressions:

<file type> ::= `file of` <type>

<type> ::= <identifier>

The elements (or components) of a file—corresponding, in the BNF definition of file type, to the nonterminal symbol type—may belong to any type, structured or not, with the exception of file types themselves. In the case of the components of a file being structured types, this restriction extends to the elements that compose the structured types. Figure 13.1 shows examples of the definition of file types and declaration of variables of those types. In this figure, `IntegerFile` is a `file` type whose components are integers; `Grades` is a variable of type `IntegerFile`. `StudentFile` is a `file` type whose elements are `StRecord`. Figure 13.2 shows an example of an illegal definition of a file. Notice that one of the fields of `StRecord`, `Courses`, is itself a file, and thus the file type `Students` contains elements that, in turn, contain files.

Although the variables of type `file` are a kind of variables, they differ from the variables that we have used so far: They cannot appear in an assignment statement; at any moment they can either be inspected or modified, but not both; and they *must* be transmitted by reference to subprograms.

File variables are mainly used through a buffer variable: The declaration of a variable of type `file`, say `MyFile`, automatically introduces a variable, called a **buffer variable** (denoted by `MyFile^`), of the type of the components of `MyFile`. For example, referring to Figure 13.1, the declaration of the variable `Text1` introduces the buffer variable `Text1^` of type `char`. The buffer variable acts as a "window" through which we can access the components of the file. The buffer variable is automatically moved by certain file operations; it corresponds to the input and output pointers discussed in Chapter 6.

FIGURE 13.1 Definition of type `files`.

```
type Name = packed array [1..10] of char;
     StRecord = record
                  StID   : integer;
                  StName : Name
                end; { StRecord }
     IntegerFile = file of integer;
     StudentFile = file of StRecord;
     MyText = file of char;

var Text1, Text2 : MyText;
    Class : StudentFile;
    Grades : IntegerFile;
```

FIGURE 13.2 Illegal definition of a type `file`.

```
{ Illegal definitions }

type Name : packed array [1..10] of char;

     CoursesTaken = record
                      CourseID : Name;
                      Grade    : (A, B, C, D, F)
                    end; { CoursesTaken }

     StRecord = record
                  StID    : integer;
                  Courses : file of CoursesTaken
                end; { StRecord }

     Students = file of StRecord;
```

Figure 13.3 schematically represents a file of characters and the associated buffer variable. Each component of this file is a character, represented inside a square. The buffer variable, represented by an individualized square, has an arrow that points to the character E. If this file was being used by the computer, the only element of the file that could be accessed, at this particular moment, is the character E.

FIGURE 13.3 File of char and its buffer variable.

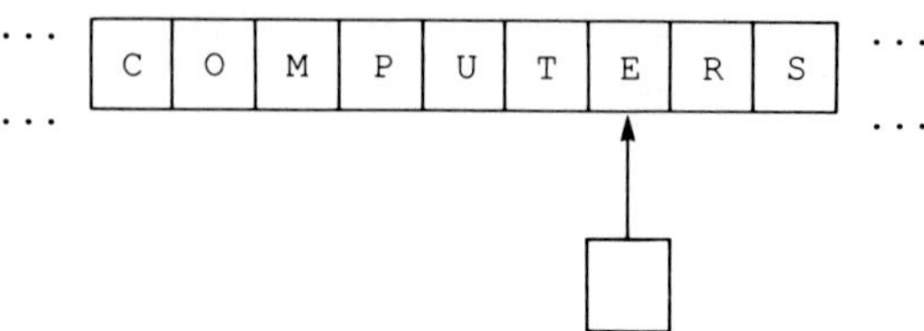

13.2 File operations

All variables that we have considered up to now can be accessed and modified, at any given moment. The variables of the type `file` differ from the other variables in the sense that they must be in one of two different states: They are being used for input (read from the file) or they are being used for output (written into the file). When we use a file we must tell the computer whether we want to input its values or to output into it. Pascal supplies two procedures, `reset` and `rewrite`, to do this:

1. The procedure call `reset(MyFile)`, where `MyFile` is a variable of type `file`, puts `MyFile` in input mode. The buffer variable associated with `MyFile` is placed at the beginning of the file: `MyFile^` contains the first component of the file.
2. The procedure call `rewrite(MyFile)`, where `MyFile` is a variable of type `file`, puts `MyFile` in output mode. The file becomes empty, any previous contents are lost, and the buffer variable associated with `MyFile`, `MyFile^`, becomes undefined.

There are two standard procedures, `get` and `put`, to read information from a file and to write information into a file.

1. The procedure call `get(MyFile)`, where `MyFile` is a variable of type `file` and `MyFile` is in input mode, assigns the file's next component to the buffer variable `MyFile^`. It generates an error if we are at the end of the file `MyFile`. To avoid this error, the function call `eof(MyFile)` should be used.
2. The procedure call `put(MyFile)`, where `MyFile` is a variable of type `file` and `MyFile` is in output mode, appends the buffer variable `MyFile^` to the end of `MyFile`. After this operation, the buffer variable becomes undefined, hence the buffer variable must be given a value before the next call to `put`. Notice that `eof` is always `true` for a file being used for output.

FIGURE 13.4 Equivalent operations with `get` and `read`.

`reset(MyFile);`
`Var1 := MyFile^;`
`get(MyFile);`
`Var2 := MyFile^;`
`get(MyFile);`
	`reset(MyFile);`
	`read(MyFile, Var1, Var2);`

FIGURE 13.5 Equivalent operations with `put` and `write`.

`rewrite(MyFile);`
`MyFile^ := Var1;`
`put(MyFile);`
`MyFile^ := Var2;`
`put(MyFile);`
	`rewrite(MyFile);`
	`write(MyFile, Var1, Var2);`

These procedures allow us to manipulate the information on files but are somewhat awkward to use. For example, the operation of reading values from a file and assigning those values to variables requires, if we want to resort to the `get` procedure, two separate and sequential steps: getting the values from the file and assigning the buffer variable to the variable we want to have the value read. We have been using these operations in a single step through the procedure `read`. Likewise, if we want to write values into a file and if we resort to the procedure `put`, we need two sequential operations: copying the output value to the buffer variable and outputting its value through the procedure `put`. Again, the procedure `write` performs these two operations in one single step.

To simplify the use of files in Pascal, the procedures `read` and `write` can be used to read from and write into files. Assuming that `MyFile` is a variable of type `file` and that `Var1` and `Var2` are of the same type as the components of `MyFile`, then Figure 13.4 shows equivalent input operations using `get` and `read`. Notice that after the procedure call `reset(MyFile)` the buffer variable contains the first component of the file, and thus we can use the assignment statement `Var1 := MyFile^` to assign to `Var1` the first component of `MyFile`. We then move the buffer variable `MyFile^` and assign its next value to `Var2`. Because the buffer variable now becomes undefined, it is a good practice to move it to the next component of the file as shown in Figure 13.4.

Figure 13.5 shows equivalent output operations using `put` and `write`. As an exercise, follow the statements on the left-hand side of this figure and convince yourself that they are equivalent to those on the right-hand side.

The advantage of using `read` and `write` instead of `get` and `put` is mainly a conceptual simplicity because the manipulation of the buffer variable is hidden. However, the buffer variable may be useful as a "look-ahead" device, to manipulate the values of the file without explicitly assigning a variable to them. Besides, an understanding of `put` and `get` clarifies the use and implementation of files.

As a final remark, whenever reading from a file, make sure that the file is in input mode, and whenever writing into a file, make sure that the file is in output mode.

13.3 Text files

Pascal provides a special kind of file, the textfile, a file of characters. Because textfiles are the most commonly used files, Pascal provides a predefined type, `text`, to denote a textfile. Thus, the following two definitions are equivalent:

```
MyText = file of char
MyText = text
```

Besides the file operations discussed in the previous section, there are three operations that can *only* be performed on textfiles: `readln`, `writeln`, and `eoln`. These operations are related with a special character that can be stored in textfiles, the end-of-line character, represented by `[EOLN]`. If `MyFile` is a textfile, the function `eoln(MyFile)` is `true` just in case the buffer variable `MyFile^` contains the character `[EOLN]`. (At this point, you should review Section 6.2, which contains an early introduction to the input and output operations as well as to the use of the functions `eof` and `eoln`.) Figure 13.6 shows a textfile with two lines (as an exercise, convince yourself about this fact). The buffer variable associated with this file "points" to the character `R`.

In textfiles we can store not only characters but also `integer` and `real` values. The computer automatically translates from the character string representation of the number to their internal representation and vice versa. However, if you have a file of `integer` or `real`, you should declare it as such (and not as a textfile) because this automatic translation places an extra burden on the execution of the program.

FIGURE 13.6 Textfile with two lines.

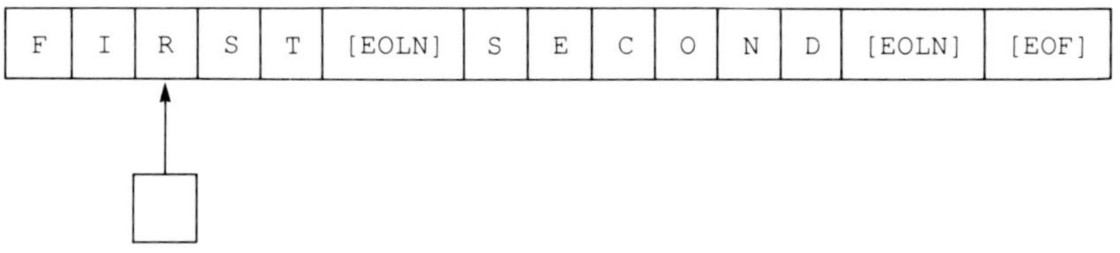

13.4 External and internal files

Taking into account the lifetime of a `file` variable, we can divide them into two distinct groups: internal and external files. **Internal files** are files whose existence is limited to the execution of the block where they are declared. The lifetime of internal files is no different from the lifetime of any variable used up to now. **External files,** however, exist independently of a program's execution: They may exist before the execution of the program that uses them and remain in existence (maybe after some modification is performed upon them) after the execution of the program that uses them.

A Pascal external file should be created by a Pascal program. In some operating systems (for example, in VAX/VMS), it cannot be created or modified by the computer's text editor. In these operating systems, it can neither be printed nor inspected using the computer's standard programs because a Pascal external file has a specific internal structure, known only by Pascal. There is one exception to these limitations, however: textfiles. A Pascal textfile can be created, modified, or printed using the computer's standard editor and printing commands.

External files are named as file identifiers in the program header (see Chapter 3). Every file identifier, besides `input` and `output`, that appears in the program's header represents an external file. This identifier *must* be declared as a file in the variable declaration part of the program. The way these identifiers are linked to the actual files they represent is implementation-dependent and is not discussed here. (For example, in the VAX/VMS operating system, this is done by the statement `open`—see Figure 13.8.) After appearing in the program's header, external files are treated just like ordinary files.

As an example of a program that uses both internal and external files, consider a program to solve the following problem: The Department of Motor Vehicles (DMV) uses a file that contains information about all the registered vehicles, the owners, and the corresponding license plate (this file is sorted by license plate). Everyday there are plates being returned, meaning end of ownership. At the end of the day, the DMV updates its ownership file, removing information about all the vehicles whose plates were returned. This updating is accomplished using two files of different types: a file containing information about ownership (`Registrations`), which will be updated, and a file containing information about the plates returned (`Returns`), which will be used to update the ownership information.

We want to write a program that "filters" the file `Registrations`, removing from it all the ownership registrations corresponding to the plates in the file `Returns`. Because we cannot read and write a single file at the same time, we need an auxiliary file, `Temp`, where the information about ownership will be written during the "filtering" operation. We define a procedure, `Filter`, that takes as parameters the files `Registrations` and `Returns` and produces the file `Temp` with the registration information updated. Afterward, we want to copy the file `Temp` back to the file `Registrations`. Although `Temp` and `Registrations` are of the same type, the assignment

```
Registrations := Temp
```

is not allowed because the file variables cannot appear in assignment statements. To perform the updating, we define a procedure, `Copy`, that takes as arguments two files and copies the first argument to the second argument. Figure 13.7 shows the main subproblems to be solved. In this program, we assume that the file `Returns` is also sorted by license plate. This makes the procedure `Filter` more efficient. For a description of how to sort files, refer to Barron and Bishop (1984), Knuth (1973b), or Wirth (1976).

The complete program is shown in Figure 13.8. Let us first take a look at the information contained in the files `Registrations` and `Returns`. The file `Registrations` contains records of ownership—a relation between a person (owner) and a vehicle (car), represented by a license plate and an expiration date. Figure 13.8 shows the record `Ownership` as well as the definition of the file types `MVFiles` and `PlatesGone`. The files `Registrations` and `Temp` are of type `MVFiles` (a file of `Ownership`); the file `Returns`, which contains the plates that were returned on a particular day, is of type `PlatesGone`.

FIGURE 13.7 Main subprograms.

```
program UpdateOwners (Registrations, Returns);

   ...

begin
  Filter(Registrations, Returns, Temp);
  Copy(Temp, Registrations)
end. { UpdateOwners }
```

FIGURE 13.8 Registration-update program.

```
program UpdateOwners (output, Registrations, Returns);

{ This program updates the file Registrations by removing from
  it all the records whose plate appears in the file Returns.
  If there is a returned plate not in the file Registrations,
  a message is sent to the user }

const WordLen = 5;
      LongWordLen = 15;
      PlateLen = 7;

type Word = packed array [1..WordLen] of char;
     LongWord = packed array [1..LongWordLen] of char;
     PlateType = packed array [1..PlateLen] of char;

     Date = record
              Month : 1..12;
              Day   : 1..31;
              Year  : integer
            end; { Date }
```

(continued)

FIGURE 13.8, *continued.*

```
    Person = record
                Name    : LongWord;
                Address : LongWord
             end; { Person }
    Vehicle = record
                 YearMan : integer;
                 Make    : Word;
                 Typ     : Word;
                 Color   : Word;
                 IDNb    : LongWord
              end; { Vehicle }
    Ownership = record
                   Owner    : Person;
                   Car      : Vehicle;
                   Plate    : PlateType;
                   ExpDate  : Date
                end; { OwnerShip }
    MVFiles = file of Ownership;
    PlatesGone = file of PlateType;

var Registrations, Temp : MVFiles;
    Returns : PlatesGone;

   procedure Filter (var Original : MVFiles;
                     var Returns  : PlatesGone;
                     var Updated  : MVFiles);
   { This procedure "filters" the file Original, removing
     from it all the records whose plate appears in the file
     Returns. It assumes that both Original and Returns are
     sorted by license plate }

   var RegInfo : Ownership;

   begin
     reset(Original);
     reset(Returns);
     rewrite(Updated);
```

(continued)

FIGURE 13.8, *continued.*

```
    while (not eof(Returns)) and (not eof(Original)) do
      begin
        read(Original, RegInfo);
        while RegInfo.Plate < Returns^ do
          begin
            write(Updated, Reginfo);
            read(Original, RegInfo)
          end;
        if RegInfo.Plate = Returns^ then
           { do nothing -- RegInfo deleted }
        else
           writeln('Error ... the plate ,'Returns^,' not in',
                   ' the Registrations file');
        get(Returns)
      end;
      if not eof(Returns) then
         writeln('Error ... there are plates not in the ',
                 'Registrations file');
      while not eof(Original) do
          begin
            write(Updated, Reginfo);
            read(Original, RegInfo)
          end
  end; { Filter }

  procedure Copy (var FromFile, ToFile : MVFiles);
  { Copies the file FromFile to the file ToFile }
  var Item : Ownership;
  begin
    reset(FromFile);
    rewrite(ToFile);
    while not eof(FromFile) do
      begin
        read(FromFile, Item);
        write(ToFile, Item)
      end
  end; { Copy }
```

(continued)

FIGURE 13.8, *continued.*

```
begin
  { The next statement is implementation-dependent - It links
     the file Registrations to the operating system file
     MotorVehicles.dat }
  open(Registrations, 'MotorVehicles.dat', history := old,
       sharing := readwrite);
  { The next statement is implementation-dependent - It links
     the file Returns to the operating system file
     ReturnedPlates.dat }
  open(Returns, 'ReturnedPlates.dat', history := old);

  Filter(Registrations, Returns, Temp);
  Copy(Temp, Registrations)

end. { UpdateOwners }
```

One aspect that is worth noticing about this program concerns the procedure `Filter`. This procedure does not modify the files `Registrations` nor `Returns`, and thus, apparently, they should be transmitted by value. However, this is *not* possible with files because they must be passed by reference; thus, the arguments of this procedure must be passed by reference. Also, notice that because this program does not ask questions to the user, the file `input` does not exist in the program header.

Summary

This chapter introduced the `file` type. A file is a sequential structure whose elements are all of the same type. We can either read or write a Pascal file, but these operations cannot be done simultaneously.

In a file we can move toward the end of the file, one component at a time, but the only way to move toward the beginning of the file is through the procedure `reset`. The procedure `rewrite` creates a brand new file, and the computer gets ready to write information into it.

In Pascal there is a distinguished type of files, textfiles, that, unlike ordinary files, can be created, modified, or inspected by the computer's text editor and printing routines. Besides, textfiles allow the use of some operations not allowed in ordinary files.

Suggested readings

You can explore the topics presented in this chapter more deeply by consulting the following books:

Tremblay, J., and Sorenson, P. 1976. *An Introduction to Data Structures with Applications.* New York: McGraw-Hill.
Chapter 7 of this book takes a detailed look into files. It covers sequential files, indexed sequential files, and direct files and discusses file-access methods and the devices that are used to store files.

Wirth, N. 1976. *Algorithms + Data Structures = Programs.* Englewood Cliffs, NJ: Prentice-Hall.
This book discusses in detail the data type `file` and considers sequential files and methods for sorting files.

Exercises

1. ✓ Give a syntax chart for the file type.
2. ✓ Suppose that we want to assign to `Var1` the first element of `MyFile`. What is wrong with the following piece of code?

```
reset(MyFile);
Get(MyFile);
Var1 := MyFile^;
```

3. ? Suppose that `MyFile` is a file variable and that `Var1` and `Var2` are of the same type as the components of `MyFile`. Rewrite the following sequence of statements using `read` and `write`. If any of them generates an error, explain why.

a.
```
reset(MyFile);
Get(MyFile);
Var1 := MyFile^;
Get(MyFile);
Var2 := MyFile^;
```
b.
```
reset(MyFile);
Var1 := MyFile^;
Get(MyFile);
Var2 := MyFile^;
Get(MyFile);
```
c.
```
reset(MyFile);
Get(MyFile);
Get(MyFile);
Var1 := MyFile^;
Var2 := MyFile^;
```

d.
```
rewrite(MyFile);
MyFile^ := Var1;
Put(MyFile);
MyFile^ := Var2;
Put(MyFile);
```
e.
```
reset(MyFile);
MyFile^ := Var1;
Put(MyFile);
MyFile^ := Var2;
Put(MyFile);
```

4. **?** Give a suitable definition of a file type to hold the student record described in Chapter 11.
5. **?** Using the definition from Exercise 4, write a Pascal program to search an existing file of students for all the students with a given major.
6. **!** Using the definition from Exercise 4, write a Pascal program that takes two student files, sorted by student number, and creates a new file by merging them. The resulting file should be sorted by student number and should contain no duplicates. Whenever a duplicate is found, it should be placed in the file `Duplicates`.
7. **?** Suppose that `MyFile` is the file of Figure 13.6, that `MyFile` is being used for input, and that `int` is a variable of type `integer`. What are the values of `MyFile^`, `eoln(MyFile)`, and `eof(MyFile)` after the execution of each of the following statements?
   a. `Get(MyFile)`
   b. `Get(MyFile); Get(MyFile); Get(MyFile)`
   c. `for int := 1 to 10 do Get(MyFile)`
   d. `for int := 1 to 11 do Get(MyFile)`
8. **?** What is the file produced by the following program? What is the source of the problem?

```
program WrongOne (MyFile);
var MyFile : text;
begin
  rewrite(MyFile);
  writeln(MyFile, 'Here is the first line');
  rewrite(MyFile);
  writeln(MyFile, 'Here is the second line')
end. { MyFile }
```

9. **!** How can you insert something in the middle of a file? Notice that when you call the procedure `rewrite`, the contents of the file are erased. (HINT: Use an auxiliary file.)

10. **!** Write a word-processing program in Pascal. Your program should ask the user the name of the file that contains the source text (text and word-processor commands) and the name of the file that contains the final text (because these operations are implementation-dependent, refer to your local Pascal manual and find out how this can be done). Then begin the word-processing task, generating text with the following default values:

a. Each page has room for 66 lines.
b. The number of lines printed on each page is 58.
c. The left margin begins at column 9.
d. The right margin ends at column 79.
e. Single spacing (no blank lines inserted between the lines of text).
f. The pages are automatically numbered, their number being placed at the upper-right corner of the page.
g. Paragraphs (indicated in the source file by a line beginning with a blank) are indented 8 positions to the right and separated from the previous text by a blank line.
h. Each line of text begins at the left margin and ends on or before the right margin.

These default values can be changed by giving commands to the word processor. Each command is written on a separate line and has a $ on the first column. The commands available are

`$ nl`

which causes the beginning of a new line.

`$ jp` <n>

The nonterminal symbol n represents a positive integer. This command causes the insertion of n blank lines. It takes spacing into account.

`$ ce` <text>

The nonterminal symbol text represents a string of characters. This command skips to the next line and centers the string represented by the nonterminal symbol on the page.

`$ fi`

After execution of this command, each line of text begins at the left margin and ends at the right margin, although the number of characters per line may vary from line to line. The word processor justifies text by padding short lines with extra spaces to make the right margin flush.

`$ nf`

After execution of this command, each line begins at the left margin and ends at or before the right margin. No padding is done.

$ rm <n>

The nonterminal symbol n represents a positive integer. After execution of this command, the right margin becomes the column n. If the value of n is less than or equal to the value of the left margin, the word processor generates an error message and ignores this command.

$ lm <n>

The nonterminal symbol n represents a positive integer. After execution of this command, the left margin becomes the column n. If the value of n is greater than or equal to the value of the right margin, the word processor generates an error message and ignores this command.

`$ pa`

This command causes a jump to the beginning of the next page, except if this command is found at the beginning of a page.

(HINT: Use an array of characters to hold the line currently being formed. Your program should get words from the source file. Decide whether they can fit in the current line. If so, add them to the current line; otherwise, flush the line to the output file—maybe after some processing is done—and insert the word read in the next line.)

11. **!** Modify the word-processing program of Exercise 10 with the addition of an automatic, index-generating feature. Some words in your text are to appear in an index at the end of the text. This index contains all the specified words, followed by the page numbers on which they appeared. To signal that a word should be placed in the index, the word is preceded by the symbol @. For example, if we write `This @thing goes in the index`, the word `thing` will be placed in the index. The index will have all its words listed alphabetically. Be careful about punctuation symbols that may be attached to index words. For example, `@thing,` should place the word `thing` in the index, but not `thing,`! (HINT: Use an array of records. Each record contains the index words and the page numbers on which it appeared. Keep this array sorted. It will be easier to decide whether a given word has been placed in the index.)
12. **?** Write a Pascal program that takes as input a file for your word-processing program and counts how many lines and words it contains. Be careful not to count the word-processing commands as words.
13. **?** Suppose that `MyFile` is a textfile. Using the functions `get` and `eoln`, write a piece of a program that is equivalent to the statement

readln(MyFile). Remember that after this statement the buffer variable is placed immediately after the first occurrence of the character [EOLN].

14. **?** In Section 10.5 we discussed a program to supply phone numbers. A program of this kind typically uses a file that contains names and the corresponding phone numbers and searches the file when a phone number is requested. Modify the program of Section 10.5 to follow this approach. (HINT: Instead of parallel arrays, you need a file of records.)
15. **?** Modify the program of Exercise 14 so that when a phone number is not found, it asks the user to supply it and stores the appropriate information in the phone numbers file.
16. **?** Redo the program of Section 13.4 (Figure 13.8) assuming that the file Registrations was sorted by last name of the owner. Discuss the disadvantage of this approach.
17. **?** Write a Pascal program that takes two files of the same type and appends the second file to the end of the first file.
18. **!** The circulation department of a magazine has all the information about its subscribers in a file of Subscriber, where Subscriber is defined by the following record:

```
Subscriber = record
                Name    : RepName;
                Street  : RepStreet
                City    : RepName
                State   : RepState
                ZIP     : integer
                ExpDate : Date
             end; { Subscriber }
```

The circulation department wants to produce mailing labels automatically; to send a letter to all subscribers whose subscriptions will expire within the next two months, informing them of the impending expiration; and to delete from the file all those subscribers whose subscriptions have expired. Write a Pascal program that receives the file of subscribers, asks the user what is today's date, and generates labels of the following form

```
****           Jan 89
Santa Claus
15 Happiness Road
White Christmas
Alaska 98765
```

for all subscribers whose subscriptions are in effect (in the upper-right corner of the label, the subscription-expiration date is shown). These labels are stored in the file `Labels`. In addition, it removes all subscribers whose subscriptions have expired and places the corresponding information in the file `Deletions`. It also writes a letter to all those subscribers whose subscriptions will end within the next two months (these will be placed in the file `Letters`).

19. **?** Suppose that the DMV wants to update the ownership information by adding the new registrations that were made on a particular day. Write a Pascal program to update the file `Registrations`.

20. **!** Write a Pascal program for the DMV that takes the file `Registrations`, the file `Returns`, and a file of new registrations and updates the file `Registrations` in one single pass.

CHAPTER 14

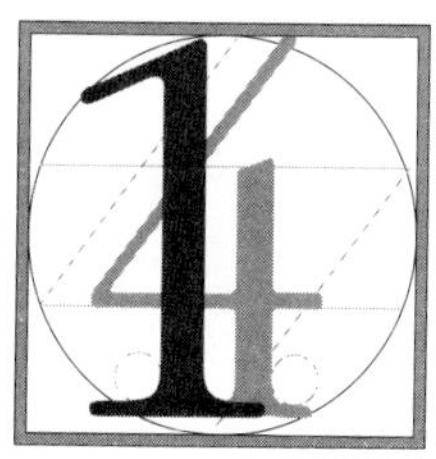

This chapter introduces a data type, the pointer, that enables the creation of structures whose size is not predetermined. We discuss how pointers are created, manipulated, and destroyed, and show some examples of the use of pointers. Techniques of memory management—manual updates (used in Pascal), reference counters, and garbage collection—are presented.

DYNAMIC DATA TYPES: POINTERS

Here's a path that leads straight to it—at least, no, it doesn't do that— . . . but I suppose it will at last. But how curiously it twists!
Lewis Carroll, *Through the Looking Glass*

All the variables discussed so far share a common characteristic: They are **static.** This means that when the execution of the block where the variable is declared begins, the computer allocates a certain amount of storage and associates the name of the variable with that storage area. The values of the variable will be kept in that storage area, which remains allocated as long as the block where the variable was declared is being executed (refer to the discussion of lifetime of a variable in Chapter 9). The value of a variable is accessed by referring to the name of the variable.

This chapter discusses other kinds of variables, called dynamic variables. A **dynamic variable** can be created and destroyed "dynamically" at any point during the execution of a program. Furthermore, the value of a dynamic variable is accessed not by referring to its name but through a link or pointer to the storage area where its value is located.

In Pascal dynamic variables are implemented through the type `pointer`. Pointers are not very interesting by themselves. The great usefulness of pointers is seen when they are considered as the connecting links between the elements of a data structure. This chapter introduces Pascal's type `pointer`, explains how pointers are manipulated, and shows some simple examples that use pointers. Chapters 16–18 present programs that use pointers.

14.1 The notion of a pointer

A **pointer** is something that points. In computer science, a variable of type `pointer` "points" to some location in memory. Whereas with a static variable, we are interested in the value of the variable (that is, the contents of the memory cell associated with the variable); with a pointer variable, we are interested in the *valued pointed to* by the variable. The value of the pointer itself is not our concern.

Suppose that the memory of our computer is composed of ten memory locations, numbered `1` through `10` (Figure 14.1). Furthermore, assume that we are using a program with two variables: `Int`, of type `integer`, and `Ptr`, of type `pointer`; that the value of `Int` is stored in the first memory location and that the value of `Ptr` is stored in the second memory location. If main memory contains the values shown in Figure 14.1, then the value of the variable `Int` is `5`. Because `Ptr` is a pointer variable, we are not interested in the contents of the memory cell that stores the value of `Ptr` but rather in the contents of the memory cell whose address is `6` (the cell "pointed to" by the variable `Ptr`).

FIGURE 14.1 Contents of main memory.

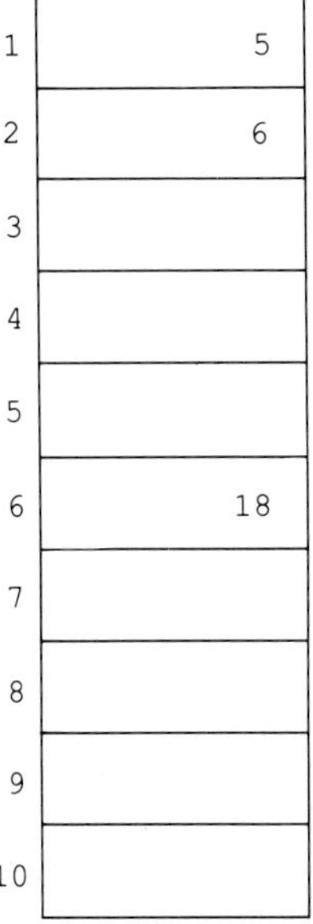

FIGURE 14.2 Pictorial representation of variables.

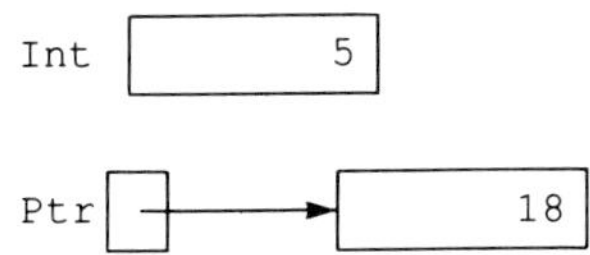

Pictorially, we represent a nonpointer variable by the name of the variable, together with a box that contains the value of the variable; we represent a pointer variable by its name, together with a box that has an arrow pointing to the value of the variable. Figure 14.2 shows the variables `Int` and `Ptr` of our example using this pictorial representation. It is a good practice to resort to these diagrams whenever you directly work with pointers.

14.2 Pointers in Pascal

A pointer variable in Pascal is a variable that is declared to be of pointer type. A pointer type is syntactically defined in the following way.[1]

<pointer type> ::= ^ <type identifier>

The semantics of a definition of the form `type` ptr = ^ basetype is to define a new type, ptr, whose variables are pointers. The variables of this type point to objects of type basetype. For example, the definition

```
type IntPointer = ^integer
```

defines the type `IntPointer`, whose variables point to integer values. This definition is read "The type `IntPointer` is a pointer to an `integer`." The declaration

```
var Iptr :  IntPointer
```

declares a variable, `Iptr`, as being of type `IntPointer`: `Iptr` points to `integer` values. In a block where this declaration is found, the variable

1. Either a circumflex or an up-arrow (↑) can be used in pointer types. Some Pascal implementations use the symbol @ in place of the circumflex.

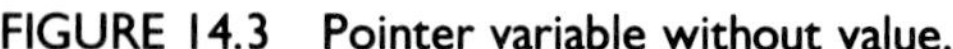

FIGURE 14.3 Pointer variable without value.

Iptr ?

FIGURE 14.4 Pointer variable pointing to a cell without a value.

`Iptr` is created. Even though `Iptr` exists at this time, the value it is pointing to does not yet exist. The declaration `var Iptr: IntPointer` leaves `Iptr` as shown in Figure 14.3, where ? represents *undefined.* A pointer variable is of no use unless there is something to which it can point. To create a cell to which it can point, Pascal has a procedure, `new`, that takes as argument a variable of type `pointer` and creates a variable (of the type pointed to by the pointer variable) to which the pointer variable points. For instance, the statement `new(Iptr)` creates a variable of type `integer` that is pointed to by `Iptr` (Figure 14.4). The value of this variable is undefined.

A variable to which a pointer variable points is called a referenced variable. A **referenced variable** is thus a variable accessed not by name but through a pointer variable. (A referenced variable is also called an **anonymous variable.**) The procedure `new` thus creates a referenced variable (whose value is undefined) that is pointed to by the pointer variable that is the argument of the procedure `new`.[2]

If a referenced variable is anonymous, how do we access it? By using its pointer! A referenced variable is defined in the following way:

<referenced variable> ::= <pointer variable> ^

According to what we just said, `Iptr^` is a referenced variable of type `integer`. So the statement `Iptr^ := 19` has the effect of assigning the

2. The variables created with the procedure `new` remain allocated for the duration of program execution, even if they are created within a subprogram. The only process to deallocate these variables is the procedure `dispose`, discussed in Section 14.4.

FIGURE 14.5 Pointer variable pointing to a cell whose value is 19.

FIGURE 14.6 p1 and p2 have no value.

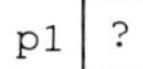

FIGURE 14.7 Both p1^ and p2^ have the value 6.

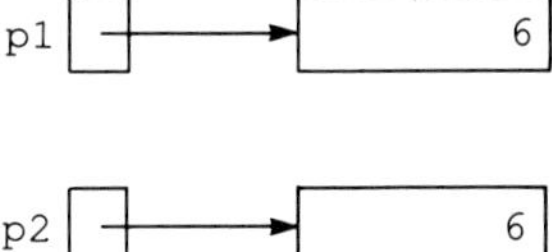

value 19 to the referenced variable Iptr^. After execution of this assignment statement, Iptr points to a cell whose contents are 19 (Figure 14.5).

It is important to distinguish between a pointer variable and the value to which it points (a referenced variable). Let us consider that both p1 and p2 are declared as of type Iptr. The declaration var p1, p2 : Iptr creates two variables, p1 and p2, which are pictorially represented in Figure 14.6. If we execute the statements

```
new(p1);
new(p2);
p1^ := 6;
p2^ := 6;
```

the variable p1 points to a cell containing the value 6 and the variable p2 points to a cell containing the value 6 (Figure 14.7). In this case, the

FIGURE 14.8 `p1` and `p2` point to the same location.

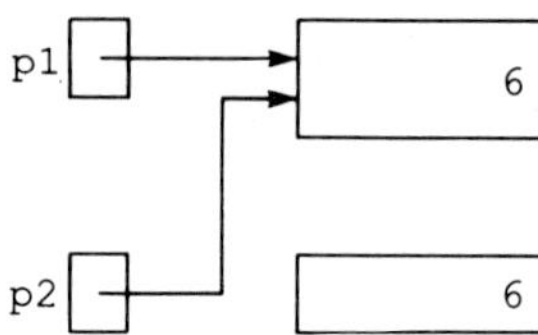

FIGURE 14.9 `p2` now points to a new referenced variable.

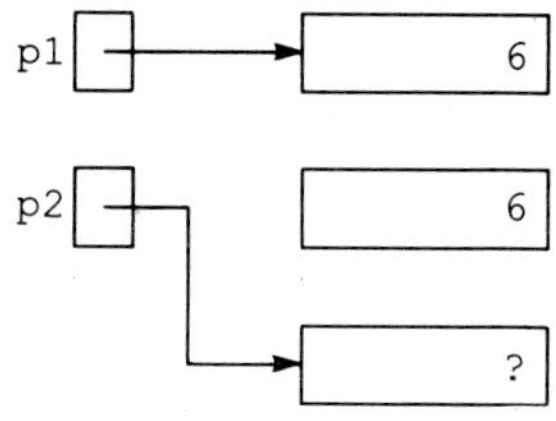

expression `p1^ = p2^` is `true`, but the expression `p1 = p2` is `false` (because `p1` and `p2` point to different cells, and thus the values of the pointer variables themselves are different).

The statement `p2 := p1` has the effect of changing the pointer `p2` so that it points to the same cell that `p1` points to (in other words, they both reference the same variable), as shown in Figure 14.8. Now, both expressions `p1^ = p2^` and `p1 = p2` have the value `true`. There are two aspects worth mentioning about this new situation:

1. Because both `p1` and `p2` point to the same memory location, changing the value pointed to by one of them will have the effect of changing the value pointed to by the other. (Notice that this is what happens when call by reference is used in a subprogram.)
2. The old value of `p2` is no longer accessible. The referenced variable with the value 6 still exists (still occupies memory space), but there is no way we can have access to it. It is called **garbage.**

If the statement `new(p2)` is now executed, it will have the effect of creating a new referenced variable to which `p2` points (Figure 14.9). The value of `p2^` is now undefined. Notice that the value that `p2` used to point to before the assignment `p2 := p1` was not used, but rather a new cell was created.

FIGURE 14.10 A Pascal program that uses pointers.

```
program ExamplePointer (input, output);
type CharPointer = ^char;
var  Cptrl, Cptr2 : CharPointer;
begin
  new(Cptrl);
  Cptrl^ := 's';
  writeln('Cptrl points to: ',Cptrl^);
  new(Cptr2);
  Cptr2^ := 'p';
  writeln('Cptr2 points to: ',Cptr2^);
  Cptr2^ := Cptrl^;
  writeln('Cptrl points to: ',Cptrl^,', Cptr2 points to: ',Cptr2^);
  Cptrl^ := 'm';
  writeln('Cptrl points to: ',Cptrl^,', Cptr2 points to: ',Cptr2^);
  Cptr2 := Cptrl;
  writeln('Cptrl points to: ',Cptrl^,', Cptr2 points to: ',Cptr2^);
  Cptrl^ := 'j';
  writeln('Cptrl points to: ',Cptrl^,', Cptr2 points to: ',Cptr2^)
end. { ExamplePointer }
```

FIGURE 14.11 Output produced by the program of Figure 14.10.

```
cpl points to: s
cp2 points to: p
cpl points to: s, cp2 points to: s
cpl points to: m, cp2 points to: s
cpl points to: m, cp2 points to: m
cpl points to: j, cp2 points to: j
```

Figure 14.10 shows a Pascal program that uses these concepts, and Figure 14.11 shows the output it produces. As an exercise, trace through this program and compare the results obtained with the results of Figure 14.11.

Sometimes it is useful to state that a given pointer variable does not have an associated referenced variable. In this case, if `Ptr` is a pointer variable, we write `Ptr := nil` to state that `Ptr` does not have an associated referenced variable—that is, `Ptr` does not point to anything. The word nil is a reserved name in Pascal. Any pointer variable can be assigned the value nil. The advantage of a nil pointer over one that is simply undefined is that with the value nil we can test whether the pointer has a value: If Ptr = nil, then Ptr does not have a value; otherwise, Ptr has a value. With an undefined value we cannot do such a test.

The main application of pointer variables is to define **dynamic data structures,** structures whose size varies during program execution. The next section discusses how dynamic data structures can be created in Pascal.

Another application of pointers is related with the values returned by functions. In Chapter 9 we saw that functions in Pascal can return simple types but not records or arrays. However, Pascal functions can also return pointers. This provides another useful application of pointers: They allow the definition of functions that return referenced variables of type array or record. Let us suppose that we have the type

```
MyArray = array [1..10] of integer
```

and we want to write a function that would return an element of type MyArray. Pascal does not allow us to do such a thing. However, we can define MyArrayPointer as

```
MyArrayPointer = ^MyArray
```

and write a function whose value is of type MyArrayPointer. This function returns a referenced variable of type MyArray. Chapters 16–18 present several functions that use this technique.

14.3 Structures with pointers

One of the main applications of pointers is the definition of structures whose size varies during the execution of a program (dynamic data structures). This section discusses how this can be done.

The most common technique for building dynamic data structures is to define record types, some of whose fields contain pointers to the record type itself; that is, they are recursive data structures. We then dynamically allocate a series of records and link them with pointer fields. Consider, for example, the type definition in Figure 14.12.[3] This type definition may

3. We purposely avoid naming this structure—we simply call it structure. The reason for doing this is that, at this stage, we just want to show how dynamic data structures can be built without concern for the properties and applications of the structures themselves.

FIGURE 14.12 Dynamic data structure.

```
type StructPointer = ^ Structure;
     Structure = record
                   Field1 : integer;
                   Field2 : char;
                   Field3 : StructPointer;
                   Field4 : StructPointer
                 end; { Structure }
```

FIGURE 14.13 Value pointed by S1.

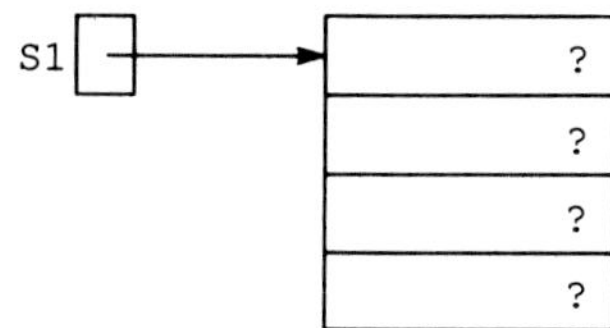

seem strange. Notice that `StructPointer` is defined as a pointer to the type `Structure`, whose definition appears further on. It might seem that the definition of `Structure` should be placed before the definition of `StructPointer`; however, the definition of `Structure` also uses `StructPointer`! To avoid this problem, pointer type definitions in Pascal may precede the definition of their referenced types as long as they are all defined in the same type definition part. However, the reverse is not true; that is, the referenced types may not appear before the definition of the pointer types.

Suppose that, in a program where the definition of Figure 14.12 appears, we have the declaration: `var S1, S2 : StructPointer`. The statement `new(S1)` has the effect of creating the structure shown in Figure 14.13. In this figure, `S1` points to a large rectangle that encloses four smaller rectangles. The large rectangle represents the record `Structure`, and each one of the enclosed rectangles represents one field of the record: The first

FIGURE 14.14 New values of S1 and S2.

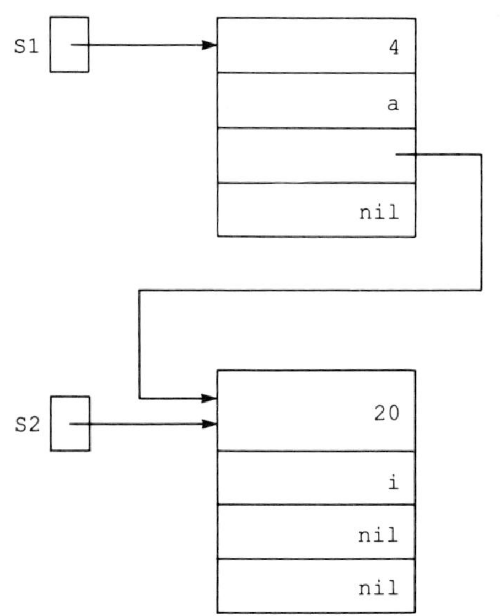

rectangle represents Field1, the second rectangle represents Field2, and so on. Suppose that we now execute the following statements:

```
new(S2);
S1^.Field1 := 4;
S1^.Field2 := 'a';
S1^.Field3 := S2;
S1^.Field4 := nil;
s2^.Field1 := 20;
s2^.Field2 := 'i';
s2^.Field3 := nil;
s2^.Field4 := nil;
```

These statements have the effect of creating the structure shown in Figure 14.14. If the statement new(S2) is now executed, it has the effect of creating a new referenced variable to which S2 points (Figure 14.15). This newly created record can be linked to the existing structure, which will keep growing as long as we want (and have available memory—see Section 14.4).

Chapters 16–18 present several dynamic data structures and discuss their properties and how to implement and manipulate them.

FIGURE 14.15 Structure of Figure 14.14 after `new(S2)`.

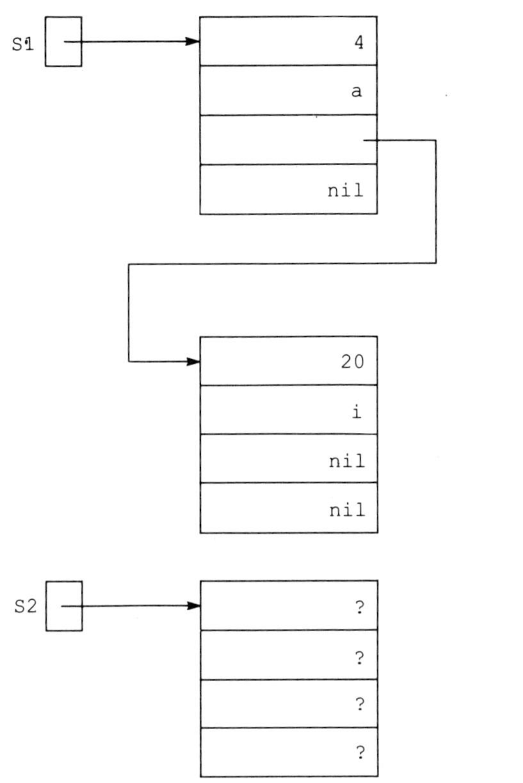

14.4 Memory management

At the beginning of this chapter we said that dynamic variables could be created and destroyed at any point during the execution of a program. So far, we have only discussed how dynamic variables are created. This section gives an insight into several techniques used to destroy dynamic variables.

Any programming language that allows the use of dynamic variables keeps a collection of memory cells to be used for the allocation of dynamic variables. This collection of cells is called a **heap.** The procedure `new` retrieves memory cells from the heap, which will store the value of the newly generated referenced variable. Cells that have been allocated but are no longer needed should be returned to the heap. There are basically three methods for returning no-longer-needed cells to the heap: manual updates, reference counts, and garbage collection.

The **manual-updates method** (which is the method used in Pascal) relies on the programmer to explicitly return the no-longer-needed cells to the heap. Pascal supplies the procedure `dispose` that takes as argument a pointer variable and returns to the heap the cell to which the variable points. After the execution of the procedure `dispose(Ptr)`, in which `Ptr` is a pointer variable, the value of `Ptr` is undefined and the cell that was allocated to `Ptr` is placed back in the heap. This method may seem the natural recovery technique for heap storage; however, it can give rise to two serious problems: garbage and dangling references.

Garbage can be generated when all the links to a structure have been destroyed without the structure itself being returned to the heap. This problem was discussed in Section 14.2; a garbage cell is shown in Figure 14.9. Garbage has the effect of producing memory cells that are no longer accessible.

Dangling references present a more serious problem. **Dangling references** are produced when a structure is destroyed (and thus returned to the heap) before all links to the structure are destroyed. In this case, the remaining links become dangling references: They point to something that no longer exists. (In fact, they point to a cell that is in the heap. If this cell is allocated again—through the procedure `new`—they will keep pointing to this cell, which may now have a completely different meaning for the program.) Figure 14.16 shows a fragment of a Pascal program that generates a dangling reference.

To avoid dangling references, an alternative method for returning cells to the heap has been proposed: the reference-counting technique. The basic concept underlying **reference counts** consists of allocating some extra space within each element of the heap (the *reference count*) that counts how many pointers point to it. This technique is used in a language called SLIP (Weizenbaum, 1963). When a cell is allocated from the heap, its reference count is set to 1; whenever a new pointer to the cell is created, its reference count is increased by 1; and whenever a pointer to the cell is destroyed, the reference count is decreased by 1. Whenever the reference count of a cell reaches 0, the cell is free and can be returned to the heap. This method avoids dangling references, but, in some cases, it may still allow the generation of garbage. This problem is associated with circular structures, an example of which is shown in Figure 14.17. This figure shows a pointer variable, `Ptr`, that points to a structure that contains three elements (labeled `A`, `B`, and `C`). The element labeled `C` points back to the beginning of the structure. If the pointer `Ptr` is changed (for example, by the statement `Ptr := nil`), the circular structure becomes inaccessible (and thus garbage); however, the reference count of each element of the structure is still 1.

The **garbage-collection** technique (which is used by LISP) allows garbage to be generated. When there are almost no more cells in the heap and more storage is needed, the execution of the program is suspended

FIGURE 14.16 Generating a dangling reference.

```
program Dangling (input,output);
type IntPointer = ^integer;
var  v1,v2 : IntPointer;
begin
     new(v1);
     new(v2);
     v1^ := 3;
     v2 := v1;
     dispose(v1); {v2 becomes a dangling reference}
     ...
end. { Dangling }
```

FIGURE 14.17 Circular structure.

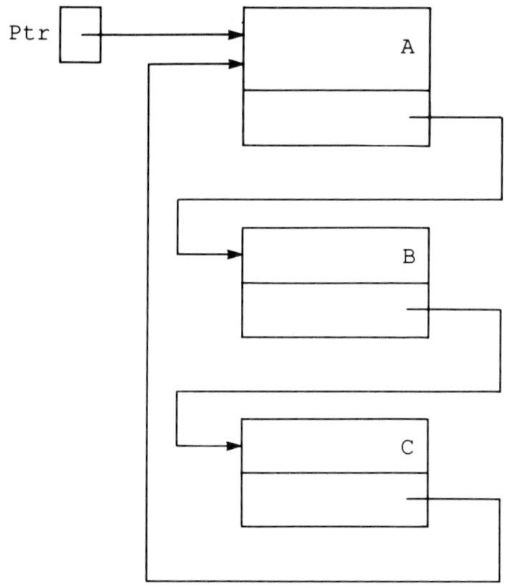

temporarily, and another procedure is executed: the garbage-collection procedure. This procedure identifies garbage and returns it to the heap. The basic principle underlying garbage collection is that, at any point during computation, all cells that do not contain garbage are reachable from the existing variables. Because garbage collection is done only rarely, it is allowed for it to be fairly costly. There are two phases involved in garbage collection:

1. The **mark phase,** in which every nongarbage element is marked. In this phase, every cell that is reachable from a variable in the program is marked as nongarbage.
2. The **sweep phase,** in which the entire memory allocated for data is scanned, and every cell not marked as nongarbage is returned to the heap.

We conclude this section by reminding you that Pascal uses the manual-updates technique to return cells to the heap. It is, thus, your responsibility to use the function `dispose` to return no-longer-needed cells to the heap. The use of `dispose` should be done with care to avoid dangling references.

Summary

This chapter introduced the notion of a pointer. When using a variable of type `pointer`, we are not interested in the value of the variable by itself but rather in the value to which it points. Variables of type `pointer` can be created and destroyed at will during the execution of a program.

Dynamic data structures—that is, structures whose size can grow and shrink during the execution of a program—were introduced. The variation in the size of these structures is obtained by manipulating the pointers that link their components.

Pointers also can be used to allow functions to return structured data types. The functions do not actually return the structured data type but rather a pointer to it.

Finally, three techniques for memory management—manual updates, reference counts, and garbage collection—were briefly introduced.

Suggested readings

The techniques of memory management introduced in this chapter are very important in computer science. These concepts were covered here at a very superficial level. You can explore the topics presented in this chapter more deeply by consulting the following publications:

Allen, J. 1978. *Anatomy of LISP.* New York: McGraw-Hill.
This book describes in detail the use of pointers in LISP and the process of garbage collection.

Cohen, J. 1981. "Garbage Collection of Linked Data Structures," *Computing Surveys,* 13 (3):341–367.
This is a tutorial on garbage collection. It discusses both the classical garbage-collection algorithms and the recently proposed ones. It gives an exhaustive bibliography on garbage collection.

Knuth, D. 1973a. *The Art of Computer Programming, Vol. 1, Fundamental Algorithms.* Reading, MA: Addison-Wesley.
This book discusses pointers, structures using pointers, dynamic storage allocation, and memory-management techniques, all in great depth.

Pratt, T. 1984. *Programming Languages: Design and Implementation,* 2d ed. Englewood Cliffs, NJ: Prentice-Hall.
This book presents an excellent survey of memory-management techniques.

Exercises

1. ✓ Give a syntax chart for pointer type.
2. ? Consider the following statements:

```
type Rp = ^real;
var Mp :  Rp;
```

   Is the following legal: `Mp^ := nil`? Why?
3. ? Assume the following definitions and declarations:

```
type Structure = ^StructRep;
     StructRep = record
                   Fieldl : integer;
                   Field2 : Structure
                 end;

var sl,s2 : Structure;
```

   Which of the following calls are legal?
   a. `new(sl)`
   b. `new(Structure)`
   c. `new(StructRep)`
   d. `new(sl^.Fieldl)`
   e. `new(s2^.Field2)`
4. ? Assuming the declarations of Exercise 3, which of the following statements are legal?
   a. `sl := nil`
   b. `sl := s2`
   c. `sl := s2^.Fieldl`
   d. `sl := s2^.Field2`

5. **?** What is the output produced by the following program?

```
program Test (input,output);
var a,b : ^integer;
begin
  new(a);
  new(b);
  a^ := 5;
  b^ := 15;
  writeln('a = ' a^ : 3,' b = ',b^ : 3);
  a := b;
  a^ := 10;
  writeln('a = ' a^ : 3,' b = ',b^ : 3)
end.
```

6. **?** Consider the following definition of a dynamic structure and the following assignments:

```
type  StructPointer = ^Structure;
      Structure = record
                    Field1 : integer;
                    Field2 : StructPointer
                  end; { Structure }
var   MyStructure, AuxStruct : StructPointer;

 new (MyStructure);
 new (AuxStruct);
 MyStructure^.Field1 := 5;
 MyStructure^.Field2 := AuxStruct;
 AuxStruct^.Field1 := 10;
 New(AuxStruct);
 MyStructure^.Field2^.Field2 := AuxStruct;
 AuxStruct^.Field1 := 15;
 AuxStruct^.Field2 := nil;
```

Now, suppose that the procedure

```
procedure Mystery (S : StructPointer);
begin
   if S <> nil then
      begin
         Mystery(S^.Field2);
         writeln(S^.Field1)
      end
end
```

is called with the variable MyStructure. What will be printed? (HINT: A diagram of MyStructure may help.)

7. **?** Explain why the program in Figure 14.16 produces a dangling reference.

8. **✓** What problems may be caused by manual updates of the heap?

9. **?** A linked list of integers can be created by the following type definition:

```
type  List = ^ListElem;
      ListElem = record
                   Value : integer;
                   Next  : List
                 end ; { ListElem }

var  MyList : List;
```

A list with the elements 4, 7, and 2 can be represented as follows:

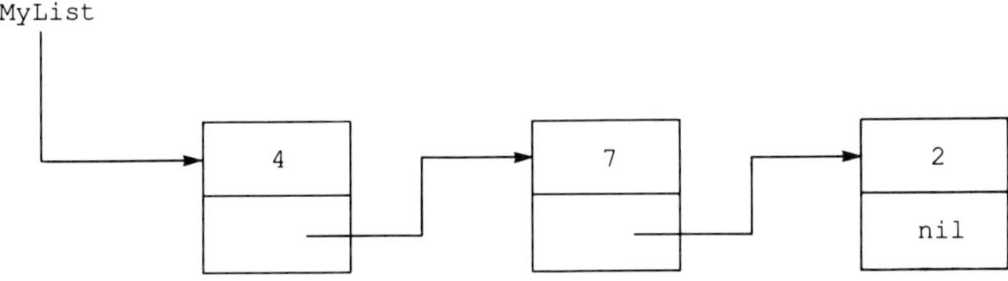

Write a procedure that reads a sequence of integer numbers and inserts them into a list. When inserting a new element, you can either scan the entire list to find its last element and then insert the new element, or you can keep a pointer to the last element of the list, which is updated whenever a new element is inserted. Compare the advantages and disadvantages of each approach.

10. **!** Using the list structure in Exercise 9, write a procedure that takes as arguments a list and an integer and deletes from the list *all* elements whose value is equal to the integer. Notice that deleting an element from the list corresponds to changing one pointer first and then executing the procedure dispose on the element that we want to delete. As an example, if we want to delete the element that stores the value 7 in the list of the previous exercise, we have:

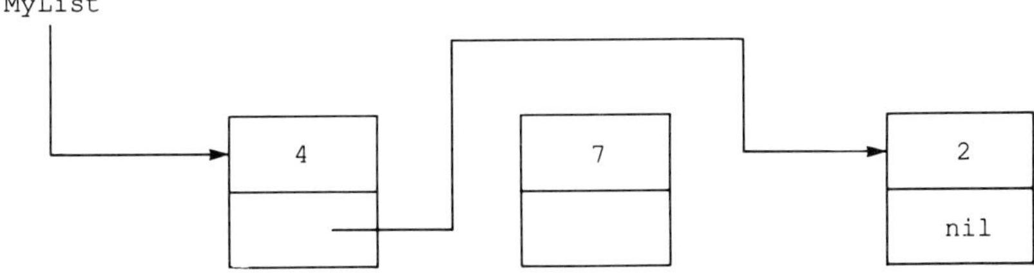

Notice that we did not represent the pointer to the element that contains the value 7: We don't care about it. After disposing of this element, it will be returned to the heap and reused whenever needed. (HINT: Use an auxiliary pointer that will be moved along the list, searching for the desired element or elements.)

11. ❗ Using the list structure that we have been describing, write a procedure that inserts a new element at the front of the list.

12. ❓ Write a procedure that accepts as input two lists and concatenates them into a single list; that is, the last element of the first list points to the first element of the second list.

13. ❓ Write a function that takes as argument a list structure and returns the length of the list.

14. ❓ Write a procedure that takes as argument a list structure and outputs all its elements.

15. ❗ Lists whose elements are characters can be used to represent character strings. The advantage of this representation over the `string type` (represented by a packed array) is that there is no predetermined upper bound on the length of the string. Using this type of representation, reimplement the procedure `substring` and the function `match` described in the exercises of Chapter 11.

16. ❓ Write a procedure that takes as argument a list and creates another list with the same elements but in reverse order. (HINT: Use recursion.)

17. ❓ Suppose that in a Pascal program where the type `List` of the previous exercise was defined we declare the variables `A`, `B`, and `C` as

```
var A,B,C : List
```

Furthermore, suppose that after some manipulation we have the following situation:

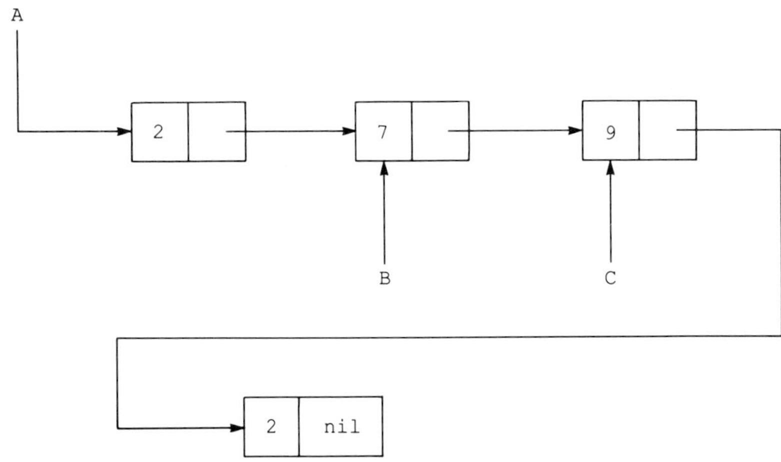

Explain what the following statements do. (If a statement causes an error, explain what is wrong.)

a. `A^.Next^.Value := 4`

b. `B := C`

c. `A^.Next = nil`

d. `A^.Next^.Next^.Value := nil`

e. `dispose (B)`

18. A binary tree of integers can be defined as follows:

```
type  Tree = ^ Node;
      Node = record
                Left  : Tree;
                Value : integer;
                Right : Tree
             end; { Node }
```

Suppose that in a program where the type `Tree` is defined, we declare the variables `T1` and `T2` as

```
T1, T2 :  Tree;
```

Furthermore, suppose that after some manipulation we have the following situation:

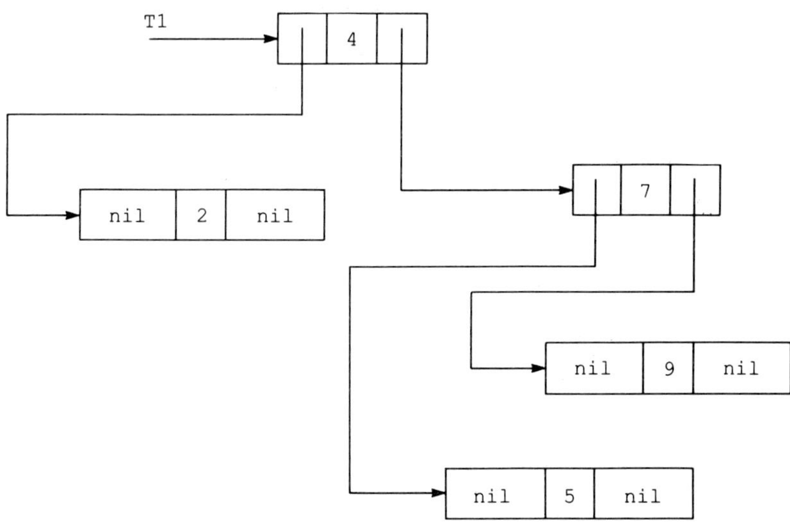

Write statements to insert a new node on the left of the node whose value is 9. Assume that the value of this new node is 8. (HINT: Use `T2` as an auxiliary variable.)

19. **!** Using the tree defined in Exercise 18, write a Pascal program that reads a sequence of integers and inserts them into a tree according to the following algorithm: The first value goes to the top of the tree (also called the *root* of the tree, corresponding to the node with value 4 in the previous exercise). The following elements are inserted in the following way: If they are greater than the element at the root, then they are inserted (using the same algorithm) in the tree on the right; otherwise, they are inserted in the tree on the left.
20. **!** Passing pointers by reference has the same effect as passing pointers by value. Explain.

CHAPTER 15

This chapter introduces the concept of an abstract data type. The advantages of using abstract data types and the methodology to be followed to define and implement them are discussed. The methodology introduced in this chapter is used in the next three chapters.

ABSTRACT DATA TYPES

I never get your limits, Watson . . . there are unexplored possibilities about you.
Sir Arthur Conan Doyle, *The Sussex Vampire*

Chapter 1 introduced two terms, *procedural abstraction* and *data abstraction*. We used procedural abstraction with procedures and functions. We made some use of data abstraction in the sense that when we used a data type (for example, an integer or an array), we abstracted (ignored) the way the data type was actually implemented in the language. However, we did not yet use data abstraction as we used procedural abstraction—that is, in the construction of new objects. We used procedural abstraction to create new procedures and functions; now you will learn how to use data abstraction to create new data types.

Having completed the study of the data types available in a programming language, for example, Pascal, we face the following question: What if we need a data type that is not available in the language that we use? For example, what if we need a data type that is not available in Pascal?[1] This chapter answers this question of how to extend a language by creating new data types. The methodology for doing so is relatively recent. It was developed mainly during the late 1970s and is still an active area of research.

---

1. You may be wondering if there is really a need to define and use new data types. You will have a good understanding of such a need by the end of the next three chapters.

With this methodology, we can develop a program that makes use of user-defined data types without thinking about how to implement those data types. This is done by considering each data type as an object that is contained in a module or capsule and that the only communication between the program and the data type is done through functions that represent the characteristics of the data type.

The methodology relies heavily on the use of abstractions, and the data types developed using it are called **abstract data types.** It was introduced by Liskof and Zilles (1974). Recent programming languages—for example, Ada (Gehani 1983), CLU (Liskof, Snyder, Atkinson, and Schaffert 1977), Mesa (Geschke, Morris, and Satterthwaite 1977), and Modula-2 (Wirth 1983)—provide facilities for abstract data types.

15.1 Abstraction in computer science

An **abstraction** is a simplified description or specification of an object that emphasizes some of the object's properties while suppressing others. A good abstraction specifies the important properties and ignores the details. Because the properties to be abstracted from an object depend on the use of the object, the term *good abstraction* is always associated with a particular application of the object.

Consider, for example, a group of people. Each person has several attributes: name, sex, date and place of birth, eye color, hair color, weight, height, place of employment, Social Security number, yearly salary, and so on. It is important to notice that when we talk about attributes such as eye color or hair color, we are already using an abstraction. For example, the iris (the part of the eye that is used to characterize the eye color) is not a uniform color. It may present hues of the same color or even a mixture of different colors (for example, green and brown). When we use the term *eye color,* we *abstract* from all these aspects and just refer to the dominating color.

Furthermore, suppose that this group of people is being considered for the purpose of processing tax information. In this case, attributes such as sex, hair color, and eye color are not relevant. In this application, a good abstraction should consider the person's name, Social Security number, yearly salary, and so on, and should disregard the person's sex, eye color, and hair color. Suppose that, instead, we were developing an application for a dating agency. In this case, the attributes sex, eye color, hair color, height, and weight would be of fundamental importance, whereas attributes such as Social Security number, place of employment, and yearly salary could be left out. In summary, the properties that we consider, or *abstract* from the real object (in our example, the person), depend on the application at hand.

Abstraction is a key concept in modern programming. Historically, the earliest applications of abstraction in programming languages were the symbolic assemblers (see Chapter 19), which abstract from the internal representation of machine-language instructions and addresses (strings of 0s and 1s) and use symbolic names to refer to parts of those instructions. In the late 1950s and early 1960s, abstraction in high-level programming languages concentrated on the development of subprograms (procedural abstraction).

By the early 1970s, programming techniques that used procedural abstraction (top-down design and stepwise refinement) were widespread: Using these techniques, a first version of the program is written in terms of higher-level constructs (which are abstractions of actions and structures of the program), without concern about how they will be implemented. Only the fundamental concepts (the *abstraction*) that are applicable to the problem at hand are considered. When the first version is concluded, the same technique is applied again for each of the problems generated in the previous stage. Successive steps of program development add details to the program; each detail added brings the program closer to the programming language being used. These steps are repeated until the program has been completely expressed using the operations and data types of the programming language being used.

Separating the operations used in a program from the way the operations are implemented helps in decomposing complex problems into smaller, fairly independent modules.

The top-down program-development technique leads to procedural abstraction. **Procedural abstraction** means that subprograms are used taking into account *what* the subprograms do, not *how* they are implemented. The details of how a subprogram is implemented can be suppressed, and the particular subprogram itself can be replaced by another one that has the same overall behavior.

Later in the 1970s, most research activity in abstraction concentrated on developing methods for abstracting the fundamental properties of **data.** The collection of techniques developed is called the **theory of abstract data types.** The main idea behind the abstract data type techniques consists of identifying the fundamental properties of a given data object and packaging that entire information into a single module. The resulting module contains the information necessary to treat the data object and its associated operations as a type. The definition of a new abstract data type has the effect of extending the set of data types available in a given programming language.

The analogue of procedural abstraction for data is called data abstraction. **Data abstraction** is a methodology used to separate the abstract properties of an object from the details of how it is implemented. Using data abstraction, we can write programs that manipulate abstract data objects without concern for their implementation. We can replace the particular *implementation* of a data object without having to change the *program* that uses that object, provided that the new implementation has the same overall behavior—that is, provided that the new implementation represents, in fact, the same abstract object.

15.2 Theory of abstract data types

Just as a given numerical function can be computed by many different computational processes, there are many ways in which a given data structure can be represented in terms of simpler objects, and the choice of representation can have significant impact on the time and space requirements of processes that manipulate the data.
Abelson, Sussman, and Sussman (1985, p. 90)

A **data type** is a set of objects, called the **elements** of the data type, together with a collection of **operations** that can be performed on those objects. These operations create, build up, destroy, and pick apart instances of the objects. Data types come in two varieties: elementary (or atomic) data types and structured data types.

The theory of abstract data types considers the definition of new data types in two separate and independent phases: the study of the properties of the type and the implementation details. The essence of data abstraction is thus to separate the parts of a program that deal with how data objects are *used* from the parts of a program that deal with how data objects are *represented.*

We now consider each of these in detail. To make the presentation easier to follow, we will consider a case study and draw all the examples from it. Suppose, then, that we need to write a program that deals with rational numbers. A **rational number** is a number of the form a/b in which both numerator a and denominator b are integers. Our program should be able to add, subtract, multiply, and divide rational numbers; it has to test whether two rational numbers are equal; it should be able to construct rational numbers from pairs of integers; and so on.

With the knowledge that you have about Pascal, you could define a "rational number type," for example, as a record (Figure 15.1) and use the fields of that record to select the numerator and denominator of rational numbers. For example, if `Rat1`, `Rat2`, and `Rat3` are of type `Rational`, in order to add `Rat1` and `Rat2`, giving `Rat3`, we could use the statements:

```
Rat3.Numerator := Rat1.Numerator * Rat2.Denominator +
                  Rat2.Numerator * Rat1.Denominator;
Rat3.Denominator := Rat1.Denominator * Rat2.Denominator;
```

FIGURE 15.1 A representation of rational numbers.

```
type Rational = record
                  Numerator   : integer;
                  Denominator : integer
                end; { Rational }
```

However, if rational number were a predefined type in Pascal, you wouldn't need to bother with those details. For example, if rational numbers were predefined in Pascal and had a function `AddRat` associated with them, the previous operation would be achieved by the statement:

```
Rat3 := AddRat(Rat1, Rat2).
```

A program of this sort would be much easier to write if rational numbers were a predefined type in the programming language. One of the goals of the abstract-data-type methodology is to allow you to treat new types—for example, rational numbers—as if they were predefined in the language.

With this setting in mind, we begin by considering the part that deals with *how data objects are used.* The basic idea underlying this part consists of identifying, for each data type, the basic set of operations that can be performed on the elements (or objects) of that type. These operations fall into four categories: constructors, selectors, recognizers, and tests.

Constructors specify how to generate (construct) new objects of the type. In our example, we can devise five constructors for rational numbers: `NewRat`, a function that takes as arguments two integer numbers and creates a rational number whose numerator is the first argument and whose denominator is the second argument (that is, this function builds rational numbers from scratch), and `AddRat`, `SubRat`, `MultRat`, and `DivRat`, which perform the arithmetic operations with rational numbers. These functions take two rational numbers as arguments and return a rational number.

Selectors specify how to access (select) the elements that compose the objects of the type. In the case of rational numbers, we can "pick apart" its two components: the numerator and the denominator. As selectors, we need the function `Numerator`, which takes as argument a rational number and returns its numerator, and the function `Denominator`, which takes as argument a rational number and returns its denominator.

Recognizers recognize basic properties of the objects of the type. Among the recognizers for rational numbers we may have `IsInteger`, which tests whether the denominator is 1 (or if the numerator is a multiple of the denominator), and `IsZero`, which tests whether the numerator is 0 (and the denominator is different from 0).

Tests make comparisons among the elements of the type. In our example, the operation `EqRat` takes as arguments two rational numbers and decides whether they are equal.

Constructors, selectors, recognizers, and tests are called the **basic operations** (or **basic functions**) of a data type. Their job is to add elements to the data type (constructors), take elements out of the data type (selectors), and answer questions about the elements of the data type (recognizers and tests).

We must also consider the transformations between the abstract-data-type notation and the notation of the underlying representation. In our example, the abstract-data-type notation for rational numbers is `a/b`, and the underlying representation is, for example, a record. The operations that correspond to such specifications are called **input/output transformations.** There are two input/output transformations: the **read operation,** which maps the abstract objects into their representation, and the **write operation,** which maps the representation into the abstract objects. In our example, the read function, which may be called `ReadRat`, reads an object of the form `a/b` (where `a` and `b` are integers) as a rational number and stores that object as a record (if records are used to represent rational numbers); the write operation, which may be called `WriteRat`, takes a variable of the type rational number (represented by a record) and outputs it in the form `a/b`.

When we specify these operations (the basic operations together with the input/output transformations), we create an extension of our high-level programming language that has our data type as a predefined type. We can then write programs that manipulate objects of the new data type in terms of the constructors, selectors, recognizers, tests, and the input/output transformations even *before* we actually implement the data type. In this way, we obtain a true separation of the use of a data type from its particular implementation.

Finally, we must consider *how data objects are implemented.* We need to devise a *representation* for the data objects in terms of existing types and, based on that representation, to implement the basic operations and the input/output transformations in terms of existing types. The collection of operations, together with the representation of the data type, is called the **module** that implements the data type. In our example, we could represent a rational number as shown in Figure 15.1 and write the basic operations and the input/output transformations in terms of this representation (other representations are possible). These operations, together with the definition of `Rational`, constitute the module for rational numbers.

After both steps are concluded (defining how data objects are used and how they are implemented), we can then put these two parts together to produce a program that uses the data type as if it were predefined in the language. The program has access to a set of operations that are specific to the type and, in fact, characterize the behavior of the new type. Any manipulation of an object of a given type should be done *exclusively* through the use of the basic functions of its type.

High-level programming languages that were developed prior to the advent of the abstract-data-type methodology do not have specific mechanisms for guaranteeing that the only use of a given type is done using the operations that are specific for that type. More recent programming languages (for example, Ada, CLU, Mesa, and Modula-2) guarantee that the manipulations done with the elements of a given type use the basic operations for that type. These new languages rely on design methodologies called **data encapsulation** and **information hiding:** The module that represents a data type *encapsulates* all information concerning the data type. Furthermore, this module *hides* a secret, the representation chosen for the implementation of the data type. The *only* access we have to the elements of the data type is through the basic operations, which are defined within this module and which completely specify the expected behavior of the data type.

To clarify data encapsulation and information hiding, let us return to our example of rational numbers. Suppose that, based on the representation shown in Figure 15.1, we have implemented the basic operations and the input/output transformations for the rational numbers. We can now put together the module that defines rational numbers and the program that uses them to produce a working program that manipulates rational numbers. In programming languages based on the abstract-data-type methodology, we only use the data type `Rational` through its basic operations. That is, although we might know that rational numbers are represented by records, we *cannot* access or use them by referring to the fields of records. In Pascal and other programming languages not based on the definition of abstract data types, the situation is different. If we knew that the data type were represented by a record, we could then directly manipulate the representation and thus manipulate the data type by performing operations on records. That is, if our Pascal program that uses rational numbers had the declaration

```
var Rat1, Rat2, Rat3 :  Rational;
```

we could *directly* add `Rat1` and `Rat2` giving `Rat3`, using the following assignment statements:

```
Rat3.Numerator := Rat1.Numerator * Rat2.Denominator +
                  Rat2.Numerator * Rat1.Denominator;
Rat3.Denominator := Rat1.Denominator * Rat2.Denominator;
```

However, you should be warned that *this is a bad programming practice.* There are two reasons for this:

1. Directly manipulating the representation of a data type makes the program dependent on the representation. If, after completion of the development of the program, we decide to change the representation of rational numbers from records to arrays, we would have to scan the entire program, looking for references to the records representing rational numbers, and change them to references to arrays.
2. It also makes the program difficult to write and to read. In fact, if we manipulate the representation directly, while writing the program, whenever we use an element of type rational number, we have to think of it in terms of its representation, not its abstract properties. Likewise, when reading the program, we would have to remember the representation of the data elements and "interpret" the references to the representation as references to the data objects themselves.

The advantage of the languages based on abstract data types over the older languages resides in the fact that they *prevent* the use of a data type by direct manipulation of its representation. All information concerning the data type is *encapsulated* in the module that implements the type; furthermore, the module *hides* from the outside program the method used to represent the data type.

Summary

The abstract-data-type methodology allows the effective separation of the abstract properties of an object from the details of how it is used. This separation improves the task of program development and the readability of the programs. Furthermore, it makes programs independent of the representation used for the new data types.

According to the abstract-data-type methodology, whenever we want to introduce a new data type, we should take the following steps:

1. *Specify the basic operations.* We abstract the properties of the new data type by specifying the constructors, selectors, recognizers, and tests.
2. *Choose the underlying representation.* We choose a representation for the data type in terms of existing data types.
3. *Implement the basic operations as concrete operations.* We write functions and/or procedures that mirror the behavior of the basic operations, in terms of the representation chosen for the data type.
4. *Implement the input/output transformations.* We supply functions and/or procedures that map the abstract objects to and from their internal representation.

One topic not discussed in this chapter (and not considered in the book) concerns the question of whether the set of basic functions that we define for the data type does in fact characterize the data type that we are implementing. This question may be answered by giving an **axiomatization** of the data type. An axiomatization consists of the rigorous statement of the properties of the data type. As examples of axiomatization, refer to Hoare (1972) or Manna and Waldinger (1985).

Suggested readings

You can explore the topics presented in this chapter more deeply by consulting the following publications:

Allen, J. 1978. *Anatomy of LISP.* New York: McGraw-Hill.
This book is mainly about LISP but discusses fundamental concepts of data structures (using abstract data types).

Bastani, F. B., and Iyengar, S. S. 1987. "The Effect of Data Structures on the Logical Complexity of Programs," *Communications of the ACM,* 30 (3):250–261.
This paper discusses the relation between the readability of a program and the level of abstraction used in its data types.

Bishop, J. 1986. *Data Abstraction in Programming Languages.* Reading, MA: Addison-Wesley.
This is a small book that introduces the main concepts of data abstraction and discusses the influence of data abstraction on programming methodology and the way we think about programs.

Ghezzi, C., and Jazayeri, M. 1982. *Programming Language Concepts.* New York: Wiley.
This is a book on programming languages. It discusses the influence of abstraction on programming-language design and describes several languages that use the abstract-data-type concept and the mechanisms provided by those languages to define new data types.

Hoare, C. A. R. 1972. "Notes on Data Structuring" in *Structured Programming,* edited by O. Dahl, E. Dijkstra, and C. A. R. Hoare. New York: Academic Press.
This is an excellent paper written by the pioneer of data abstraction. It discusses the advantages of using abstraction, draws a clear distinction between abstraction and representation, and studies several data types, presenting their axiomatization and a discussion of possible representations.

Shaw, M. 1984. "Abstraction Techniques in Modern Programming Languages," *IEEE Software,* 1 (4):10–26.
This article discusses the role of abstraction in programming languages, presenting a historical account of the use of abstraction in computer science; describes the abstraction tools in modern programming languages; and talks about the programming languages that support data abstraction and abstract data types.

Exercises

1. ? Implement the basic operations for rational numbers, using the representation of Figure 15.1.
2. ? Using the representation of Figure 15.1, implement the input/output transformations for rational numbers.
3. ? Write a Pascal program that deals with rational numbers. Your program should read a rational number, an operation, and another rational number. It then performs the operation on the two numbers read and displays the result.
4. ? An alternative way to represent rational numbers is to use an array rather than a record. Using the definition

```
type    position = (n, d);
        Rational = array [position] of integer;
```

   reimplement the basic operations and the input/output transformations for rational numbers.
5. ? Modify the program of Exercise 3 so that it uses the representation in Exercise 4. Then, to appreciate the advantage of the abstract-data-types approach, discuss the amount of work involved in such modification if the abstract-data-types methodology had not been used.
6. ? Suppose that after working with the rational numbers program for a while, you realize that you want to see the rational numbers reduced to their lowest terms. For example, $2/6$ will be shown as $1/3$. What parts of the program have to be modified to attain this goal? Write them.
7. ! Specify the constructors, selectors, recognizers, and tests that will be needed to specify the data type `array`.
8. ! Specify the constructors, selectors, recognizers, and tests that will be needed to specify the data type `record`.
9. ? Some programming languages (for example, FORTRAN) do not have, as predefined, the data type "record." In these languages the data type "record" has to be implemented with existing structured data types. Using the functions of the previous exercise, define a data type `MyRecord` that corresponds to the data type record, and is implemented using arrays.
10. ? Specify the constructors, selectors, recognizers, and tests that will be needed to specify the data type `set`.
11. ? Implement the data type `set` using arrays.
12. ! Specify the constructors, selectors, recognizers, and tests that will be needed to specify the data type `pointer`.
13. ! Implement the data type `pointer` using arrays. (HINT: You may need to define a large array to represent the heap and have functions that fetch and return cells to the heap.)

CHAPTER 16

This chapter introduces stacks as an abstract data type and discusses possible ways of representing stacks and their corresponding basic operations. An example that uses stacks and the corresponding program is presented.

THE STACK AS AN ABSTRACT DATA TYPE

It occurred to her that she might as well look and see what was on the top of it.
Lewis Carroll, *Alice's Adventures in Wonderland*

In this chapter, we apply the methodology of abstract data types in the definition of a new type: `Stack`. A **stack** is a data type that is similar to a stack of physical objects (for example, a stack of cafeteria trays, a stack of books, or a stack of boxes). A stack is an ordered group of elements. Stack elements are added to the top of the stack and are also removed from the top of the stack. We cannot remove or inspect any element other than the one on the top of the stack. You can imagine a stack of books with books that are so heavy that you can only lift one book at a time. In this stack, if you want to take a look at the third book from the top you have to remove the first book from the stack, then remove the second book (which is now on the top of the stack), and only after these two operations can you pick the book that you want. Stacks in computer science behave similarly.

Stacks are widely used in computer science: Subprogram calls are implemented through a stack structure, stacks are used to evaluate expressions, stacks are even built into the hardware of some machines.

16.1 Evaluation of postfix expressions

Before discussing data type `Stack`, we show an example that uses stacks: the evaluation of Reverse Polish Notation (RPN) expressions.

When writing an arithmetic expression, we traditionally write the operator *between* the operands, as in `a + b`, rather than *before* the operands

(+ a b) or *after* the operands (a b +). The form with the operator in between the operands is called **infix notation,** the form with the operator before the operands is called **prefix notation** (or **Polish Notation**), and the form with the operator after the operands is called **postfix notation** (or **Reverse Polish Notation**). The word *Polish* is named after the Polish logician J. Lükasiewicz, who investigated the properties of this notation (Lükasiewicz 1958). Because the name Lükasiewicz is not easy to write or pronounce, the notation has become known as Polish notation.

Prefix and postfix notations have advantages over the infix notation: To evaluate an expression in either prefix or postfix notation, we do not need to specify precedence of operators, and, furthermore, any expression can be expressed without parentheses. The evaluation of expressions in either one of these notations is done with the help of a stack. This section shows how to evaluate expressions in postfix notation. For a discussion on how to convert an expression from infix notation to postfix notation, refer, for example, to Amsbury (1985), Horowitz and Sahni (1984), Singh and Naps (1985), or Tanenbaum (1976). A discussion of the evaluation of expressions in prefix notation and conversion from infix notation to prefix notation can be found in Dale and Lilly (1985).

In postfix notation a simple expression consisting of one operator and two operands is written with the two operands first, followed by the operator. Thus, the infix expression 2 + 8 becomes 2 8 +. More complex expressions are built by repeating this process with subexpressions, thus (4 + 3 * 6) + 5 * 8 becomes 4 3 6 * + 5 8 * +.

To evaluate an expression in postfix notation, we scan the expression from left to right. When we find an operator, we apply the operator to the last two operands seen and put the result back into the expression. This is repeated until the expression is reduced to a simple number, the value of the expression. As an example, consider the expression 4 3 6 * + 5 8 * +. Reading from left to right, the first operator we find is *, so we apply this operator to the last two operands seen (3 and 6), and place the result (18) back into the expression (replacing 3 6 *), which then becomes 4 18 + 5 8 * +. We keep on scanning the expression from left to right. Finding the operator +, we apply this operator to the last two operands seen (4 and 18), and place the result (22) back into the expression, which then becomes 22 5 8 * +. The next operator we find is *, and the expression becomes 22 40 +. Finally, we find the operator +, and the final value of the expression is 62.

This evaluation procedure can be implemented through a very simple algorithm that uses a stack (this stack contains the operands that we have seen). To use this algorithm, we begin with an empty stack (an **empty stack** is a stack with no elements), meaning that, at the beginning, we have seen no operands). We scan the expression from left to right. Whenever we find an operand, it is placed on the top of the stack. Whenever we find an operator, it is applied to the topmost element and the next to the topmost element of the stack. The element on the top of the stack represents the second operand. Before we apply the operation, this element is removed from the stack; the new element on the top of the stack represents the first operand (which is also removed from the stack). The operation is then performed on these two operands, and the result of the operation is placed on the top of the stack. The stack has the effect of "remembering" the last two operands seen: The last operand seen is on the top of the stack; the next-to-last operand seen is the second element of the stack.

Figure 16.1 shows the stack used for the evaluation of the expression `4 3 6 * + 5 8 * +`. At each step of the evaluation, we show the symbol being scanned (immediately above the character ^) and the contents of the stack.

The example of this section shows one of the possible applications of stacks in computer science. We now turn our attention to the stack's basic functions and a possible representation of stacks in terms of existing data types.

FIGURE 16.1 Evaluation of `4 3 6 * + 5 8 * +`.

```
Step        Expression          Stack

  1        4 3 6 * + 5 8 * +    empty
          ^

  2        4 3 6 * + 5 8 * +    | 4 |
           ^

  3        4 3 6 * + 5 8 * +    | 3 |
             ^                  | 4 |
```

(continued)

FIGURE 16.1, *continued.*

Step	Expression	Stack
4	4 3 6 * + 5 8 * + ^	6 3 4
5	4 3 6 * + 5 8 * + ^	18 4
6	4 3 6 * + 5 8 * + ^	22
7	4 3 6 * + 5 8 * + ^	5 22
8	4 3 6 * + 5 8 * + ^	8 5 22
9	4 3 6 * + 5 8 * + ^	40 22
10	4 3 6 * + 5 8 * + ^	62

16.2 The basic operations for stacks

The first step for implementing data type `Stack` is to specify its basic operations: We have to specify how to construct stacks (the constructors), how to remove elements from stacks (the selectors), how to recognize special kinds of stacks (the recognizers), and how to compare stacks (the tests).

1. *Constructors.* Whenever we define constructors, we should specify an operation that creates brand-new instances of the data type. In this case, function `NewStack` creates a brand-new, empty stack. The other way to construct a stack is to take an already existing stack and add an element to it. We know that this addition is performed by placing the new element on the top of the stack. This operation is traditionally called **push.** Therefore, the other constructor that we have is operation `Push`, which takes as arguments a stack element and a stack and constructs the stack that is obtained by pushing the element onto the stack.
2. *Selectors.* There is only one way of taking elements from a stack: removing its topmost element. This operation is traditionally called **pop.** The only selector for data type `Stack` is thus the operation `Pop`, which takes as argument a stack and removes its topmost element. The element removed is returned; in addition, the stack loses its topmost element (as a side effect).
3. *Recognizers.* These operations recognize special kinds of stacks. The only special kind of stack that we will have is the stack with no elements, the empty stack. We need one recognizer for data type `Stack`, the function `IsEmpty`, which takes as argument a stack and returns `true` if and only if the stack is empty.
4. *Tests.* The purpose of the tests is to provide a way of comparing the elements of the data type. In the case of stacks, we can just compare them for equality. Thus, function `EqualStacks` takes as arguments two stacks and returns `true` if and only if both stacks are equal—they have the same elements in the same order.

In summary, data type `Stack` has the following basic operations:

1. Constructors: `NewStack`, `Push`
2. Selector: `Pop`
3. Recognizer: `IsEmpty`
4. Test: `EqualStacks`

To use data type `Stack`, we must also define input/output transformations. As a notation for representing stacks, we use a column of elements (for

FIGURE 16.2 A representation of stacks using arrays.

```
RepStack = record
            StackItself : array [1..Maxel] of StackElm;
            Top : 1..Maxel;
            UpperBound : integer
           end; { RepStack }
```

example, integers) with its topmost element at the top. The following is an example of a stack with four integer elements, its topmost element being 20.

```
20
34
19
 5
```

The input operation for stacks (let us call it `ReadStack`) reads a sequence of elements and pushes them into a stack in the same sequence, and the output operation (called `WriteStack`) takes as argument a stack and outputs its contents in sequence from top to bottom.

We now turn to the problem of representing a stack in terms of existing data types. We explore two basic alternatives for representing stacks: using arrays and using pointers. Each of these two alternatives are discussed, and the corresponding basic operations are presented.

16.3 Stacks as arrays

We can implement **stacks as arrays,** using a one-dimensional array to store the elements of the stack. We postulate that the first element of the array stores the element at the bottom of the stack, the second element of the array stores the next element, and so on; that is, the stack grows toward the high-subscript end.[1] We also need to "remember" where the topmost element is located. Moreover, because the number of elements of an array is limited beforehand, our stacks as arrays have a limit on the maximum number of elements that they can contain (this limit is defined by the stack's implementor). Figure 16.2 shows a possible representation of stacks

1. This decision is arbitrary. For an alternative, refer to the Exercises.

FIGURE 16.3 Another representation of stacks using arrays.

```
Stack = ^RepStack;
RepStack = record
                StackItself : array [1..Maxel] of StackElm;
                Top : 1..Maxel;
                UpperBound : integer
            end; { RepStack }
```

using arrays. At this point, we don't care what the type of the elements of the stack is, and thus we use type StackElm. This may be either a predefined type or a user-defined type. Notice that a RepStack contains not only the stack itself (the field StackItself) but also additional information: the location of the top of the stack (the field Top) and the maximum stack size allowable (the field UpperBound). The need for field UpperBound will become evident when we consider the implementation of the basic operations.

Although the definition of Figure 16.2 suffices to fully represent a stack, it does not allow us to write functions that return stacks (remember, a function cannot return a record). As you will see, we want to write functions that return stacks (for example, NewStack), and because Pascal functions have to return either a simple type or a pointer type, we represent a stack as being a pointer to RepStack (Figure 16.3).

Figures 16.4–16.7 show the implementation of the stack's basic operations using the representation discussed.

There are several features of our implementation of the stack's basic operations that are worth mentioning. The first thing that may strike you in these functions is the recognizer IsFull (Figure 16.6). This recognizer was not presented when we discussed the stack's basic operations. In theory a stack may have any number of elements, and thus IsFull is not a basic operation. However, the representation that we chose for stacks sets a limit beforehand to the maximum number of elements a stack can have (the size of the array that we allocate to represent a stack), and we decided to define this new function that avoids stack overflow.

The second feature concerns the procedure Pop (see Figure 16.5). The fact that operation Pop is implemented as a procedure rather than as a function does not stem from a Pascal limitation but rather is due to the nature of operation Pop itself. Notice that Pop has two effects: It returns a value (the element on the top of the stack), and it modifies the stack (removes its topmost element). Because a function should perform no side effects, it should not be used to implement operation Pop. (An alternative could be the definition of two functions: function Top, which returns

FIGURE 16.4 Constructors for type `Stack` (using arrays).

```
function  NewStack : Stack;
{ This function returns a brand new stack }

var Stk : Stack;
begin
  new(Stk);
  Stk^.Top := 0;
  Stk^.UpperBound := Maxel;
  NewStack := Stk
end; { NewStack }


function Push (Elem : StackElm; Stk : Stack) : Stack;
{ This function returns the stack that results from pushing
  the element Elem into the stack Stk }

begin
  if Stk^.Top <> Stk^.UpperBound then
    begin
      Stk^.Top := Stk^.Top + 1;
      Stk^.StackItself[Stk^.Top] := Elem;
      Push := Stk
    end
  else
    writeln('Error ... Pushing into a full stack')
end; { Push }
```

the element at the top of the stack without modifying the stack, and function `Pop`, which returns a stack with its topmost element removed.)

The third feature worth mentioning concerns the implementation of `Push` and `Pop` (Figures 16.4 and 16.5). These include tests, respectively, of whether the stack is full or empty. They could have used the functions `IsFull` and `IsEmpty`. They don't. Our decision was exclusively an efficiency measure. Because `Push` and `Pop` manipulate the representation, we elected to directly manipulate the representation (when testing for a full or empty stack) rather than having an extra function call to functions `IsFull` and `IsEmpty`.

FIGURE 16.5 Selector for type `Stack` (using arrays).

```
procedure Pop (var Elem : StackElm; var Stk : Stack);
{ This procedure pops the top element, Elem, from the stack Stk }

begin
  if Stk^.Top <> 0 then
    begin
      Elem := Stk^.StackItself[Stk^.Top];
      Stk^.Top := Stk^.Top - 1
    end
  else
    writeln('Error ... Popping an empty stack')
end; { Pop }
```

FIGURE 16.6 Recognizers for type `Stack` (using arrays).

```
function IsEmpty (Stk : Stack) : boolean;
{ This function returns true just in case Stk is empty }

begin
  IsEmpty := (Stk^.Top = 0)
end; { IsEmpty }



function IsFull (Stk : Stack) : boolean;
{ This function returns true just in case Stk is full }

begin
  IsFull := (Stk^.Top = Stk^.UpperBound)
end; { IsFull }
```

Fourth, function `EqualStacks` (Figure 16.7) assumes that the elements of type `StackElm` can be directly compared using the relational operator =, as in the expression

```
Stk1^.StackItself[Stk1^.Top] =
                              Stk2^.StackItself[Stk2^.Top].
```

FIGURE 16.7 Test for type `Stack` (using arrays).

```
function EqualStacks (Stkl, Stk2 : Stack) : boolean;
{ This function returns true just in case Stkl and Stk2 are
  equal. It destroys the stacks }

begin
  if Stkl^.Top = 0 then
    EqualStacks := (Stk2^.Top = 0)
  else
    if Stk2^.Top = 0 then
       EqualStacks := false
    else
      if (Stkl^.StackItself[Stkl^.Top] =
          Stk2^.StackItself[Stk2^.Top])
      then
        begin
          Stkl^.Top := Stkl^.Top - 1;
          Stk2^.Top := Stk2^.Top - 1;
          EqualStacks := EqualStacks(Stkl,Stk2)
        end
      else
        EqualStacks := false
  end; { EqualStacks }
```

However, it may be the case that the elements of the stack are data types whose elements cannot be directly compared with the relational operator =. In this case, the basic operations for data type `StackElm` should provide a test for equality of its elements—let us call it `EqualElm`—and the above expression should become

```
EqualElm(Stkl^.StackItself[Stkl^.Top],
                              Stk2^.StackItself[Stk2^.Top]).
```

Fifth, function `EqualStacks` is conceptually very simple, but after its execution both stacks that are its arguments *are destroyed.* This is due to the fact that we implement stacks as pointers. Because passing pointers by reference and by value is the same (see Chapter 14, Exercise 20) and because this function changes the pointer to the stack's top elements, the

FIGURE 16.8 Alternative definition for `IsEmpty` and `IsFull`.

```
function IsEmpty (Stk : Stack) : boolean;
begin
  if Stk^.Top = 0 then
     IsEmpty := true
  else
     IsEmpty := false
end; { IsEmpty }


function IsFull (Stk : Stack) : boolean;
begin
  if Stk^.Top = Stk^.UpperBound then
     IsFull := true
  else
     IsFull := false
end; { IsFull }
```

arguments of the function are changed as a side effect. As an exercise, modify this function so that it does not destroy the stacks.

The final remark also concerns the functions `IsEmpty` and `IsFull`. You may have expected the function definitions shown in Figure 16.8. Regarding the functions of this figure, notice, for example, that `Stk^.Top = 0` evaluates to either `true` or `false` and that its value is *exactly* the value we want to assign to function `IsEmpty`. So there is no reason for the extra `if` used in Figure 16.8. Functions `IsEmpty` and `IsFull` of Figure 16.6 use redundant parentheses on the right-hand side of the assignment. These parentheses are used to increase their readability.

Figure 16.9 shows the input/output transformations for type `Stack`. In these procedures we assumed that the elements of a stack could be directly read and written using functions `readln` and `writeln`. If this is not the case, `readln` and `writeln` should be replaced by the input/output transformations for `StackElm`.

Having defined a representation for stacks and implemented the basic operations and the input/output transformations based on the representation chosen, we can now write programs that use data type `Stack`. An example of such a program is shown in Section 16.5.

FIGURE 16.9 Input/output transformations for type `Stack` (using arrays).

```
procedure ReadStack (var Stk : Stack);
{ This procedure reads a stack into the variable Stk }

var Elem : StackElm;
begin
  if  eof then
      Stk := NewStack
  else
      begin
        readln (Elem);
        ReadStack (Stk);
        Push (Elem, Stk)
      end
end;  { ReadStack }



procedure WriteStack (Stk : Stack);
{ This procedure writes the stack Stk }

var  Elem : StackElm;
begin
  if  IsEmpty (Stk) then
      writeln
  else
      begin
        Pop (Elem, Stk);
        writeln (Elem);
        WriteStack (Stk)
      end
end;  { WriteStack }
```

16.4 Stacks as pointers

The implementation of stacks as arrays has two disadvantages: It places an upper bound on the maximum number of elements that a stack can have, and whenever a new stack is created, it uses up all the storage needed for a full stack even if this stack remains empty (remember that a complete array is allocated to store the stack). To avoid these two problems, an

FIGURE 16.10 A representation of stacks using pointers.

```
type    Stack = ^RepStack;
        RepStack = record
                       Value : StackElm;
                       Next  : Stack
                   end; { RepStack }
```

FIGURE 16.11 Constructors for type Stack (using pointers).

```
function NewStack : Stack;
{ This function returns a brand new stack }

begin
  NewStack := nil
end; { NewStack }


function Push (Elem : StackElm; Stk : Stack) : Stack;
{ This function returns the stack that results from pushing the
  element Elem into the stack Stk }

var S : Stack;
begin
  new(S);
  S^.Value := Elem;
  S^.Next := Stk;
  Push := S
end; { Push }
```

alternative representation for stacks that uses pointers rather than arrays is presented.

Using this representation, a stack is a sequence of cells, each cell containing a stack element and a pointer to the next element in the stack (the element just below it). If we use pointers, a stack can be defined as shown in Figure 16.10. In this case, the maximum number of elements that a stack can have is limited only by the size of available memory, and thus the function `IsFull` is not needed. Figures 16.11–16.14 show the basic

FIGURE 16.12 Selector for type `Stack` (using pointers).

```
procedure Pop (var Elem : StackElm; var Stk : Stack);
{ This procedure pops the top element, Elem, from the stack Stk }

var StackAux : Stack;
begin
  if Stk <> nil then
    begin
      Elem := Stk^.Value;
      StackAux := Stk;
      Stk := Stk^.Next;
      dispose(StackAux)
    end
  else
    writeln('Error ... Popping an empty stack')
end; { Pop }
```

FIGURE 16.13 Recognizer for type `Stack` (using pointers).

```
function IsEmpty (Stk : Stack) : boolean;
{ This function returns true just in case the stack Stk is empty }

begin
  IsEmpty := (Stk = nil)
end; { IsEmpty }
```

operations for this representation. As an exercise, write the input/output transformations for this representation.

16.5 An evaluator for RPN expressions

This section presents a Pascal program that evaluates RPN expressions (whose operands are integer numbers), using data type `Stack`. The program uses the algorithm described in Section 16.1, and thus the stack used in this example contains integer numbers (the operands and the results of the operations): `StackElm` is of type `integer`. Figure 16.15 shows a program that evaluates RPN expressions and thus performs operations with

FIGURE 16.14 Test for type `Stack` (using pointers).

```
function EqualStacks (Stk1, Stk2 : Stack) : boolean;
{ This function returns true just in case Stk1 and Stk2 are
  equal. It destroys the stacks }

begin
  if Stk1 = nil then
    EqualStacks := (Stk2 = nil)
  else
    if Stk2 = nil then
      EqualStacks := false
    else
      if Stk1^.Value = Stk2^.Value then
        EqualStacks := EqualStacks(Stk1^.Next, Stk2^.Next)
      else
        EqualStacks := false
end; { EqualStacks }
```

FIGURE 16.15 A program to evaluate RPN expressions.

```
program RPNEvaluator (input, output);

{ This program evaluates RPN expressions using
  a stack }

const Digits = ['0'..'9'];
      Ops = ['+', '-', '*', '/'];
      Blank = ' ';

{ ------------ Representation for Stacks ------------ }

type StackElm = integer;
     Stack = ^RepStack;
     RepStack = record
                    Value : StackElm;
                    Next  : Stack;
                end; { RepStack }

{ -------- End of representation for Stacks -------- }
```

(continued)

FIGURE 16.15, *continued.*

```
var AuxStack : Stack;
    Error : boolean;
    Symbol : char;
    Result, Op1, Op2, Number : integer;
```

The stack's basic functions and the input/output transformations will be placed here.

```
   function Digit (c : char) : integer;
   { This function converts a character into a corresponding
     digit                                                    }
   begin
     Digit := ord(c) - ord('0')
   end; { Digit }

begin
  Number := 0;
  Error := false;
  AuxStack := NewStack; { The stack is created }

  writeln('Please write a postfix expression (in one line)');
  writeln('I will evaluate it ...');
  writeln;

  repeat
    read(Symbol);
    if Symbol in Digits then  { Keep reading the Number }
      begin
        repeat
          Number := Number * 10 + Digit(Symbol);
          read(Symbol)
        until not (Symbol in Digits) or eoln;
        AuxStack := Push(Number, AuxStack); { Push it onto the stack }
        Number := 0
      end
```

(continued)

FIGURE 16.15, *continued.*

```
    else
      if Symbol in Ops then  { Perform the operation }
        begin
          Pop(Op2, AuxStack);
          Pop(Op1, AuxStack);
          case Symbol of
            '+' : Result := Op1 + Op2;
            '-' : Result := Op1 - Op2;
            '*' : Result := Op1 * Op2;
            '/' : Result := Op1 div Op2
          end; { case }
          AuxStack := Push(Result, AuxStack)
        end
      else
        if Symbol <> Blank then Error := true
  until eoln or Error;

  Pop(Result, AuxStack);
  if Error or (not IsEmpty(AuxStack)) then
    writeln('Error in expression')
  else
    writeln('The value of the expression is ',Result:4)
end. { RPNEvaluator }
```

stacks. Notice that this program is written without concern about the internal representation of stacks. It is written *exactly* as if the type `Stack` were predefined in Pascal.

This example shows the usefulness of the abstract-data-type approach: Our program uses the abstraction, not the representation. For that reason, it is easy to write, easy to read, and easy to debug. Furthermore, if we decide to change the representation, the body of the program remains unchanged.

This example also shows that the ideas of data encapsulation and information hiding cannot be enforced in Pascal. In fact, the module that defines `Stack` is divided into two parts: one that appears in the type definition part and that tells how stacks are represented and another in the function-and-procedure-definition part that defines the implementation of the stack's basic operations. This means that the information concerning data type `Stack` is not encapsulated into a single part of the program. Moreover, information hiding does not exist either because the representation for stacks is known to the entire program.

However, we can use stacks as if both of these concepts were in effect, provided our program treats the stacks as a data type—that is, as if the information concerning stacks is encapsulated in a single module—and does not try to access the components of a stack using the representation chosen.

Summary

This chapter introduced you to data type `Stack`, defined the basic functions for stacks and two possible ways of implementing stacks: as arrays and as records. The representation using arrays has some serious limitations and should be avoided in Pascal. The reason that we presented it here is that it may be the only way to implement stacks in programming languages that do not have type `pointer` (for example, FORTRAN and BASIC). Finally, a complete Pascal program that uses stacks as an abstract data type was presented.

Suggested readings

You can explore the topics presented in this chapter more deeply by consulting the following books:

Dale, N., and Lilly, S. 1985. *Pascal Plus Data Structures, Algorithms, and Advanced Programming.* Lexington, MA: D. C. Heath.
This is a book on data structures using the abstract-data-type approach. It covers stacks, presenting several examples of their use.

Stubbs, D., and Werbe, N. 1985. *Data Structures with Abstract Data Types and Pascal.* Pacific Grove, CA: Brooks/Cole.
This is a book on abstract data types and Pascal, covering stacks among other structures. It discusses an application of stacks to memory management.

Exercises

1. ? Convert the following expressions into prefix notation:

a. `20 + 19 * 34 / 21 - 5`

b. `(20 + 19) * 34 /(21 - 5)`

c. `10 * 9 * 8 * 7 * 6`

2. **?** Redo Exercise 1, converting the expressions into postfix notation.
3. **?** Write a Pascal program to verify whether a given expression contains balanced parentheses: The total number of open parentheses should equal the number of closed parentheses, and, scanning the expression from left to right, the number of closed parentheses should never exceed the number of open parentheses. For example: `(a + (b + c))` has balanced parentheses, and `( a )) + (( b + c )` has not. (HINT: Use a stack to keep the open parentheses that you found.)
4. **?** Suppose that you want to represent stacks as arrays, but you want your stack to grow toward the low-subscript end; that is, the last element of the array stores the element at the bottom of the stack, the second-to-last element of the array stores the next element, and so on. Write the basic operations for stacks using this representation.
5. **?** Write the input/output transformations for type `Stack` when pointers are used in the representation.
6. **?** Modify the program of Figure 16.15 so that it uses the array representation for stacks rather than the pointer representation. Discuss what would be involved in such a modification if abstract data types had not been used.
7. **!** Redo the maze exercise of Chapter 10 using a stack. (HINT: Whenever the road divides, take one of the possible ways and push the other alternatives onto a stack. They will be helpful in the backtracking process.)
8. **?** Stacks are called last-in/first-out (LIFO) structures. Another structure that is very useful in computer science is the queue, a first-in/first-out (FIFO) structure. Queues have two ends: We insert the elements at one end of the queue and remove the elements at the other end of the queue. Queues correspond to the lines that people form when they are waiting to be served, for example, by a bank teller: The person closest to the teller (the person in the front of the queue) is the earliest arrival, and the person farthest from the teller (the person at the end of the queue) is the latest arrival. Specify the basic operations for queues: Queues have two constructors, `NewQueue` and `EnQueue`; one selector, `DeQueue`; one recognizer, `IsEmptyQueue`; and one test, `EqualQueues`.
9. **?** Choose a representation for queues and, based on your representation, implement the basic operations.
10. **?** Using the representation for queues of the last exercise, write the input/output transformations for data type `Queue`.

11. **!** Write a program that manages queues. It interacts with the user, who may supply the following commands:

N <q>

This command creates a new queue, represented by the nonterminal symbol q. If this queue already exists, it generates an error and ignores the command.

A <q> <n>

This command adds to the queue represented by the nonterminal symbol q the element represented by the nonterminal symbol n. If the queue specified does not exist yet, it generates an error and ignores the command.

D <q>

This command deletes the queue represented by the nonterminal symbol q. If the queue is not empty, it warns the user about it and ignores the command. If the queue does not exist, it generates an error and ignores the command.

R <q>

This command removes the element at the front of the queue represented by the nonterminal symbol q and shows this element to the user. If the queue is empty, it tells it to the user and does nothing. If the queue does not exist, it generates an error message and ignores the command.

P <q>

This command prints the queue represented by the nonterminal symbol q. If the queue does not exist, it generates an error and ignores the command.

E

This command terminates execution.

You should decide how to manage several queues, the syntax used to name queues, and the type of elements that may belong to a queue. You may want to include a help command to help the user.

12. **?** Write a procedure that takes a queue as argument and returns another queue with the elements in reverse order. Your procedure should use a stack to reverse the queue; that is, the original queue is emptied into the stack that is, in turn, emptied onto the new queue.

13. **!** The word *deque* (pronounced deck) is a short form for *d*ouble *e*nded *q*ueue, an ordered collection of elements with two ends. Elements can be added or deleted from either end, but no changes or inspections can be done elsewhere in the collection of elements. Specify the basic functions for the data type `Deque`.

14. **?** Choose a representation for `Deque` and, based on your representation, implement the basic functions of the previous exercise.

15 **?** The functions `EqualStacks` of Figure 16.7 and `WriteStack` of Figure 16.9 destroy the stacks that are their arguments. Modify these functions to avoid this problem.

CHAPTER 17

This chapter introduces lists as an abstract data type, discusses possible ways of representing lists and their corresponding basic operations. Some examples of functions that use data type list are shown.

THE LIST AS AN ABSTRACT DATA TYPE

Alice watched the White Rabbit as he fumbled over the list, feeling very curious to see what the next witness would be like.
Lewis Carroll, *Alice's Adventures in Wonderland*

A **list** is a data type whose elements are ordered: There is a first element on the list, a second element on the list, and so on. We can insert and delete items anywhere on the list.

We use lists in our daily life. To explain the use of lists, informally, we will look at a shopping list: The items in a shopping list are ordered, we can insert a new item anywhere into the list, and we can delete an item from anywhere in the list. In general, the insertions into a list and deletions from a list are done based on the elements already in the list. For example, suppose that we were writing a list for our weekly supermarket shopping. We can arrange the items in the list according to the products that can be found in each of the aisles of the supermarket; we can have a group with fruit juices, a group with cookies, a group with detergents, and so on (Figure 17.1). If, after creating the list, we remember that we also want to buy peanut butter cookies, we introduce this new item into the section corresponding to cookies—the position occupied by peanut butter cookies depends on the location of the cookies group in the list. The resulting list is shown in Figure 17.2. Deletions of elements from a list can be done anywhere in the list. If the first aisle we go through contains detergents, then the first item deleted from the list will be dishwasher detergent; on the other hand, if the first aisle we go through contains cookies, then the

FIGURE 17.1 Supermarket shopping list.

```
orange juice
lemonade
oatmeal cookies
chocolate cookies
crackers
dishwasher detergent
```

FIGURE 17.2 Updated supermarket shopping list.

```
orange juice
lemonade
oatmeal cookies
peanut butter cookies
chocolate cookies
crackers
dishwasher detergent
```

first item deleted from the list will be one of the cookies (the first one we find in the aisle).

In short, a list contains an ordered collection of elements. We can insert new elements anywhere in the list, and we can delete elements from anywhere in the list. Lists are widely used in computer science, and there are programming languages whose basic data type is the list, for example, LISP.[1]

17.1 Basic operations for lists

We now turn our attention to the basic operations for data type `List`. Among the constructors, there is an operation that takes a list element and a list, and inserts the element into the list. The question that should be asked about this constructor is *where* in the list the element should be

1. This is not quite true. LISP's basic data type is the S-expression, and lists are implemented as S-expressions.

inserted. The answer to this question will clearly depend on the application at hand. For example, we can have lists whose elements are sorted (using some sorting criterion), and we insert new elements so that the entire list remains sorted: We may want to insert an element in a given position of the list (the first position, second position, and so on), or we can do the insertions in some other way (for example, insert into a certain group of items that appear in the list). The idea underlying the definition of the basic operations of a data type is to define a small number of operations that *uniquely* identify the type as a separate data type. In the case of type `List`, the characteristic reflected by the constructor is that we can insert elements anywhere in the list. This chapter defines an operation that takes a list element, a list, and a position in the list and adds the element to the specified position in the list. Likewise, there are selectors that retrieve elements from a list. In the case of type `List`, the characteristic of the selectors is that we can *retrieve any* element from the list or we can *delete any* element from the list. This chapter defines two selectors, one that retrieves the *n*th element from a list and one that deletes the *n*th element from a list. Data type `List` has the following basic operations:

1. *Constructors.* `NewList` creates an empty list—a list with no elements. This function enables us to get started with lists by building lists from scratch. The function `InsertN` takes as arguments a list element, a list, and an integer indicating in which position of the list the element should be inserted and returns a new list resulting from inserting the element in the specified position of the list. If this integer is greater than the number of elements of the list, the function `InsertN` is undefined. For example, if `Lst` is the list shown in Figure 17.1 and `Elem` is `peanut butter cookies`, then `InsertN(Lst, 4, Elem)` will produce the list of Figure 17.2.
2. *Selectors.* Function `ElementN` takes as arguments a list and an integer number and returns the element of the list that is in the position specified by the number. For example, if `Lst` is the list shown in Figure 17.1, then the value of `ElementN(Lst, 2)` will be `lemonade`.[2] Function `AllButN` takes as arguments a list and an integer and returns a new list containing all the elements of the original list except for the element in the position specified by the number. For example, if `Lst` is the list of Figure 17.2, `AllButN(Lst, 4)` returns the list of Figure 17.1.
3. *Recognizers.* `IsEmpty` takes as argument a list and returns `true` just in case the list is empty.

2. We are not specifying how the elements of a list are represented. We are just assuming that they are represented in such a way that a function can return them.

4. *Tests.* EqualLists takes as arguments two lists and returns true just in case they are equal—they have the same number of elements and are in the same order.

In summary, data type List has the following basic operations:

1. Constructors: NewList, InsertN
2. Selectors: ElementN, AllButN
3. Recognizer: IsEmpty
4. Test: EqualLists

To use data type List, we also must define the input/output transformations. These operations map between the way we represent lists in our daily life and its representation used in our program. We represent a list as a sequence of items, each item being written in one line (see, for example, Figures 17.1 and 17.2). Operation ReadList reads a list from the input file and creates a corresponding list as a data structure. Function WriteList takes a list as an argument and writes it to the output file.

17.2 Lists as arrays

To write the basic operations and the input/output transformations, we must choose a representation for lists. We give two different representations: using arrays and using pointers. The representation using arrays has serious limitations and should not be used in Pascal. We present it here to show how to implement lists in programming languages that do not have type pointer, for example, FORTRAN and BASIC.

Behind both representations there is the following idea: In the implementation, each element of a list contains the element itself and an indication about which element follows it. If we represent *lists using arrays,* each element of the list is represented as an element of an array. This element contains two distinct parts: a part that stores the element itself and a part that tells where in the array the next element of the list is located. Figure 17.3 shows the representation of the list of Figure 17.1 using arrays. This representation assumes the existence of an array, called ShoppingList, each of whose elements contains a list element and the location (in the array) of the next element of the list. For example, ShoppingList[1] contains the first element of the list, orange juice, and the location of the second element of the list, ShoppingList[2]. To mark the element at the end of the list (dishwasher detergent, in our example), we say that the array element whose index is 0 (an index that does not exist) follows it. Figure 17.4 shows the shopping list of Figure 17.2, which was obtained by adding the element peanut butter cookies to the list of Figure 17.1. Notice that this addition does not entail a rearranging of the

FIGURE 17.3 A list represented using arrays.

ShoppingList[1]	orange juice	2
ShoppingList[2]	lemonade	3
ShoppingList[3]	oatmeal cookies	4
ShoppingList[4]	chocolate cookies	5
ShoppingList[5]	crackers	6
ShoppingList[6]	dishwasher detergent	0
ShoppingList[7]		
ShoppingList[8]		
ShoppingList[9]		

FIGURE 17.4 An updated list (using arrays).

ShoppingList[1]	orange juice	2
ShoppingList[2]	lemonade	3
ShoppingList[3]	oatmeal cookies	7
ShoppingList[4]	chocolate cookies	5
ShoppingList[5]	crackers	6
ShoppingList[6]	dishwasher detergent	0
ShoppingList[7]	peanut butter cookies	4
ShoppingList[8]		
ShoppingList[9]		

FIGURE 17.5 A representation of lists using arrays.

```
type List = ^ListRep;

     RepLstElem = record
                      Elem : LstElem;
                      Next : integer
                  end; { RepLstElem }

     ListRep = record
                   First     : integer;
                   Available : integer;
                   Elements  : array [1..Maxel] of RepLstElem
               end; { ListRep }
```

elements of the list, but rather a change in the "next-element information" in one list element (`oatmeal cookies`). Figure 17.5 shows a Pascal definition of lists using arrays. As we did with stacks, we define a `List` as a `pointer` to an `array` (rather than just as an `array`) to be able to write Pascal functions that return lists.

The elements of the list are stored in an array (`Elements`) whose elements (of type `RepLstElem`) contain the elements of the list itself (field `Elem` of the record `RepLstElem`) and the location of the element that immediately follows it (field `Next` of the record `RepLstElem`). At this point we don't care what the type of the elements of the list is, and thus we use the type `LstElem`. Furthermore, the representation of the list contains the location of the first element (field `First` of the record `ListRep`) and the location of the next available position for a list element (field `Available` of the record `ListRep`). The need for fields `First` and `Available` may not be apparent at first. To understand their role, suppose that in a program you have two lists. Each list is represented by an array, and these lists, most probably, have different lengths. So you must keep track of where the first element of each list is located. The right place to keep track of this information is in the list itself, thus the existence of fields `First` and `Available`. We stipulate that if `First` is zero, then the list has no elements; that

FIGURE 17.6 Constructors for type `List` (using arrays) (part 1).

```
function NewList : List;
{ This function returns a brand-new list }

var NLst : List;
    i : integer;

begin
  new(NLst);
  with NLst^ do
    begin
      First := 0;
      Available := 1;
      for i := 1 to Maxel - 1 do
          Elements[i].Next := i + 1;
      Elements[Maxel].Next := 0
    end;
  NewList := NLst
end; { NewList }
```

if `Available` is zero, then there are no more available elements; and that the last element of the list contains the integer zero in its `Next` field.

Figures 17.6–17.11 show the basic operations for type `List` using the representation of Figure 17.5. As an exercise, write the input/output transformations for lists using the representation just described.

Regarding the functions of Figures 17.6–17.11, it is important to explain how the available elements are organized. Recall from Chapter 14 that when we have a dynamic structure we must have some space (called the heap) from which we get the cells that we need. Lists are dynamic structures, thus we must implement the heap through an array. The array that stores the elements of our list has space for the maximum possible number of elements, whether or not they are used. The used elements are linked together. Field `Next` of each element points to the next element of the list. We also need some way to organize the available cells. The most natural way to do so is also to link them together as a list. In this way, all the cells that are not used are linked together as a list. Field `Available` points to the first element of the available-cells list. Whenever we get any new cell from our list, we get it from the list of available cells; whenever we return a cell to the available list, we return it to the list of available cells. This is the reason that function `NewList` (see Figure 17.6) initializes all elements of the array so that each of them points to the next one.

FIGURE 17.7 Constructors for type `List` (using arrays) (part 2).

```
function InsertN (Elm : LstElem; Lst : List;
                  Where : integer) : List;
{ This function returns the list that results from inserting
  the element Elm in the Where position of the list Lst }

var ElementsConsidered, NewCell,
    OldLocation, NextLocation : integer;

begin
  if Lst^.Available <> 0 then
    begin
      { Finding the location of the insertion }
      ElementsConsidered := 0;
      NextLocation := Lst^.First;
      while (ElementsConsidered + 1 < Where) and
            (NextLocation <> 0) do
        begin
          ElementsConsidered := ElementsConsidered + 1;
          OldLocation := NextLocation;
          NextLocation := Lst^.Elements[NextLocation].Next;
        end;
      if (ElementsConsidered + 1) = Where then
        { We skipped over "Where - 1" elements without getting to
          the end of the list }
        begin { Insert the new element }
          NewCell := Lst^.Available;
          Lst^.Available := Lst^.Elements[Lst^.Available].Next;
          Lst^.Elements[NewCell].Elem := Elm;
          Lst^.Elements[NewCell].Next := NextLocation;
          if Where > 1 then
            Lst^.Elements[OldLocation].Next := NewCell
          else
            Lst^.First := NewCell;
          InsertN := Lst
        end
      else
        writeln ('Error...the list does not have ',
                 Where:2,' elements')
    end
  else
    writeln ('Error...the list is full')
end; { InsertN }
```

FIGURE 17.8 Selectors for type `List` (using arrays) (part 1).

```
function ElementN (Lst : List;
                   Where : integer) : LstElem;
{ This function returns the element that is in the Where position of the
  list Lst }

var ElementsConsidered, NextLocation : integer;

begin
  if Lst^.First <> 0 then
    begin
      ElementsConsidered := 0;
      NextLocation := Lst^.First;
      while (ElementsConsidered + 1 < Where) and
            (Lst^.Elements[NextLocation].Next <> 0) do
        begin
          ElementsConsidered := ElementsConsidered + 1;
          NextLocation := Lst^.Elements[NextLocation].Next
        end;
      if (ElementsConsidered + 1) = Where then
        ElementN := Lst^.Elements[NextLocation].Elem
      else
        writeln ('Error...the list does not have ',
                 Where:2,' elements')
    end
  else
    writeln ('Error...the list is empty')
end; { ElementN }
```

Again, notice the existence of the recognizer `IsFull`, which was not presented when we discussed the list's basic operations. In theory, a list can have any number of elements, thus `IsFull` is not a basic operation. However, the representation that we used for lists sets a limit beforehand to the maximum number of elements a list can have (the value of `Maxel`—see Figure 17.5), and we decided to define this new function that avoids overflow.

FIGURE 17.9 Selectors for type `List` (using arrays) (part 2).

```
function AllButN (Lst : List; Where : integer) : List;
{ This function returns the list that results from removing the element in
  the Where position of the list Lst }

var ElementsConsidered, NextLocation, OldLocation : integer;

begin
  if Lst^.First <> 0 then
    begin
      ElementsConsidered := 0;
      NextLocation := Lst^.First;
      while (ElementsConsidered + 1 < Where) and
            (Lst^.Elements[NextLocation].Next <> 0) do
        begin
          ElementsConsidered := ElementsConsidered + 1;
          OldLocation := NextLocation;
          NextLocation := Lst^.Elements[NextLocation].Next
        end;

      if (ElementsConsidered + 1) = Where then
        begin
          if Where > 1 then
            Lst^.Elements[OldLocation].Next :=
                          Lst^.Elements[NextLocation].Next
          else
            Lst^.First := Lst^.Elements[NextLocation].Next;
          Lst^.Elements[NextLocation].Next := Lst^.Available;
          Lst^.Available := NextLocation;
          AllButN := Lst
        end
      else
        writeln ('Error...the list does not have ',
                 Where:2,' elements')
    end
  else
    writeln ('Error...the list is empty')
end; { AllButN }
```

FIGURE 17.10 Recognizers for type `List` (using arrays).

```
function IsEmpty (Lst : List) : boolean;
{ This function returns true just in case the list Lst is empty }

begin
  IsEmpty := (Lst^.First = 0)
end; { IsEmpty }


function IsFull (Lst : List) : boolean;
{ This function returns true just in case the list Lst is full }

begin
  IsFull := (Lst^.Available = 0)
end; { IsFull }
```

FIGURE 17.11 Test for type `List` (using arrays).

```
function EqualLists (Lst1, Lst2 : List) : boolean;
{ This function returns true just in case the lists Lst1 and Lst2 are equal }

begin
  if Lst1^.First = 0 then
    EqualLists := (Lst2^.First = 0)
  else
    if Lst2^.First = 0 then
      EqualLists := false
    else
      if (Lst1^.Elements[Lst1^.First].Elem =
          Lst2^.Elements[Lst2^.First].Elem) then
        begin
          Lst1^.First := Lst1^.Elements[Lst1^.First].Next;
          Lst2^.First := Lst2^.Elements[Lst2^.First].Next;
          EqualLists := EqualLists(Lst1,Lst2)
        end
      else
        EqualLists := false
end; { EqualLists }
```

17.3 Lists as pointers

Using arrays to represent lists is unsuitable for most list applications. These applications usually involve many lists of widely varying and unpredictable lengths. If lists are to be implemented using arrays, then the arrays must be made very large to allow for the longest possible list (recall the function `IsFull` from Figure 17.10). This approach wastes much memory space because every list requires the storage needed for the longest possible list. We can overcome this problem by representing *lists using pointers*. Also, with this second approach there is no need for us to manage the heap.

If we represent lists using pointers, we can use the representation shown in Figure 17.12. Figures 17.13–17.17 show the basic operations using the representation of Figure 17.12. Again, as an exercise, write the input/output transformations for this representation.

FIGURE 17.12 A representation of lists using pointers.

```
List = ^Elem;
Elem = record
          InfoLst : LstElem;
          Next    : List
       end; { List }
```

FIGURE 17.13 Constructors for type `List` (using pointers).

```
function NewList : List;
{ This function returns a brand new list }

begin
  NewList := nil
end; { NewList }

function InsertN (Elem : LstElem;
                  Lst : List;
                  Where : integer) : List;
{ This function returns the list that results from inserting the element Elem
  in the Where position of the list Lst }

var NewCell, OldLocation, NextLocation : List;
    ElementsConsidered : integer;
```

(continued)

FIGURE 17.13, *continued.*

```
begin
  { Finding the location of the insertion }
  ElementsConsidered := 0;
  NextLocation := Lst;
  while (ElementsConsidered + 1 < Where) and
        (NextLocation <> nil) do
    begin
      ElementsConsidered := ElementsConsidered + 1;
      OldLocation := NextLocation;
      NextLocation := NextLocation^.Next
    end;

  if (ElementsConsidered + 1) = Where then { We skipped over
    "Where - 1" elements without getting to the end of the List }
    begin { insert the new element }
      new(NewCell);
      NewCell^.InfoLst := Elem;
      NewCell^.Next := NextLocation;
      if Where > 1 then
        OldLocation^.Next := NewCell
      else
        Lst := NewCell;
      InsertN := Lst
    end
  else
    writeln ('Error...the List does not have ',
              Where:2,' elements')
end; { InsertN }
```

FIGURE 17.14 Selectors for type List (using pointers) (part 1).

```
function ElementN (Lst : List;
                   Where : integer) : LstElem;
{ This function returns the element that is in the Where position of
  the list Lst }

var NextLocation : List;
    ElementsConsidered : integer;
```

(continued)

FIGURE 17.14, *continued.*

```
begin
  if Lst <> nil then
    begin
      ElementsConsidered := 0;
      NextLocation := Lst;
      while (ElementsConsidered + 1 < Where) and
            (NextLocation^.Next <> nil) do
        begin
          ElementsConsidered := ElementsConsidered + 1;
          NextLocation := NextLocation^.Next
        end;
      if (ElementsConsidered + 1) = Where then
        ElementN := NextLocation^.InfoLst
      else
        writeln ('Error...the list does not have ',
                 Where:2,' elements')
    end
  else
    writeln ('Error...the list is empty')
end; { ElementN }
```

FIGURE 17.15 Selectors for type `List` (using pointers) (part 2).

```
function AllButN (Lst : List; Where : integer) : List;
{ This function returns the list that results from removing the element in
  the Where position of the list Lst }

var OldLocation, NextLocation : List;
    ElementsConsidered : integer;
```

(continued)

FIGURE 17.15, *continued.*

```
begin
  if Lst <> nil then
    begin
      { Finding the location of the insertion }
      ElementsConsidered := 0;
      NextLocation := Lst;
      while (ElementsConsidered + 1 < Where) and
            (NextLocation^.Next <> nil) do
        begin
          ElementsConsidered := ElementsConsidered + 1;
          OldLocation := NextLocation;
          NextLocation := NextLocation^.Next
        end;
      if (ElementsConsidered + 1) = Where then
        begin
          if Where > 1 then
            OldLocation^.Next := NextLocation^.Next
          else
            Lst := NextLocation^.Next;
          dispose(NextLocation);
          AllButN := Lst;
        end
      else
        writeln ('Error...the list does not have ',
                 Where:2,' elements')
    end
  else
    writeln ('Error...the list is empty')
end; { AllButN }
```

FIGURE 17.16 Recognizer for the type `List` (using pointers).

```
function IsEmpty (Lst : List) : boolean;
{ This function returns true just in case the list
  is empty }

begin
  IsEmpty := (Lst = nil)
end; { IsEmpty }
```

FIGURE 17.17 Test for the type `List` (using pointers).

```
function EqualLists (Lst1, Lst2 : List) : boolean;
{ This function returns true just in case the lists Lst1 and Lst2
  are equal }

begin
  if Lst1 = nil then
    EqualLists := (Lst2 = nil)
  else
    if Lst2 = nil then
      EqualLists := false
    else
      if Lst1^.InfoLst = Lst2^.InfoLst then
        EqualLists := EqualLists(Lst1^.Next, Lst2^.Next)
      else
        EqualLists := false
end; { EqualLists }
```

17.4 Manipulating lists

Having presented two alternative representations for data type `List` and defined the basic functions for each of them, we now discuss some functions that are useful in several applications that use lists. Chapter 18 presents a complete program that uses lists.

When working with data type `List`, we frequently want to compute the length of a given list. Figure 17.18 shows the function `Length`, which takes a list as argument and returns its length.

Next, we present two functions that insert and retrieve elements from a list. They differ from the basic functions in the sense that they are based on the elements of the list themselves, rather than on the positions that the elements occupy in the list. These functions assume that there is an ordering among the elements of the list and that this ordering can be tested by the function `IsGreater`, a test of data type `LstElem`: `IsGreater(a,b)` is `true` if `a` is greater than (comes after) `b` and is `false` otherwise.

The function `FirstGreater` takes as arguments a list and a list element and returns the position of the first element of the list that is greater than the element specified. It returns zero if the list is empty and returns the length of the list if no greater element is found. The function `InsertInOrder` takes as arguments a list and a list element and inserts the element in the list just before the first list element that is greater than it. These functions are shown in Figure 17.19.

FIGURE 17.18 Computing the length of a list.

```
function Length (Lst : List) : integer;
{ This function returns the length of the list Lst }

begin
  if IsEmpty(Lst) then
     Length := 0
  else
     Length := 1 + Length(AllButN(Lst,1))
end; { Length }
```

FIGURE 17.19 Searching and inserting in a list.

```
function FirstGreater (Lst : List; Elem : LstElem): integer;
begin
   if  IsEmpty(Lst) then
       FirstGreater := 0
   else
       if IsGreater(ElementN(Lst, 1), Elem) then
          FirstGreater := 1
       else
          FirstGreater := 1 + FirstGreater(AllButN(Lst, 1), Elem)
end;  { FirstGreater }


function InsertInOrder (Lst : List; Elem : LstElem) : List;
begin
   if  IsEmpty(Lst) then
       InsertInOrder := InsertN(Elem, Lst, 1)
   else
       if  IsGreater(ElementN(Lst, 1), Elem) then
           InsertInOrder := InsertN(Elem, Lst, 1)
       else
           InsertInOrder := InsertN(ElementN(Lst, 1),
                                   InsertInOrder(AllButN(Lst, 1), Elem),
                                   1)
end; { InsertInOrder }
```

Before concluding this section, we should point out that the development of the functions of Figures 17.18 and 17.19 was done without concern for the representation we chose for lists—either pointers, arrays, or something else—provided that the basic operations behave as specified in the abstract definition of type `List`. This is a fundamental result of using abstract data types.

Summary

This chapter presented another data type, `List`, using the abstract-data-type methodology. We discussed the basic operations and two possible representations for lists. Based on these representations, we implemented the basic operations. We presented two functions that manipulate lists independently of the representation we chose for lists.

Suggested readings

You can explore the topics presented in this chapter more deeply by consulting the following books:

Abelson, H., Sussman, G., and Sussman, J. 1985. *Structure and Interpretation of Computer Programs.* Cambridge, MA: MIT Press.
This book deals with abstraction in programming. It extensively deals with lists and operations on lists.

Dale, N., and Lilly, S. 1985. *Pascal Plus Data Structures, Algorithms, and Advanced Programming.* Lexington, MA: D. C. Heath.
This book on data structures uses the abstract-data-type approach. It covers lists and presents several examples of their use.

Knuth, D. 1973a. *The Art of Computer Programming, Vol. 1, Fundamental Algorithms.* Reading, MA: Addison-Wesley.
This is a classic book that extensively deals with lists. The book does not use the abstract-data-type approach but deals directly with the representation of the structures.

Exercises

1. **?** Write the input/output transformations for type `List` for the representation using arrays.
2. **?** Write the input/output transformations for type `List` for the representation using pointers.
3. **?** Rewrite the function `InsertInOrder` of Figure 17.19 using the function `FirstGreater`.
4. **?** Using a diagram, explain the behavior of the `List` basic operations for the array representation.

5. [?] Repeat Exercise 4 for the pointer representation.
6. [?] Redraw the list representation of Figures 17.3 and 17.4 taking into account the representation of the available-cells list. Assume that `Maxel = 9`.
7. [?] Write a program that reads a sequence of integer numbers and inserts them into a list.
8. [?] Write a procedure that receives as arguments a list of integers and an integer and removes from the list *all* its elements whose value is equal to the integer.
9. [?] Write a function that receives as arguments a list and a list element and inserts the element at the end of the list.
10. [?] Write a function that takes as argument a list and produces another list with the same elements but in reverse order.
11. [?] Write a function that takes as arguments two lists and returns a list resulting from concatenating them into a single list; that is, in the list produced, the element corresponding to the first element of the second argument of the function follows the element corresponding to the last element of the first argument of the function.
12. [?] Compare the solutions of Exercises 7–11 with the solutions of the equivalent exercises given at the end of Chapter 14. Admire the power of the abstract-data-type methodology.
13. [?] When inserting elements very often at the end of a list, it may be worthwhile to keep, with the representation, the location of the last element of the list. Find a representation for lists that, besides the information discussed in this chapter, stores the position of the last element of the list. Based on that representation, write the following operations:
    - **a.** `NewList`
    - **b.** `InsertN`
    - **c.** `AllButN`
    - **d.** `InsertLast`: a function that takes as arguments a list and a list element and returns a list resulting from inserting the list element in the last position of the list.
14. [?] Some applications require that each member of a list contain, besides the element itself, the location of both the element that follows it and the element that precedes it. How could you represent a list if such a condition is needed?
15. [!] Some applications of lists require that the elements of lists be, themselves, other lists. For example, in our supermarket shopping list, we could have had the elements arranged as on the next page.

```
fruit juices
     orange juice
     lemonade
cookies
     oatmeal cookies
     chocolate cookies
     crackers
detergents
     dishwasher detergent
```

We can look at this list in the following way: The list contains three elements, `fruit juices`, `cookies`, and `detergents`, and each element contains besides its name a list of items. For example, the element `cookies` contains the items `oatmeal cookies`, `chocolate cookies`, and `crackers`. Find the basic operations for this new kind of list. Notice that the main difference consists of having elements containing a name (for example, `cookies`) and a list of items. Thus, insertion and deletion must be done in two phases: finding the group and then finding the element inside the group.

16. **?** Find a representation for the lists of Exercise 15 and implement the basic operations and the input/output transformations (use the representation of Exercise 15).

17. **!** Based on the operations of Exercise 16, write a Pascal program that manages shopping lists. With this program you should be able to

a. Create new shopping lists.

b. Add new groups of items to your shopping lists.

c. Add or remove elements from groups of items.

d. Delete groups of items from your shopping list (for safety reasons, your program should only allow the deletion of the name of a group of items when the group contains no items).

e. List all the items in a group of items.

f. List all the groups in the list.

Design an interactive interface to achieve the desired interaction.

18. **?** The lists of Exercise 15 can be implemented by the list structure discussed in this chapter whose elements are another data type that also contains a list structure. Redo Exercise 17 using this approach.

19. **?** A **sparse array** is an array in which many of the elements are zero. Much space and computing time can be saved if only nonzero elements of a sparse array are explicitly stored. One method for storing sparse arrays is as a list in which each element contains three items: the row and the column of a nonzero element and the element itself. Suppose that you want to add and subtract sparse, two-dimensional arrays (arrays are added and subtracted by adding and subtracting elements in the same position), and, to do so, you want to implement two-dimensional sparse arrays as an abstract data type.

a. What basic operations do you need?
b. Implement the basic operations based on the representation described.
c. Write input/output transformations for two-dimensional sparse arrays.

20. **!** Generalize Exercise 19 for n-dimensional sparse arrays.
21. **!** Some of the functions presented in this chapter destroy the lists that are their arguments. Find them and rewrite these functions to get rid of the problem.
22. **!** Redo the program of Section 10.5 using a list representation for the names and telephone numbers. (HINTS: The elements of your list should be themselves another data type containing a name and the corresponding telephone number. Write the basic operations for this new data type. When creating the list of names and telephone numbers keep it sorted. Think carefully about the search function.)
23. **!** One way to represent polynomials is as a list in which each element contains two values: the coefficient and the exponent of each of the terms of the polynomial. For example, the polynomial: $4x^{12} + 7x^3 + 9x^2 + 10x + 5$ could be represented by the following list:

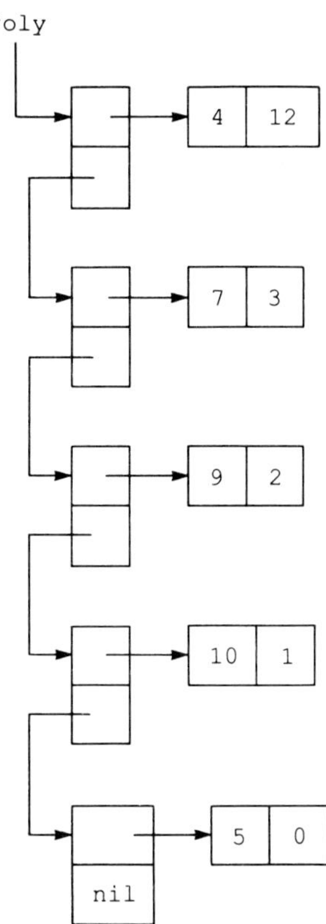

Suppose that you want to write a program that deals with polynomials and that you want to implement `Polynomial` as an abstract data type. You could devise the following basic operations: (a) *Constructors:* `AddPol`, which adds two polynomials; `SubPol`, which subtracts two polynomials; and `MultPol`, which multiplies two polynomials. (b) *Selectors:* `Coefficient`, which takes a polynomial and an exponent and returns the coefficient of the term with that exponent. (c) *Recognizers:* `IsConstant`, which tells whether the polynomial is a constant. (d) *Tests:* `EqualPol`, which tests equality of polynomials. Based on the representation described, implement the basic functions for polynomials.

24. ! Choose an abstract representation for polynomials and write the input/output transformations using the underlying list representation of Exercise 23.

25. ? Using the data type `Polynomial` write a program that reads polynomials and performs operations with them. Your program should ask the user to type polynomials and the operations to be performed with them and should show the results of the operations. Use a suitable interface language.

26. ! Write a Pascal program that asks the user to type in a polynomial and that outputs the derivative of the polynomial. (HINT: The derivative of a polynomial is the derivative of its first term plus the derivative of the polynomial without its first term.)

CHAPTER 18

This chapter introduces trees as an abstract data type, discusses possible ways of representing trees, and discusses their corresponding basic operations. An example that uses both trees and lists is presented.

THE TREE AS AN ABSTRACT DATA TYPE

So she went on, wondering more and more at every step, as everything turned into a tree the moment she came up to it.
Lewis Carroll, *Through the Looking Glass*

The last data type that we consider is a tree. We have already dealt with tree structures: Chapter 2 described the structure of a sentence and used an upside-down tree representation (Figures 2.1, 2.8, and 2.9); Chapter 5 described Pascal's data types in the form of an upside-down tree (Figure 5.1); Chapter 6 showed the order of evaluation of some expressions (Figures 6.4 and 6.5), and again, the objects shown had a tree structure; and Chapter 11 explicitly referred to a tree structure when we described records (Figures 11.5 and 11.7).

A **tree** is a structured data type that has a hierarchical relationship among its components. A tree can either be empty or composed of an element, the **root** of the tree, that dominates other trees. The terminology for trees mixes terms for natural trees with some that come from genealogical charts (family trees). A tree that dominates only empty trees is a **leaf.** The roots of the dominated trees are the **children** of the root of the dominating tree, and the root of the dominating tree is the **parent** of the roots of the dominated trees. The link between a parent and a child root is a **branch.**

In computer science, trees are usually written upside down, that is, with the root at the top. Figure 18.1 shows a tree whose root is labeled `A`. This tree dominates three trees: a tree whose root is labeled `B` (and only dominates empty trees), a tree whose root is labeled `C`, and a tree whose

FIGURE 18.1 An example of a tree.

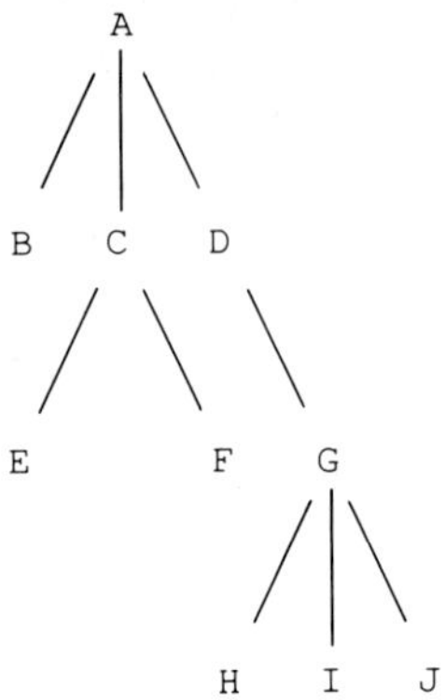

FIGURE 18.2 An example of a binary tree.

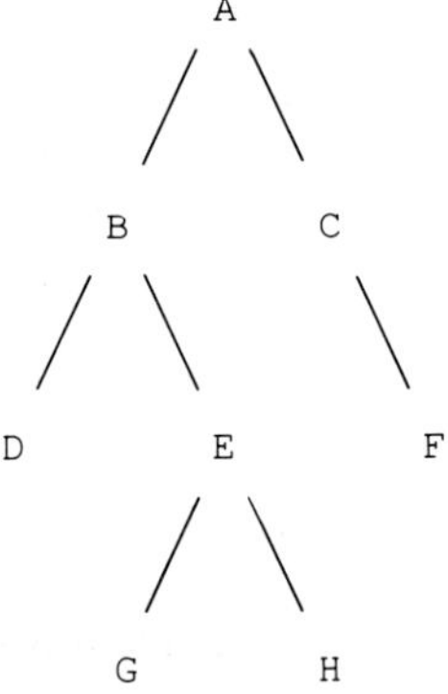

root is labeled D. A is the parent of B, C, and D. G is the child of D. The leaves of the tree are labeled B, E, F, H, I, and J.

A tree whose root dominates exactly two trees is a **binary tree.** That is, a binary tree is either empty or composed of a root that dominates two binary trees, the **left tree** and the **right tree.** The tree of Figure 18.1 is not a binary tree because some of its trees (namely, the trees whose roots are labeled A and G) dominate more than two trees. Figure 18.2 shows a binary tree. Notice that the tree whose root is C dominates the empty tree at its left and a binary tree whose root is `F` (this tree, in turn, dominates two empty trees).

This chapter only considers binary trees. This is not a serious limitation because it can be shown that any tree can be converted into a binary tree (see, for example, Knuth 1973a, Section 2.3.2). From now on, we will use the word *tree* to refer to binary tree.

18.1 Basic operations for trees

As usual, in order to study data type `Tree`, we start by defining its basic operations:

1. *Constructors.* `EmptyTree` creates an empty tree. This function enables us to get started with trees by building trees from nothing. `MakeTree` takes as arguments a root and two trees and creates a new tree with that root, whose left tree is the first tree and whose right tree is the second tree.
2. *Selectors.* `RootTree` takes as argument a tree and returns its root. `LeftTree` takes as argument a tree and returns its left tree. `RightTree` takes as argument a tree and returns its right tree.
3. *Recognizer.* `IsEmptyTree` takes as argument a tree and returns `true` just in case its argument is the empty tree.
4. *Test.* `EqualTrees` takes as arguments two trees and returns `true` just in case they represent the same tree—they have the same root, the same left tree, and the same right tree.

In summary, data type `Tree` has the following basic operations:

1. Constructors: `Emptytree`, `MakeTree`
2. Selectors: `RootTree`, `LeftTree`, `RightTree`
3. Recognizer: `IsEmptyTree`
4. Test: `EqualTrees`

We also must define the input/output transformations that map between the abstract tree and its internal representation. Procedure `ReadTree` reads data from the input file, creates a tree, and returns the tree that was read; procedure `WriteTree` takes as argument a tree and writes it to the output file. It would be nice if these procedures would read and produce a graphic representation as shown in Figures 18.1 and 18.2. However, procedures that produce output in this form and that read input in this form are very difficult to write in Pascal. Instead, we use an indented list as the external

FIGURE 18.3 A graphic representation of a tree.

```
A
 B
  D
   nil
   nil
  E
   G
    nil
    nil
   H
    nil
    nil
 C
  nil
  F
   nil
   nil
```

representation of a tree, as shown in Figure 18.3. This figure represents the tree of Figure 18.2. This representation uses the following conventions: The empty tree is represented by `nil`. The left tree and right tree of a binary tree are written on different lines, with the same indentation, and they are indented one space to the right of the root of the tree that is written on the line above. Functions `ReadTree` and `WriteTree` accept input in this form and produce output in this form, respectively.

To use data type `Tree`, our next step is to define a representation for trees and to implement the tree's basic operations and the input/output transformations based on the representation chosen.

18.2 Trees as arrays

As with stacks and lists, we can represent trees using arrays. This representation presents serious limitations but may be the only way to represent trees in languages that do not have type `pointer`. Figure 18.4 shows an array that stores the tree of Figure 18.2. A tree is represented by an element

FIGURE 18.4 A representation of the tree of Figure 18.2.

MyTree[1]	A	2	3
MyTree[2]	B	4	5
MyTree[3]	C	0	6
MyTree[4]	D	0	0
MyTree[5]	E	7	8
MyTree[6]	F	0	0
MyTree[7]	G	0	0
MyTree[8]	H	0	0
MyTree[9]			
MyTree[10]			
MyTree[11]			
MyTree[12]			

of the array. This element is a record that contains three fields: The first field contains the root of the tree, the second field contains the location (in the array) of the left tree, and the third field contains the location of the right tree. We stipulate that an empty tree is located at the position zero (a nonexistent position) of the array. Figure 18.5 defines type `Tree` using arrays. As with lists (see Figure 17.5), we use field `First` to store the root of the tree and field `Available` to store the location of the next available array location. As an exercise, implement the basic operations and the input/output transformations for this representation.

FIGURE 18.5 A representation of trees using arrays.

```
type    Tree = ^TreeRep;

        RepTreeElm = record
                          Root   : ElemType;
                          Left   : integer;
                          Right  : integer
                       end; { RepTreeElm }

        TreeRep = record
                       First     : integer;
                       Available : integer;
                       Elements  : array [1..Maxel] of RepTreeElm
                    end; { TreeRep }
```

18.3 Trees as pointers

Another way to represent trees is using pointers. In this case, a tree can be represented as shown in Figure 18.6. In this representation, a tree has a root and two pointers, one to the left tree and one to the right tree.

Figures 18.7–18.10 show the tree's basic operations for the representation of Figure 18.6. Figure 18.11 shows the function `WriteTree` for this representation. Notice that this function uses the function `WriteRoot`, which is the output transformation for the data type represented by the root of the tree. As an exercise, write the procedure `ReadTree`.

FIGURE 18.6 A representation of trees using pointers.

```
type Tree = ^TreeRep;

     TreeRep = record
                    Root  : ElemType;
                    Left  : Tree;
                    Right: Tree
                 end; { TreeRep }
```

FIGURE 18.7 Constructors for type `Tree` (using pointers).

```
function EmptyTree : Tree;
{ This function returns an empty tree }

begin
  EmptyTree := nil
end; { EmptyTree }


function MakeTree (R : ElemType; Lt, Rt : Tree) : Tree;
{ This function returns a tree with root R, left tree Lt,
  and right tree Rt }

var Nt : Tree;
begin
  new(Nt);
  Nt^.Root := R;
  Nt^.Left := Lt;
  Nt^.Right := Rt;
  MakeTree := Nt
end; { MakeTree }
```

FIGURE 18.8 Selectors for type `Tree` (using pointers).

```
function RootTree (T : Tree) : ElemType;
{ This function returns the root of the tree T }

begin
  if T <> nil then
    RootTree := T^.Root
  else
    writeln ('Error...taking the root of an empty tree')
end; { RootTree }


function LeftTree (T : Tree) : Tree;
{This function returns the left tree of the tree T }
```

(continued)

FIGURE 18.8, *continued.*

```
begin
  if T <> nil then
    LeftTree := T^.Left
  else
    writeln ('Error...taking the left tree of ',
             'an empty tree')
end; { LeftTree }


function RightTree (T : Tree) : Tree;
{This function returns the right tree of the tree T }

begin
  if T <> nil then
    RightTree := T^.Right
  else
    writeln ('Error...taking the right tree of ',
             'an empty tree')
end; { RightTree }
```

FIGURE 18.9 Recognizer for type `Tree` (using pointers).

```
function IsEmptyTree (T : Tree) : boolean;
{ This function returns true just in case the tree T is empty }

begin
  IsEmptyTree := (T = nil)
end; { IsEmptyTree }
```

FIGURE 18.10 Test for type `Tree` (using pointers).

```
function EqualTrees (T1, T2 : Tree) : boolean;
{This function returns true just in case the trees T1 and T2 are equal }

begin
  if T1 = nil then
    EqualTrees := (T2 = nil)
  else
    if T2 = nil then
      EqualTrees := false
    else
      EqualTrees := (T1^.Root = T2^.Root) and
                    (EqualTrees(T1^.Left, T2^.Left)) and
                    (EqualTrees(T1^.Right, T2^.Right))
end; { EqualTrees }
```

FIGURE 18.11 An output transformation for type `Tree`.

```
procedure WriteTree (T : Tree);
{This procedure writes the tree T }

   procedure WriteAuxTree(T : Tree; Indent : integer);
   begin
     if  T <> nil then
       begin
         write(' ':Indent);
         WriteRoot(T^.Root);
         writeln;
         WriteAuxTree(T^.Left, Indent + 2);
         WriteAuxTree(T^.Right, Indent + 2)
       end
     else
       writeln(' ':Indent,'nil')
   end; { WriteAuxTree }

begin
  WriteAuxTree(T, 0)
end; { WriteTree }
```

18.4 Tree sort

This last section presents an application that uses trees: tree sorting. **Tree sorting** is an efficient sorting algorithm that is done in two steps: It first takes the sequence of elements to be sorted and places them in a tree (this tree is a **binary search tree**); then it "walks through" (or **traverses**) the tree in a certain fashion, "visiting" the roots of the trees that compose it. This visiting is done so that the first root visited contains the smallest element, the next one visited contains the next to the smallest, and so on. Let us consider each of these steps.

The binary search tree is constructed in the following way: Starting with an empty tree, insert the elements to be sorted in this tree, one at a time. An element is inserted in an empty tree by creating a new tree whose root contains the element and whose left tree and right tree are empty. An element is inserted in a nonempty tree by first comparing the element with the root of the tree: If the element being inserted is smaller than the element at the root of the tree, then the element is inserted (using the same algorithm) in the left tree; otherwise, the element is inserted (using the same algorithm) in the right tree.

As an example of this procedure, suppose that we want to construct a binary search tree with the elements `5`, `14`, `8`, `2`, and `20`. First, create an empty tree and insert the element `5` in it, producing a tree whose root contains `5` and whose left and right trees are empty. Next, insert `14` in this tree. Because `14` > `5` (remember that `5` is the root of the tree), `14` is inserted in the right tree, producing the tree shown in Figure 18.12. The next element to be inserted is `8`. Because `8` > `5`, it is inserted in the right tree; furthermore, because `8` < `14` (`14` is the root of the right tree), it is inserted in the left tree of the tree whose root is `14`, producing the tree shown in Figure 18.13. The next element to be inserted is `2`; because `2` < `5`, it is inserted in the left tree, producing the tree shown in Figure 18.14. Finally, the last element to be inserted is `20`, generating the tree shown in Figure 18.15.

Using the tree's basic operations and assuming the existence of procedure `GetElement`, which gets the next element to be inserted in the tree, and function `ElementsExist`, which tells whether there are more elements to be inserted in the tree,[1] the algorithm that we have just described can be implemented by function `CreateTree` shown in Figure 18.16.

Once a tree is created, we must walk through the tree, visiting the roots of its trees. The roots are visited by the sorted order of the elements

1. Procedure `GetElement` could be, for example, the input transformation for the elements at the root of the tree, and function `ElementsExist` could be, for example, the function `eof`.

FIGURE 18.12 The tree after the insertion of 5 and 14.

FIGURE 18.13 The tree after the insertion of 8.

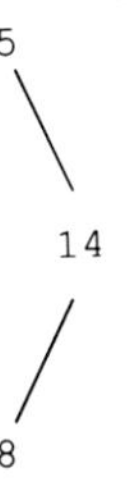

FIGURE 18.14 The tree after the insertion of 2.

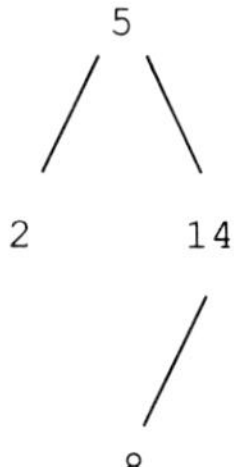

FIGURE 18.15 The tree after the insertion of 20.

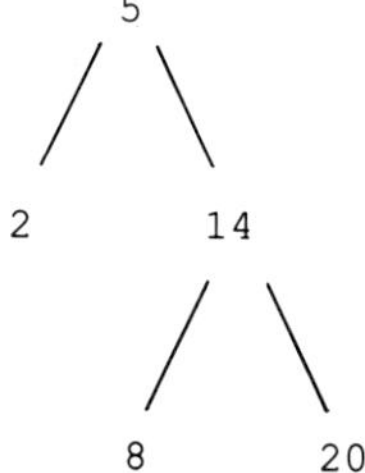

FIGURE 18.16 Constructing the tree.

```
function CreateTree : Tree;

var   Elem : ElemType;
      AuxTree : Tree;

  function InsertInTree (E : ElemType; T : Tree) : Tree;
  begin
    if  IsEmptyTree(T) then
        InsertInTree := MakeTree(E, EmptyTree, EmptyTree)
    else if E > RootTree(T) then
        InsertInTree := MakeTree(RootTree(T),
                                 LeftTree(T),
                                 InsertInTree(E, RightTree(T)))
    else
        InsertInTree := MakeTree(RootTree(T),
                                 InsertInTree(E, LeftTree(T)),
                                 RightTree(T))
  end; { InsertInTree }

begin
  AuxTree := EmptyTree; { We start with an empty tree }
  while ElementsExist do
    begin
      GetElement(Elem);
      AuxTree := InsertInTree(Elem, AuxTree)
    end;
  CreateTree := AuxTree
end; { CreateTree }
```

in the tree. The algorithm for tree traversal is the following: Traversing an empty tree causes no action to be taken; to traverse a nonempty tree, we first traverse its left tree, then we visit the root, and finally we traverse the right tree.

As an example, we apply this procedure to the tree of Figure 18.15. Because this tree is not empty, we must traverse its left tree, visit its root, and then traverse its right tree. To traverse its left tree (whose root contains 2), we must traverse the left tree, which is empty; we then visit the root,

FIGURE 18.17 The procedure for inorder traversal.

```
procedure InOrder (T : Tree);
begin
    if not IsEmptyTree (T) then
      begin
          InOrder (LeftTree (T));
          ProcessRoot (RootTree (T));
          InOrder (RightTree (T))
      end
end; { InOrder }
```

which contains the value 2; finally, we traverse the right tree, which is also empty. We are done with the traversal of the tree whose root is 2. We now visit the root of the original tree, which contains 5. The next step is to traverse its right tree—the tree whose root contains 14—and so on. As an exercise, convince yourself that the sequence of the roots visited is 2, 5, 8, 14, and 20. This method for traversing the tree is called inorder traversal.

Using the tree's basic operations and assuming the existence of a procedure `ProcessRoot`, which processes the root of the tree when this is visited, the algorithm that we have described can be implemented by procedure `InOrder` shown in Figure 18.17.

Figure 18.18 presents a Pascal program that implements tree sort. This program reads a sequence of integers, places them in a list that is then given to the sorting algorithm. The sorting algorithm writes the integers read in increasing order. Again, it should be stressed that this program uses data types `List` and `Tree` without concern for how they are implemented. Notice also that in function `CreateTree` of Figure 18.18, procedure `GetElement` of Figure 18.16 corresponds to selector `ElementN`, and `ElementsExist` of Figure 18.16 corresponds to test `IsEmpty`.

Tree sorting uses one of the most common operations performed on trees: tree traversal. The **traversal** of a tree consists of systematically processing the roots of the trees that belong to a given tree. We can traverse a binary tree in three ways: preorder, inorder, and postorder. In **preorder traversal,** we process the root of the tree and then traverse (in preorder) the left tree and the right tree. In **inorder traversal,** we traverse the left tree (in inorder), process the root, and then traverse the right tree (in inorder). In **postorder traversal,** we traverse (in postorder) the left tree, then the right tree (in postorder), and then process the root of the tree.

FIGURE 18.18 Program that implements tree sort.

```
program TreeSorting (input,output);

{ ---------- Representation of List and Tree ---------- }

type ElemType = integer;
     Tree = ^TreeRep;
     TreeRep = record
                   Root  : ElemType;
                   Left  : Tree;
                   Right : Tree
               end; { TreeRep }

     LstElem = integer;
     List = ^Elem;
     Elem = record
                InfoLst : LstElem;
                Next    : List
            end; { Elem }

{ ------ End of Representation of List and Tree ------ }

var Lst : List;
    Number : integer;
```

The basic functions of the data types List and Tree are placed here.

```
procedure TreeSort (Lst : List);

   procedure InOrder (T : Tree);
   begin
     if not IsEmptyTree(T) then
       begin
         InOrder(LeftTree(T));
         writeln(RootTree(T));
         InOrder(RightTree(T))
       end
   end; { InOrder }
```

(continued)

FIGURE 18.18, *continued.*

```
function CreateTree (Lst : List) : Tree;

var Element:LstElem;

   function InsertInTree (E : ElemType; T : Tree) : Tree;
   begin
     if IsEmptyTree(T) then
       InsertInTree := MakeTree(E, EmptyTree, EmptyTree)
     else if E > RootTree(T) then
       InsertInTree :=
             MakeTree(RootTree(T),
                      LeftTree(T),
                      InsertInTree(E,RightTree(T)))
     else
       InsertInTree :=
            MakeTree(RootTree(T),
                     InsertInTree(E,LeftTree(T)),
                     RightTree(T))
   end; { InsertInTree }
   begin
     if IsEmpty(Lst) then
       CreateTree := EmptyTree
     else
       begin
         Element := ElementN(Lst, 1);
         CreateTree :=
              InsertInTree(Element,
                           CreateTree(AllButN(Lst, 1)))
       end
   end; { CreateTree }

begin
  InOrder(CreateTree(Lst))
end; { TreeSort }
```

(continued)

FIGURE 18.18, *continued.*

```
begin
  Lst := NewList;
  writeln ('Please type an integer');
  writeln('(Control Z to terminate)');
  while not (eof) do
    begin
      readln (number);
      Lst := InsertN(number, Lst, 1)
      writeln ('Please type an integer');
      writeln('(Control Z to terminate)');
    end;
  TreeSort(Lst)
end. { TreeSorting }
```

FIGURE 18.19 Tree traversal procedures.

```
procedure PreOrder(T : Tree);
begin
   if not IsEmptyTree(T) then
      begin
        ProcessRoot(RootTree(T));
        PreOrder(LeftTree(T));
        PreOrder(RightTree(T))
      end
end; { PreOrder }


procedure PostOrder(T : Tree);
begin
   if not IsEmptyTree(T) then
      begin
        PostOrder(LeftTree(T));
        PostOrder(RightTree(T));
        ProcessRoot(RootTree(T))
      end
end; { PostOrder }
```

Procedures for preorder and postorder tree traversal are shown in Figure 18.19. It is worthwhile noting that these procedures use procedure `ProcessRoot`, which processes the root of the tree. Once again, notice that these functions were written without concern for how trees are represented: They were defined just in terms of the tree's basic operations.

Summary

This chapter presented data type `Tree` using the abstract-data-type methodology. We discussed the tree's basic operations and two possible representations for trees. Based on one of these representations, we implemented the tree's basic operations. Finally, an application that uses trees, tree sort, was discussed.

Suggested readings

You can explore the topics presented in this chapter more deeply by consulting the following books:

Dale, N., and Lilly, S. 1985. *Pascal Plus Data Structures, Algorithms, and Advanced Programming.* Lexington, MA: D. C. Heath.
This book on data structures uses the abstract-data-type approach. It covers trees and presents examples of their use.

Knuth, D. 1973a. *The Art of Computer Programming, Vol. 1, Fundamental Algorithms.* Reading, MA: Addison-Wesley.
This is a classic book that extensively deals with trees. The book does not use the abstract-data-type approach but deals directly with the representation.

Wirth, N. 1976. *Algorithms + Data Structures = Programs.* Englewood Cliffs, NJ: Prentice-Hall.
This book deals with data structures and contains a section devoted to trees. It deals with representation of trees in Pascal and covers binary trees, balanced trees, and optimal search trees. It addresses the problem of deleting nodes from a tree.

Exercises

1. ✓ Consider the following binary tree:

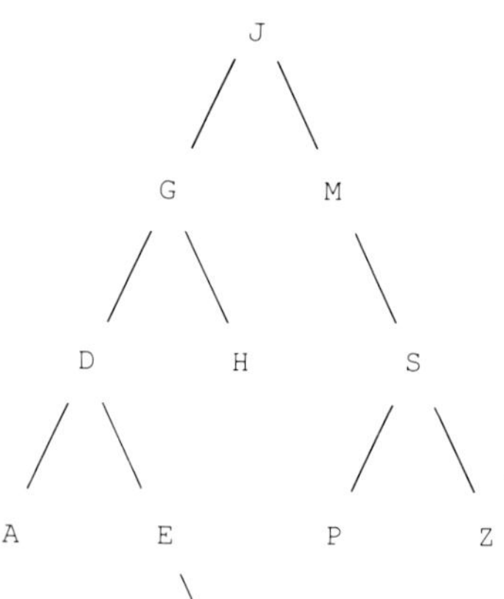

   a. What are the children of `G`?
   b. What is the parent of `S`?
   c. What are the labels of the leaves of the tree?
   d. List the labels of all the roots in preorder.
   e. List the labels of all the roots in inorder.
   f. List the labels of all the roots in postorder.
2. ? Draw the binary search tree that the function `CreateTree` of Figure 18.16 would produce with the following input: `G H A B C Z A A F G H J`
3. ! Write the basic operations for type `Tree` for the representation using arrays. (HINT: You may need to organize the available elements as a list.)
4. ? Write the input/output transformations for type `Tree` for the representation using arrays.
5. ? Define the basic operations and the input/output transformations for data type `NaryTree`: a tree whose root dominates at most `N` trees. Choose a representation for `NaryTree` and implement the basic operations and the input/output transformations.
6. ? The maximum depth of a tree can be defined as the depth of its longest branch. For example, the depth of the tree of Figure 18.2 is 3, and the depth of the tree of Figure 18.15 is 2. Write a function that takes as argument a tree and returns its depth.
7. ! Write function `ReadTree` that maps a tree in the format shown in Figure 18.3 in its internal representation (use the internal representation shown in Figure 18.6).

8. **!** Rewrite procedure `WriteTree` so that it displays a binary tree in the format shown in Figure 18.2.
9. **?** The order of evaluation of an expression can be specified using a tree. For example, the expression `(4 + 2) * 7` could be represented by the following tree:

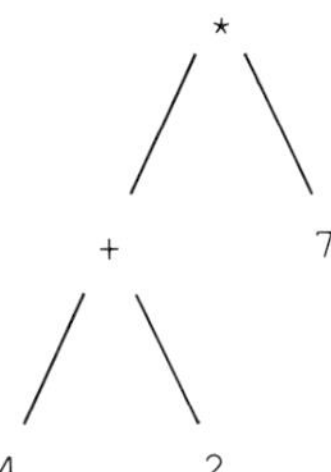

We first add `4` and `2`, and the result is multiplied by `7`. Choose a representation for trees that can be used to specify the order of evaluation of expressions. (HINT: Be careful with the type of the root of your tree.)

10. **!** Write a function that takes as argument a tree as described in Exercise 9 and returns the value of the expression that the tree represents.
11. **!** Modify the function of Exercise 10 so that variables could be allowed in your expressions. You will need a table that associates with each variable name its corresponding value. Whenever a variable is found, its value is looked up in the table. If the variable is not in the table, the error message `Unbound variable` <variable name> is printed, and the evaluation aborts. Create a mechanism to allow the user to assign values to variables.
12. **?** Rewrite the program discussed in Section 10.5 so that the names and phone numbers are stored in a binary search tree (a binary tree constructed using the algorithm of Section 18.4). Notice that in this tree the root contains two different pieces of information: the name of the person and the person's phone number. Write the function `Search` so that it searches through this binary tree.
13. **?** Modify the algorithm of Exercise 12 so that it handles the case where a person can have several phone numbers. (HINT: The root of your tree should contain the name of the person and a *list* containing all of the person's phone numbers.)
14. **?** Write a function that takes as argument a binary tree and counts the number of binary trees it contains. Your function should exclude the empty tree. For example, the tree of Figure 18.2 contains eight binary trees (one corresponding to each root).

15. **?** Write a function that takes as argument a binary tree and counts how many leaves it has. For example, the tree of Figure 18.2 contains four leaves.
16. **?** Another method of tree traversal is called **breadth-first traversal** and consists of traversing the tree level by level. In other words, the root of the tree is visited first, then all of its children are visited, then all of the children of its children are visited, and so on. Write a procedure that takes as argument a binary tree and traverses it using the breadth-first method.
17. **?** A tree is said to be balanced if (a) the number of roots on the left tree differs by at most one from the number of roots on the right tree and (b) both the right tree and the left tree are balanced. Write a function that takes as argument a binary tree and returns `true` if it is balanced and `false` otherwise.
18. **?** Redo Exercise 17 for a `NaryTree`.
19. **?** The width of a tree can be defined as the number of trees on its widest level. Write a function that takes as argument a tree and returns its width. (HINT: Use breadth-first traversal.)
20. **?** Modify function `CreateTree` of Figure 18.16 so that duplicated elements are ignored.

CHAPTER 19

A computing system is a collection of machines and programs—hardware and software—whose goal is to manipulate information. **Hardware** refers to the physical machines themselves, and **software** refers to the programs that dictate the behavior of the machines. This chapter introduces the main hardware components of a computer. It introduces the concept of an abstract machine and discusses the options available for building an abstract machine. We present the levels of a modern computer, discussing what each level does.

HARDWARE AND SOFTWARE

You really are an automaton—a calculating machine . . . there is something positively inhuman in you at times.

It is of the first importance not to allow your judgment to be biased by personal qualities.

Sir Arthur Conan Doyle, *The Sign of Four*

19.1 Main hardware components

The modern computer is one of the most complex machines ever built by human beings. As with every complex mechanism, it is useful to consider it as consisting of several components, each of which has a specific function. This section considers the main hardware components of a computer and the function of each.

A computer consists of several interconnected units working together under the command of a central processing unit. Most of the units that constitute a computer are called **peripherals,** and their goals are to transmit information from the outside world to the computer, to transmit information from the computer to the outside world, and to store the large amounts of information necessary for the proper functioning of the computer. A **central processing unit (CPU)** coordinates the functioning of all of these units. Besides the CPU and the peripheral units, there is a memory unit, the **main memory,** which stores the program being executed and the information being manipulated.

FIGURE 19.1 Hardware components of the PDP-11 computer.

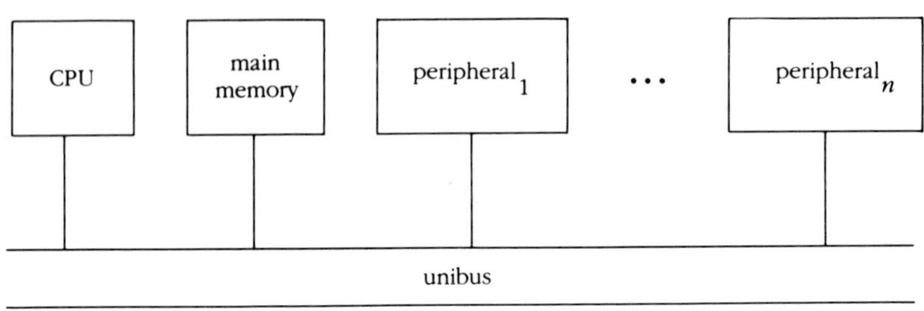

Figure 19.1 shows the main hardware components of the PDP-11 computer built by Digital Equipment Corporation: the CPU, the brain of the computer; the main memory, which stores the program being executed and the information being manipulated; and a series of peripheral units. All these components communicate with each other through a single connecting medium, the **unibus.**

19.1.1 CPU

The CPU is the brain of the computer. It fetches instructions from the main memory, decodes the instructions, and executes them. It is composed of a control unit, an arithmetic and logic unit, and internal registers. Figure 19.2 shows the CPU components of the PDP-11 computer.

The **control unit** transmits the signals that command the functioning of the computer and acts as the supervisor of the functioning of the computer as a whole. The control unit receives the instructions of the program being executed and analyzes them, one by one, finding out which action should be taken. After deciding what should be done, it sends signals to the unit that performs the action, which then executes the instruction.

The **arithmetic and logic unit (ALU)** executes arithmetic and logic operations. This unit works with binary numerals (numerals composed only of the symbols 0 and 1). It executes operations such as addition, subtraction, multiplication, and division. It can also compare two numbers and decide whether they are equal. These operations are executed at a very high speed. Even the slowest computers can execute thousands of operations per second.

The **internal registers** (the PDP-11 has eight) are high-speed memories that belong to the CPU. These registers are used to store temporary results of the operations and some control information (this is discussed later on in this chapter).

FIGURE 19.2 CPU components for the PDP-11 computer.

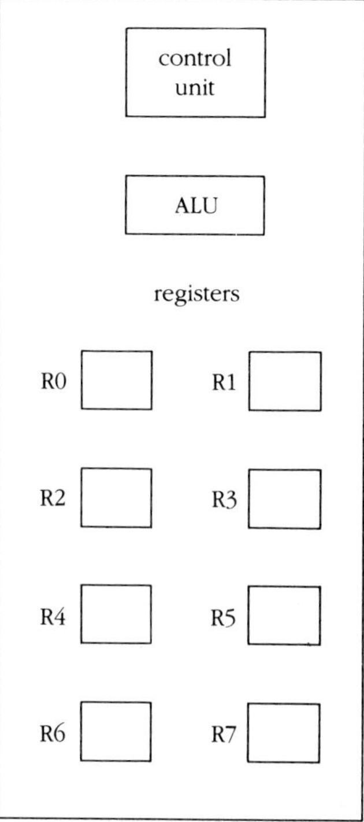

19.1.2 Main memory

Main memory is the component that stores the program being executed and the information being manipulated. The information is represented inside the main memory using only 0s and 1s. Each memory element that stores either a 0 or a 1 is called a **bit** (abbreviation of *b*inary dig*it*). Main memory is composed of an ordered set of cells, and each cell is composed of a fixed number of bits. The number of bits per cell is fixed for each computer, but it varies from computer to computer. For example, the PDP-11 has 8 bits per cell; the IBM/370 has 32 bits per cell; and the CDC Cyber 170 has 60 bits per cell. Each cell is uniquely identified by an **address.** A memory with n cells has addresses that go from 0 to $n - 1$. Whenever information is fetched from main memory or stored in main memory, we have to supply the address of the cell where the information is located.

The size of main memory is measured in thousands of cells. The symbol K is used to represent approximately 1000 cells, 1024 to be precise.

This means that a memory of 64K cells contains 64 × 1024 cells. It is important to note that if a memory of 64K cells is composed of 8-bit cells, it will have 64 × 1024 × 8 = 524,288 bits; if it is composed of 32-bit cells, it will have a total of 64 × 1024 × 32 = 2,097,152 bits. For this reason we usually use the word **byte** that corresponds to 8 bits to measure the size of main memory. For example, a memory of 500K bytes has 500 1024 × 8 = 4,096,000 bits.

Main memory has three characteristics that set it apart from the other kinds of memory that exist in a computer:

1. **Random-access memory (RAM).** This means that the access time to any cell in memory is constant and thus independent of the location of the cell inside main memory. (The **access time** can be defined as the interval of time that lasts from the instant at which an order is given to fetch information from main memory until the instant at which that information is available.)
2. **High-speed memory.** This means that the access time to the memory cells is very short. In the PDP-11 the typical access time is about one millionth of a second (a **microsecond**).
3. **Read/write memory.** This means that information can be read from memory and written into memory. Furthermore, these two operations have comparable duration.

The fundamental points to be remembered about main memory are (a) main memory is composed of cells, each of which has a fixed number of bits; (b) all cells of main memory have the same length; and (c) each cell has a unique address.

19.1.3 Peripheral units

Peripheral unit refers, in general, to hardware components other than the CPU or main memory. Typical examples of peripheral units are the following:

1. **Input devices.** They are, for example, terminals, optical readers, and measuring devices. These devices transfer information from the outside world into the computer.
2. **Output devices.** They are, for example, terminals, printers, and plotters. These devices transfer information from the computer to the outside world.
3. **Auxiliary memory devices** (also called secondary memory devices). They are, for example, magnetic-disk devices and magnetic-tape devices. These devices store a large amount of information and are necessary because it is not feasible (for cost and technologic reasons) to store every program and data file in main memory. In this way, programs

FIGURE 19.3 Magnetic-tape device.

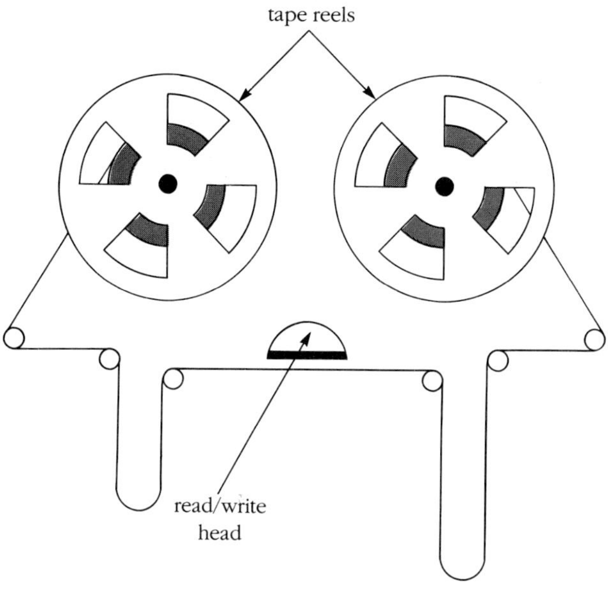

and data that are not being used are stored away in auxiliary memory devices. The most commonly used auxiliary memory devices are magnetic tapes and magnetic disks.

Magnetic-Tape Devices. Magnetic tapes used by computers are very similar to magnetic tapes used in tape recorders (Figure 19.3); however, instead of storing analog information, they store binary digital information. The tape is composed of a flexible material coated with a magnetizable material (iron oxide). The information is recorded on the tape by the magnetization of the magnetic coating in one of the two possible directions (Figure 19.4).

Typically, each symbol (character) is recorded on the tape using 8 bits. (See Appendix A for methods of character coding.) These bits are recorded across the tape. Magnetic-tape devices are not as reliable as CPU or main memory (errors can be caused by specks of dust on the read/write head or on the tape).

Magnetic tapes are **sequential access** devices. This means that the information is read in the same order in which it was written. If the read/write head is positioned at the beginning of the tape and the information that we want to read is close to the end of the tape, the magnetic-tape unit

FIGURE 19.4 Recording on a magnetic tape.

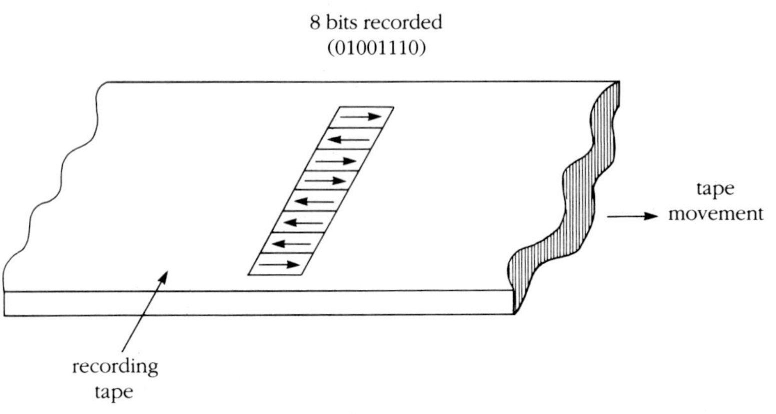

must read almost the complete tape, which can take several minutes. Magnetic tapes are cheap, have a large storage capacity, and are easily transportable but have the disadvantage of being slow. They represent a medium for "hand-carrying" information from one computer to another or for storing information that may not be used for long periods of time.

Magnetic-Disk Devices. A magnetic disk is a metal disk, about the same size as an LP phonograph record, that is coated with a magnetizable layer. Once placed in the disk drive, the disk continuously rotates at a constant speed (about 2400 rotations per minute). This kind of disk made out of metal is usually called a **hard disk.**

The information is recorded in a number of concentric circles, called **tracks** (Figure 19.5). In general, there are several hundred tracks on one disk. The tracks are, in turn, divided into **sectors;** in general, there are between 10 and 100 sectors per track, each of which contains a certain number of bits. Associated with each surface of the disk is a read/write head that can move from track to track. This head reads or writes information on one track at a time.

A disk drive often has several disks stacked vertically (Figure 19.6). In this type of device, there is one read/write head per surface of the disk. The read/write heads may be connected to form a read/write arm, which moves as a whole. For disk devices with several disks, a **cylinder** is the set of every track in the same vertical column.

Magnetic-disk devices are called **semirandom,** or **direct-access, devices.** This stems from the fact that, as opposed to magnetic-tape devices,

FIGURE 19.5 Magnetic-disk.

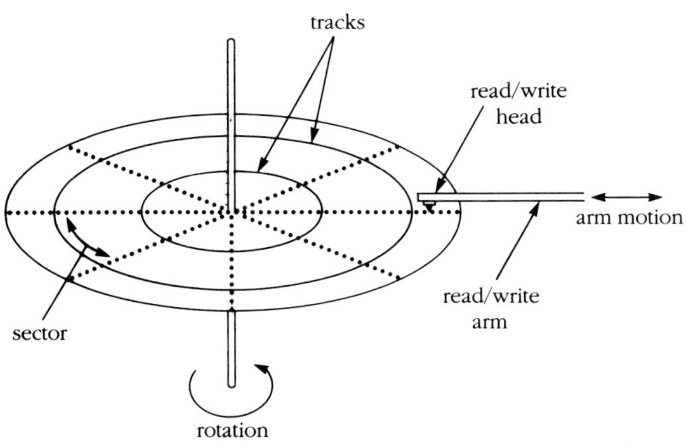

FIGURE 19.6 Magnetic-disk device.

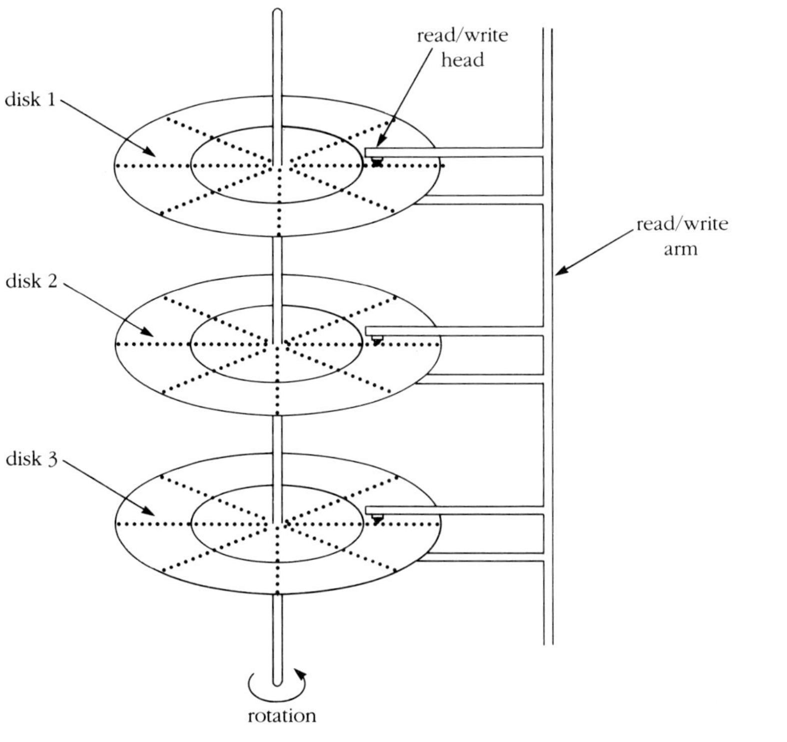

FIGURE 19.7 Floppy disk (diskette).

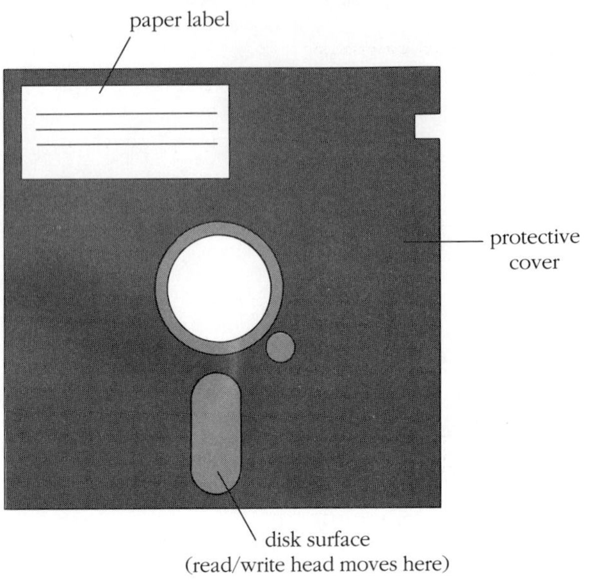

the information is not necessarily read in the same order in which it was written. To perform an **information transfer** operation (a read or write operation) on a magnetic-disk device, the track and sector where the information begins must be specified. Before the information transfer begins, the read/write head must be placed on the appropriate track. This first step is called **seek.** Once the read/write head is properly placed, it is necessary to wait until the desired sector is placed underneath it. This second waiting time is called **rotational latency time** and may go from zero seconds to the time it takes to perform a complete rotation. The **access time** is the sum of the seek time and the rotational latency time.

Magnetic-disk devices are used widely. Although their capacity is smaller and their price is higher than magnetic tapes, they have the advantage of having a much faster access time, which makes them the ideal storage device for frequently used programs and data.

There is another kind of disk widely used in personal computers: The **floppy disk,** or **diskette.** A floppy disk (Figure 19.7) is smaller than a hard disk, and it is made of a flexible plastic substrate coated with iron oxide. Floppy disks, which can be easily handled, store much less information than do hard disks (for example, a floppy disk for the Apple II

Computer[1] under the DOS-operating system contains thirty-five tracks, each track having sixteen sectors).

19.2 Fetch–execution cycle

Having studied the main hardware components of the computer, let us now discuss how the computer executes the instructions of a program. Assume that the program and data are already placed in main memory and coded in the binary system.

The CPU executes each instruction of a program through a sequence of small steps. Before considering what this sequence is, consider what information the CPU should receive to carry out a given instruction. First, the CPU should know the *memory address where the instruction to be executed is located* (remember that the instructions of the program being executed are stored in main memory); second, from the memory cell in that location, it should be able to find out *what operation* must be performed, where the *data needed for the operation* are located, and where the *result of the operation* should be placed. There is a register in the CPU, the **program counter,** that contains the address of the next instruction to be executed. (The first step before the execution of a program begins should thus be the initialization of the program counter so that it contains the address of the first instruction of the program.)

During the execution of a program, the CPU performs the following steps:

1. It fetches, from main memory, the next instruction to be executed—the address of this instruction is found in the program counter—and places that instruction in the instruction register. The **instruction register** contains the instruction that is being executed. During the execution of the program, the instruction register is used whenever the CPU needs any information about the instruction being executed (for example, the memory location of the operands, or in which memory location the result of the operation should be stored).
2. It updates the program counter to contain the address of the next instruction to be executed. Because the instructions of a program are stored sequentially in main memory, this step is normally done by incrementing the program counter by one.

1. The word *Apple* is a registered trademark of Apple Computer, Inc.

3. It decodes the instruction placed in the instruction register in order to decide what kind of operation should be performed.
4. It finds out whether the instruction being executed needs information from main memory. If so, it computes the memory location of the information needed.
5. If the instruction needs information from memory, it fetches that information from main memory and places it in appropriate CPU registers.
6. Once it knows the operation to be executed and has fetched the necessary information from main memory, the CPU executes the instruction; that is, it carries out the operation prescribed by the instruction.
7. If the execution of the instruction produced a result, it stores the result in the appropriate location in main memory.
8. It then goes back to Step 1.

From this discussion of the fetch–execution cycle, it may seem that once the execution of a program begins, these eight steps are continuously repeated and the execution never stops. To avoid this problem, there is the **halt instruction,** which has the effect of stopping the execution of the program; thus, the fetch–execution cycle is repeated until the halt instruction is executed.

While talking about the fetch–execution cycle, recall that the CPU finds out the type of instruction to be executed and fetches from main memory the operands needed for the execution of the instruction. Each instruction supplied to the CPU should therefore contain information about what operation should be performed, in which memory locations the operands for that instruction are stored, and in which memory location the result of the operation should be placed.

An instruction for the CPU is a **machine-language instruction** because it is written in the language that the computer understands. It consists of an operation code, which determines which operation should be executed, followed by a certain number (possibly none) of memory addresses. Before going on, it should be clear that a machine-language instruction is a string of 0s and 1s. In general, this string corresponds to one memory cell.[2] This string contains both the operation code and the memory addresses. One question that may be raised at this point is how the computer knows where the operation code ends and where the addresses begin. This decision is made by the computer manufacturer. When a computer is designed, it is decided that a certain number of bits in its instructions correspond to the operation code and a certain number of bits correspond to the memory address. Information built into the hardware tells where the operation code ends and where the addresses begin. Operation

2. In some computers, it may span several memory cells.

TABLE 19.1 Operation codes.

Operation code	*Meaning*
0001	Performs an addition
0010	Copies the contents of a cell
1101	Stops the execution

codes for the machine language are determined by the computer manufacturer when it decides which operations the computer should execute. For example, let us consider a hypothetical computer that, among others, can perform the operations represented in Table 19.1. This table presents the operation codes for three operations: addition, cell-contents copy, and the halt instruction.

The operation code is the only piece of information that cannot be left out of the machine-language instructions. All remaining information can be removed provided that certain rules are followed. Depending on the number of addresses specified in the machine-language instructions, computers can be classified into four-address (also called three-plus-one-address) machines, three-address machines, two-address machines, one-address machines, and zero-address machines. We consider here the instructions for a two-address machine. For a discussion of the other kinds of machines, refer to Eckhouse (1975) or Hayes (1978).

A **two-address machine** (for example, the PDP-11 and the IBM System 360) obeys instructions composed of an operation code and two addresses. We can represent these instructions as

`opcode`	`op1`	`op2`

In this instruction, `opcode` represents the operation code and determines the type of the operation to be performed, and `op1` and `op2` represent memory addresses. The operation represented by `opcode` is performed on the contents of the cells whose addresses are `op1` and `op2`, and the result of the operation is stored in the address of the second operand (that is, in the address represented by `op2`).

Assume that we want to use a two-address machine to add the contents of the memory cells whose addresses are 11101100 and 01111011, storing the result of the operation in the memory location whose address is 00011010. Assuming that the operation code for addition is 0001 and that the operation code for copying contents of memory cells is 0010 (see Table 19.1), this operation would be written in machine language using the following two instructions (in which blanks separate the fields containing the opcode and the addresses)[3]:

```
0010 11101100 00011010
0001 01111011 00011010
```

Because using binary codes makes our presentation very hard to follow, in the rest of this discussion we will replace the binary addresses by symbolic names that represent those addresses. Let us use `A` to represent the memory address 11101100, `B` to represent the memory address 01111011, and `C` to represent the memory address 00011010. Let us represent the operation code for addition by `ADD` and the operation code of the cell-contents copy operation by `MOV`. Using this notation, the two instructions given above would be written as

```
MOV A C
ADD B C
```

This convention is merely to make our presentation easier; whenever we actually want to communicate with the CPU, we *must use binary code.*

If we represent by [X] the contents of the memory cell whose address is X, then the actions executed by the previous instructions can be expressed in the following way:

`[C]` takes the value `[A]`
`[C]` takes the value `[B] + [C]`

The need for two instructions to perform a simple addition may seem strange at first. As an exercise, convince yourself that the single instruction `ADD A B` won't do the desired job.

Before ending this section, we should stress once again that a user does not have to worry about the details that have been described. Most computer users write their programs in a high-level programming lan-

3. In actual machine-language instructions, there are no spaces.

guage such as Pascal. Users do not even need to know on which type of machine their programs are being executed (that is, they do not need to know whether the program is being executed on a two-address machine, a four-address machine, or a zero-address machine). However, our short discussion on the format of the two-address machine-language instructions and about the way they are executed should make it easier to understand how a computer works.

19.3 Abstract, physical, and virtual machines

The cheapest, fastest, and the most reliable components of a computer system are those that aren't there.
Gordon Bell (Bentley 1985)

At the outset of this chapter, we said that a computing system consists of software and hardware. Section 19.1 discussed hardware, and Section 19.2 discussed how the hardware executes programs. Let us now consider the software.

There are two different classes of software: The first one consists of programs designed to help the writing and execution of other programs. This class of programs is called **systems software.** The second one consists of programs that execute the information manipulation required by specific applications. This class of programs is called **problem-oriented software.**

Whenever a new piece of software is added to a computer, the computer behaves as if it were a different machine. It does things it wasn't able to do before. It is as if a new machine were built on top of the existing one. The purpose of this section is to give you an idea of how these multilevel machines are created. To do so, we define three different types of machines: abstract, physical, and virtual machines.

19.3.1 Abstract machine

An **abstract machine** is a machine that only exists in our imagination or on paper. It is a machine that does not have a physical reality. An abstract machine is defined by a combination of specifications that determine which commands (instructions) the machine should accept (obey), which operations should be carried out for each command, what type of information should be received, what type of information should be produced, and what should be done when an error is detected. The definition of an abstract machine completely specifies the behavior of the machine without taking into account the way that the machine is built.

As an example, we define an abstract machine that is a calculator that only executes four arithmetic operations on integer numbers.[4] This machine has a set of sixteen keys (with the symbols 1, 2, 3, 4, 5, 6, 7, 8, 9, 0, +, −, ×, /, =, C) through which a person communicates with the machine and a display through which the machine communicates with the person. In the display the machine shows the number that the person is entering and the result of the operations executed by the machine. The machine has two memories, one to store the first operand of the arithmetic operations, the other to store the operation that should be performed. When the calculator is turned on, both memories are cleared, and the display shows nothing. For the sake of explanation, assume that the machine can accept and produce arbitrarily long numbers.

The following is a description of the behavior of the machine for each of the keys pressed:

1. Pressing one of the keys 1, 2, 3, 4, 5, 6, 7, 8, 9, or 0: The digit corresponding to the key pressed is placed to the right of the number in the display, and the result is shown in the calculator's display.
2. Pressing one of the keys +, −, ×, or / : It memorizes (in the memory containing the first operand) the number shown in the display, memorizes (in the memory containing the operation) the operation corresponding to the key pressed, clears the display, and gets ready to accept a new number, and the display shows 0.

   If there is already a memorized operation, it shows an indication of an error, both memories are cleared, the calculator gets ready to accept a new number, and the display shows 0.
3. Pressing the key =: It executes the memorized operation using the memorized number (first operand) and the number in the calculator's display (second operand), shows the result of the operation, clears both memories, gets ready to accept a new number, and shows the results of the operation on the display.

   If there is no memorized number or no memorized operation, it shows an indication of an error (in the display), both memories are cleared, the calculator gets ready to accept a new number, and the display shows 0.

   If the memorized operation is / and the number in the display is 0, it shows an indication of an error (in the display), both memories are cleared, the calculator gets ready to accept a new number, and the display shows 0.
4. Pressing the key C: It clears the memorized operation and the memorized number, gets ready to accept a new number, and shows 0 in the display.

4. A very similar machine was discussed in Chapter 12.

These actions define the behavior of a calculator without concern about the method of construction of this machine. This description could have been given hundreds of years ago by someone creative enough. This person would have imagined an ideal machine without having to worry about its method of construction. In short, the fundamental aspect of the definition of an abstract machine is *the specification of its behavior independently of its physical construction.*

19.3.2 Physical machine

When an abstract machine is directly implemented in hardware without using software, we obtain a **physical machine.** One of the alternatives to building our calculator would be to use electronic circuits. We can buy electronic circuits that have the behavior prescribed for each of the different operations to be executed by the calculator and connect them in such a way that the machine as a whole has the described behavior. In this way we obtain a calculator as a physical machine. The machine physically exists and only performs the job for which it was built. We can point to the electronic circuits that execute each of the operations.

19.3.3 Virtual machine

An alternative to building our calculator is to resort to programming. Suppose that we have access to a medium-sized computer, but we need a calculator. Generally, this type of computer does not directly accept instructions to execute arithmetic operations. (What it accepts are instructions for the operating system.) Thus, although we have available a machine capable of executing arithmetic operations, we cannot directly execute them in the machine. However, we can write a program that when executed by the computer allows the direct execution of arithmetic operations. When the computer executes this program, it acts as if it were a calculator. With this approach, we obtain the behavior of our abstract machine through a program that is executed by another machine.

When an abstract machine is implemented by a program executed by another machine (as we have just described), we obtain a **virtual machine.** This machine is called a virtual machine not only because it does not have a physical existence, but also because it only behaves as such while the program is being executed. In this case each command (instruction) given to the virtual machine is not executed directly by the hardware but causes the execution of part of the program.

The same abstract machine can be obtained by virtual machines implemented in different physical machines. Because these virtual machines are implementations of the same abstract machine, they have the same external behavior; that is, they answer the same way when they are supplied with the same data, but they are produced by different programs. Chapter 12 presented a Pascal program that represents an implementation of our abstract calculator as a virtual machine.

An abstract machine does not have to be implemented directly in a physical machine. It can be implemented using another virtual machine. Thus, we can imagine a **multilevel machine,** each of its levels corresponding to the implementation of an abstract machine on a physical or virtual machine. At the lowest level we have a physical machine; at all the other levels we have virtual machines. Each of these levels corresponds to an abstract machine, accepting a given set of commands. The set of commands accepted by a virtual or physical machine is called a **language.**

Most modern computers are composed of two or more levels, which are discussed in Section 19.5. Before presenting the function of these levels, we will study the process of implementing a virtual machine.

19.4 Implementation of virtual machines

This section presents how virtual machines can be implemented. Before considering the implementation of virtual machines, let us assume that we are given a sheet of paper with a set of instructions written in a foreign language (for example, Portuguese), and let us suppose furthermore that we do not understand Portuguese. If we want to carry out the sequence of instructions written on that sheet of paper, there are two possible alternatives. Either we could hire an interpreter, or we could hire a translator.

Suppose that we hire an **interpreter.** An interpreter is someone who knows both English and Portuguese and who translates the instructions one by one as we carry them out. The interpreter is next to us while we are executing the instructions and translates one instruction from Portuguese into English; we then carry out that instruction. Afterward, the interpreter translates the next instruction from Portuguese into English, and so on. This is repeated until all instructions are executed. This process has the advantage of having the interpreter next to us: If there is any question concerning the English version of the Portuguese instruction, the interpreter is able to help us in disambiguating this instruction. However, this approach has the drawback that if the set of instructions that we are executing contains a loop, the interpreter has to translate those instructions into English everytime we execute the instructions in the loop.

The other alternative consists of handing the sheet of paper containing the instructions to a **translator,** who hands back to us another sheet of paper containing the same instructions translated into English. The translator then goes away, and we are on our own to carry out the instructions written in a language that we can understand. This approach has the drawback that if there is any question on our part concerning one of the English instructions, the translator is no longer around to help us. On the other hand, if there is a subset of instructions that we must carry out over and over again, the translator would have only had to translate them once. The

FIGURE 19.8 Interpretation.

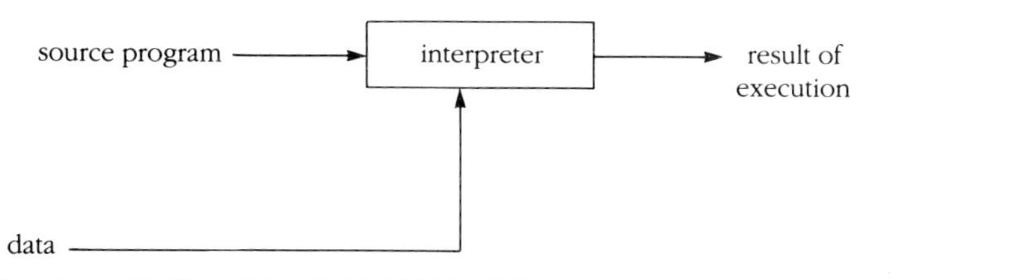

translator does not have to worry about the number of times we will execute the instructions.

The process of implementing a virtual machine is very similar. When we are implementing a virtual machine, we want to supply the virtual machine with a program written in a given language, a language that is not understood by the machine that is going to execute the program—that is, by the machine in which the virtual machine is implemented. A fundamental aspect of implementing virtual machines is that each instruction given to the virtual machine causes the execution of a sequence of instructions by a machine below it (either physical or virtual).

Suppose, then, that a program is executed by a virtual machine. How is the virtual machine going to execute this program? The two possible alternatives are called interpretation and translation.

1. During **interpretation** the virtual machine translates and executes one instruction at a time. It gets an instruction from the program, analyzes it, and executes the sequence of instructions that on the lower-level machine correspond to that instruction. Only after the complete execution of this set of instructions (and thus the execution of the instruction given to the virtual machine) does it consider another instruction (Figure 19.8).

   The program that implements this kind of solution is called an interpreter. During interpretation the instructions of the program are directly executed by the interpreter: Each instruction of the program being executed is analyzed by the interpreter in order to decide the set of instructions to execute; the interpreter executes them immediately before the analysis of the next instruction of the program.
2. During **translation** the virtual machine takes the complete set of instructions (the **source program**) and analyzes each one of them *before beginning their execution.* It then replaces each source-program instruction by the set of instructions that implements it, thus creating a new program, called the **object program.** This new program is equivalent to the first one—because with the same data it

FIGURE 19.9 Translation.

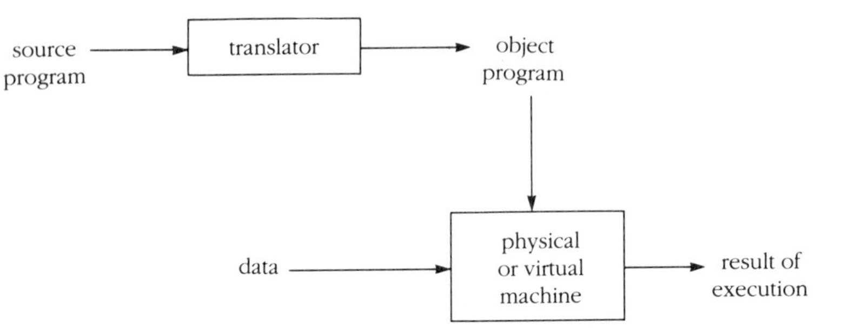

produces the same results—but it is formed by instructions that are directly executable by the machine in which the virtual machine is implemented. Finally, it executes the new program. Using translation the execution of a program goes through two different phases: first, the creation of a new program; second, the execution of the program created (Figure 19.9).

The program that implements this kind of solution is called a translator. There are two types of translator, depending on the type of translation being made: a **compiler** and an **assembler.** We will distinguish between these two notions later in this chapter. During translation the translator receives the program to be executed and creates a new program equivalent to the first one, but composed of instructions that are understood by the machine at the level immediately below. This new program is then executed by the machine at the lower level.

Interpretation and translation have advantages and disadvantages. Interpretation is slower than translation (typically 10 to 100 times slower) and requires more memory. Translation makes it harder to detect errors in the program and has less flexibility in the execution of the program. Let us now consider each of these in detail.

Concerning the speed of execution, if we remember that during interpretation the instructions are analyzed one by one immediately prior to their execution and if we imagine a situation in which part of the program is repeatedly executed, we can understand that each instruction of the loop is analyzed every time the loop is executed. This does not happen during translation because the program is translated all at once *before the beginning of the execution.* Each one of the instructions is analyzed only once, independently of the number of times it is going to be executed.

As for the required amount of memory, we can informally say that during interpretation two different groups of instructions must be kept in memory: the group that analyzes the instructions to be executed and the group that executes the instructions. During translation these groups of instructions are not simultaneously required. During the first phase (the creation of the object program), only the group that analyzes the instructions is needed; during the second phase (the execution of the object program), only the group that executes the instructions is needed.

Debugging is one source of headaches for programmers. During debugging we often need to know what the values of certain variables were when an error occurred and in which instruction this happened. With interpretation these two problems are easily solved. Because the instructions are analyzed and executed one at a time, when an error appears we know immediately in which instruction it occurred: The error is in the instruction that is being executed. Also, because the interpreter must necessarily have some way to associate each variable in the program with the memory location that stores its value, it can inform us about the values of the variables. During translation the situation is completely different: After the creation of the object program from the source program, the source program is forgotten because the virtual machine does not need it anymore. There is now a new program, the object program, that the machine understands and is able to execute. This new program has more instructions than the source program because each instruction in the source program was replaced by several instructions in the object program. Suppose now that an error is found during the execution of the object program. This error is detected in an instruction of the object program, but we cannot know which original instruction generated it. Also, during translation each variable of the source program is replaced in the object program by a variable in a different language. For instance, if the object program is in machine language, each variable in the source program is replaced by the address of the memory cell that contains the value of the variable. Thus, when an error occurs, it is no longer possible (or else it is very difficult) to know the value a variable had when the error occurred. This situation is rapidly changing with the introduction of a class of programs called debuggers. **Debuggers** are programs whose goal is to help the user of a compiled language in correcting the errors in his or her program. They provide error-correcting facilities that are similar to those supplied by interpreted languages.

Another consideration is the flexibility of program execution. During interpretation, once we can access the value of a variable, we can also change it. In certain cases, after detecting an error we can change the value of one or several variables and resume the execution of the program from the instruction where the error was found. This is not possible in translation. If we find an execution error during translation, we have to follow three steps: (a) Change the source program to remove the error; (b) create a new object program; and (c) execute the object program.

19.5 Levels of a computer

Most modern computers are composed of two or more levels. Systems with five levels, like the one shown in Figure 19.10, are common. This section describes the functions of each of these levels.

19.5.1 The microprogramming level

The lowest level has instructions that are directly executed by the electronic circuits of the computer. This level is called the **microprogramming level,** and the programs it executes are called **microprograms.** The set of microprograms is called **firmware.**

FIGURE 19.10 A machine with five levels.

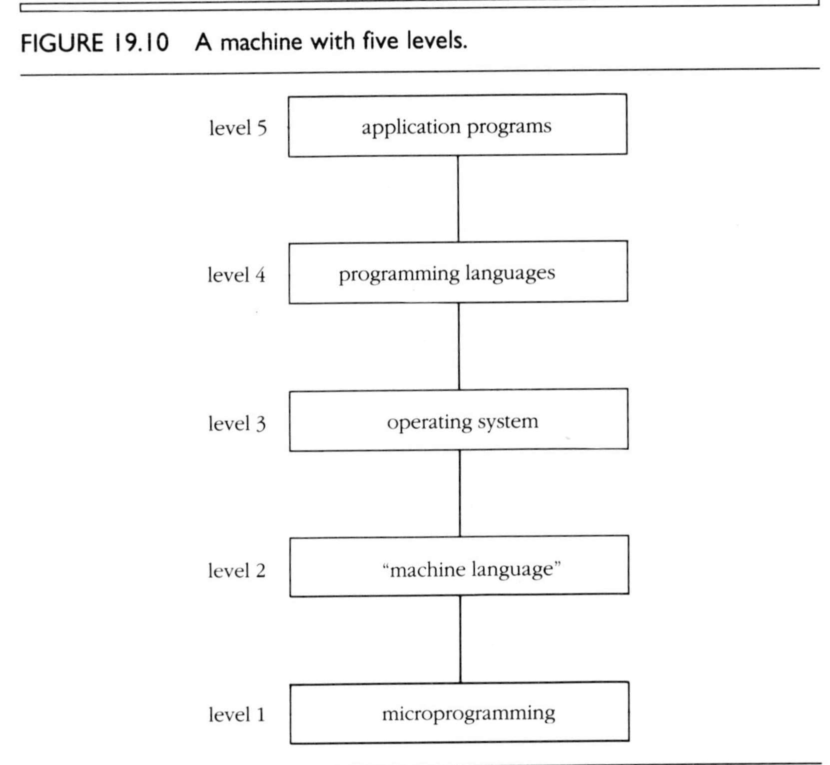

FIGURE 19.11 Hard-wired control.

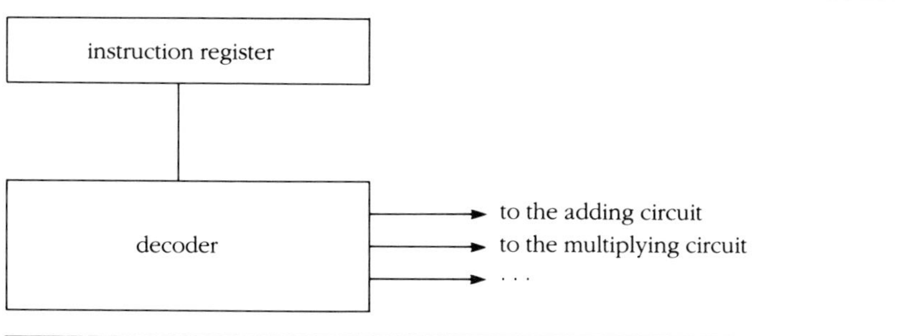

In early computers machine-language instructions were directly executed by the electronic circuits of the computer. These machines had a hardware component corresponding to each operation code. Whenever a machine-language instruction was executed, the corresponding hardware component was selected (Figure 19.11). Using this approach, each possible operation code in a machine-language instruction corresponds to an electronic circuit that executes the instruction.

The notion of microprogramming was introduced in 1951 by Maurice Wilkes (Wilkes 1951). However, its generalized use didn't start until the 1970s. It can be described as follows: Each machine-language instruction is executed by a program (the microprogram) that is stored in a special memory, the **control memory.** Each operation code corresponds to a location in the control memory, a location that contains the first microinstruction of the microprogram corresponding to the instruction to be executed (Figure 19.12).

Microprogramming can considerably reduce the number of hardware circuits needed to execute specific operations. For example, without microprogramming we need a hardware component to execute multiplications; with microprogramming we can perform a multiplication through the execution of a sequence of additions, thus not needing a multiplication component. When a computer uses microprogramming, what was described here by "machine language" is not, in fact, the language directly executed by the hardware.

The first microprogrammed computers had control memories that could not be modified. However, it has been shown that it is useful to provide read and write operations in control memories, and, at present, most computers that use microprogramming have control memories that make reading and writing possible. The capability of writing microprograms, and thus of defining the instructions of the "machine language,"

FIGURE 19.12 Microprogrammed control.

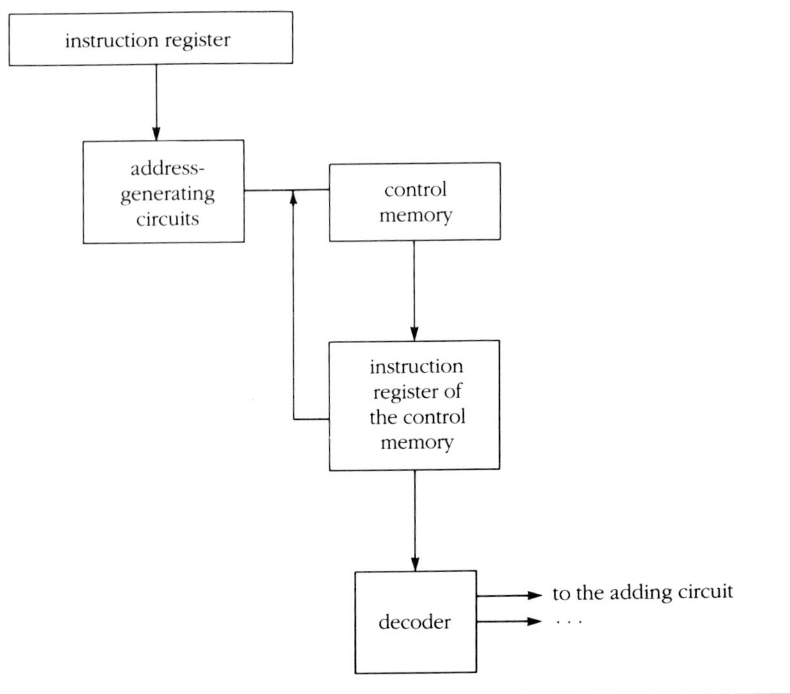

has several advantages compared with the use of computers with a fixed machine language:

1. The programmer can design the "machine language" according to the specific needs of a particular application. In fact, the programmer (or, better, the microprogrammer) can create a "machine language" suitable to a particular application.
2. The programmer can simulate other computers by writing microprograms to define the "machine language" of the other computer.
3. The useful lifetime of a computer can be increased. If new concepts about the set of the instructions in the machine language are developed, microprogramming allows the introduction of those concepts in the "machine language" of the existing machine. This also could be obtained through simulation—that is, through the creation of a virtual machine that would simulate the new "machine language." However, this second solution is very inefficient.

The main disadvantage of microprogramming compared with the hard-wired-control approach concerns the speed of execution of programs and production costs. Without microprogramming, machine-language instructions are directly executed by the hardware; whereas with microprogramming, the execution of each instruction in the "machine language" causes the execution of several microinstructions (typically, ten microinstructions). To increase the speed of execution of the machine-language instructions, more advanced technologies are used in the construction of control memories. These technologies allow an increase in the speed of execution but are more expensive.

19.5.2 The conventional-machine level

Level 2, the **conventional-machine level,** uses "machine language." "Machine language" appears in quotes because, as noted in the previous section, this may not be the language that the machine directly understands. Hereafter, we will not use the quotes in this expression, but remember that in certain computers—the ones that use microprogramming—this language does not correspond to machine language. In the case of microprogrammed computers, each machine-language instruction is implemented by a microprogram. This means that the execution of a machine-language instruction causes the execution of a microprogram, which, because it is executed in a physical machine, acts directly on the electronic circuits of the computer.

Machine language is composed of instructions that have an operation code and one or more memory addresses, as described in Section 19.2. These instructions are coded using the binary system. For example, suppose that in a certain two-address machine the addition operation has the code 0110 and that we want to add the contents of memory cell whose address is 01111101 with the contents of the memory cell whose address is 11100111. The machine-language instruction that executes this command is 01100111110111100111. Programming in machine language is very hard. Some of the reasons are:

1. The programmer must memorize all operation codes or constantly consult a manual.
2. The programmer must remember all memory addresses that contain information (constants, variables, or instructions).
3. Because the program and data are sequentially stored in main memory, the addition or deletion of instructions from the program can cause the alteration of every address in the program and consequently the alteration of the entire program.
4. Programming is error-prone. If a 0 is changed to a 1, or vice versa, the meaning of an instruction changes.

FIGURE 19.13 The assembly-language level.

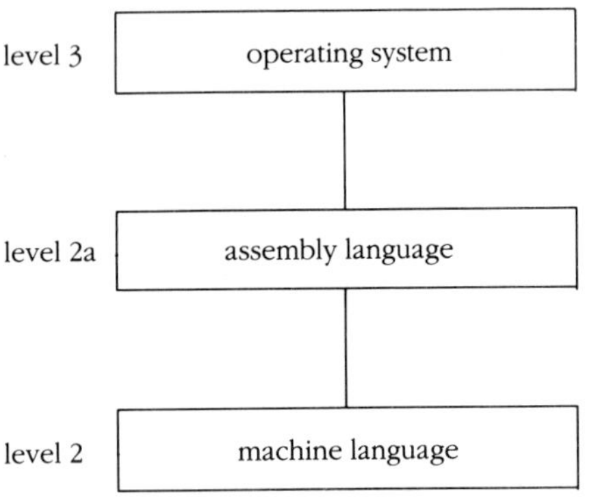

To avoid these disadvantages a new language, basically similar to machine language, was created. In this language the operation codes of the machine language are replaced by mnemonics representing the operations, and the memory addresses of variables are replaced by symbolic names. Considering the previous example, if `ADD` is the mnemonic that represents the operation code for addition, and `A` and `B` represent the variables whose values are found in the memory cells whose addresses are 01111101 and 11100111, respectively, then instruction to add the contents of memory location 01111101 and 1110111 is written `ADD A B`. This is **assembly language** and corresponds to a level located between levels 2 and 3 of Figure 19.10 (Figure 19.13). The assembly-language level is considered an intermediate level between levels 2 and 3 (and not a new level) because each instruction of the assembly language corresponds exactly to an instruction of the machine language (except for so-called macro instructions). Each assembly-language program is translated to the machine language by a translator called an **assembler.** This translator receives the program in assembly language and replaces each of its instructions by an equivalent instruction in machine language; finally, the program is executed in machine language. Although assembly language does not have the disadvantages pointed out for machine language, it has three other disadvantages (which are also disadvantages of machine language):

1. Each instruction corresponds to a very basic operation (addition, subtraction, and so on), thus producing long programs. Complicated programs, if written in assembly language, can have hundreds of thousands of instructions.

2. The language is oriented toward the machine instead of being oriented toward the application. The programmer must think in terms of the organization of the machine (internal registers, memory locations, number of addresses to use, and basic operations, for example) instead of thinking in terms of the application for which the program is being written.
3. An assembly-language program written for a given machine cannot be executed by a different machine (without using microprogramming or simulation).

19.5.3 The operating-system level

Level 3 contains a set of instructions that control the execution of all the programs in the computer. This level, the **operating-system level,** acts as a supervisor of every action executed by the computer.

The operating system supplies instructions that free the user from having to pay attention to the particularities of each of the devices that compose a computer. The programmer supplies the operating system with instructions such as "execute a given program," "store certain information," "print the result of the execution of the program," and so on; each of these instructions triggers the execution of a program at the operating-system level, which carries out the desired action. Besides making it easier to use the computer, the operating system allows different users to share the computing resources.

The **operating system** is the set of programs that allows the interaction between the electronic and mechanical components of a computer in such a way that they constitute an efficient data-processing system. The operating system has different functions according to the point of view of the user or the point of view of the computing center. According to the user's point of view, the function is to supply an easy and economical way to execute programs. According to the computing center point of view, the function is to allow the sharing of the computing resources among users in order to maximize both the execution speed of programs and the use of the computing resources.

From the user's point of view, the operating system supplies, among others, the following services:

1. *Creates, maintains, and accesses files.* The operating system allows programmers to give names to each of their files and to manipulate the information contained in the files just by referring to the name of the file and to the type of manipulation to be performed on the contents of the file.

2. *Transfers programs and data between peripheral devices and between them and main memory.* The operating system "hides" from the user all the details necessary to communicate among devices. For example, to transfer a file from the disk to the printer, you give a print command (typically, `print`) followed by the name of the file, and the operating system executes the transfer. You don't need to know the location of the file on the disk (that is, on which tracks and sectors it is stored) or the necessary operations to initiate the functioning of the printer.
3. *Allows file security, which gives access only to authorized users.* When there are several users on the same computer, one of the users might not want other users to have access to the information in his or her files. The operating system guarantees this protection, preventing unauthorized access to files. If, on the other hand, users want to share the information contained in their files with certain other users, they can tell this to the operating system, which, in turn, allows those users (and only those) to access those files.
4. *Maintains library programs.* **Library programs** are programs frequently used by certain classes of users. They are supplied by the manufacturer or by the group in charge of the computer. The operating system allows users to have access to these programs. Examples of library programs include translators and interpreters for the languages used on the computer, the text editor, and so on.
5. *Allows the use of electronic mail.* Users may send messages to other users (either on the same system or on systems connected to it). This facilitates communication and sharing of information among users.

From the computing center point of view, the operating system supplies, among others, the following services:

1. *Allows the use of the computer in multiprogramming mode.* The CPU can execute millions of operations per second. The operations executed by some peripheral devices (for example, input and output devices) are much slower than the operations executed by the CPU. For this reason, when the CPU must execute an operation that uses a peripheral device, it must wait until the peripheral device terminates processing. During this interval of time, the CPU could have done a great amount of work. Thus, keeping the CPU waiting for a slow device to finish the work it is currently doing is not economical. This led to the idea of keeping a program running until it needs a slow device, letting the program start the slow device, and then beginning (or resuming) the execution of another program that is waiting to be executed; this program is executed until the slow device terminates its work. This type of behavior is called **multiprogramming.** Most computers use multiprogramming. Using multiprogramming, there are several programs that are partly executed and waiting to resume

execution, and there is one program currently being executed by the CPU. Each program is usually given a certain amount of time for execution (which may vary between 0.1 and 100 seconds); at the end of this time, the program currently being executed is temporarily stopped and replaced by another program that is waiting to be executed. In addition, when one program starts a slow peripheral device, it is immediately replaced by another program.

2. *Allows the use of priorities in the execution of programs.* With multiprogramming there are several programs waiting to be executed by the CPU. A question that can be raised is which of them should be executed first. The operating system assigns a priority to each of these programs and executes the one with the highest priority.
3. *Gives the users the idea that the computer has a main memory bigger than it really is.* Certain operating systems use the concept of **virtual memory;** this simulates the existence of a much bigger main memory than there in fact is. In a very simplified way, an operating system that supplies virtual memory uses a disk to help simulate the existence of a memory bigger than the main memory. When the program being executed needs the information that is in the disk (this information can either be data or part of the program being executed), the operating system seeks for that information in the disk and places it in the main memory. All this is done without the user's awareness.
4. *Maintains an internal accounting system.* The use of a computing system is not free of charge. There are rates for CPU usage, printed lines, space in occupied secondary memory, and so on. The operating system takes care of keeping records of each user's time on the computer.

19.5.4 The programming-languages level

Level 4 is composed of the different programming languages that the computer supplies. Remember that both machine language and assembly language presented several disadvantages from the user's point of view. To avoid the disadvantages, new programming languages called **high-level programming languages** started to appear in the 1950s. A high-level programming language is characterized by the following aspects:

1. It uses a notation that is similar to the notation used by people when solving the problems for which the language was created. The statements `A = B + C`, `A := B + C`, and `ADD B C GIVING A` are examples in FORTRAN, Pascal, and COBOL, respectively, of instructions that add the values of the variables `B` and `C` and assign the result of the addition to the variable `A`. (Compare these instructions both with the machine-language and assembly-language instructions that perform the same operation.)

2. It can be used by a person with no knowledge of how the computer works. To use a high-level programming language, it is not necessary to know how the computer executes the machine-language instructions.
3. Programs written in a high-level programming language are largely independent of the computer that is going to execute them. This means that the same program can be executed on different computers with (almost) no changes.
4. When a program written in a high-level programming language is translated into machine language, each one of its instructions produces several machine-language instructions (with rare exceptions).

High-level programming languages have many advantages over machine language and assembly language: They are easier to learn, and programs in high-level languages are easier to write, to debug, and to understand. High-level programming languages are usually aimed at a given application, and consequently the number of these languages is almost as big as the number of different applications. According to Sammet (1983), in 1980 there were more than 200 high-level programming languages, out of which only a few were widely used. Among the most widely used high-level programming languages are the following (in order of their development):

1. *FORTRAN* (*FOR*mula *TRAN*slation). This language was introduced in 1956 by John Backus of IBM. It emphasizes scientific applications. FORTRAN has gone through several versions (FORTRAN II, FORTRAN IV, FORTRAN 77) that reflect the evolution of concepts about programming languages and that try to keep FORTRAN competitive. Nowadays, FORTRAN is still widely used for technical problems. The books by Sammet (1969) and Wexelblat (1981) present a detailed history of the development of the language.
2. *COBOL* (*CO*mmon *B*usiness *O*riented *L*anguage). This language was introduced in 1960 by a group of important computer users, including manufacturers and government agencies. Its development was carried out in the United States. It is a commercial, business-oriented language. Nowadays, it is the most commonly used language not only because it has many commercial applications—accounting, personnel management, and so on—but also because it was adopted by the U.S. Department of Defense. A detailed history of the development of COBOL is given in Sammet (1969) and Wexelblat (1981).
3. *ALGOL* (*ALGO*rithmic *L*anguage). ALGOL (Naur 1963) was introduced in 1960 by an international committee. It is a language with a scientific flavor, developed to allow the easy specification of algorithms; it is mainly used in Europe. ALGOL had a very influential role in the research and development of programming-languages concepts and has influenced most modern programming languages. Again, Sammet (1969)

and Wexelblat (1981) present a detailed history of the development of ALGOL up to 1968.

4. *LISP* (*LIS*t *P*rocessing). This language was introduced in 1960 by John McCarthy of the Massachusetts Institute of Technology (McCarthy et al. 1965). It is both a formal mathematical language and a programming language. It emphasizes symbolic computation. In the last twenty years, LISP has been the main language used in research in Artificial Intelligence. The history of the language, as told by its creator, can be found in Wexelblat (1981).
5. *APL* (*A* *P*rogramming *L*anguage). This language was introduced in 1962 by Kenneth Iverson of Harvard University (Iverson 1962). It was not developed with the goal of being a programming language but rather as a notation to express important algorithms. It is a scientific language that emphasizes array manipulation.
6. *BASIC* (*B*eginner's *A*ll-Purpose *S*ymbolic *I*nstruction *C*ode). This language was introduced in 1965 by John Kemeny and Thomas Kurtz (Kemeny and Kurtz 1967) of Dartmouth College. Their goal was to develop a language that was easy to learn and economical to use and implement so that it could be used by many people. Their goal was totally achieved, and BASIC is the most common language among personal computer users.
7. *PL/1* (*P*rogramming *L*anguage *One*). This language was introduced in 1965 by an IBM–organized committee. Its goal was to be a universal language, applicable both for scientific and commercial problems. The history of the language can be found in Sammet (1969).
8. *SNOBOL* (*S*tri*N*g-*O*riented Sym*BO*lic *L*anguage). This language was designed during the 1960s at Bell Telephone Laboratories as a language for manipulating character strings. It has evolved through a series of versions, SNOBOL4 (Griswold, Poage, and Polonsky 1971) being the most powerful one.
9. *Pascal* [named after the French mathematician Blaise Pascal (1623–1662)]. This language was introduced in 1971 by Niklaus Wirth of the Institut für Informatik, ETH (Eidgenossische Technische Hochshule), Zurich, Switzerland (Jensen and Wirth 1974). Pascal was based on ALGOL and was developed to teach structured programming. It is oriented toward both scientific and commercial applications. It also is designed for easy development and maintenance of large programs.
10. *PROLOG* (*PRO*gramming in *LOG*ic). This language was introduced in 1972 by Alain Colmerauer of the University of Aix-Marseille (France) (Clocksin and Mellish 1981). It is a language based on predicate logic and used in Artificial Intelligence applications. It was the language selected by the Japanese fifth-generation project (Feigenbaum and McCorduck 1983).

11. *C*. This language was developed by Dennis Ritchie at the Bell Telephone Laboratories around 1972 (Kernighan and Ritchie 1978). It was developed for writing systems software for the PDP-11 computer. It is currently implemented on a large number of computers. The main characteristic of C is that it allows a programmer to manipulate objects that are usually only accessible through assembly- or machine-language instructions, while retaining aspects of a high-level language.
12. *Modula-2*. This language is strongly based on Pascal and developed by Niklaus Wirth (Wirth 1976, 1978). Modula-2 is a language for programming using abstract data types.
13. *Ada* [named after Ada Byron (1815–1852), Countess of Lovelace, the daughter of the poet Lord Byron and considered to be the first programmer]. This language was developed in 1980 by a committee organized by the U.S. Department of Defense (Gehani 1983 and Pyle 1981). It is used for scientific and commercial applications, numeric applications, development of systems software, and real-time processing. It replaced COBOL in the programs developed by the Department of Defense.

High-level programming languages can be classified into two main groups: imperative languages and functional languages. **Imperative languages** account for the large majority of high-level programming languages (for instance, FORTRAN, COBOL, and Pascal). They are based on the traditional idea of the behavior of a computer [called von Neumann's model; see Backus (1978) or Harland (1984)]. That is, they depend on the existence of variables (which correspond to memory cells) and on the assignment of values to variables. Programs in these languages consist of sequences of instructions (also called **statements**) that are executed one after the other. **Functional languages** (for example, LISP) are based on the notion of function application. A program in a functional language is a function that uses values produced by other functions. In these languages the notion of a variable is not that important.

Each high-level programming language defines an abstract machine that accepts that language as its "machine language." This abstract machine is almost always implemented as a virtual machine, and it can use either interpretation or translation. A translator program for a high-level language is called a **compiler.**

19.5.5 The application-programs levels

Level 5 (and the levels that can be built above it) are formed by application programs written by computer users. A programmer who writes a program is defining a virtual machine whose goal is to solve the problem for which the program was developed. For example, if we write a program to play chess, we are creating a virtual machine that accepts commands to make chess moves. This is the level for which this book was written.

Summary

A computing system is composed of hardware and software. The main hardware components of a computer are the CPU, main memory, and peripherals. The CPU executes the instruction, the main memory stores the program being executed and the data being manipulated, and the peripherals serve multiple purposes such as holding large amounts of data and communicating with the outside world.

Machine language was introduced. From the format of machine-language instructions, we saw that programming directly in machine language is not pleasant. The concept of a multilevel machine was introduced, and we went through the several levels of a modern computer: microprogramming level, machine-language level, operating-system level, programming-languages level, and applications level. You also learned how a new level can be implemented: through translation or through interpretation.

Thus grew the tale of Wonderland:
Thus slowly, one by one,
Its quaint events were hammered out—
And now the tale is done,
And home we steer, a merry crew
Beneath the setting sun.
Lewis Carroll, *Alice's Adventures in Wonderland*

Suggested readings

You can explore the topics presented in this chapter more deeply by consulting the following publications:

Denning, P. 1970. "Virtual Memory," *Computing Surveys,* 2 (3):153–189.
This article is an excellent introduction to the virtual-memory concept and its implementations.

Eckhouse, R., Jr. 1975. *Minicomputer Systems: Organization and Programming (PDP-11).* Englewood Cliffs, NJ: Prentice-Hall.
This book presents a good discussion of the several machine-language formats and describes in detail the organization and structure of the PDP-11 computer. It also describes the machine language of the PDP-11 computer.

Hayes, J. 1978. *Computer Architecture and Organization.* New York: McGraw-Hill.
This book covers topics such as memory organization, CPU architecture, and instruction formats and discusses microprogramming and several alternatives to designing microinstruction formats.

Hill, F., and Peterson, G. 1978. *Digital Systems: Hardware Organization and Design.* New York: Wiley.
This book presents the organization of a computer at the hardware level, describing in great detail the fetch–execution cycle, memory-access processes, and so on. It describes hardware components at the level of electronic components, discusses machine language and a microprogramming language, and

presents a notation to write programs in machine language and microprograms for a hypothetical computer, the SIC, describing its functioning at the hardware level.

Ralston, A., and Reilly, E., Jr. 1983. *Encyclopedia of Computer Science and Engineering,* 2d ed. New York: Van Nostrand Reinhold.
This encyclopedia covers every topic related to computer science. The topics are presented in clear and understandable language.

Siewiorek, D., Bell, C., and Newell, A. 1982. *Computer Structures: Principles and Examples.* New York: McGraw-Hill.
This book exhaustively covers the main computers built up to 1982.

Stone, H. 1975. *Introduction to Computer Architecture.* Chicago: Science Research Associates.
This is a collection of papers related to computer architecture.

Tanenbaum, A. S. 1984. *Structured Computer Organization*, 2d ed. Englewood Cliffs, NJ: Prentice-Hall.
This very well-written book presents the organization of a computer in general and analyzes (in detail) Digital's PDP-11, the IBM series 360 and 370, and the Motorola 68000. It deals with several levels of a computer and the historic evolution of multilevel machines. It presents in detail the multiprogramming level, conventional machine-level, assembly language, and operating systems.

Tanenbaum, A. S. 1987. *Operating Systems: Design and Implementation.* Englewood Cliffs, NJ: Prentice-Hall.
This book is an excellent introduction to operating systems, providing a good balance between theory and practice. The book covers all fundamental concepts in detail and discusses one particular operating system—Minix—in detail, up to the point of providing the complete source code listing for study.

Tsichritzis, D., and Bernstein, P. 1974. *Operating Systems.* New York: Academic Press.
This book is a good introduction to operating systems, emphasizing topics such as memory management, virtual memory, and file systems.

Wexelblat, R. 1981. *History of Programming Languages.* New York: Academic Press.
This book presents the complete record of a 1978 conference on the history of programming languages. A very interesting book because it presents the opinions of the main scientists involved in the development of high-level programming languages.

Exercises

1. ✓ Answer true or false:
   - **a.** Disk memory is the main memory of a computer.
   - **b.** On magnetic disks, information is stored sequentially.
   - **c.** The CPU contains a control unit, ALU, and associated registers.
   - **d.** Magnetic disks are the fastest of secondary memory devices.
2. ✓ What are the components of the CPU? What is the role of each?
3. ? Rewrite the fetch–execution cycle using a Pascal-like language.
4. ✓ Describe the main hardware components of a computer.
5. ✓ What are internal registers, and what are they used for?

6. ✓ Explain how information is read from a magnetic disk. Be sure that you explain the two waiting times involved in this operation.
7. ? Explain why we need two instructions to perform the addition operation described in Section 19.2.
8. ? A four-address machine obeys instructions of the following format:

opcode	ad1	ad2	ad3	ad4

Here, opcode is the operation code, ad1 and ad2 are the memory addresses of the operands, ad3 is the memory location where the result of the operation is to be stored, and ad4 is the address of the next instruction to be executed.

a. Explain why a four-address machine does not need a program counter.

b. What is the instruction for a four-address machine to perform the operation discussed in Section 19.2 for a two-address machine?

c. Discuss the advantages and disadvantages of four-address machines over two-address machines.

9. ? Consider the following operation codes, their assembly-language counterparts, and English explanation of their meaning:

Opcode	*Assembly-language symbol*	*Meaning*
001	ADD	Perform an addition
010	SUB	Perform a subtraction
011	MOV	Copy cell contents
100	HLT	Halt the execution

Suppose that these operation codes were part of a two-address machine language and consider the following assembly-language program:

```
MOV  A  C
ADD  B  C
SUB  D  C
HLT
```

Furthermore, suppose that `A` refers to the contents of the cell whose address is 10011, `B` to the contents of the cell whose address is 00110, `C` to the contents of the cell whose address is 11101, and `D` to the contents of the cell whose address is 00111.

a. Explain how this program is executed if translation is used (generate its machine-language equivalent).

b. Explain how this program is executed if interpretation is used.

10. **!** Taking into account what was said about physical and virtual machines, discuss the sense in which hardware and software are equivalent.

11. **?** Suppose that a hard disk rotates at 2400 rotations per minute, has 250 cylinders (a cylinder is the set of every track in the same vertical column), and 50 sectors per track. Furthermore, suppose that the seek time to move n cylinders is given by the following expression (in milliseconds):

$$seek(n) = \begin{cases} 8 + 3n & \text{if } n < 10 \\ 25 + 5\frac{n}{4} & \text{if } 10 \leq n < 100 \\ 125 + 2\frac{n}{3} & \text{if } n \geq 100 \end{cases}$$

Compute:

a. The lowest possible access time (be sure to consider the seek and the rotational latency time).

b. The highest possible access time.

c. The average access time.

12. **!** Write a Pascal program to handle requests to a disk. Your program should receive requests containing the cylinder and the sector where the desired information begins and the number of bits that we want to read or write (that is, the number of bits in the information transfer operation). Your program should output for every request the amount of time needed to complete the request. Assume the values from Exercise 11 and suppose that information can be transferred at a rate of 1500 bits per millisecond. Assume also that the requests are queued using a first-in/first-out queue (see Exercise 8 of Chapter 16).

13. **!** Modify the program from Exercise 12 so that we let the read/write head sweep across the disk from the inner to the outer tracks. Any requests that are in the front of the head in the direction that it is traveling will be served, and the requests that fall behind it will be left pending. When the head has satisfied the last request that it finds in front of it, it turns around and starts a reverse sweep from the outer tracks to the inner tracks. Think carefully about the data type to use before you start working on your program.

APPENDIX A

REPRESENTATION OF CHARACTERS

A computer receives information in the form of numbers, characters, or words. After processing the information, the computer writes it in the form of numbers, characters, or words. However, the information is not stored inside the computer in the same way that it is perceived by a user. The information is stored inside the computer using **bistable circuits,** that is, circuits that have only two possible states, which are represented by 0 and 1. This appendix discusses the internal representation of characters.

To represent characters inside the computer, we need a **character code**—a standard scheme for representing characters by a combination of bits. There is more than one such code in use. The most widely used codes are the **ASCII** code (American Standard Code for Information Interchange) and the **EBCDIC** code (Extended Binary Coded Decimal Interchange Code). The ASCII code uses seven bits to represent each character. This allows the representation of 128 different characters. The 128 ASCII characters can be divided into two groups; the first is composed of characters used to control the hardware (printers and terminals) and in general cannot be seen on the screen of a terminal; the second group is composed of 95 characters and contains the "visible" characters (characters that can be printed or seen on the screen of a terminal).

Table A.1 shows the ASCII characters that are not visible, the so-called **control characters.** This table presents the symbolic representation of each control character, its ASCII code in binary, the equivalent value in decimal, and an explanation of the action produced by the character. Table A.2 shows the "visible" ASCII characters. This table has three columns. Each column contains a character, its ASCII binary code, and the equivalent value of this code in the decimal system.

TABLE A.1 Nonvisible ASCII characters.

char	*Representation*		*action*
	binary	*decimal*	
NUL	0000000	0	CONTROL/SHIFT/P
SOH	0000001	1	CONTROL/A
STX	0000010	2	CONTROL/B
ETX	0000011	3	CONTROL/C
EOT	0000100	4	CONTROL/D
ENQ	0000101	5	CONTROL/E
ACK	0000110	6	CONTROL/F
BEL	0000111	7	CONTROL/G, Bell
BS	0001000	8	CONTROL/H, Back space
HT	0001001	9	CONTROL/I, Horizontal tab
LF	0001010	10	CONTROL/J, Line feed
VT	0001011	11	CONTROL/K, Vertical tab
FF	0001100	12	CONTROL/L, Form feed
CR	0001101	13	CONTROL/M, Carriage return
SO	0001110	14	CONTROL/N
SI	0001111	15	CONTROL/O
DLE	0010000	16	CONTROL/P
DC1	0010001	17	CONTROL/Q
DC2	0010010	18	CONTROL/R
DC3	0010011	19	CONTROL/S
DC4	0010100	20	CONTROL/T
NAK	0010101	21	CONTROL/U
SYN	0010110	22	CONTROL/V
ETB	0010111	23	CONTROL/W
CAN	0011000	24	CONTROL/X
EM	0011001	25	CONTROL/Y
SUB	0011010	26	CONTROL/Z
ESC	0011011	27	CONTROL/SHIFT/K, Escape
FA	0011100	28	CONTROL/SHIFT/L
GS	0011101	29	CONTROL/SHIFT/M
RS	0011110	30	CONTROL/SHIFT/N
US	0011111	31	CONTROL/SHIFT/O
DEL	1111111	127	Delete

TABLE A.2 Visible ASCII characters.

char	Representation		char	Representation		char	Representation	
	binary	*decimal*		*binary*	*decimal*		*binary*	*decimal*
	0100000	32	@	1000000	64	‘	1100000	96
!	0100001	33	A	1000001	65	a	1100001	97
”	0100010	34	B	1000010	66	b	1100010	98
#	0100011	35	C	1000011	67	c	1100011	99
$	0100100	36	D	1000100	68	d	1100100	100
%	0100101	37	E	1000101	69	e	1100101	101
&	0100110	38	F	1000110	70	f	1100110	102
’	0100111	39	G	1000111	71	g	1100111	103
(	0101000	40	H	1001000	72	h	1101000	104
)	0101001	41	I	1001001	73	i	1101001	105
*	0101010	42	J	1001010	74	j	1101010	106
+	0101011	43	K	1001011	75	k	1101011	107
,	0101100	44	L	1001100	76	l	1101100	108
-	0101101	45	M	1001101	77	m	1101101	109
.	0101110	46	N	1001110	78	n	1101110	110
/	0101111	47	O	1001111	79	o	1101111	111
0	0110000	48	P	1010000	80	p	1110000	112
1	0110001	49	Q	1010001	81	q	1110001	113
2	0110010	50	R	1010010	82	r	1110010	114
3	0110011	51	S	1010011	83	s	1110011	115
4	0110100	52	T	1010100	84	t	1110100	116
5	0110101	53	U	1010101	85	u	1110101	117
6	0110110	54	V	1010110	86	v	1110110	118
7	0110111	55	W	1010111	87	w	1110111	119
8	0111000	56	X	1011000	88	x	1111000	120
9	0111001	57	Y	1011001	89	y	1111001	121
:	0111010	58	Z	1011010	90	z	1111010	122
;	0111011	59	[	1011011	91	{	1111011	123
<	0111100	60	\	1011100	92	|	1111100	124
=	0111101	61	]	1011101	93	}	1111101	125
>	0111110	62	^	1011110	94	~	1111110	126
?	0111111	63	_	1011111	95			

APPENDIX B

SYNTAX OF THE PASCAL LANGUAGE

This appendix presents a BNF grammar for the complete syntax of the Pascal language. This grammar corresponds to Standard Pascal (Cooper 1983). The initial symbol for the grammar is the nonterminal symbol Pascal program. To increase the readability of the grammar, the production rules are sorted by the nonterminal symbol on their left-hand side.

<actual parameter> ::= <expression> |
<variable> |
<procedure identifier> |
<function identifier>

<actual parameters> ::= <actual parameter> |
<actual parameter> , <actual parameters>

<adding operator> ::= + | - | or

<array type> ::= array [<index types>] of <component type>

<array variable> ::= <variable>

<assignment statement> ::= <variable> := <expression> |
<function identifier> := <expression>

<base type> ::= <simple type>

<block> ::= <label declaration part>
<constant definition part>
<type definition part>
<variable declaration part>
<function and procedure declaration part>
<statement part>

<body of case> ::= <case element> |
<case element> ; <body of case>

<case element> ::= <case labels> : <statement>

<case label> ::= <constant>

<case labels> ::= <case label> |
<case label> , <case labels>

<case statement> ::= `case` <expression> `of` <body of case> `end`

<character> ::= A | B | C | D | E | F | G | H | I | J | K | L | M | N |
O | P | Q | R | S | T | U | V | W | X | Y | Z | a | b |
c | d | e | f | g | h | i | j | k | l | m | n | o | p |
q | r | s | t | u | v | w | x | y | z | 0 | 1 | 2 | 3 |
4 | 5 | 6 | 7 | 8 | 9 | ! | @ | # | $ | % | ^ | & | * |
(|) | _ | - | + | = | { | } | [|] | ; | : | ' | " |
< | > | , | . | / | ? | ~

<characters> ::= <character> | <character> <characters>

<complete variable> ::= <variable identifier>

<component type> ::= <type>

<compound statement> ::= `begin` <statements> `end`

<conditional statement> ::= <if statement> | <case statement>

<constant> ::= <unsigned number> |
<sign> <unsigned number> |
<constant identifier> |
<sign> <constant identifier> |
<string>

<constant definition> ::= <identifier> = <constant>

<constant definition part> ::= `const` <constants> ; |
<empty>

<constant identifier> ::= <identifier>

<constants> ::= <constant definition> |
<constant definition> ; <constants>

<control variable> ::= <identifier>

<declaration of function> ::= <function header> <directive> |
<function header> <block> |
<function identification> <block>

<declaration of procedure> ::= <procedure header> <directive> |
<procedure header> <block> |
<procedure identification> <block>

<declaration of procedure or function> ::= <declaration of procedure> |
<declaration of function>

<digit> ::= 0 | 1 | 2 | 3 | 4 | 5 | 6 | 7 | 8 | 9

<digits> ::= <digit> | <digit> <digits>

<directive> ::= `forward;` | <identifier> ;

<element> ::= <expression> | <expression> . . <expression>

<elements> ::= <element> | <element> , <elements>

<empty> ::=

<empty statement> ::= <empty>

<enumerated type> ::= (<identifiers>)

<expression> ::= <simple expression> |
<simple expression> <relational operator>
<simple expression>

```
<expressions> ::= <expression> |
                  <expression> , <expressions>

<factor> ::= <variable> |
             <unsigned constant> |
             ( <expression> ) |
             <function designator> |
             <set> |
             not <factor>

<field designator> ::= <record variable> . <field identifier>

<field identifier> ::= <identifier>

<field list> ::= <fixed part> |
                 <fixed part> ; <variant part> |
                 <variant part>

<file buffer> ::= <file variable> ^

<file identifier> ::= <identifier>

<file identifiers> ::= <file identifier> |
                       <file identifier> , <file identifiers>

<file type> ::= file of <type>

<file variable> ::= <variable>

<final value> ::= <expression>

<fixed part> ::= <records>

<for list> ::= <initial value> to <final value> |
               <initial value> downto <final value>

<formal parameters> ::= <formal parameter section> |
                        <formal parameter section> ; <formal parameters>

<formal parameter section> ::= <parameter group> |
                               var <parameter group> |
                               <function heading> |
                               <procedure heading>
```

<for statement> ::= **for** <control variable> := <for list> **do** <statement>

<function and procedure declaration part> ::= <declaration of procedure or function> ; |
<function and procedure declaration part> |
<empty>

<function designator> ::=
<function identifier> |
<function identifier> (<actual parameters>)

<function header> ::= <function heading> ;

<function heading> ::=
function <identifier> : <result type> |
function <identifier>
(<formal parameters>) : <result type>

<function identification> ::= **function** <identifier> ;

<function identifier> ::= <identifier>

<go to statement> ::= **goto** <label>

<identifier> ::= <letter> |
<letter> <letters or digits>

<identifiers> ::= <identifier> |
<identifier> , <identifiers>

<if statement> ::= **if** <expression> **then** <statement> |
if <expression> **then** <statement>
else <statement>

<indexed variable> ::= <array variable> [<expressions>]

<index type> ::= <near-ordinal type>

<index types> ::= <index type> |
<index type> , <index types>

<initial value> ::= <expression>

<label> ::= <unsigned integer>

<label declaration part> ::= **label** <labels> | <empty>

<labels> ::= <label> | <label> , <labels>

<labels field> ::= <field identifier> | <empty>

<letter> ::= A | B | C | D | E | F | G | H | I |
J | K | L | M | N | O | P | Q | R |
S | T | U | V | W | X | Y | Z | a |
b | c | d | e | f | g | h | i | j |
k | l | m | n | o | p | q | r | s |
t | u | v | w | x | y | z

<letter or digit> ::= <letter> | <digit>

<letters or digits> ::= <letter or digit> |
<letter or digit> <letters or digits>

<member designator> := <elements> | <empty>

<multiplying operator> ::= * | / | div | mod | and

<near-ordinal type> ::= <char> |
<boolean> |
<enumerated type> |
<subrange type>

`<parameter group> ::= <identifiers> : <type identifier>`

<Pascal program> ::= <program header> <block>

<pointer type> ::= ^ <type identifier>

<pointer variable> ::= <variable>

<procedure header> ::= <procedure heading> ;

<procedure heading> ::= procedure <identifier> |
procedure <identifier> (<formal parameters>)

<procedure identification> ::= procedure <identifier> ;

<procedure identifier> ::= <identifier>

<procedure statement> ::= <procedure identifier> |
<procedure identifier> (<actual parameters>)

<program header> ::= `program` <identifier> (<file identifiers>) ;

<records> ::= <record section> |
<record section> ; <records>

<record section> ::= <identifiers> : <type> | <empty>

<record type> ::= `record` <field list> `end`

<record variable> ::= <record variable> |
<record variable> , <record variable>

<record variable> ::= <variable>

<record variable list> ::= <record variable>

<referenced variable> ::= <pointer variable> ^

<relational operator> ::= = | <> | < | <= | >= | > | `in`

<repeat statement> ::= `repeat` <statements> `until` <expression>

<repetitive statement> ::= <for statement> |
<repeat statement> |
<while statement>

<result type> ::= <type identifier>

<scale factor> ::= <unsigned integer> |
<sign> <unsigned integer>

<set> ::= [<member designator>]

<set type> ::= `set of` <base type>

<sign> ::= + | -

<simple expression> ::=

<term> |
<sign> <term> |
<simple expression> <adding operator> <term>

```
<simple statement> ::= <assignment statement> |
                       <procedure statement> |
                       <go to statement> |
                       <empty statement>

<simple type> ::= <enumerated type> |
                  <subrange type> |
                  <type identifier>

<statement> ::= <unlabeled statement> |
                <label> : <unlabeled statement>

<statement part> ::= <compound statement>

<statements> ::= <statement> |
                 <statement> ; <statements>

<string> ::= ' <characters> '

<structured statement> ::= <compound statement> |
                           <conditional statement> |
                           <repetitive statement> |
                           <with statement>

<structured type> ::= <unpacked structured type> |
                      packed <unpacked structured type>

<subrange type> ::= <constant> .. <constant>

<term> ::= <factor> |
           <term> <multiplying operator> <factor>

<type> ::= <simple type> |
           <structured type> |
           <pointer type>

<type definition> ::= <identifier> = <type>

<type definition part> ::= type <types> ; |
                           <empty>

<type identifier> ::= <identifier>

<types> ::= <type definition> |
            <type definition> ; <types>
```

<unlabeled statement> ::= <simple statement> |
<structured statement>

<unpacked structured type> ::= <array type> |
<record type> |
<set type> |
<file type>

<unsigned constant> ::= <unsigned number> |
<string> |
<constant identifier> |
`nil`

<unsigned integer> ::= <digits>

<unsigned number> ::= <unsigned integer> |
<unsigned real>

<unsigned real> ::= <unsigned integer> . <digits> |
<unsigned integer> . <digits> `E` <scale factor> |
<unsigned integer> `E` <scale factor>

<variable> ::= <complete variable> |
<variable component> |
<referenced variable>

<variable component> ::= <indexed variable> |
<field designator> |
<file buffer>

<variable declaration> ::= <identifiers> : <type>

<variable declaration part> ::= `var` <variables> ; |
<empty>

<variable identifier> ::= <identifier>

<variables> ::= <variable declaration> |
<variable declaration> ; <variables>

<variant> ::= <case label list> : (<field list>) |
<empty>

<variant part> ::= `case` <labels field>
<type identifier> `of` <variants>

<variants> ::= <variant> |
<variant> ; <variants>

<while statement> ::= `while` <expression> `do` <statement>

<with statement> ::= `with` <record variable list> `do` <statement>

APPENDIX C

PASCAL IDENTIFIERS

This appendix presents a complete list of the reserved and standard names of the Pascal language. Chapter 5 stated that the set of **reserved names** consists of every identifier that is used by Pascal for a specific purpose. A reserved name can only be used in the context for which it is defined. For example, `begin` and `end` are reserved names. We cannot use variables whose name is `begin`, nor can we have procedures or functions whose name is `begin`. The set of **standard names** consists of every identifier that has a predefined meaning in Pascal but whose meaning can be changed, if necessary. For example, `sqrt` is the symbolic name for the square-root function. We are allowed to define a function whose name is `sqrt`. For example, this function may compute the square of a number rather than its square root. However, once `sqrt` is redefined, it cannot be used with the original meaning for the rest of the program.

Reserved names

```
and          end          nil
array        file         not
begin        for          of
case         function     or
const        goto         packed
div          if           procedure
do           in           program
downto       label        record
else         mod          repeat
```

set	type	while
then	until	with
to	var	

Standard names

Constants

false	maxint	true

Types

boolean	integer	text
char	real	

Program parameters

input	output

Functions

abs	exp	sin
arctan	ln	sqr
chr	odd	sqrt
cos	ord	succ
eof	pred	trunc
eoln	round	

Procedures

get	put	rewrite
new	read	unpack
pack	readln	write
page	reset	writeln

REFERENCES

Abelson, H.; Sussman, G.; and Sussman, J. 1985. *Structure and Interpretation of Computer Programs.* Cambridge, MA: MIT Press.

Aho, A., and Ullman, J. 1977. *Principles of Compiler Design.* Reading, MA: Addison-Wesley.

Allen, J. 1978. *Anatomy of LISP.* New York: McGraw-Hill.

Amsbury, W. 1985. *Data Structures: From Arrays to Priority Queues.* Belmont, CA: Wadsworth.

Backus, J. 1978. "Can Programming Be Liberated from the von Neumann Style? A Functional Style and Its Algebra of Programs," *Communications of the ACM,* 21 (8):613–641.

Barron, D. W., and Bishop, J. M. 1984. *Advanced Programming, a Practical Course.* Chichester, England: Wiley.

Bastani, F. B., and Iyengar, S. S. 1987. "The Effect of Data Structures on the Logical Complexity of Programs," *Communications of the ACM,* 30 (3):250–261.

Bentley, J. 1984. "Programming Pearls: How to Sort," *Communications of the ACM,* 27 (4):287–291.

———. 1985. "Programming Pearls: Bumper-Sticker Computer Science," *Communications of the ACM,* 28 (9):896–901.

Bishop, J. 1986. *Data Abstraction in Programming Languages.* Reading, MA: Addison-Wesley.

Brainerd, W., and Landwebber, L. 1974. *Theory of Computation.* New York: Wiley.

Brooks, F. 1975. *The Mythical Man-Month.* Reading, MA: Addison-Wesley.

Brown, P. J. 1974. "Programming and Documenting Software Projects," *Computing Surveys,* 6 (4):213–220.

Chomsky, N. 1957. *Syntactic Structures.* The Hague, Netherlands: Mouton.

———. 1959. "On Certain Formal Properties of Grammars," *Information and Control,* 2:137–167.

Clocksin, W., and Mellish, C. 1981. *Programming in PROLOG.* Berlin, West Germany: Springer-Verlag.

Cohen, J. 1981. "Garbage Collection of Linked Data Structures," *Computing Surveys,* 13 (3):341–367.

Cooper, D. 1983. *Standard Pascal Reference Manual.* New York: Norton.

Dahl, O.; Dijkstra, E.; and Hoare, C. 1972. *Structured Programming.* New York: Academic Press.

Dale, N., and Lilly, S. 1985. *Pascal Plus Data Structures, Algorithms, and Advanced Programming.* Lexington, MA: D. C. Heath.

Dale, N., and Orshalick, D. 1983. *Introduction to Pascal and Structured Design.* Lexington, MA: D. C. Heath.

Denning, P. 1970. "Virtual Memory," *Computing Surveys,* 2 (3):153–189.

Dijkstra, E. 1968. "GO TO Statement Considered Harmful," *Communications of the ACM,* 11 (3):147–148.

———. 1976. *A Discipline of Programming.* Englewood Cliffs, NJ: Prentice-Hall.

Donon, J. 1959. *The Classic French Cuisine.* New York: Knopf.

Dromey, R. 1982. *How to Solve It by Computer.* Englewood Cliffs, NJ: Prentice-Hall.

Eckhouse, R., Jr. 1975. *Minicomputer Systems: Organization and Programming (PDP-11).* Englewood Cliffs, NJ: Prentice-Hall.

Feigenbaum, E., and McCorduck, P. 1983. *The Fifth Generation: Artificial Intelligence and Japan's Challenge to the World.* Reading, MA: Addison-Wesley.

Friedmann, D., and Shapiro, S. C. July 1974. "A Case for While-Until," *SIGPLAN Notices*:7–14.

Gehani, N. 1983. *Ada: An Advanced Introduction.* Englewood Cliffs, NJ: Prentice-Hall.

Geschke, C.; Morris, J.; and Satterthwaite, E. 1977. "Early Experience with Mesa," *Communications of the ACM,* 20 (8):540–553.

Ghezzi, C., and Jazayeri, M. 1982. *Programming Language Concepts.* New York: Wiley.

Ginsburg, S. 1966. *The Mathematical Theory of Context-Free Languages.* New York: McGraw-Hill.

Gordon, M. 1979. *An Introduction to the Denotational Description of Programming Languages.* Berlin, West Germany: Springer-Verlag.

Green, J. 1982. *A Dictionary of Contemporary Quotations.* London, England: Pan Books.

Griswold, R.; Poage, J.; and Polonsky, I. 1971. *The SNOBOL4 Programming Language.* Englewood Cliffs, NJ: Prentice-Hall.

Harland, D. 1984. *Polymorphic Programming Languages.* Chichester, England: Ellis Horwood.

Hayes, J. 1978. *Computer Architecture and Organization.* New York: McGraw-Hill.

Hennie, F. 1977. *Introduction to Computability.* Reading, MA: Addison-Wesley.

Hermes, H. 1969. *Enumerability, Decidability, Computability,* 2d revised ed. New York: Springer-Verlag.

Hill, F., and Peterson, G. 1978. *Digital Systems: Hardware Organization and Design.* New York: Wiley.

Hoare, C. A. R. 1969. "An Axiomatic Basis of Computer Programming," *Communications of the ACM,* 12 (10):576–580.

———. 1972. "Notes on Data Structuring," in *Structured Programming,* edited by O. Dahl, E. Dijkstra, and C. Hoare. New York: Academic Press.

Hopcroft, J., and Ullman, J. 1969. *Formal Languages and Their Relation to Automata.* Reading, MA: Addison-Wesley.

Horowitz, E. 1983. *Fundamentals of Programming Languages.* Rockville, MD: Computer Science Press.

Horowitz, E., and Sahni, S. 1984. *Fundamentals of Data Structures in Pascal.* Rockville, MD: Computer Science Press.

Ingerman, P. 1961. "Thunks," *Communications of the ACM,* 4 (1):55–58.

Iverson, K. 1962. *A Programming Language.* New York: Wiley.

Jensen, K., and Wirth, N. 1974. *Pascal, User Manual and Report.* New York: Springer-Verlag.

Jensen, K.; Wirth, N.; Mickel, A.; and Miner, J. 1985. *Pascal, User Manual and Report—ISO Pascal Standard,* 3d ed. New York: Springer-Verlag.

Kemeny, J., and Kurtz, T. 1967. *BASIC Programming.* New York: Wiley.

Kennedy, K., and Schwartz, J. 1975. "An Introduction to the Set Theoretical Language SETL," *Journal of Computer and Math with Applications 1*:97–119.

Kernighan, B., and Plauger, P. 1978. *The Elements of Programming Style.* New York: McGraw-Hill.

Kernighan, B., and Ritchie, D. 1978. *The C Programming Language.* Englewood Cliffs, NJ: Prentice-Hall.

Kleene, S. 1974. *Introduction to Metamathematics.* 7th reprint. New York: American Elsevier.

Knuth, D. 1969. *The Art of Computer Programming, Vol. 2, Seminumerical Algorithms.* Reading, MA: Addison-Wesley.

———. 1973a. *The Art of Computer Programming, Vol. 1, Fundamental Algorithms.* Reading, MA: Addison-Wesley.

———. 1973b. *The Art of Computer Programming, Vol. 3, Sorting and Searching.* Reading, MA: Addison-Wesley.

———. 1977. "Structured Programming with GO TO Statements." Pp. 140–194 in *Current Trends in Programming Methodology,* edited by R. Yeh. Englewood Cliffs, NJ: Prentice-Hall.

Koffmann, E.; Miller, P.; and Wardle, C. 1984. "Recommended Curriculum for CS1, 1984," *Communications of the ACM,* 27 (10):998–1001.

Koffmann, E.; Stemple, D.; and Wardle, C. 1985. "Recommended Curriculum for CS2, 1984," *Communications of the ACM,* 28 (8):815–818.

Ledgard, H. 1975. *Programming Proverbs.* New York: Hayden.

Lehnert, W., and Ringle, M. 1982. *Strategies for Natural Language Processing.* Hillsdale, NJ: Lawrence Erlbaum.

Liskof, B.; Snyder, A.; Atkinson, R.; and Schaffert, C. 1977. "Abstraction Mechanisms in CLU," *Communications of the ACM,* 20 (8):564–576.

Liskof, B., and Zilles, S. 1974. "Programming with Abstract Data Types," *SIGPLAN Symposium on Very High Level Languages—SIGPLAN Notices 9,* (4):50–59.

Lükasiewicz, J. 1958. *Aristotle's Syllogistic.* New York: Oxford University Press.

Lyons, J. 1977. *Semantics.* Cambridge, England: Cambridge University Press.

Manna, Z., and Waldinger, R. 1985. *Logical Basis for Computer Programming, Volume 1: Deductive Reasoning.* Reading, MA: Addison-Wesley.

McCarthy, J.; Abrahams, P.; Edwards, D.; Hart, T.; and Levin, M. 1965. *LISP 1.5 Programmer's Manual.* Cambridge, MA: MIT Press.

Mills, H. 1971. "Top-Down Programming in Large Systems" in *Debugging Techniques in Large Systems,* edited by R. Rustin. Englewood Cliffs, NJ: Prentice-Hall.

Milne, R., and Strachey, C. 1976. *A Theory of Programming Language Semantics.* London, England: Chapmann & Hall.

Naur, P. 1960. "Documentation Problems: ALGOL 60," *Communications of the ACM,* 3 (5):299–314.

———. 1963. "Revised Report on the Algorithmic Language ALGOL 60," *Communications of the ACM,* 6 (1):1–17.

Organick, E.; Forsythe, A.; and Plummer, R. 1978. *Programming Language Structures.* New York: Academic Press.

Pratt, T. 1975. *Programming Languages: Design and Implementation.* Englewood Cliffs, NJ: Prentice-Hall.

———. 1984. *Programming Languages: Design and Implementation,* 2d ed. Englewood Cliffs, NJ: Prentice-Hall.

Pyle, I. 1981. *The Ada Programming Language.* Englewood Cliffs, NJ: Prentice-Hall.

Ralston, A., and Reilly, E., Jr. 1983. *Encyclopedia of Computer Science and Engineering,* 2d ed. New York: Van Nostrand Reinhold.

Rohl, J. S. 1984. *Recursion via Pascal.* Cambridge, England: Cambridge University Press.

Sammet, J. 1969. *Programming Languages: History and Fundamentals.* Englewood Cliffs, NJ: Prentice-Hall.

———. 1983. "Programming Languages." Pp. 1228–1232 in *Encyclopedia of Computer Science and Engineering,* 2d ed., edited by A. Ralston and E. Reilly, Jr. New York: Van Nostrand Reinhold.

Schneider, G. M.; Weingart, S.; and Perlman, D. 1978. *An Introduction to Programming and Problem Solving with Pascal.* New York: Wiley.

Shaw, M. 1984. "Abstraction Techniques in Modern Programming Languages," *IEEE Software,* 1 (4):10–26.

Shell, D. 1959. "A Highspeed Sorting Procedure," *Communications of the ACM,* 2 (7):30–32.

Siewiorek, D.; Bell, C.; and Newell, A. 1982. *Computer Structures: Principles and Examples.* New York: McGraw-Hill.

Simon, H. 1969. *The Sciences of the Artificial.* Cambridge, MA: MIT Press.

Singh, B., and Naps, T. 1985. *Introduction to Data Structures.* St. Paul, MN: West.

Stone, H. 1975. *Introduction to Computer Architecture.* Chicago: Science Research Associates.

Stubbs, D., and Werbe, N. 1985. *Data Structures with Abstract Data Types and Pascal.* Pacific Grove, CA: Brooks/Cole.

Tanenbaum, A. S. 1976. *Structured Computer Organization.* Englewood Cliffs, NJ: Prentice-Hall.

———. 1984. *Structured Computer Organization,* 2d ed., Englewood Cliffs, NJ: Prentice-Hall.

———. 1987. *Operating Systems: Design and Implementation.* Englewood Cliffs, NJ: Prentice-Hall.

Taylor, A. L. 16 April 1984. "The Wizard Inside the Machine," *TIME,* 123 (16):42–49.

Tremblay, J., and Sorenson, P. 1976. *An Introduction to Data Structures with Applications.* New York: McGraw-Hill.

Tsichritzis, D., and Bernstein, P. 1974. *Operating Systems.* New York: Academic Press.

van Tassel, D. 1974. *Program Style, Design, Efficiency, Debugging and Testing.* Englewood Cliffs, NJ: Prentice-Hall.

Wegner, P. 1972. "The Vienna Definition Language," *Computing Surveys,* 4 (1):5–63.

Weinberg, G. 1971. *The Psychology of Computer Programming.* New York: Van Nostrand Reinhold.

Weizenbaum, J. 1963. "Symmetric List Processor," *Communications of the ACM,* 6 (9):524–544.

Wexelblat, R. 1981. *History of Programming Languages.* New York: Academic Press.

Wilkes, M. V. 1951. "The Best Way to Design an Automatic Calculating Machine." Pp. 16–18 in Report of the Manchester University Computer Inaugural Conference, Manchester University. Also in Swartzlander, E. 1976. *Computer Design Development: Principal Papers.* New York: Hayden.

Wirth, N. 1971. "The Programming Language Pascal," *Acta Informatica,* 1:35–63.

———. 1973. *Systematic Programming: An Introduction.* Englewood Cliffs, NJ: Prentice-Hall.

———. 1974. "On the Composition of Well-Structured Programs," *Computing Surveys,* 6 (4):247–259.

———. 1976. *Algorithms + Data Structures = Programs.* Englewood Cliffs, NJ: Prentice-Hall.

———. 1978. "Modula-2," *Technical Report 27,* Institut für Informatik, ETH, Zurich.

———. 1983. *Modula-2.* New York: Springer-Verlag.

Yohe, J. M. 1974. "An Overview of Programming Practices," *Computing Surveys,* 6 (4):221–245.

INDEX

NOTE: Page numbers in **boldface** indicate pages on which terms are defined; page numbers in *italics* indicate figures.